Repentance

and the Return to God

Repentance
and the Return to God

Tawba in Early Sufism

Atif Khalil

SUNY
PRESS

Cover photo © Museum Associates / LACMA / "A Sufi in a Landscape"
(Iran, Isfahan, circa 1650–1660)

Published by State University of New York Press, Albany

For information, contact State University of New York Press, Albany, NY
www.sunypress.edu

Library of Congress Cataloging-in-Publication Data

Names: Khalil, Atif, author.
Title: Repentance and the return to God : tawba in early Sufism / Atif Khalil.
Description: Albany : State University of New York Press, [2018] | Includes bibliographical references and index.
Identifiers: LCCN 2017021794 (print) | LCCN 2017022192 (ebook) | ISBN 9781438469133 (ebook) | ISBN 9781438469119 (hardcover) | ISBN 9781438469126 (pbk.)
Subjects: LCSH: Repentance—Islam. | Sufism—Doctrines.
Classification: LCC BP166.79 (ebook) | LCC BP166.79 .K43 2018 (print) | DDC 297.4/46—dc23
LC record available at https://lccn.loc.gov/2017021794

10 9 8 7 6 5 4 3 2 1

I am the Prophet of Repentance.

—ḥadīth

Repentance is that you be unto God a face without a back,
Just as you were previously unto Him a back without a face.

—Ibrāhīm al-Daqqāq

Every saint has a past, and every sinner has a future.

—Oscar Wilde

Contents

Acknowledgments ix

Introduction 1

PART I
THE SEMANTICS OF *TAWBA*

1 Is *Tawba* "Repentance"? A Lexical and Semantic Survey 13

2 The Internal Structure and Semantic Field of *Tawba* in the Qur'ān 23

PART II
EARLY SUFI APPROACHES TO *TAWBA*

3 *Tawba* as Interior Conversion 61

4 The States, Stations, and Early Sufi Apothegmata 77

5 Four Early Approaches to *Tawba* 97

6 *Tawba* in the Writings of al-Ḥārith al-Muḥāsibī 123

7 *Tawba* in the *Nourishment of Hearts* of Abū Ṭālib al-Makkī 145

Conclusion 175

Notes 181

Bibliography 241

Index 257

Acknowledgments

This monograph grew out of a PhD dissertation completed at the University of Toronto's Department of Religious Studies under the able supervision of Professor Todd Lawson. It is only fitting that I begin by thanking him for his guidance and unfailing support throughout my doctoral years, since it was under his tutelage that I began to explore the world of early Sufism and the idea of this study first conceived. To the committee members—Professors Amir Harrak, Walid Saleh, and Maria Subtelny—I am grateful for the generous feedback offered at various stages of the writing process. The wealth of knowledge and critical insight shared by Professor Ahmet Karamustafa, the external examiner and one of the foremost experts in the field of early Sufism, proved particularly invaluable. The late Professor Michael Marmura, also on the committee, deserves special mention for playing a formative role in my intellectual maturation by nurturing an interest in Islamic philosophy and theology that stretches back almost two decades. To this day I carry vivid memories of the pre-Islamic poetry he would recite off the cuff in his seminars, hypnotically carrying us back to an almost mythical age of warriors and poets. Other teachers from whom I benefitted include Professors Deborah Black, William Chittick, James DiCenso, Lloyd Gerson, Timothy Gianotti, Sebastian Günther, Wael Hallaq, Jane McAullife, Thomas McIntire, Seyyed H. Nasr, Robert Sinkewicz, and the late Willard Oxtoby. It was a privilege to have worked with such a distinguished group of scholars, all of whom contributed to my intellectual development in more ways than the present work reveals.

I must also express my thanks to Shaikh Mahmoud al-Hoda and his Shadhili disciples in Aleppo for graciously welcoming me into their community in the summer of 2004. It was with them that I closely read some of the textual material that became the basis of this book. As Syria fragments into political and sectarian infighting, one can only hope that the more inward, contemplative, and compassionate approach to Islam offered by Shaikh Mahmoud, his disciples, and other likeminded inheritors of the Sufi tradition in the region, will serve to heal the wounds of the traumas inflicted by war in the years to come.

This book would not have been possible without the enduring support of my parents, Ahmed and Shaheen Khalil. My father in particular was a constant source of encouragement as we shared many stimulating late-night conversations about Sufism, *tawba*, and the conversion-narratives of early figures central to Muslim piety. He is now an avid reader and admirer of Abū Ṭālib al-Makkī, whose Urdu translation of the *Nourishment of Hearts* has become something of his own nourishment. I credit the intellectual curiosities that took me down the road of academia to the influence of his probing mind. To Saima, Amir, Tariq, Nimra bhabi, ummy, Shadi, Amber, the Ahmads, Rehmans, and Kalims, I thank for the joy and laughter they brought to my frequent visits to Toronto, Montreal and Calgary.

I must also thank the University of Lethbridge's Department of Religious Studies as well as our superb Administrative Assistant Bev Garnett for graciously welcoming me into the Department in 2007, tolerating my Nag Champa incense addiction, and for providing an amicable and stimulating atmosphere that has made teaching and scholarship exciting in the prairies of southern Alberta.

To my close friend Professor Mohammed Rustom I am grateful for reading and commenting on earlier drafts of this piece. He saved me from many embarrassing errors and oversights. To Professor Yusuf Mullick, I must express the same appreciation. Nancy Ellegate at SUNY, the news of whose untimely death came as the final edits of this manuscript were being completed, deserves special mention: her editorial advice and sagacious suggestions were much appreciated.

Last but not least, I cannot forget the close friends and teachers whose encouragement and support contributed to the completion of a study that has long been in gestation. Among them, I must mention the names of S.H. Ali, the late C. Bruchet, the Fereigs, Rabbi A. Glazer, Rev. V. Grandfield, H.T. Ibrahim, Shaikh Muhammad al-Kabir, Dr. Z. Mian, J. Richmond, A. Qurayshi, Professor S. Sheikh, T. al-Tayeb, and Dr. Eric Winkel. Finally, to Br. Camil Xerri I remain forever indebted for opening up to me the world of Islam's sapiential tradition. Others whose names have not been mentioned have not been forgotten—absent in form, they are present in spirit.

A shorter, edited version of chapter 7 originally appeared in the *Oxford Journal of Islamic Studies* as "*Tawba* in the Sufi Psychology of Abū Ṭālib al-Makkī (d. 996 CE)," 23, no. 3 (2012): 294–324. An excerpt from chapter 3 also appeared in the *Journal of Sufi Studies* as "A Note on Interior Conversion in Early Sufism and Ibrāhīm b. Adham's Entry into the Way," 5 (2016): 189–198.

Introduction

It can be argued that the consciousness of sin is as old as human consciousness itself. From the first glimmerings of human history, human beings—as *homo religiosi*—have exhibited an acute awareness of their transgressions against a moral or supernatural order, and often suffered, as a consequence, under a distressing self-condemnation. Whether one considers the ancient Egyptians, the Aztec communities of America, the Hebrew prophets of Israel, or the Vedic Hindus of the Indus Peninsula, the sense of sin has gone hand in hand with the larger existential dramas of human existence.[1]

Yet, alongside this awareness of sin, humans have also sought ways to mend the ruptures created with the supernatural world as a result of their misdeeds, and to protect themselves from the consequences of their own actions. The fact that some believed these consequences appeared in the form of divine retribution, and others as a karmic response due to the violation of *dharma,* is ultimately of secondary importance. At the heart of this sense of sin there often lay a belief in a cosmic law of cause and effect, a belief that without some mitigating or atoning factor, one was condemned to face the consequences of one's transgressions, and that if those consequences did not appear in this life, they would in the next. The consciousness of sin was therefore almost always accompanied by measures, introduced by tradition, to protect the sinner from his own moral and sacrilegious crimes. Historically, these measures ranged from such responses as priestly sacrificial rites, elaborate purification rituals, the invocation of certain litanies or formulas, to extreme forms of self-mortification and even self-immolation.

In the Abrahamic religions, the cornerstone of these restorative strategies lay in "repentance." Although many of the common presumptions about the nature of the concept derive from Christian theology—indeed the term itself, as we shall see, is of a peculiarly Christian origin—it is still possible to speak of repentance within Judaism and Islam provided certain preliminary qualifications are made. Keeping in mind that we should remain cautious of artificially imposing the categories of one religious tradition onto another, even when the other tradition belongs to the same family of faiths, only an extreme reductionism would prevent one from acknowledging the presence of repentance outside of a Christian context. If, however, one understands the concept in the broadest sense as a religious mechanism to cancel, redress, or atone for one's previous wrongs or past misdoings, then we can indeed speak of repentance not only in the Abrahamic faiths, but also across the spectrum of world religions.[2] But this, as noted, requires that one not inadvertently impose the particular features associated with this concept in one tradition onto another, even if those features are linguistically intrinsic to the term itself.

The purpose of the present study is to bring to light approaches to *tawba*, commonly translated as "repentance," from the early period of Sufism. To date, not a single academic monograph has been published on *tawba* in Islam, let alone one of its intellectual subtraditions. The scholarly lacuna is surprising considering the central place of *tawba* in the Qur'ān and the wider Islamic tradition. Indeed, Islam's founding Prophet is to have declared, "I am the Prophet of repentance" (*anā nabī al-tawba*).[3] While a number of short studies have appeared in the form of journal articles or book chapters exploring *tawba*[4] in the Qur'ān,[5] *fiqh* (Islamic jurisprudence),[6] *kalām* (Islamic theology),[7] Shī'ism,[8] literature,[9] or the relation of the concept to "conversion,"[10] or "redemption,"[11] this study aims to be the first full-length treatment of *tawba* in Islam, with a unique focus on early Sufism.[12]

The period analyzed in our study runs primarily from the eighth through eleventh centuries, with a particular focus on the middle two. In light of the periodization introduced by Michael Sells,[13] we shall look at two phases of the formative period of Sufism. The first consists of that of the "founders" of the tradition, and runs from the late seventh and early eighth centuries to the middle of the tenth century. It includes such figures as Ibrāhīm b. Adham (d. 778–9), 'Abd Allāh b. al-Mubārak (d. 797), Dhū al-Nūn al-Miṣrī (d. 860), Sarī al-Saqaṭī (d. 867), Junayd al-Baghdādī (d. 910), Sahl al-Tustarī (d. 896), and Abū Sa'īd Aḥmad al-Kharrāz (d. 899). The second consists of the "formative period of Sufi literature," and begins in the middle of the tenth century with the appearance of some of the first comprehensive texts in which Sufism is presented as a "self-conscious mode of spirituality embracing all aspects of life and society."[14] This phase begins with the writings of Abū Bakr al-Kalābādhī

(d. 994–5), Abū Naṣr al-Sarrāj (d. 988), and Abū Ṭālib al-Makkī (d. 996), and ends with those of Abū al-Qāsim al-Qushayrī (d. 1072) and ʿAlī b. ʿUthmān al-Hujwīrī (d. 1077). Although the focus on this second phase in the course of this study will be on its earlier period, and even here, with particular attention to the thought of Makkī (for reasons outlined below), some of the later works of this phase will not be excluded from our broader analysis, especially for *tawba* narratives and sayings as they have been transmitted to us in some key eleventh-century sources.

A study of this nature faces a few challenges from the outset. The most significant of these is that our knowledge of the earliest period of Sufism is still quite rudimentary.[15] This is not simply because relatively little research has been carried out in this area, a problem which, on its own, can be rectified by more research. As in the case of our understanding of the pre-Socratics, much of this has to do with meagerness of sources and scarcity of documentation. While many scholars agree that the origins of the phenomenon that came to be defined as Sufism (*taṣawwuf*) can be traced back to the interior life of the Prophet of Islam—particularly, to certain pivotal events in his mission, such as the first descent of revelation, or the famous nocturnal ascent (*miʿrāj*)—we do not have a very clear picture of the beginnings of Sufism insofar as we are dealing with a distinct expression of Islamic piety.[16] Although it is generally believed that Sufism gradually emerged out of a movement of renunciants (*zuhhād*) and devout worshippers (*ʿubbād, nussāk*) who had spread across the empire during the late Umayyad and early Abbasid period—a movement that was composed of individuals who saw themselves as inheritors of the spiritual message of the Prophet and who may have been reacting through their ascetic renunciation to the newfound wealth of the empire[17]—we have little knowledge of the exact nature of the theological and mystical doctrines that were in circulation during this period and shortly afterward. Many of the "founders" of the Sufi tradition who emerged out of this movement wrote very little, and many of the works of those who did write have either been lost or come down to us in the form of partial or fragmentary manuscripts. For many of these figures, all we have are a few aphorisms, glosses on Qurʾānic verses, or anecdotes passed on through oral tradition until they eventually appeared in later Sufi treatises. In many cases it is difficult to comprehend the actual import or meaning of these sayings because they are so removed from their initial contexts. In the course of this study we shall see how, for example, the same saying could be interpreted in conflicting and contradictory ways by later authors. Because we lack, for the most part, extensive texts until the formative period of Sufi literature, our understanding of the doctrines of the earliest Sufis remains quite hazy. The difficulties this can present for a historical analysis of a single concept in the earliest phases of Sufism are self-evident. For this reason, our inquiry into the various perspectives on *tawba* prevalent in this period cannot be exhaustive. In some instances, an element of speculation will guide our conceptual reconstruction of early notions of *tawba*.

Although many figures played important roles in the intellectual development of early Sufism, this study will focus largely on the views of those individuals from whom important contributions to early notions of *tawba* can be drawn. Thus, some personalities of the early period will be given negligible or no attention. These include such men as Ḥasan al-Baṣrī (d. 728), considered by many to be the patriarch of Islamic mysticism, and Manṣūr al-Ḥallāj (d. 922), whose dramatic execution by the Abbasid polity brought tensions between the more esoteric and exoteric strains of Islam to a climax, thus marking a turning point in the unfolding of the tradition. The reason for this exclusion is not because these and other such personalities were peripheral players in the formation of the tradition, but because no more than a few cursory (and seemingly inconsequential) remarks of theirs have been transmitted on the theme of *tawba*.[18] On the other hand, an entire chapter will be given to exploring the views of a figure like al-Ḥārith b. Asad al-Muḥāsibī (d. 857), who lived between the time of Ḥasan and Ḥallāj, because we have a number of his written texts, including a short treatise still in manuscript form entitled the *Iḥkām al-tawba* (*The Establishing of Repentance*). The range of works by him that are currently available remains a rather unique exception to the general dearth of texts that characterizes the earliest phases of Sufism. A study of early approaches to *tawba* would be incomplete without including Muḥāsibī.

It should be clear that the criterion that will determine our selection of figures whose ideas will be explored will not depend solely on how much they might have addressed the concept under study. In other words, the criterion is not simply quantitative. Since one of the aims of this study is to shed light on some of the principal theoretical trajectories of early views of *tawba*, we will also look into the views of certain figures who played an important role in some of the early debates surrounding the concept, even if no more than a handful of sayings on *tawba* have been transmitted from them.

The most comprehensive and sustained single treatment of *tawba* that we have up to the end of the tenth century is to be found in Makkī's chapter on *tawba* in the *Qūt al-qulūb* (*Nourishment of Hearts*). On account of its breadth and depth, a significant part of this study will focus on this important Sufi author's discussion of this topic as it appears in his seminal Sufi text. Although Sarrāj and Kalābādhī, who wrote in the same period as Makkī, also devote chapters to repentance in the *Kitāb al-lumaʿ* (*Book of Flashes*) and *Taʿarruf li madhhab ahl al-taṣawwuf* (*An Introduction to the Way of the Folk of Sufism*), respectively, their treatments of the subject are brief and succinct. But despite the brevity of their comments, their views shall be included in this study as well as those of other figures who came shortly afterward.

One of the salient characteristics of early discussions of *tawba*, and one that will become quickly apparent over the course of this study, is the extent to which they are centered on the most practical concerns of the path. The most extensive inquiries into the nature of *tawba* that have been transmitted to us focus not so much on abstract, metaphysical issues but on practical considerations. Although inquiries into the former were certainly not absent in the early period, a fact we shall also see in this study, the main focus of the most well known of the early works was on *praxis* (*muʿāmala*), that is to say, in aiding the spiritual seeker to grow and mature on the path, and in protecting him from the trappings of his own psyche and inner world. This point has been highlighted by Laury Silvers, when she writes that "the treatises and manuals that are the most visible face of early Sufism and the early institutional period tend to focus on the basics of the spiritual path and less so on theoretical questions."[19]

An accurate way to describe this *praxis*-oriented Sufism would be as a spiritual psychology, one whose aim was to direct the spiritual traveler toward an experience and knowledge of God through an inner cleansing and purification of the self.[20] Though principally pragmatic, this "practical Sufism"[21] did not consist of a simple list of injunctions and prohibitions of the path drawn through an analytic study of the formal precepts of scripture. Were that to have been the case, there would have been little to separate this science from jurisprudence. Although, like jurisprudence, it was prescriptive in nature, its foundations lay largely in meditative introspection and self-examination on the one hand, and reflection on revelation, particularly those passages dealing with the inner life of the believer, on the other. Even though many of the most well-known early representatives of this science had close ties to jurisprudence and its culture, the science developed out of the fruits of their asceticism, contemplation, prayer, inner life, and single-minded devotion to God. Describing this inner science in the early period, Fritz Meier writes that the Sufi thinkers "established a scheme of ethical and epistemological principles and mapped out the boundaries of what was permitted in the way of spiritual adventuring; in short, they evolved an intricate moral psychology [. . .] intended to guide the initiate in his pilgrimage towards the purification of the soul."[22] It was only later that the more metaphysical and esoteric treatises came into prominence, though, as noted, such conversations were also taking place early on.

In the context of *tawba*, the aim of this "practical Sufism" was to help free the *tāʾib*—the one who repents and returns to God—from the seductive power of sin. This involved directing him to a certain course that would ensure he remained true to his *tawba*. The Sufi thinkers did not simply stipulate a set of conditions that had to be met in order for *tawba* to be accepted by God. Although they did discuss these conditions in detail, in the longer treatises they laid out a comprehensive regimen that would help protect the aspirant from lapsing in his *tawba*. In the process, they drew attention to the various internal impulses and maladies of the heart that could draw the *tāʾib* back to his misdeeds and the means through which he could overpower them. They thus prescribed a course of action through which the cravings of the lower soul, which were the ultimate causes of many of the sins, could be tamed and brought into control. One also finds in Sufi discussions *tawba* presented as an all-consuming process of returning to God—indeed, as the first stage or station (*maqām/manzil*) of the spiritual path. Insofar as it is presented as a comprehensive spiritual process, *tawba* is tied to other essential virtues of the path, such as patience (*ṣabr*), gratitude (*shukr*), and inner struggle (*mujāhada*).[23] The nature of the unity of the virtues in Sufi thought will become clearer by the end of this study.

The Structure of this Study

This work has been divided into two broad sections. The first consists of two chapters that examine the semantic field of *tawba*. In the first chapter, we shall explore the meaning of *tawba* through an inquiry into the most established and authoritative lexicons of classical Arabic. In the process, we will define the parameters of the semantic field of the term both from a linguistic (*taʿrīf al-tawba fī al-lugha*) and religious (*taʿrīf al-tawba fī al-sharʿ*) perspective. Most important, we shall highlight the central problems involved in conceptualizing *tawba* simply as "repentance." Although many of the problems in this equation will be brought out, it will be shown that, in the final analysis, repentance can function as a viable translation of *tawba* provided one does not lose sight of the principal lexical sense of the Arabic term, namely, that of a "return." The chapter will demonstrate the importance of being conscious of this principal lexical sense in order to appreciate the full range of meanings conveyed by its use in the Islamic tradition. One of the main reasons that it will be concluded that the commonly employed English word can act as a reasonable though not unproblematic translation of the Arabic term is because the underlying meaning of the former corresponds closely to the religious meaning of the latter (at least in relation to the human being), and moreover, because English lacks an altogether adequate alternative. The focus of this chapter, however, will be on demonstrating not the converging but diverging meanings of repentance and *tawba*. This is simply because it is usually taken for granted, even in scholarly studies, that the two function as neat equivalents.

The second chapter offers a detailed and meticulous analysis of *tawba* in the Qur'ān. One of the purposes of including such an inquiry in a study of Sufi approaches to this concept is to demonstrate the Qur'ānic background to many later Sufi ideas. As we shall see in subsequent chapters, many of the issues brought up for discussion by the early Sufis had strong scriptural precedents. By employing a method used by the remarkable Japanese scholar Toshihiko Izutsu in his studies of the Qur'ān, this chapter will attempt to define the semantic field of *tawba* through an internal analysis of Islam's sacred text. Although we shall occasionally consult external literature, such as *tafsīr* (exegetical commentaries), the primary intention is to draw out the Qur'ānic meaning of *tawba* through the text itself. This will involve examining not only the derivatives of the root **t-w-b**, but also those terms that tend to cluster around our point of focus. As a semantic analysis, particular attention will be given to the root meanings of those terms that congregate around *tawba* on a recurring basis. This will involve analyzing both its Qur'ānic synonyms and antonyms. By the end of this chapter we shall have a clearer idea of how *tawba* fits into the larger *Weltanschauung* of Muslim scripture.

Part II of this study consists of four chapters. Here, we begin to look at early Sufi notions of *tawba*. We shall begin in chapter 3 by exploring the idea of *tawba* as "interior conversion." That is to say, we shall examine how early Sufis understood *tawba* not simply as an act of turning away from a particular sin, but as an overall conversion experience in which a nominal allegiance to the faith one was born into was replaced by a whole-hearted commitment to God and the spiritual life. To this end, we shall look at the conversion or *tawba*-narratives of some of the Sufis of the early period, such as Ibrāhīm b. Adham and Fuḍayl b. ʿIyāḍ, as they have been portrayed in the biographical and hagiographical literature. In the process of this analysis, we shall identify and categorize the various means through which these conversions to the Sufi path were brought about. The purpose of this chapter is not to scrutinize or determine the veracity of these conversion narratives, which from a purely historical perspective remain suspect,[24] but to observe instead how the narratives were presented in the tradition. These stories, as we shall see, were not meant to function as existentially irrelevant historical accounts. Instead they had, as the authors of these narratives often openly confess, the specific goal of encouraging would-be mystics to submit themselves completely to God, just like the heroes of these narratives, or of allowing readers to draw some level of inspiration from them. By analyzing these narratives phenomenologically, we will highlight the various ways through which the Sufi tradition depicted the life-altering *tawba* and conversion experiences of some its most important early figures. This analysis is possible because we are fortunate enough to have rather elaborate accounts of the conversions of some of the early figures, particularly from the eighth and ninth centuries.

Chapter 4 is divided into two subsections. In the first part, we shall develop our understanding of the theme introduced in the previous chapter by further exploring *tawba* as a life-transforming alteration. This shall be done by situating *tawba* into the larger journey of the soul as it strives to ascend into the divine presence. In the process, we shall explore the Sufi understanding of the virtues essential for the spiritual ascent, particularly insofar as they are embodied in the states (*aḥwāl*) and stations (*maqāmāt*). This shall be followed by a brief analysis of the role wisdom sayings and aphorisms (*ḥikam*) played in the transmission of early Sufi ideas, as well as what they reveal to us about early notions of *tawba*. As part of our analysis, we shall examine the various levels of mystical realization or attainment from which a given concept could be conceived by underscoring the important function of what has been identified as the "ethical perspectivalism" of Sufi thought.

After this we shall proceed, in chapter 5, to explore *tawba* in the thought of four key figures from the early period: Kharrāz, Sahl al-Tustarī, Junayd, and Abū Bakr al-Wāsiṭī (d. 936). These individuals have not been randomly selected. Kharrāz is of importance because (with the exception of Muḥāsibī) his *Kitāb al-ṣidq* presents us with one of the earliest treatments of *tawba* in Sufism, particularly in relation to the larger scheme of ascending stations. As for Sahl al-Tustarī, his importance lies in the central place he assigned *tawba* in the spiritual life. He stands unique among early Sufis in emphasizing the necessity of continuously turning to God in *tawba*, regardless of one's state or degree of spiritual maturation. By studying the views of Sahl, we will also be in a better position to appreciate the views of Makkī, who was an heir to the Sahlian tradition as it was transmitted through his disciples. As for Junayd, although we have very few of his sayings on repentance, he is considered by many to be the most critical figure in the theoretical formation and development of Sufism. We shall look at his ideas on repentance because of the central role he played in the theoretical formation of the early tradition. Although Wāsiṭī was not as prominent as the other three, he was by no means insignificant in early Sufism. His ideas of repentance represent the most theoretically sophisticated views of the subject from the early period with respect to the metaphysics of *tawba*.

In chapter 6 we shall turn to examine in detail the views of Muḥāsibī, whose primary importance within the tradition rests on the role he played in developing a science of moral psychology. While it would have made sense to approach him before Kharrāz, at least if we were following a strict chronological order, the reason he will be examined independently in a separate chapter, immediately before Makkī, is because his writings offer, like the author of the *Qūt al-qulūb*, a relatively comprehensive treatment of *tawba* in the early period. In the interests of conceptual development, he will be studied alongside Makkī. In this chapter, we shall see how his many treatises are concerned not so much with mystical experiences, but with practical measures the aspirant should adopt in order to draw closer to God, and at the heart of which lies the practice of *muḥāsaba* or self-examination—from which he derives his name. In order to draw out his particular understanding of repentance, we shall consult more than a dozen of his treatises. The themes covered in this chapter include the obligatory nature of *tawba*, the relation of *tawba* to the larger return to God, the means by which the aspirant may overcome temptation, the danger of breaking one's resolve never to repeat the sin, and the importance of turning away from both outward and inner sins.

The final chapter is an analysis of *tawba* as it appears in Makkī's *Qūt al-qulūb*. As noted above, the book was one of the most influential and widely read works in early Sufism. Makkī's analysis of repentance in this work, to which he devoted an entire chapter, remains the lengthiest sustained single discussion of the concept in Sufi literature up to the tenth century. Despite overlaps with Muḥāsibī in his analysis, particularly because, like Muḥāsibī, he is concerned primarily with Sufi *praxis*, Makkī's psychology bears the stamp of Sahl al-Tustarī more than anyone else. The themes to be covered in this final chapter include the obligatory nature of *tawba*, the process and conditions of *tawba*, the importance of resolve and regret, the method through which the *tāʾib* can protect himself from falling back into sin, the merit of effortlessly abandoning sins, the importance of rectifying past wrongs, the categories of the *tāʾibūn*, and the highly contested question of whether the process of repentance ever comes to an end.

Readers who wish to avoid the technical analyses of *tawba* in Arabic and the Qurʾān may simply begin with the second part of this study, which holds together on its own and does not require a close reading of the first two chapters.

Part I

The Semantics of *Tawba*

Chapter 1

Is *Tawba* "Repentance"?

A Lexical and Semantic Survey

The purpose of this short chapter is to explore the semantic relation between "repentance" and the Arabic word commonly accepted as its equivalent. One of the purposes of this inquiry is to demonstrate that although the English term conveys many of the underlying connotations of the Arabic one, it neither sufficiently captures the semantic range nor the primary lexical sense of *tawba*. The absence of a precise English equivalent of *tawba*, in turn, occasionally obscures our understanding of the subtle and intricate use of the word both in the Qurʾān and the broader Islamic tradition, particularly in the writings of those representatives of the tradition who paid close attention to the language of Islamic revelation. At the same time, although repentance, as we shall see, is no more than a partial equivalent of *tawba*, it remains an adequate translation nonetheless, at least insofar as *tawba* is envisaged at the human level. Moreover, English does not offer us a better alternative to capture the range of meanings conveyed by the Arabic. Repentance can therefore be used as a relatively viable translation of *tawba* provided one remains aware of its intrinsic limitations within an Islamic context. This chapter will explore some of those limitations.

Repentance refers primarily to a feeling of grief, sorrow, contrition, or regret for something one has either done or left undone.[1] The word entered Modern and Middle English through the Old French *repentaunce* (v. *repentir*). Structurally, it is formed from a combination of the intensifying prefix *re* with the Latin *paenitēre*, from which the word ultimately derives, which means to experience dissatisfaction, sorrow, regret, or even torture.[2] The Latin root conveys the principle meaning of the English term, which refers to the negative psychological experience that follows in the wake of the commission of an ethical or religious wrong.[3]

The primary and most basic meaning of *tawba* (root **t-w-b**), on the other hand, is that of a "return" (*rujūʿ*).[4] This return, according to the classical lexical authorities, is either a "return to God from sin," a "return to God from something" (*min kadhā* or *ʿan kadhā*), a "return to God," a "return to obedience after sin," or simply a "return from sin."[5] *Tawba* thus entails a fundamental reorientation, a change of direction, toward a moral, ethical, or even ontological higher ground. Since it can never imply turning away from God or what is virtuous, its meaning is always positive. For *tawba* to be complete, it must be accepted by God. Thus, one of the poets sings in a couplet cited by Ibn Manẓūr (d. 1311):

> I have turned in *tawba* towards You, so accept my *tawba*
> And I have fasted my Lord, so accept my fast.[6]
>
> *Tubtu ilayka fa taqabbal tābatī*
> *Wa ṣumtu rabbī fa taqabbal ṣāmatī*

Tawba, unlike repentance, can also be an act of God. As a divine act, it means to relent, forgive, accept, turn, or return toward the human being in mercy and compassion.[7] This turning or returning can either be from divine wrath to mercy, from rejection to acceptance, or from punishment to forgiveness. It can also refer to a divine initiative that ultimately leads to the first glimmerings of human *tawba.* In all of these cases, the turning or returning is an act of mercy, compassion, and grace, and for the ultimate felicity of the human soul. The subject of the verbal form of *tawba* can usually be identified by the preposition that follows it: *tāba ʿalā* usually refers to divine *tawba; tāba ilā* usually refers to human *tawba.* But this is not, strictly speaking, always the case.[8] In the Qurʾān, however, this is the norm.

The primary sense of *tawba* as "return" can be illustrated by a word that many of the lexical authorities consider to be a derivate of **t-w-b**, namely *tābūt,* which refers to a chest or box (*ṣundūq*). Zabīdī (d. 1790) explains this derivation on the grounds that "whatever is taken out of it always returns to it."[9] *Tābūt* can also refer to the ribs, bosom, or chest (*aḍlāʿ*), and what they contain, such as the heart and lungs. The reason for this is almost certainly because the blood and air that leave the organs enclosed within the chest return back, so that what lies within it, like a *ṣundūq*, is not lost.[10] *Tabūt* is also used in the Qur'ān to refer to the Ark of the Covenant, which in biblical tradition held God's self-revelation in the form of the sacred tablets received by Moses at Mt. Sinai, and in which, says the Qur'ān, "is peace from your Lord" (*fīhi sakīna*[11] *min rabbikum*) (Q 2:248). This may have been—though it is mere speculation—because it was through the contents of the *tābūt*[12] that the fallen and exiled human being was able to return to God.

Tawba also has another meaning that cannot be extrapolated simply through linguistic analysis, namely that of "regret" or "contrition." The *ḥadīth* on which this meaning rests is often cited by the lexicographers alongside the religious sense of the term: *al-nadam tawba,* "regret is [a sign of] of *tawba.*"[13] This was the Prophet's response on being asked by his companions, "what is the sign of *tawba*?"[14] But many of the leading lexicographers, such as Khalīl b. ʿAyn (d. 776–791), Zamakhsharī (d. 1144), Ibn Sīda (d. 1065), Fīrūzābādī (d. 1413), Fayyūmī (d. 1368), Ibn Durayd (d. 933), and Ibn ʿAbbād (d. 995), to name but a few, exclude *nadam,* which can also mean "remorse," "contrition," "sorrow," or "sadness,"[15] altogether from their definitions of *tawba.* This is most likely because it lies outside of *taʿrīf al-tawba fī al-lugha,* that is to say, the principally linguistic meaning of the term. Thus, al-Rāghib al-Iṣfahānī (d. 1060) in his *Mufradāt alfāẓ al-qurʾān* includes *nadam* under a separate subsection on the religious meaning of the term (*tawba fī al-sharʿ*).[16]

It is also of some relevance to note that the advent of Islam has been called *zaman al-tawba,* the "time of return." This is because Islam caused the polytheists to turn away from *shirk* and return to God.[17] *Tawba* in this sense carries the general meaning of "conversion,"[18] insofar as it entails a return to One God, and a concomitant "aversion" from polytheism, even though the usual word for the idea is *aslama* (lit. "he surrendered").[19] In this light we can see why, as Ibn ʿAbbād contends, "*tawba* is Islam [itself]" (*al-tawba al-islām*).[20]

The semantic field of *tawba* can be more fully grasped by drawing attention to three words besides *rujūʿ* that are frequently used to explain its meaning. The lexicographers also employ *ināba,* and to a lesser extent, *awba* and *ʿawd,* to define *tawba.* Ibn Manẓūr, Ibn Sīda, and Zabīdī write that one who performed *tawba* to God, "*anāba* and *rajaʿa* from sin towards obedience."[21] Ibn Manẓūr, citing a previous authority, adds that the one who performed *tawba,* " *ʿāda* towards God, *rajaʿa* and *anāba.*"[22] All of these terms, like *rujūʿ*, convey the basic idea of "return," but with different emphases. *ʿAwd* and *awba,* along with their respective roots, **ʿ-w-d** and **ʾ-w-b**, are closest in their meanings to *rujūʿ*. Like it, they are neutral terms that can be used for nonreligious acts such as "returning home." But they can also take on very significant religious senses. *Al-maʿād*, from the same root as *ʿawd*, is used for the Hereafter or Resurrection. Literally, it is a "place to which one returns." As such, it is also a name of Mecca, because pilgrims frequently return to it.[23] A *maʾāb*, from the same root as *awba*, carries the same meaning, and is used to refer to "that place to which one is translated, or removed, by death."[24] The *maʾāb* can therefore also be God Himself (Q 36:13, 38:78). The *awwāb*, from the same root, is one who frequently turns to God in *tawba*.[25] *Ināba*, from the root **n-w-b**, includes among its meanings, "to replace," "to substitute," and "to come by in turns."[26] *Ināba* also means "to do *tawba* and return."[27] An act of *ināba* may, unlike these other terms, imply the necessity of obedience to God.[28] A *munīb*, like a *tāʾib*, is one who turns to God in obedience. But *munīb* can also more neutrally refer to a person who makes "another supply his or another's place," or even to "copious rain."[29] Perhaps the most significant difference between *tawba* and the aforementioned terms is that derivatives of **t-w-b** are almost entirely marked by an ostensible ethical coloring. In other words, they are almost exclusively of a religious nature (with *tābūt* remaining one of the notable exceptions). This cannot be said to the same degree of the derivatives of the other roots, **n-w-b**, **ʿ-w-d**, and **ʾ-w-b**.

Another important term that we should draw attention to, but one which has been curiously ignored by the lexical authorities in their explications of *tawba* and its root, is the root **th-w-b**. Its primary meaning is to return to a place after having left, or to "return after one's departure."[30] The semantic emphasis of *thāba* is on a return to a familiar place or state. Thus, the Arabic word for "raiment" or "garment," *thawb*, derives from this root because it is an item of clothing to which one repeatedly returns. The verbal root *thāba* can also be used to describe the gathering together and coming of a people, as well as the collecting of water.[31] Derivatives of the root **th-w-b** also take on significant religious meanings. An important Qurʾānic word for "reward" or "recompense," *thawāb*, derives from this very root, as it is that which one gains as a return for one's deed.[32] This return can either be a reward or a punishment.[33] The Kaʿba is also described in the Qurʾān as a *mathāba*[34] because it is a place to which people gather together and return,[35] or because it is where people are rewarded—that is, "given returns"—for their pilgrimages. This latter interpretation, however, is that of a minority.[36] A *mathāba* can also refer to that place from which water is drawn from a well,[37] presumably because people return to it.

For our purposes, it is important to observe that the relation between *thāba* and *tāba* is explicitly mentioned by Ibn Manẓūr when he writes in the opening of his entry for **th-w-b**: " 'so-and-so *thāba* towards God, and *tāba*,' with a [letter] *thā'* and *tā'*, that is to say, 'he came back and returned to obedience to Him' " (*ʿāda wa rajaʿa ilā ṭāʿatihi*).[38] He then notes that the words *tawwāb, awwāb, munīb,* and *thawwāb* all share the same meaning. The same observation reappears in Zabīdī. It is of interest to note here not only the semantic but morphological overlap between *tāba* and *thāba*: both words are separated only by a simple dot. Ibn Manẓūr seems to highlight this by his words, either "by a [letter] *thā'* or *tā'*." Curiously, many of the major lexicographers exclude the idea of *tawba* altogether in their definitions of *thāba*: Jawharī (d. 1007), Zamakhsharī, Ibn Fāris (d. 1004), Fayyūmī, Ibn ʿAbbād, Ibn Durayd, Ibn Sīda, Khalīl b. ʿAyn, Ṣaghānī (d. 1261), and Fīrūzābādī do not mention, even in passing, **t-w-b** or any of its derivatives in their entries for **th-w-b**. It is true that many of these authors are not particularly concerned with providing exhaustive definitions of terms. Ibn Fāris, for example, will simply give us the most elemental meaning of a word. But the absence of any reference to *tawba* is at least of some import in the works of Jawharī, Ibn Sīda, Fīrūzābādī, and to a lesser extent Zamakhsharī, in view of their more comprehensive definitions of terms.[39] Perhaps this absence reflects a point of scholarly disagreement over the very question of whether *tawba* was to be subsumed under **th-w-b**'s range of meanings. This disagreement might also have something to do with the fact that **th-w-b** and its derivatives, which appear in the Qur'ān twenty-eight times, never take on the meaning of *tawba*. That *tāba* appears as a definition of *thāba* in the *Lisān al-ʿarab* and the *Tāj al-ʿarūs*, the two most exhaustive Arabic dictionaries in the history of Arabic lexicography, however, gives us good reason to accept its inclusion in the semantic field of **th-w-b**.

We are now in a better position to understand some of the difficulties involved in translating *tawba* as repentance. The primary meaning of the latter, as we have already seen, is that of remorse, regret, and contrition for a past wrong. Its linguistic emphasis is on the painful psychological or emotional experience of the repentant individual. This emphasis has been well summarized by Karl Burger when he writes:

> [R]epentance is the feeling of pain experienced by man when he becomes conscious that he has done wrongly or improperly in thought, word, or deed. It always presupposes knowledge of fault, and is usually combined with judgment. It is a natural and involuntary feeling of pain, and is not the result

> of education, habit, or reflection [. . .] In dogmatic theology repentance is "godly sorrow" (II Cor. vii 10) and pain caused by having wronged God through sin (Ps. li. 4). This contrition is carefully distinguished from attrition, which fears only the punishment and evil consequences of sin.[40]

Tawba involves, on the other hand, as we have seen, a psycho-spatial reorientation, a return to God from what is other than God, or a return to virtue from vice, or, in the case of God, a turning toward the human being in mercy and forgiveness. Only secondarily does *tawba* potentially signify regret or contrition for a past wrong. But even though this latter meaning, as we have also seen, does not lie within the linguistic sense of the term, many of the lexicographers include it within the wider range of meanings it subsumes. From this point of view, *tawba* and repentance overlap, even though their centers do not.

A much closer equivalent to *tawba* is the Hebrew *teshubah*, a word that derives from the root **sh-w-b**, the primary meaning of which is to "turn back" or "return."[41] William Holladay, in the introduction to his monograph on this Hebrew root in the Old Testament, observes that the Arabic *thāba* has "exactly the central meaning which we shall assign to *shub*."[42] He also notes that the Hebrew *shūb*, along with the Aramaic *tūb*, are both Semitic cognates of the Arabic term, which, as we saw above, is remarkably close both morphologically and in meaning to *tāba*. This principle etymological relation between the three Semitic words, (*shūb*, *tūb*, *thāba*), is confirmed by others.[43] To this family of Semitic cognates should also be added the Ugaritic *thb* ("to return, bring word, answer") and the Syriac *tāb* ("to return, hand back").[44]

The similarity between the Arabic *tawba* and the Hebrew *teshubah* is highlighted by the fact that *shūb* is frequently, but not always, used in the Hebrew Bible in the same way *tāba* is used in the Qurʾān: to describe an act of return, either by God or the human being, tied in some way to the leaving of sin, vice, or impiety. *Shūb* and *tāba* are close lexical counterparts and are employed within the sacred discourse of their respective religious traditions in remarkably similar fashion. Thus we read, for example, in the Hebrew Bible, such passages as, "Turn Thou unto us O Lord, and we shall be turned" (Lamentations 5:21), and "Rend your heart and not your garments, and turn unto the Lord your God" (Joel 2:13), in which *shūb* is used for each instance of "turn." These uses of the Hebrew word bear a striking resemblance to the uses of *tāba* in the Qurʾān, where we find such passages as, "Then God turned to them that they might return to Him" (Q 24:31), and "Turn to God with a sincere returning" (Q 66:8), in which *tāba* is also used for each instance of "re/turn."

There are, however, some differences between uses of the two words. First of all, *shūb*, as used in the Bible, can take on not only the neutral meaning of "returning," but also, and more importantly, the negative meaning of apostasy or turning away from God.[45] This, as we know, is unlike the use of *tāba* and its cognates in the Qur'ān, which always carry a positive sense. The Qur'ān employs an altogether different term to express the opposite idea of *tawba*, namely *tawallā*, and to a lesser extent, *irtadda*. This shall be explored in greater detail in the following chapter. Second, the noun *teshubah* does not occur in the Bible in a religious sense; only the verb *shūb* does.[46] *Teshubah* is a uniquely religious term coined by rabbinic authorities, but one that nevertheless captures the central teachings of the Hebrew Bible regarding the human being's return to God after sin. Although the rabbis invested *teshubah* with a technical religious meaning, they did not originate the thoroughly biblical concept it represented. The rabbinic authorities eventually came to define *teshubah* as "a turning away from sin and a turning towards God,"[47] much the same way the Arabic lexicographers defined *tawba*. In the Muslim and Jewish traditions, therefore, *tawba* and *teshubah* remain close if not exact lexical counterparts even though they may not necessarily encapsulate the same constellation of theological doctrines.[48]

Keeping in mind the similarities between these two terms, it is not surprising that some Jewish scholars have found repentance to be an inadequate translation of the Hebrew word. In his article on the biblical concept of *teshubah*, Jacob Petuchowski expressed this discontentment when he wrote:

> I have as much as possible, tried to avoid translating teshuvah as "repentance." Our English "repentance" comes to us from the Latin. Its basic meaning is "to make sorry." To feel sad and sorry about our sins is indeed an essential part of the process of regeneration. But, as Bible and Talmud see it, it is only a part.[49]

Petuchowski's observation that sadness and sorrow are "only a part" of the restorative process of *teshubah* is of significance, since, as we saw, regret is also a religious component of *tawba*. But Hebrew, like Arabic, has an altogether different word to express this sense of regret, remorse, sadness, and sorrow, namely *naham*.[50] Regret emerges as a component of *tawba / teshubah* when we probe into the deeper human psychological experience of returning to God from some spiritual deficiency or moral shortcoming. But the linguistic emphasis of both terms is on the act of returning and not on the negative psychological state which usually accompanies it. *Nadam* and *naham* are constituents of *tawba* and *teshubah* but they are not its central elements, at least from a purely lexical sense. *Naham* and *nadam* come very close, on the other hand, to the linguistic meaning of repentance. Montefiore astutely notes this with regard to the Hebrew word when he writes that "the verb . . . [**n-h-m**] seems to mean 'to be sorry, to feel pain or regret,' and thus closely corresponds to the root meaning of our word 'repentance.'"[51] *Naham* as employed in the Hebrew Bible usually signifies divine regret or repentance. It is used to mean human regret or repentance no more than seven times.[52] *Shūb* and its cognates, on the other hand, appear more than a thousand times. It is the standard "Old Testament" word to signify what we have in mind by *tawba*.

This brings us to a closer understanding of the theological origin of the very word *repentance*. One of the peculiar differences between the Septuagint—that is, the Greek translation of the Hebrew Bible—and the New Testament (authored as it was in Greek), in particular in the gospels, is of the terminology employed for the *teshubah* concept. In the Septuagint, the Hebrew *shūb* is consistently translated by the Greek *epistrepho*.[53] This word has very much the same meaning as *shūb*. In its verbal form, it can mean anything from "turn about," "turn around," and "turn toward," to "return" or even "convert."[54] Like *shūb*, it can carry both a neutral as well as more religious meanings. The word *naham* on the other hand is translated in the Septuagint by the Greek *metanoia*, and to a lesser extent, *metamelomai*[55] (both of which are sometimes used as synonyms).[56] It is *metanoia*, however, that is of primary interest to us. In its strictest etymological sense, it means "change of mind" or "afterthought," being, as it is, a combination of the Greek "meta" ("after") and "noia" (cognate of *nous* = "mind," "thought"). But it also means to "regret" or "repent," which is why it was employed as a suitable translation of *naham*.[57] It was for this reason that Nave was so easily able to highlight the various ways *metanoia* captured the idea of regret or remorse in classical Greek literature.[58] *Epistrepho*, however, like the root *shūb*, does not connote regret or remorse the way *metanoia* does. Yet when we come to the New Testament gospels, the gospel writers employ *metanoia*, rather than, as we would expect, *epistrepho*, to convey the idea of *teshubah*. This is despite the fact that Jesus the Jew would have spoken of *teshubah*,[59] and despite the fact that in Jewish literature in Greek, *epistrepho* is repeatedly used to describe *teshubah*.[60] Although an exploration of the underlying reasons behind this terminological shift would take us too far into the realm of New Testament scholarship,[61] it is important at least to note that such a shift occurred, and its role in shaping some of our assumptions about the nature of repentance.

To summarize the findings of our brief overview, repentance is a relatively adequate translation of *tawba* because the semantic fields of both words sufficiently overlap to allow them to function as general equivalents. Repentance, in this light, remains a suitable term to express the idea of *tawba*. This is particularly the case because insofar as repentance places an accent on the negative emotional aftermath of sin, its meaning intersects with the religious meaning of *tawba* (*ta'rīf al-tawba fī al-shar'*), which is that of regret, remorse, contrition, and sorrow (= Arabic *nadam*; Hebrew *naham*). At the same time, the central and most defining features of *tawba* and repentance are not semantically shared, and for this reason it remains no more than a partial equivalent. Repentance is not an exact translation of *tawba*, nor does it capture the primary sense of the term (= *rujū'*). This is partly evident by the fact that, as we shall see more closely in the following chapter, we can speak of divine and human *tawba* in the Qur'ān and the Islamic tradition, but not of divine and human repentance.[62] The very act of *tawba* is a part of a dialectical relationship between God and the human being, in which the two jointly partake of a process of turning and returning: God turns to the human being in *tawba*, after he falls, through an act of mercy; the human being responds in *tawba*, partly out of regret (= repentance); then God accepts in *tawba*, through an act of relenting and forgiveness. We cannot postulate a similar dynamic of repentance. It is for this reason that, at least in the following chapter on *tawba* in the Qur'ān, *tawba* will be translated almost entirely through its primarily lexical sense of "re/turn." This is to enable us to appreciate the way *tawba* figures into the wider divine–human relationship that is so vividly presented in the Qur'ān. In the subsequent chapters (3–7), however, we shall freely alternate between *tawba* and repentance, having clarified from the outset the limitations of the latter. One of the reasons that repentance will be used for *tawba* in these later chapters is that, because most of this study focuses on the literature of "practical Sufism," our attention will be directed primarily to the human dimension of *tawba*, and even here, to the preliminary stages of the Sufi journey. Regret, as we shall see, plays a central role in these early stages. To speak of *tawba* as a re/turn alone would be to ignore the emotional element that accompanies the Arabic.

Chapter 2

The Internal Structure and Semantic Field of *Tawba* in the Qur'ān

An Izutsian Method of Semantic Analysis

Having analyzed the meaning of *tawba* on the basis of a survey of the classical lexicons, we shall now turn to explore the meaning of *tawba* more specifically in the Qur'ān. This shall be done by employing a method of semantic analysis previously utilized by Toshihiko Izutsu in two of his own central studies of the text.[1] One of the distinguishing features of this method is that it approaches the terms and concepts of the Qur'ān as they stand in relation to each other, the purpose of which is to define the semantic boundaries of these terms, principally, but not exclusively, through an internal analysis of the text itself. This method will be of particular benefit for our purposes because it will allow us to isolate, to the best of our abilities, the idea of *tawba* in the Qur'ān, so that we may then compare it later in this study with the sense it has in the Sufi tradition. We will also be able to see the importance that terms which semantically congregate around *tawba* in the Qur'ān take in various Sufi texts, ranging from those of Kharrāz and Muḥāsibī to Sarrāj and Makkī. A preliminary chapter of this kind will be particularly beneficial because of the extent to which Sufi discussions are grounded in Islam's primary text.[2]

Izutsu's method of semantic analysis is premised on a distinction he draws, following the lead of other semanticists, between the "basic" and "relational" meanings of terms in any given language.[3] The "basic" meaning of a term is its most elementary meaning, something it carries in whatever system—philosophical, theological, mystical, or literary—it functions within. As a linguistic constant, it is an element inherent within the term itself and which remains unchanged. The "relational" meaning, on the other hand, is the meaning the term acquires within a given system of thought or cultural milieu. It is the sense the word takes on when it stands in multiple and diverse relations to a range of other words, all of which form, as a whole, the vocabulary of that given system. Izutsu explains this distinction through a simple example from the Qur'ān:

> The word *kitāb*, for example, means basically the same thing whether it is found in the Koran or outside the Koran [. . . but . . .] In the Koran context, the word *kitāb* assumes an unusual importance as the sign of a very particular religious concept surrounded by a halo of sanctity. This comes from the fact that in this context the word stands in a very close relation to the concept of divine Revelation, or rather various concepts having direct reference to Revelation. This means that the simple word *kitāb* with its simple basic meaning "book," once introduced into a particular system and given a certain definite position in it, acquires a lot of new semantic elements arising out of this particular situation, and also out of the various relations it is made to bear to other major concepts of that system [. . .] Thus in this case, the word *kitāb*, as soon as it is introduced into the Islamic conceptual system, is put into close connection with such important Koran words as Allāh, *waḥy* "revelation," *tanzīl* "sending down (of divine words)," *nabīy* "Prophet," *ahl* "people" (in the particular combination of *ahl al-kitāb* "the people of the Scripture" meaning peoples who possess a Book of Revelation like Christians and Jews, etc.). Henceforward, the word in the characteristically Koranic context will have to be understood in terms of all these related terms, and this association alone gives the word *kitāb* very special semantic coloring, that is, very complex and particular meaning structure which it would never have acquired if it remained outside of this system.[4]

We might also add here that the degree of connotative difference between a term's basic and relational meaning varies from one term to another. The word *kitāb* is itself a rather neutral word but acquires, in the Qur'ān, a uniquely religious import. Yet if we look at another word, such as *īmān* ("faith"), it already in its most elemental form seems to carry a strong religious connotation, and so the difference between its basic and relational meaning is not as wide. The difference of degree, it should also be noted, may depend on the particular kind of system in which the word functions. Despite varying degrees of difference, however, a clear distinction can still be drawn between the conceptual core of a word and the larger meaning it acquires relationally. It is also of some importance to keep in mind, that, as Izutsu argues, the basic meaning is a mere "methodological concept" that lacks any kind of concrete existence in the real world. This is because words are always situated in an elaborate web of associations and never exist outside of a network of highly complex relations. As a methodological concept, the basic meaning of a word allows one to "analyze the meaning of a word scientifically." It thereby functions as a scientific tool to help one determine the larger meaning of a word within any given system of thought; this, even though it remains, in and of itself, a mere abstraction.

Izutsu's main purpose in employing a method of semantic analysis was to map out the ethical and ontological worldview of Islam's primary sacred text. Our purpose, though more modest, is to do the same for the idea of *tawba*. And we shall attempt this in much the same way Izutsu did for such central Qur'ānic concepts as *kufr, waḥy, islām, īmān,* and *dīn,* by analyzing those concepts that cluster around our point of focus. A semantic analysis is of particular use for our intended purpose because it is essentially a conceptual analysis. By relationally defining a term we are, in effect, determining the parameters of the concept it denotes. And this is because, as Izutsu writes,

> the linguistic is simply the other side of the conceptual. A "concept," however it may be defined, is in itself but an extremely elusive wooly thing, hard to grasp and always with a blurred outline. It begins to exist as an independent entity with a more or less fixed contour and stability only when it comes to be couched in a linguistic form, i.e. a word.[5]

Our particular semantic analysis of *tawba* shall therefore consist of exploring just how *tawba* is employed in the Qur'ān. We shall look primarily at those terms that tend to accompany it, those that are paired with it as synonyms or near synonyms, and those that serve to express opposing meanings. We will also pay attention to the frequency in which some of these words appear in the "*tawba* verses," that is, those verses in which a derivative of the root **t-w-b** occurs. We shall also look at less directly related terms, the analysis of which will contribute to shedding more light on the larger Qur'ānic concept under consideration. In the course of our study, we will pay particular attention to the underlying meanings conveyed by the roots of Qur'ānic terms. For this, occasional use shall be made of Iṣfahānī's authoritative lexicon of Qur'ānic Arabic, the *Mufradāt alfāẓ al-qur'ān,* of which some use was made in the previous chapter. Because, however, the very nature of our inquiry is, first and foremost, an internal analysis of the Qur'ān itself, minimal use will be made, on the whole, of extra-Qur'ānic sources. In those few instances where such sources will be employed, it will simply be to illuminate an obscure or puzzling feature of the Qur'ān's use of *tawba.* The intention behind this strategy, as already noted, is to better enable us to understand the range of meanings *tawba* takes on in the Qur'ān so that we can then compare it with the sense it has in the Sufi tradition.[6]

Forms of *Tawba* in the Qur'ān

The root **t-w-b** and its cognates appear in the Qur'ān a total of eighty-seven times spread out in sixty-nine verses. God is the subject of *tawba* thirty-four times, in more than a third of its occurrences. When applied to God, the word occurs as a verb (*tāba, yatūbu/a, atūbu, tub*), in intensive active participle form (*tawwāb*), or as a verbal noun (*tawba*). In its verbal form, it can express, besides its primary sense of "re/turn," anything from "pardon," "forgive," "relent," "accept," "guide," "show mercy," "readily accept a human *tawba,*" or even "cause a human *tawba.*" In intensive active participle form, as *tawwāb,* it simply emphasizes any of the meanings of its verbal form. *Tawwāb* ("Oft-returning") as a divine attribute occurs in the Qur'ān a total of ten times, usually at the end of a verse or cluster of verses addressing some aspect of human *tawba.* The occurrence of God as *Tawwāb* at the very end of the verses seems to highlight the ultimacy of divine *tawba.* As a verbal noun, as *tawba,* the word occurs only twice, and this in two consecutive verses (Q 4:17–18),[7] where, as the context makes clear, it means either divine "relenting," "pardoning," "accepting," or "forgiving." These specific verses, along with the nature of divine *tawba,* will be analyzed further below.

In reference to the human being, the word *tawba* appears as a verb (*tāba, tābā, tubtu, tubtum, tatūbā, yatūbu, yatūbū, yatūbūna, tūbū*), in active participle form (*tā'ib, tā'ibūn, tā'ibāt*), in intensive active participle form once (*tawwābīn*), as a verbal noun (*tawba, tawbatuhum, al-tawb*), and once as an accusative noun (*matāb*). The general meaning of the word in relation to the human being varies from its basic sense of a "re/turn to God or obedience from sin," to "seek divine forgiveness," to "repent" or "seek divine acceptance." In reference to the human being, *tawba* most frequently occurs in its plural verbal form.

Tawba and Rectification

The Root ṣ-l-ḥ

One of the most striking characteristics of human *tawba* as it appears in the Qurʾān is that, as a religious act, it is not restricted, as one might expect, to the average, fallible believer. The subject of human *tawba* in fact encompasses virtually the entire spectrum of human types, ranging from the hypocrite, disbeliever, and sinful believer to the pious believer and even prophet. The reason for this is quite simply because no one, not even the recipient of divine revelation, is entirely faultless. The nature of the *tawba* on the part of the human being corresponds to the particular nature of his ethico-religious crime or short-falling, and this, in turn, varies from one individual to the next and depends largely on where he stands in the Qurʾānic hierarchy of human types. The sins one must turn away from range from the most heinous, of associating partners with God (*shirk*), hypocrisy (*nifāq*), and disbelief (*kufr*) to major sins (*kabāʾir*) and minor sins (*ṣaghāʾir*).

It is of some importance to note that the particular kind of *tawba* that is called for is occasionally made evident by a particular kind of religious act or virtue that is mentioned alongside *tawba*—the same religious virtue that, in most cases, the person lacks. *Tawba* in itself is simply a return, but what does this return entail? How might this return be possible? The Qurʾān does not always remain silent on this matter and sometimes goes beyond its general call to *tawba* by specifying the act or acts that must accompany it. This is because God does not, as we shall shortly see, accept every *tawba*. Thus when Q 4:145–146 claims, in no uncertain terms, that "the hypocrites will be in the fire," and then qualifies this assertion immediately afterward with the words, "except those who return (*tābū*)," the qualification does not end there. In order for the hypocrites to be saved, the Qurʾān adds the need to make amends, hold fast to God, and, most important, make one's religion pure for God (*akhlaṣū dīnahum li Allāh*). These additional qualifications, particularly the last one, make complete sense, for it is precisely the insincerity of the hypocrites that destines them to perdition. Since their profession of faith is not matched by an inner sincerity, their *tawba* must involve a self-surrender marked by genuine *ikhlāṣ* and an unswerving commitment to God. Only then will they be "with the *mu'minīn*" and entitled to an "immense reward" in the afterlife. Similarly, when the Qur'ān speaks of the *tawba* of the polytheists in Q 9:5 and 9:11, it adds as a requisite to their act of *tawba,* in both cases, the establishment of ritual prayer and the payment of alms in order for their Islam to be accepted. Only then, the Qur'ān continues, are they "your brothers in faith" (*ikhwānukum fī al-dīn*). Here the Qur'ān demands, alongside *tawba,* key Islamic rituals that distinguish the Muslims from polytheists and other non-Muslims, whereas no such demand was made of the hypocrites in the previous verse. This is simply because they already conformed to the external rites of Islam. Yet another example of this kind occurs in Q 2:159–160, when the Qur'ān castigates those who "conceal the proofs and guidance which God has revealed" (*yaktumūna mā anzalnā min al-bayyināt wa al-hudā*), warning them of the curse of God. Then the Qur'ān continues by asserting that only those shall escape the curse who perform *tawba,* make amends, and "reveal the proofs (*bayyanū*)"—the same kinds of proofs (*bayyināt*) that they previously concealed.

In most cases, however, the Qur'ān does not specify the precise nature of the *tawba* that is demanded or the kind of act that must accompany it. But it does recurringly emphasize the importance of *iṣlāḥ,* roughly translated as "the making of amends," "setting aright," "rectification," or "reform."[8] This was evident in two of the three previous examples cited above, where the specification came only after the general quality of "making amends" was mentioned. In fact, the verbal form of *iṣlāḥ—aṣlaḥa*—is more frequently coupled with the verbal form of human *tawba* than any other word. It appears immediately alongside *tawba* in almost a sixth of its total occurrences—seven out of forty. The syntactic structure of this coupling, which is always very similar, highlights the close connection between these two concepts:

> Except such of them as *tābū, aṣlaḥū,* and make manifest the truth . . . (Q 2:160).

> Except those who *tābū, aṣlaḥū,* and hold fast to God . . . (Q 4:146).

> Except those who *tābū* after that, and *aṣlaḥū*. Surely God is Forgiving . . . (Q 3:89).
>
> Except those who *tābū* after that, and *aṣlaḥū*. Surely God is Forgiving . . . (Q 24:5).
>
> And if they *tābā* and *aṣlaḥā,* then let them be (Q 4:16).
>
> And he who *tāba* after his wrongdoing, and *aṣlaḥa* . . . (Q 5:39).
>
> Whoso of you does wrong in ignorance, and then *tāba* after that, and *aṣlaḥa* . . . (Q 6:54).

The close pairing makes it rather clear that in the Qur'ānic *Weltanschauung, tawba* is not simply a "feeling of regret" or "remorse," as we might conclude from the etymology of "repentance," a central point highlighted in the previous chapter, but ties, instead, very closely to the idea of rectification. This is confirmed by other instances in which the term *iṣlāḥ* appears surrounding a *tawba* verse and where the connection between the two concepts becomes clear upon closer scrutiny. One such instance of this kind occurs in the sūra of *Hūd*: shortly after Shu'ayb tells his people that "I desire only *iṣlāḥ* [for you]," he calls them to "seek forgiveness of your Lord and re/turn to Him (*thumma tūbū ilayhi*)" (Q 11:88–90), intertwining thereby these two notions. The close relation between *tawba* and "setting aright" finds further evidence in Q 4:92. Although neither *iṣlāḥ* nor any of its cognates appear in this verse, the idea of restoration is clearly present. The verse addresses the topic of the accidental killing of a believer, and the two forms of compensation that are to be made by the guilty party, namely the paying of blood money and the freeing of a believing slave. For one who does not have the means to compensate, however, the verse goes on to say that a fast of two consecutive months is required. This fast is referred to as a "*tawba* from God"—a *tawba,* because, as an act of penance, it serves to absolve the guilty party of his crime. As our examples make clear, *tawba* is not simply an emotional or psychological experience, but a re/turn to God accompanied by restorative acts that attempt to eliminate the disorder that was introduced, at either the individual or collective level, or both, by the commission of an ethical or religious wrong.

It is also of some interest to observe that in the Qur'ān, *iṣlāḥ,* like *tawba,* is not restricted to the human being. *Iṣlāḥ* insofar as it is an act of God and the human being furnishes us with an example of the symmetrical relationship that often characterizes the ethical relationship between God and the human being. Like human *iṣlāḥ*, divine *iṣlāḥ* also entails the eradication of a moral or ethical fault and the setting of things aright.[9] Unlike human *tawba*, however, *iṣlāḥ* is not generally coupled in the Qurʾān with divine *tawba*. In only one of the verses in which *tawba* appears is there any mention of divine *iṣlāḥ*.[10]

The central place that "right action" occupies in *tawba* is reinforced by another closely related expression that also appears alongside *tawba*, that of *ʿamila ṣāliḥan*, "to perform a righteous act." Both *aṣlaḥa* and *ṣāliḥ* ("righteous deed") derive from the same **ṣ-l-ḥ** root, but whereas the emphasis of the former is on the rectifying quality of the act, in the latter it is on the goodness of the deed itself and does not imply the presence of a pre-existent wrong. There are five instances of *ʿamila ṣāliḥan* immediately alongside *tawba*.[11] Even though the wording in one of these slightly varies (*ʿamila ʿamalan ṣāliḥan*), its meaning remains essentially the same.

> Except for the one who *tāba, āmana,* and *ʿamila sāliḥan* (Q 19:60).
>
> As for the one who *tāba, āmana,* and *ʿamila ṣālihan* . . . (Q 28:67).
>
> I am Forgiving to him who *tāba, āmana,* and *ʿamila sāliḥan* . . . (Q 20:82).
>
> And who *tāba* and *ʿamila ṣālihan* (Q 25:71).
>
> Except for one who *tāba, āmana,* and *ʿamila ʿamalan sāliḥan* (Q 25:70).

The most obvious feature of this group of verses, at least for our concerns, lies in the interposition of *īmān* between righteous deeds and *tawba* (except in the case of Q 25:71, but this verse follows another one with the aforementioned characteristic). The main reason for this seems to be that all of these verses immediately follow other verses that single out various serious religious crimes typically associated with disbelief—associating others with God, corrupting the teachings of prophets, causing discord in the earth—deserving of God's chastisement. In order to escape chastisement, the Qurʾān specifies that the guilty one must re/turn to God through faith and righteous deeds. The verses illustrate not only the well-known relation between *īmān* and *ṣāliḥāt*, but also between the latter and *tawba*.[12] This latter relationship is particularly reinforced by the manner in which Q 25:71 ends. The Qur'ān says that the one who does *tawba* and performs righteous deeds "verily re/turns to God with a true re/turning." Iṣfahānī notes that this final part of the verse emphasizes the complete and perfect nature of this *tawba* (*al-tawba al-tāmma*) because through it the individual brings together both "abandonment of the (morally) repugnant (*qabīḥ*) and pursuit of the (morally) beautiful (*jamīl*)."[13]

Tawba and Forgiveness

The Root gh-f-r

Another concept even more closely tied to the notion of *tawba*—both divine and human *tawba*—is forgiveness: "seeking forgiveness (*istighfār*)" in the case of the human being and granting it (*maghfira, ghufrān*) in the case of God. The most commonly used words for forgiveness in the Qur'ān, as well as those most closely related to *tawba* in the Qur'ān, derive from the root **gh-f-r**. Although the Qur'ān also employs the root **ʿ-f-w**, it occurs much less frequently than **gh-f-r**, and on only two occasions does it appear in the *tawba* verses. Some observations shall be made about **ʿ-f-w** later, as well as the root **ṣ-f-ḥ**. Our primary analysis of the relation between *tawba* and forgiveness shall, for the time being, focus on the **gh-f-r** root.

Derivatives of **gh-f-r**, as we just noted, are very closely tied in the Qur'ān to **t-w-b**. The human being is the subject of *istighfār* on nine occasions in the *tawba* verses. In five of these, *istighfār* is coupled immediately alongside *tawba*, as in the case of *iṣlāḥ* earlier. Four of these pairings, moreover, occur in the same sūra. The reason for this becomes clearer upon analysis of the sūra's order and contents. It opens with the Prophet Muḥammad being commanded to call his community to "serve none but God" (Q 11:2) and "*istaghfirū* [seek forgiveness from] your Lord, then *tūbū'* to Him" (Q 11:3). It then goes on to recount the stories of previous prophets and the opposition that they, like the Prophet of Islam, also encountered. The sūra highlights not only the extent to which the call of these prophets remained essentially the same, but the central place of *tawba* and *istighfār* in that call. The Prophet is shown to be fundamentally no different from previous warners, and his message is essentially the same as those who received revelation before him. In the sūra, the prophets Hūd, Ṣāliḥ, and Shuʿayb are all shown to have beseeched their communities in the same words as the Prophet.

Hūd: O my people, serve God. You have no god but Him . . . And *istaghfirū* your Lord, then *tūbu* to Him . . . (Q 11:50, 52).

Ṣāliḥ: O my people, serve God. You have no god but Him . . . *fastaghfirū* Him, then *tūbū* to Him . . . (Q 11:61).

Shuʿayb: O my people, serve God. You have no god but Him . . . *wastaghfirū* your Lord, then *tūbū* to Him . . . (Q 11:84, 90).

The ordering of these pairs should not lead one to believe that *tawba* necessarily follows *istighfār*. This is because in the other instance of this pairing, the order is reversed: "Will they not *yatūbūna* to God and *yastaghfirūna* Him" (Q 5:74).

Beyond these examples, there is further, perhaps even stronger, evidence for the proximity of these two concepts. This lies in the fact that the Qurʾān on occasion presents divine *maghfira* (forgiveness) as the response to human *tawba*, and divine *tawba* as the response to human *istighfār* (seeking forgiveness). Examples for the former are found in Q 20:82, when God says, "I am Forgiving (*Ghaffār*) to him who *tāba* to Me," and in Q 40:7, when the angels pray, "Our Lord! You encompass all things in mercy and knowledge. Forgive those who *tābū* to you." Examples for the latter can be found in Q 4:64, when the Prophet is told that if a certain group of Muslims who had sinned had "come to you and asked for God's forgiveness, and the Messenger had asked forgiveness for them, they would have found God *Tawwāb*," that is to say, they would have found God forgiving.[14] And in Q 110:3, we read God commanding the believers to "celebrate the praises of your Lord and seek His forgiveness. Surely He is *Tawwāb*." Here, once again, divine *tawba* is presented as the response to the human being's prayer for forgiveness.

These instances serve to illustrate not only the proximity between human *istighfār* and human *tawba*, but also divine *maghfira* and divine *tawba*. This is not to make a redundant claim because all concepts that directly relate to human *tawba* do not necessarily relate to divine *tawba*, and vice versa. *Iṣlāḥ*, for example, does not play a paramount role in divine *tawba*. Forgiveness, on the other hand, plays such a role in both. The concept of forgiveness is in fact so closely tied to the notion of *tawba* that derivatives of the root **gh-f-r** appear a total of twenty-eight times in twenty-five of the sixty-nine *tawba* verses—more than a third of them. If our criterion is to be purely quantitative, forgiveness remains the most closely related concept to *tawba* envisaged at both the divine and human level.

But we should also note that the concept of divine *maghfira* seems to have a particularly close relation to divine *tawba*, closer, in fact, than human *tawba* does to human *istighfār*. And there seems to be both quantitative and semantic evidence for this in the Qur'ān. At the quantitative level, we find that, in the *tawba* verses, God is almost twice as often the subject of a **gh-f-r** derivative as the human being—seventeen as opposed to nine, to be precise (in the other two cases it is the angels seeking forgiveness for believers). Fifteen of these seventeen occurrences appear at the end of a verse, usually in the form, "God is *Ghafūr*, Merciful," to remind the reader of this overarching divine quality. In the other two, God is described as *Ghāfir al-dhanb*, "The Forgiver of Sin" (Q 40:3) and in the intensive form, *al-Ghaffār*, "The Oft-Forgiving" (Q 20:82). All three of the major divine attributes of *maghfira*—*Ghāfir*, *Ghafūr*, and *Ghaffār*—therefore appear in the *tawba* verses. This is of some significance because *Ghāfir* appears in only one other instance in the Qur'ān, and *Ghaffār* in only four others. Now if, beyond this, we also consider that God is the subject of *tawba* in about two-fifths of the total occurrences of **t-w-b**, and that, as just noted, twice the number of **gh-f-r** derivatives in these verses have God, as opposed to man, as their subject (excluding the angels), we realize that, at least insofar as numbers are concerned, **gh-f-r** derivatives are significantly more often coupled with the idea of divine *tawba* than they are with human *tawba*. For the fifty-three instances of human *tawba* in the *tawba* verses, there are nine instances of human *istighfār*, and for the thirty-four instances of divine *tawba*, there are seventeen instances of divine *maghfira*. This means that for roughly every instance of human *istighfār*, there are six instances of human *tawba*, and for every instance of divine *maghfira*, there are two instances of divine *tawba*, giving us the following ratios: human *tawba* to human *istighfār* is 6:1, and divine *tawba* to divine *maghfira* is 2:1. Even if we were to factor into our ratio the fact that **gh-f-r** derivatives, are, on the whole, more commonly used of God than of the human being in the Qur'ān, this still would not weaken our conclusion that divine *maghfira* and *tawba* are more frequently coupled together than human *istighfār* and *tawba* in the *tawba* verses.

But the stronger evidence for the affinity of these two concepts lies in their close semantic relationship. We see this perhaps most clearly when we analyze the terms the Qurʾān tends to employ as the opposites of the terms we are considering. We find, for example, that although the opposing terms the Qurʾān tends to employ for human *tawba* and *istighfār* remain different, those that it employs for divine *tawba* and *maghfira* are the same. The opposite of human *tawba* is almost always the second or fifth form of **w-l-y**, *tawallā* and *tatawallā*, both of which literally mean, in the *tawba* contexts, "to turn away."[15] Two examples from sūra *al-Tawba* illustrate this opposition:

> So if you *tubtum*, it is better for you, but if you *tawallāytum*, know that you cannot escape God . . . (Q 9:3).

> If they *yatūbū* it will be better for them. And if they *yatawallaw*, God will punish them with a painful punishment in this world and the next . . . (Q 9:74).

As for *istighfār*, the Qurʾān does not employ an opposing term other than the word itself prefaced by the negative participle *lā* or *lam*. Thus we read, for example, such verses as these:

> *Istaghfir* for them or *lā tastaghfir* for them . . . (Q 9:80).

> It is the same for them whether you *astaghfarta* for them, or *lam tastaghfir* for them (Q 63:6).

Although it is true that *tawallā* is seemingly used as an opposite of *istighfār* in Q 11:3 and Q 11:52, this, we can be quite certain, is only because *tawba* is coupled in these instances with *istighfār*, and that *tawallā* is either being used as the opposite of *tawba*, or as the opposite of *istighfār* and *tawba* combined, but not of *istighfār* alone. There are no instances in the Qurʾān where *tawallā* is directly employed as the opposing term for *istighfār* when the latter appears by itself, as in the case of *tawba*, and in which the polarity is immediately apparent. This does not mean that in the broader semantic sense *tawallā* does not stand at the opposite end of *istighfār*. Indeed, anyone who refuses to seek the forgiveness of God has, in the Qurʾānic perspective, definitely "turned away" from God's mercy and exposed himself to His wrath. This becomes quickly apparent when we see how the Qur'ān describes those who neglect to seek God's forgiveness. But insofar as the Qur'ān singles out certain words as opposites of others, *tawallā* does not stand as the negative counterpart to *istighfār* in the way *tawba* does.[16]

As for both divine *tawba* and *maghfira,* the term the Qur'ān almost always uses to express the opposite meanings of these terms is *ʿadhāb,* or "punishment" (root **ʿ-dh-b**). If God does not re/turn to the servant or forgive his sin, He punishes him. Some examples of how this oppositional pairing is expressed appear in the following instances:

> It is no concern for you (O Muḥammad) whether He *yatūba* to them, or whether He *yuʿadhdhiba* them (Q 3:128).
>
> So God *yuʿadhdhiba* hypocritical men and hypocritical women, idolatrous men and idolatrous women, and He *yatūba* towards believing men and believing women . . . (Q 33:73).
>
> God *yaghfiru* whom He wills, and He *yuʿadhdhibu* whom He wills . . . (Q 2:284).
>
> He *yuʿadhdhibu* whom He wills, and He *yaghfiru* whom He wills . . . (Q 5:40).

It is also of some importance to note here that *tawallā,* the opposite of human *tawba,* is frequently paired with *ʿadhāb,* the opposite of divine *tawba* and *maghfira.* The Qur'ān describes this *ʿadhāb* as a consequence of the human being's "turning away" from God instead of toward Him, as when we read, ". . . And if they *yatawallaw,* God will *yuʿadhdhib* them with a painful *ʿadhāb*" (Q 9:74). There are two other examples of this kind in the *tawba* verses (Q 9:3, 11:3), and many others spread throughout the Qur'ān.[17] What these examples demonstrate to us is that there is something of a symmetrical relationship between these concepts in that the opposites of divine and human *tawba* are themselves paired together as correlates.

ʿadhāb —— opposite —— divine *tawba*

Divine Wrath | | Divine Mercy

tawallā —— opposite —— human *tawba*

Insofar as *ʿadhāb* is a consequence of God's wrath, protection from it is a consequence of His mercy. It is no surprise, then, to find a profound relationship between divine *tawba* and mercy. A close relation also exists between divine mercy and forgiveness, but before we come to that and compare the role of mercy in *tawba* and forgiveness, let us, for a moment, examine more closely the relation between divine mercy and *tawba*.

The basic semantic sense of *tawba*, as we have already seen, is that of a re/turn. But this re/turn is not simply a neutral act. Unlike its Hebrew cognate, *teshubah*, in the Bible, there are no instances of a secular or nonreligious use of *tawba* in Islam's sacred text. If there is one overarching quality that we are to identify about the nature of this re/turn, particularly where God is concerned, it has to be the element of mercy. The human being's *tawba* is also deeply tied into mercy, but as the subject of *tawba*, he is either the recipient of mercy or he asks for it, unlike God, who is its very fount and origin. Divine *tawba* is always an act of God re/turning to the human being in mercy. But it is also more. The divine re/turn has a purpose, namely to facilitate the spiritual re/turn and ascent of the human being to a holier and more inspired state. Here the human being experiences the very opposite of what he would experience were he to be deprived of divine *tawba*.

The central role that mercy plays in divine *tawba* is made evident by the fact that the divine attribute one most frequently encounters in verses addressing *tawba* is *al-Raḥīm*. In the sixty-nine verses in which *tawba* appears, this attribute occurs twenty-five times—more than any other divine attribute, including *al-Tawwāb*, which appears a total of ten times, or even *al-Ghafūr*, *al-Ghaffār*, and *al-Ghāfir* combined. In fact, the divine name *al-Raḥīm* is coupled in some way with *tawba* in just a little more than a fifth of the total occurrences of *al-Raḥīm* (which occurs 115 times in the Qurʾān). It is no surprise, then, to find Izutsu remarking that human *tawba* "is, as it were, a counterpart of God's unfathomable mercy."[18] We certainly see this, for example, in such verses as Q 6:54, where, immediately before the Qurʾān calls the human being to re/turn, he is reminded that, "Your Lord has prescribed for Himself *al-raḥma*," with the verse ending with yet another reminder of God's infinite mercy.

We should also note that *tawba* is not just tied to mercy, but a particular kind of mercy that seems to be associated with forgiveness and the effacing of the human being's sins. This is because the attribute *al-Raḥīm*, which so frequently occurs at the end of the *tawba* verses, also seems to have a peculiarly strong relationship with divine forgiveness.

In its 115 instances, this attribute is also coupled with *Ghafūr* more than seventy times, more than any other divine attribute, and usually in the form, God is "*Ghafūr, Raḥīm*." To this we should also note its nine occurrences with the attribute *Ra'ūf*, "Full of Pity," an attribute that can also be associated with God's compassionate response to the ethical and spiritual shortcomings of the human being. All of this suggests that the kind of *raḥma* conveyed by the attribute *al-Raḥīm* has a potentially unique connection to God's relationship with the human being insofar as the latter falls short of his ethical potential.

Some Differences between Human *Tawba* and *Istighfār*

Thus far, we have looked primarily at the intersections between *tawba* and *maghfira*/*istighfār*. Although these concepts are closely related, as we have just seen, there are still some key differences between them, and these are particularly evident at the human level. We have already seen one of these differences qua human *istighfār* and *tawba* when we drew attention to the differing terms the Qur'ān uses as their opposites. Let us now explore some of the other differences, starting with human *tawba* and *istighfār*.

To begin with, while no individual can undertake *tawba* for the transgressions of another human being, one can, on the other hand, seek God's forgiveness for them. The Qur'ān presents scenarios of Moses seeking forgiveness for himself and his brother (Q 7:151), of Noah seeking forgiveness for his parents and the believers (Q 71:28), of Abraham seeking forgiveness for the believers and his parents (Q 14:41), of the Prophet as one whose *istighfār* should be sought (Q 4:64), of the believers seeking forgiveness for each other (Q 59:10), and even of the angels seeking forgiveness for the believers (Q 40:7). No such relation is possible with *tawba*, quite simply because one can only re/turn for himself. We should also note, as a point of qualification, that although one may seek forgiveness for others, this request can only be efficacious provided the one prayed for is not guilty of the unforgivable sin of *shirk*; if this is the case, no such prayers should be made at all (Q 9:113). It is true that Abraham is described on more than one occasion as seeking forgiveness for his idolatrous father (Q 14:41, 19:47), but the Qur'ān clarifies that he did this only because of a promise made to him, and that he later desisted (Q 9:114). There is nothing in the Qur'ān to suggest his prayer had any effect in alleviating his father's ultimate punishment.

Closely related to this difference, we may also note that *tawba* forms a dialectical relationship exclusively between the human being and God. The human being re/turns to God alone, and God, in turn, re/turns to man alone. Even though this re/turn on the part of the human being may carry with it an element of communal reform or rectification, this rectification is only there to facilitate one's felicitous re/turn to God. This is not the case with forgiveness insofar as humans forgive and seek the forgiveness of others whom they might have wronged—a virtue, which, in the former case, the Qurʾān lauds (Q 42:43, 45:14, 64:14). No such human-to-human relation is possible with *tawba*.[19]

Another difference between *tawba* and *istighfār* is that while the doors of the former close at death (Q 4:18),[20] one may continue to seek forgiveness even after entry into the other world. In one instance, the Qurʾān has the believers asking God, on the Day of Judgment, to "perfect our light for us and forgive us (*waghfirlanā*)" (Q 66:8). The dialectic of divine–human *tawba* therefore ends at death, while the dialectic of seeking and granting forgiveness may continue beyond the confines of this life, but only for the believer.

The final and perhaps most significant difference between human *tawba* and *istighfār* is that the latter is a less "practical" religious act. *Tawba*, as we saw earlier, is closely tied into the notion of restoration, making amends, and righteous deeds. We do not find in the Qurʾān such a close relation between *istighfār* and redeeming, penitentiary acts. In this sense, we might say that *istighfār* represents more of the psychological experience that accompanies one in the wake of their sin, insofar as that person seeks forgiveness by turning to God in supplication and prayer. It embodies, from this vantage point, the more emotive and personal side of *tawba*. *Iṣlāḥ*, on the other hand, achieves this for its more practical and tangible side.

Some Differences between Divine *Tawba* and *Maghfira*

The differences between divine *maghfira* and *tawba* are fewer, subtler, and more difficult to detect. This is because the semantic points of convergence between these Qurʾānic concepts outnumber those of their divergences, a fact that should not come as a surprise considering what our analysis of these two concepts has yielded so far. But despite their commonalities, some of which are striking, the two concepts are still not identical. To begin with, the semantic field of *tawba* is larger than that of divine *maghfira*. This becomes evident simply by observing the basic meaning of the term, which is that of a re/turn. Although this re/turn often entails forgiveness and relenting, to restrict it to this meaning is to confine its semantic breadth. Divine *tawba*, though it includes the concept of divine *maghfira*, is not limited to it. As we saw in some of our previous examples, there are cases—and these, it is true, are the majority—where *tawba*, used of God, can very well be understood to mean forgiveness. But divine *tawba* can also take on other related meanings, and this becomes evident once we encounter those Qur'ānic passages in which "forgiveness" or even "relenting" do not function as adequate translations. Some of these examples will be highlighted below.

We should also draw attention to another significant feature of the terms under consideration. Even in those instances where *tawba* does express the idea of divine forgiveness, it expresses a particular kind of forgiveness that is not identical to that of a **gh-f-r** derivative. In those occurrences in the Qur'ān where *tawba* refers to God's forgiveness, the more precise rendition of the Arabic would be to "turn toward the human being in forgiveness," and, on the part of the human being, "to turn toward God to receive this forgiveness." The *tawba* metaphor insofar as it expresses the sense of "turning" also therefore implies having previously been "turned away," and as a "returning," implies having previously been "away." Izutsu draws attention to this feature of the term when he writes,

> Man 'turns' towards God in repentance, and God 'turns' towards man with His grace. There is clearly a correlative relationship of 'turning' between God and man, and this is reflected in the semantic behavior of the word *tawbah*.[21]

This feature has even more emphatically been expressed by Denny, in regards particularly to the human aspect of *tawba*:

> The orientative dimension is predominantly spatial, in that most of the repentance terms and concepts describe the human condition in terms of right directions, turning about, ways to follow, goals to be reached (or shunned)—in short, proper orientation.[22]

The importance that this spatial element of the *tawba* metaphor plays in the language of the Qur'ān finds confirmation in the term, as we saw earlier, the Qur'ān tends to employ as the opposite of human *tawba*, *tawallā*, or "turning away." We should also note here the one instance in the Qur'ān where it says, "God wants to *yatūba* towards you. But those who follow their desires want for you to *tamīlū maylan ʿaẓīman*." This final expression, which means to "swerve away mightily," or to "go tremendously astray," captures, yet again, the spatial dimension of the *tawba* metaphor—in this case, as the effect of being deprived of divine *tawba*.

Now when we come to the idea of forgiveness contained in the root **gh-f-r**, we encounter, once again, a metaphor, but a different kind of metaphor. Iṣfahānī says that the verbal noun *ghafr* refers to "the covering of something with what preserves it from dirt" (*ilbās al-shayʾ mā yaṣūnuhu ʿan al-danas*).[23] The underlying sense of **gh-f-r** is therefore of concealment, preservation, and protection. Iṣfahānī goes on to add, "*al-ghufrān* and *al-maghfira* from God is His preserving the servant from punishment" (*huwa an yaṣūna al-ʿabd min an yamassahu al-ʿadhāb*).[24] The idea of forgiveness expressed by **gh-f-r** therefore contains within its semantic field notions (concealment, protection, preservation) entirely absent in the core semantic field of **t-w-b**. If we extend the **gh-f-r** metaphor, we also realize that to be deprived of *maghfira* means to be naked and unprotected, exposed to the blistering heat of divine punishment. To be deprived of *tawba* is also to experience punishment, but here it is because one has turned away from mercy in the direction of wrath. The semantic field of **gh-f-r** consequently conjures up a different notion of forgiveness once we pay close attention to the imagery expressed by the root's primary meaning.

This subtle distinction between the two terms, although lost in translation, is present in the Arabic for those sufficiently familiar with the classical language. Such distinctions, moreover, far from being trivial, add to the literary and poetic religious force of the Qur'ān. We need simply draw attention to those instances where derivatives of **gh-f-r** appear alongside those of **k-f-r**, in which the "concealing of sins" is, at the positive end, implicitly contrasted with the "concealing of truth" at the negative end; or where **gh-f-r** is paired with the second form of the root **k-f-r**, which, in the Qur'ān, takes on a positive meaning almost exactly synonymous to *ghafara*. In such scenarios, the literary effect of encountering a **gh-f-r** instead of a **t-w-b** derivative alongside a **k-f-r** derivative can be appreciated in the primary language only by one familiar with the subtle nuances of the classical vocabulary. The English reader who consistently encounters the rather bland but generally workable translations of "forgiveness" and "disbelief" for such terms will be unable to appreciate the intricate and multilayered tapestry that makes up the poetic fabric of Qur᾽ānic Arabic.[25]

The Root ʿ-f-w

Thus far, our comparative analysis of *tawba* and forgiveness has focused on the relation of the former to the root **gh-f-r**. But a few remarks should now be made about **ʿ-f-w**, a related root that frequently carries the meaning of forgiveness and pardon and whose derivatives appear alongside both **gh-f-r** and **t-w-b**. These observations will also help illuminate some of the differences between *tawba* and forgiveness. Derivatives of **ʿ-f-w**, however, occur in the Qur᾽ān only thirty-five times, much less frequently than those of **t-w-b** and **gh-f-r**. Moreover, as noted earlier, there are only two instances in which an **ʿ-f-w** word appears in the *tawba* verses. Due, however, to the proximity of the root's meaning to **t-w-b**, and the manner in which it is coupled with its derivatives, it deserves to be mentioned in our analysis. The underlying sense of **ʿ-f-w** in relation to forgiveness[26] is that of an "erasing" or "effacing" of sins, like that of wind blowing away traces in sand.[27] This imagery, insofar as it differs from that of "concealing" or "turning," reveals to us another dimension of the Qur᾽ānic language of forgiveness.

In the Qur᾽ān, the root **ʿ-f-w** is applied to both God and the human being. When applied to God as a divine attribute, *al-ʿAfūw* means, in the most literal sense, the Effacer of sins (Q 4:99, 4:149, 22:60, 58:2). Ghazālī (d. 1111) says that although this meaning is close to that of *Ghafūr*, it is "more expressive than that, for 'all-forgiving' [*Ghafūr*] connotes concealment while 'effacer' [*ʿAfūw*] suggests erasing, and erasing is more effectual than concealment."[28] If we are to accept Ghazālī's remark, this more forceful quality of *ʿAfūw* is lost in the usual English translations of "Forgiving" or "Pardoning," where its meaning is more or less indistinguishable from *Ghafūr*.[29]

Derivatives of **ʿ-f-w**, as we just noted, appear on only two occasions in the *tawba* verses. In the first, the verbal form of this root occurs immediately alongside God's *tawba*: "And He *tāba* towards you, and *ʿafā* towards you" (Q 2:187), which is to say, He turned toward you and effaced your sins. The two words are presented here as different stages of the forgiveness process, with *tawba* involving the preliminary act that makes *ʿafw* possible. In the second instance, it is coupled with the human being's *tawba*, but on the side of God's reception of it: "He accepts the *tawba* of his servants and *ya'fū* ugly deeds" (Q 42:25). Here God's response to the human being's *tawba* by way of acceptance, that is to say, His *tawba,* is directly equated with the effacing of his sins. Once again, the divine acceptance of *tawba* seems to precede His *'afw*. It seems to involve, like *maghfira,* the direct encounter of God and the human being, with *tawba* expressing the turn that allows the encounter to take place. We should also add here that the semantic affinity between divine *'afw* and *tawba,* as well as *maghfira,* is highlighted by the fact that in at least one instance, the Qur'ān presents *'adhāb* as a consequence of the deprivation of *'afw*: "If We *na'fu* one party of you, We will *nu'adhdhibu* (punish) another party because they were guilty" (Q 9:66). *'Adhāb* therefore also stands at the opposite end of divine *'afw,*[30] as we earlier saw in the case of divine *tawba* and *maghfira.*

Just as the human being asks for God's *tawba* and *maghfira,* he also asks for God's *'afw* (Q 2:286). A relationship of *'afw* can also exist between humans.[31] The Qur'ān, in fact, frequently encourages this kind of mutual pardoning, and presents it as a mark of piety (Q 2:109, 2:237, 4:149, 5:13, 24:22, 64:14). In one instance, humans are encouraged to show both *maghfira* and *'afw* to each other in the same verse (Q 64:14). Insofar as *'afw* and *maghfira* can exist between humans, many of the differences between human *tawba* and *istighfār* drawn out earlier also hold for human *tawba* and *'afw*. In this regard, *'afw* and *maghfira* stand closer to each other than to *tawba.*[32]

The Root ṣ-f-ḥ

This brings us to our last important key Qur'ānic term for forgiveness, one that never appears in a *tawba* verse, but which, despite this absence, comes close to inversely mirroring **t-w-b**'s primary meaning. This is the word *ṣafḥ,* from the root **ṣ-f-ḥ**.[33] Derivatives of this root appear in the Qur'ān on eight occasions. With the exception of one instance (Q 43:5), the derivatives express the idea of forgiveness. In four of these occurrences it is paired, in its verbal form, directly beside the verbal form of **'-f-w** (Q 2:109, 5:13, 24:22, 64:14) suggesting thereby a unique relationship with the latter. In only one instance does it accompany **gh-f-r**, also in its verbal form, but here too it is accompanied by **'-f-w**, so that all three terms appear together. What is peculiar about this term, for our concerns, is that the Qur'ān uses it only to describe forgiveness between humans. It is never employed to depict the idea of divine forgiveness. Of the four forgiveness terms in the Qur'ān, *ṣafḥ* therefore stands at the opposite end of *tawba* insofar as the former applies only to human relations, and the latter to relations between God and humans. It is for this reason, we can safely assume, that the word never appears in the immediate context of a *tawba* verse.

Why does the Qur'ān never employ *ṣafḥ* for divine forgiveness? The answer, or at least a part of it, may lie in the underlying imagery of forgiveness conveyed by its root. This imagery in relation to forgiveness is that of "turning away." Ibn Manẓūr cites the expression *ḍarabtu ʿanhu ṣafḥan* in his definition of the term, which Lane translates as "I turned away from him and left him."[34] The word therefore expresses the idea of forgiveness to the extent that one "turns away" from the offender. Thus the expression *ṣafaḥtu ʿan al-dhanb,* which means, "I forgave the sin (or crime)," translates in the most literal sense to "I turned away from the sin (or crime)."[35] Iṣfahānī draws attention to this literal sense when he notes in the opening of his definition that the *ṣafḥ* of a face is its side;[36] it is what one sees when the person turns slightly away. Although this sense of "turning away" conveyed by **ṣ-f-ḥ** might accurately express the human experience of forgiveness, insofar as the wronged party turns away from the offender and does not seek retribution, it does not seem to be an appropriate way to describe divine forgiveness, and it may be for this reason it is not used to describe an act of divine mercy. Divine forgiveness, it appears, does not involve turning away and leaving the guilty party, but its contrary, turning toward and returning to her in mercy, and concealing or effacing her sins. When God turns away from a person, the consequences, in the language of the Qur'ān, are always negative. This is confirmed by the one instance in the entire text in which *ṣafḥ* does apply to God—the word conveys not the sense of turning away in forgiveness and pardon, but in abandonment. "Shall We take away our remembrance from you *ṣafḥan,*" the Qur'ān asks, "because you are transgressors?" (Q 43:5).[37] Although the precise translation of this verse varies, as expected, from one translator to another, the negative sense of *ṣafḥ* as "turning away" or even "repelling" is consistently brought out.[38] This negative sense is also confirmed by the classical Qur'ān commentaries.[39]

We can close our present analysis by reiterating some of our main observations thus far. The Qur'ān, as we have seen, employs four roots to express the idea of forgiveness. Each one of these roots, moreover, expresses a different imagery of forgiveness. With **t-w-b**, it is that of a "returning" or "turning toward in mercy;" with **gh-f-r**, it is of "concealing" and "protecting;" with **ʿ-f-w**, it is of "effacing" and "erasing;" and with **ṣ-f-ḥ**, it is of "turning away." Of these four roots, **gh-f-r** and

ʿ-f-w are the only ones that can be applied to both God–human and human–human relations; **t-w-b** is used only in God–human relations; and **ṣ-f-ḥ**, the only one for human–human relations. **Gh-f-r** and **ʿ-f-w** are also more closely related through a similar imagery of the sin, in some form, being removed from sight. **T-w-b** and **ṣ-f-ḥ**, on the other hand, are both directional, spatial terms, but with opposing orientational meanings. Insofar as these terms are used in the Qurʾān, however, **gh-f-r** is most frequently paired with **t-w-b**, and **ṣ-f-ḥ** with **ʿ-f-w**. **Ṣ-f-ḥ** and **ʿ-f-w** are also much less commonly used in the Qurʾān, as a whole, in comparison to **t-w-b** and **gh-f-r**.

Further Observations on Divine *Tawba*: The Threefold Dialectic

Now that we have completed, for the most part, our inquiry into the relation between *tawba* and forgiveness, we should turn our attention to some final observations about the nature of divine *tawba* in the Qurʾān. Although our comparative analysis so far has illustrated some of the central and most salient features of divine *tawba*, some further remarks will enable us to more thoroughly comprehend this complex and multifaceted concept.

We have seen that *tawba* denotes a dialectical relationship between God and the human being. The human being re/turns to God seeking his mercy in the wake of an ethico-religious fall, and God re/turns to the human being by way of granting His mercy in the form of an acceptance. But although this is the most common pattern in the Qurʾān, it is not the only one. There are a few instances where it becomes clear that God may actually initiate the *tawba* process, so that, at least in some scenarios, human *tawba* depends on God's originating act. The clearest example of this occurs in sūra *al-Tawba* when the Qurʾān asserts, "then He *tāba* to them so that they might *yatūbū* [to Him]" (Q 9:118).[40] By placing the initiative on the divine side,[41] the Qurʾān raises the *tawba* relationship from a simple twofold process of man initiating and God responding to one in which both parties may initiate and respond. This verse, and others of a similar kind, introduce, in effect, the possibility of a threefold dialectic in which (1) God mercifully re/turns to the human being to facilitate his felicitous re/turn; (2) the human being, conscious of his sin, re/turns seeking a *tawba* of acceptance; and (3) God responds to this request out of His unfathomable mercy. The Qur'ān does not, we should emphasize, explicitly mention anywhere that the human being's *tawba* is always necessarily preceded by God's *tawba,* even though such a position was held by many of the leading representatives of *kalām* and *taṣawwuf.* But it does, as we just noted, seem to allow for the possibility of a catalyzing divine act to set forth the unfolding of this process.

This feature of the dialectical relationship is not simply a trivial detail, but has, on the contrary, some important implications. Most substantially, it implies that divine *tawba* is not simply forgiveness insofar as we conceive of forgiveness as the desired outcome of *istighfār* or seeking *ʿafw.* The divine act of *tawba,* as the end process of the dialectic, may well be understood as "forgiveness" in the most general sense, but as a primary divine act it is more meaningful simply to conceive of it as a Merciful divine re/turn to facilitate the human being's re/turn. In this wider semantic sense, this originary divine act might take on a form of guidance, to reveal to the guilty individual his own ethical or religious shortcoming, as well as his need for God's final pardon. It might also serve to transfigure his state from one of rebellious defiance to penitentiary regret, and thereby spark a deeply felt need for *tawba.*

This wider sense of the term is expressed, for example, when the Qur'ān asserts in Q 33:24 that God may "punish the hypocrites, if He so wills, or *yatūbu* towards them." Since the hypocrites are a class of disbelievers, they cannot possibly engage in *tawba* because *tawba,* as an act of faith, requires *īmān.* The most reasonable sense of divine *tawba* in this context, then, would have to be a form of divine guidance—a guidance that elicits a genuine re/turn to God, from hypocrisy, through faith. It is no surprise to find that this interpretation is confirmed in most of the major Qur'ānic commentaries. Ṭabarī's observation that divine *tawba* toward the hypocrites in this verse means that "He guides them to faith (*yahdīhim li al-īmān*)"[42] is echoed, along more or less similar lines, in the seminal commentaries, both major and minor, of exegetes ranging from Ibn al-Jawzī and Ibn al-Kathīr to Suyūṭī, Bayḍāwī, Qurṭubī, and Rāzī, to name but a few.[43] Zamakhsharī remains one of the major exceptions, understanding God's *tawba* in this verse as a response to the initial *tawba* of the hypocrites themselves. His commentary runs: "And He punishes them 'if He so wills' if they do not *yatūbū* 'or He *yatūba* towards them' if they *tābū.*"[44] The reason for this peculiar reading, which involves deriving a meaning by interjecting words that are not directly in the text, however, is not hard to discern: it is based on a Muʿtazilite theological perspective[45] according to which God does not initiate or create man's actions. The *tawba* of the human being must emerge, for Zamakhsharī, as an act of man's own volition. This free-will premise, rooted in a theological vision that attempts to safeguard a particular notion of divine justice, prevents him from accepting the more obvious sense of the Qur'ānic expression,[46] one that was accepted by the other exegetes, and rather enthusiastically by the Ashʿarites as well as the Sufis, as we shall later see. However, according to Rāzī in his commentary on Q 3:128, a verse that is similar in content to our verse above—"it is no concern at all for you (O Prophet) whether He *yatūba* towards them, or punish them. They are evil-doers"—the Muʿtazilites do not always understand such references to divine *tawba* as a divine "acceptance of [man's] *tawba*" (*qubūl al-tawba*). They might also, adds Rāzī, conceive of it as an "act of [divine] benevolence" (*fiʿl al-alṭāf*).[47] Even for the Muʿtazilites, therefore, the semantic field of *tawba* qua God includes more than simply forgiveness and can refer to an act of divine benevolence that might, to some degree, facilitate or aid the *tawba* process.[48]

We should also note here that the close relation that divine *tawba* can have with guidance is made clear in a few instances by the way the Qur'ān couples them together, as expressions of divine mercy and benevolence, to aid the human being to attain ultimate salvation. Thus we read such passages as the following:

> God wants to make clear to you, and *yahdiyakum* by the examples of those before you, and He [wants to] *yatūba* towards you (Q 4:26).

> Then his Lord chose him [Adam] and *tāba* towards him, and *hadā* [him] (Q 20:122).

> And Lo! I verily am Forgiving towards him who *tāba* towards Me, believes, and does right, and is afterward *ihtadā* (guided) (Q 20:82).

Divine *hidāya* and *tawba*, therefore, are joined together in the larger Qur'ānic vocabulary alongside a cluster of other divine qualities such as *rahma, maghfira,* and *ʿafw* that are associated with human felicity. These are the qualities all believers hope to encounter, and they have their counterparts in the human virtues associated with the "people of paradise."

Further Observations on Human *Tawba*: Negative Terms

The Roots r-d-d, ḍ-l-l, and ẓ-l-m

So far in our analysis we have looked primarily at the words positively associated with human *tawba,* such as *iṣlāḥ, al-ʿamal al-ṣāliḥ, īmān, istighfār, maghfira, ʿafw, ṣafḥ,* and *hidāya.* We should now turn briefly to some of the negative terms, besides the two that we have already looked at (*tawallā* and *ʿadhāb*) that stand at the other end of the *tawba* spectrum. We have seen that *tawba* is a directional term whose opposing meaning in relation to the human being tends to be *tawallā.* We should also note here the word *irtadda,* the eighth form of the root **r-d-d**, which can mean to "turn away," "return," or even "apostatize." Although it is never counter-posed directly alongside *tawba* in the same verse, it can convey a contrary meaning,[49] as it does, for example, in Q 47:25 ("Those who *irtaddū ʿalā adbārihim* [have turned back] after the guidance has become clear to them") and Q 5:54 ("Oh ye who believe, whoever of you *yartadda* from his religion, God will bring a people whom He loves and who love Him . . ."). Insofar as *tawba* can be used to describe the turn away from *nifāq* and *kufr, irtadda* can be used to express the exact opposite, the turn from guidance toward *kufr.*[50]

Another related term is *ḍalāla,*[51] from the root **ḍ-l-l**. It is also orientational, and is one of the most frequently employed terms in the Qur'ān to describe the state of disbelief. According to Iṣfahānī, it stands as the Qur'ānic opposite to *hidāya,* both semantically insofar as it connotes "being astray," "in error," "wandering," or "lost," as well as in its Qur'ānic employment.[52] In one instance, the Qur'ān says that God will not accept the *tawba* of those who grow in disbelief after faith, describing them as *ḍāllūn* (Q 3:90). Insofar as human *tawba* falls within the larger Qur'ānic category of guidance (since only the guided one seeks to re/turn), ignoring *tawba* falls under the larger Qur'ānic category of *ḍalāla.*

The most frequently used negative term in relation to *tawba,* however, besides its direct opposite *tawallā,* is either *ẓulm* or one of its cognates. The root **ẓ-l-m** expresses ideas primarily of "injustice," "wrongdoing," and "oppression," but also of "darkness" and "ignorance." Unlike *tawallā,* both nominal and verbal forms of **ẓ-l-m** are used in the *tawba* verses, and with varying subjects. The Qur'ān describes those who do not engage in *tawba* as *ẓālimūn* (Q 49:11). This idea is also expressed in Q 3:128: "It is no concern for you (O Prophet) whether He *yatūba* towards them or punishes them. They are the *ẓālimūn*." In another place, God's *tawba* is guaranteed for one who "*tāba* after his *ẓulm* (*ẓulmihi*) and makes amends (*aṣlaḥa*)" (Q 5:39). A similar idea is expressed in Q 4:64, where it is explicitly stated that the very object of *ẓulm* is the wrongdoer himself: "And had they, when they had *ẓalamū* themselves, come to you and asked God's forgiveness, and the Messenger had asked forgiveness for them, they would have found God *Tawwāb*, Merciful." The Qur'ān even says that the one who engages in *tawba*, has faith, and does righteous deeds will not himself become the object of *ẓulm* in the next world (*lā yuẓlamūna shay'an*) (Q 19:60).

More on the Conditions of Human *Tawba*: Promptness and Sincerity

We saw earlier the importance that *iṣlāḥ* and *ṣāliḥāt* play in *tawba*. We learned that each *tawba* seems to require a particular kind of "rectification" that will facilitate the re/turn of the human being to God, whether this rectification amounts to an abandoning of disbelief or hypocrisy, or fasting as a form of penance. *Tawba* in itself does not guarantee a divine *tawba* of acceptance. The genuineness of one's *tawba* is, in this light, demonstrated by the extent to which the guilty party makes efforts to correct past wrongs. But the Qur'ān also adds another quality to a virtuous *tawba*, the element of "promptness." The guilty party must re/turn as soon as he realizes his sin. One cannot expect God to accept one's re/turn by putting off or delaying *tawba*, especially until the moment of death. This is most explicitly expressed in sūra *al-Nisā'* when the Qur'ān unequivocally states,

> *Tawba* is only incumbent on God for those who do wrong in ignorance then *yatūbūna* soon afterwards (*min qarīb*). These are they toward whom God *yatūbu*. And God is ever Knowing, Wise.
>
> *Tawba* is not for those who do wrong (*sayyi'āt*) until when death comes to one of them, he says, 'I *tubtu* now.' Nor yet for those who while they are disbelievers. For such we have prepared a painful punishment (Q 4:17–18).

The elements of rectification and promptness are essential components to a sound *tawba*. Although the Qur'ān generally calls the human being simply to *tawba,* it is clear that God does not accept every *tawba.* The Qur'ān seems to emphasize this point when, in sūra *al-Taḥrīm,* the believers are exhorted to re/turn to God with a *tawba naṣūḥa,* that is, a "sincere" or "right" *tawba.* The particular ethical components of this *tawba naṣūḥa* became a central concern for the later Qur'ān commentators, of both Sufi and non-Sufi inclinations. *Tawba naṣūḥa* implies that there are *tawba*s that fall short of eliciting divine acceptance. But this should also not be misunderstood to mean that the standards of proper *tawba* are so stringent that only rarely is it met with God's approval. The Qur'ān makes it clear that God *desires* (*yurīdu*) to turn to the human being in *tawba* (Q 4:26–27). The frequency and readiness with which God re/turns is made clear by the fact that He is always described by the intensive active participle *Tawwāb,* and never, as in the more typical case of the human being, simply as *Tā'ib.*

The Place of Remorse (*Nadam*) in Human *Tawba*

The Root n-d-m

Having briefly touched on the Qur'ānic conditions of *tawba,* we should now turn to another key term, but one whose relation to *tawba* emerges primarily outside of the Qur'ānic context. This is the concept of *nadam* ("remorse" or "regret"), which Iṣfahānī defines as "the grief [that arises] from a change of perspective regarding an elapsed matter" (*al-taḥassur min taghayyur ra'y fī amr fā'it*).[53] *Nadam* was identified by the leading theologians, jurists, and Sufis as one of the central components of a sound *tawba.* This view was largely based on the Prophetic tradition that we cited in the previous chapter according to which regret is one of the signs of *tawba* (*al-nadam tawba*). The close relation that *nadam* has to *tawba* in the Islamic tradition, does not, however, find a parallel in the Qur'ān. To begin with, none of the two derivatives of **n-d-m**—*nadāma* ("regret" or "remorse") and *nādimīn* ("those filled with remorse" or "regret")—that occur a total of eight times in the Qur'ān appear in any of the *tawba* verses. Nor does the word, for that matter, appear along-side any of the other significant *tawba* concepts, such as *iṣlāḥ* or *istighfār.* Equally significant is Denny's astute observation about the use of the term in the Qur'ān:

> In most of its Qur'ānic occurrences there is a sense more of being caught out and exposed, or at best of simply being

terribly sorry, than there is a true change of heart, a *metanoia,* such as can be discerned in the other terms, especially *tawba.*[54]

Thus we find, for example, that when the Qurʾān declares that Cain "became one of the remorseful (*aṣbaḥa min al-nādimīn*)" after he killed his innocent brother, there is no subsequent mention of a desire for *tawba* or forgiveness on his part in the context of the verse (Q 5:31). In fact, the exact opposite appears to be the case when in the previous verse we read that on account of his crime, "he became one of the losers" (*aṣbaḥa min al-khāsirīn*). The parallel use of *nādimīn* and *khāsirīn* suggests that his was not a remorse that brought about a re/turn to God. This is further confirmed by the fact that the Qurʾān recurringly describes the "people of the fire" as *khāsirūn,* those who will experience the ultimate loss in the world to come.[55] In another instance, God consoles Noah after he pleads, "My Lord help me because they deny me," by informing him that, "in a little while they surely will become *nādimīn*" (Q 23:40). Once again, this remorse is associated with the ultimate consequence of rejecting the divine message. In yet another instance, the *nādimīn* are those whose remorse ensues from a good fortune that comes over the Muslims (Q 5:52) and is not connected in any way to any form of virtue.

Perhaps even more relevant to our general inquiry is the manner in which *nadam* is associated with divine punishment. In three instances, it is presented as the human response to encountering God's final *ʿadhāb*:

> They will be filled with *nadāma* when they see the *ʿadhāb*. But it has been judged fairly between them . . . (Q 10:54).
>
> When they see the *ʿadhāb* they will be filled with *nadāma.* We shall put iron collars on the necks of those who disbelieved . . . (Q 34:33).
>
> But they [the people of Thamūd] hamstrung her [the camel], and then became *nādimīn.* For the *ʿadhāb* [predicted by the prophet Ṣāliḥ] seized them. Verily in this there is a sign, but most of them are not believers (Q 26:157–158).

Divine *ʿadhāb,* as we have already seen, functions as the Qurʾānic opposite of divine *tawba,* and as we have also seen, results from "turning away" from God. What these examples, along with our three earlier ones, confirm is that this concept has, in Qurʾānic idiom, a closer relation to the cluster of negative qualities (*ḍalāla, kufr, irtidād, nifāq,* and *ẓulm*) that stand at the very opposite end of *tawba* than it does to *tawba* itself. The close association of *nadam* with *tawba* is, as noted earlier, a characteristic feature of the post-Qur᾽ānic tradition but not grounded in the general use of the term in the Qur᾽ān itself.

There is however one instance in the Qur᾽ān where *nadam* is ascribed to the *mu᾽minūn*, and it may be partly from this particular example that the term derives its association with *tawba* in the wider Islamic tradition. The verse reads:

> O believers, if a transgressor (*fāsiq*) brings you tidings, verify it, in case you harm others in ignorance (*tuṣībū qawman bi jahālatin*) and afterwards become *nādimīn* over what you have done (Q 49:6).

This example demonstrates that *nadam* is not, as a rule, tied to the fate of wrongdoers. Were it so, it probably would have been difficult to Qur᾽ānically justify its positive association with *tawba*. We should also note that in the verse just quoted, the nature of this wrong, "in ignorance" (*bi jahālatin*), is the kind of wrong that the believers ideally re/turn to God from, and also the kind of wrong that God readily forgives. The Qur᾽ān says, for example, "Whoso of you does wrong in ignorance (*sū᾽ bi jahālatin*), and then *tāba* after that, and makes amends (for him) lo! God is Forgiving, Merciful" (Q 6:54). This idea is again repeated in Q 16:119: "those who do wrong in ignorance (*sū᾽ bi jahālatin*) and *tābū* after that, and make amends, lo! Your Lord is afterward indeed Forgiving, Merciful." Insofar as verse Q 49:6 ties in the experience of *nadam* to the sins and mistakes of the believers, there is no reason for us to deny the larger conceptual relation between this concept and *tawba*. Nevertheless, the Qur᾽ānic emphasis in *tawba* is not on the negative feelings of remorse, but on *istighfār* and the positive and restorative acts of *iṣlāḥ* that must accompany it. With the exception of Q 49:6, *nadam* is always associated with the response of wrongdoers in the face of an impending and inescapable divine punishment.

Tawba in the Wider Context of the Human Return

The Root r-j-ʿ

We shall close the chapter by turning to a final analysis of the relation between human *tawba* and the wider concept of "return." There is no better term to begin with than the root **r-j-ʿ**, which expresses precisely this wider meaning. Although *rujūʿ* is frequently employed in the Qurʾān, for the most part it is associated not with the voluntary return of the pious, but with the involuntary return of all of creation to its Origin.[56] In this regard, the term lacks the same moral and ethical force as *tawba,* which is a virtue exclusively associated with the righteous. The absence of a strong ethical tenor to this word is also confirmed by its occasional neutral use to describe the return of a person to a group of people, an abode, or a city (as in Q 7:150, 12:62; 12:81, 24:28, 63:8). There are, however, a few instances where the term does acquire a positive ethical sense. This occurs when it is associated with the voluntary religious return of human beings to God from some form of impiety or rebellion. In these cases its meaning often overlaps with that of *tawba*. The Qurʾān says for example, that God details His revelations (*nufaṣṣil al-āyāt*) "so that they might return (*laʿallahum yarjiʿūn*)" (Q 7:174). In other places, God afflicts the impious with punishment, also "so that they might return" (Q 43:48). Verse 32:21 clarifies that the punishment meted out in this world to elicit a return (*rujūʿ*) is the "lower punishment (*al-ʿadhāb al-adnā*)," different from the "greater punishment (*al-ʿadhāb al-akbar*)" that awaits the unrighteous in the next world. In another instance, the same idea is repeated, with the transgressors being made to taste something of their own deeds in this life, once again, "so that they might return" (Q 30:41). These later uses of the term demonstrate to us an important parallel with *tawba*. In Q 9:126, for example, the Qurʾān states, "See they not that they are afflicted (*yuftanūna*) once or twice every year? Still they do not *yatūbūna,* nor do they remember (*yadhdhakkarūn*)." In both cases, God is shown to afflict a people to have them return, by *rujūʿ* and *tawba,* from a sinful or misguided life to one of obedience, surrender, and worship. This parallel between *tawba* and *rujūʿ* is also noted by Iṣfahānī in verse 21:95, which reads, "There is a ban on any community which we have destroyed. They shall not *yarjiʿūn*." For Iṣfahānī it as if God is saying, "We have banned (or prevented) them to *yatūbū* and *yarjiʿū* from sin as an admonition that there is no *tawba* after death."[57]

The Root n-w-b

A more closely related word to *tawba,* but one that occurs only a total of eighteen times in the Qurʾān, is *ināba*. The primary sense of its root **n-w-b** is that of a return characterized by recurrence. According to Iṣfahānī, the nominal root *al-nawb* refers to "the return of something time after time" or "one time after another" (*rujūʿ al-shayʾ marra baʿda ukhrā*).[58] The Qurʾān employs only the fourth form of the root, either in its verbal (*anāba*) or active participial form (*munīb*). This form conveys the basic ethical and directional sense of *tawba,* but with the added sense of repetition—a feature of the term noted in the previous chapter.[59] According to Iṣfahānī, when this fourth form is used with God as the object, as in the expression, *al-ināba ilā Allāh taʿālā,* it refers to "returning to Him through *tawba* and sincere action."[60] Since God is always the object of *ināba* in the Qurʾān, the term never takes on a negative or even neutral sense. Moreover, the God–human dialectic that so uniquely characterizes *tawba* is also absent: God is never *munīb.*

As in the case of *tawba,* the Qurʾān employs *ināba* to describe "conversion" insofar as the human being turns away from falsehood and toward God. In one verse it is paired with *ijtināb,* the eighth form of **j-n-b**, which means to "turn aside" or "turn away" from something. In this instance, the human being's *ināba* toward God is accompanied by a concomitant *ijtināb* from false gods (*al-ṭāghūt*) (Q 39:17). In another instance, the human being is commanded to both *anībū* and submit (*aslimū*) to God in order to avoid the ultimate punishment (*ʿadhāb*), thereby also conveying the sense of "conversion."

The Qurʾān also seems to emphasize the element of sincerity in *ināba,* as Iṣfahānī's definition highlighted. The manner in which the term is used in two verses makes this rather apparent:

> And when some affliction touches people, they call out to their Lord, *munībīn* towards Him. Then when they have tasted of His mercy, lo! A party of them attribute partners to their Lord! (Q 30:33).

> And when some affliction touches man, he calls out to His Lord, *munīban* towards Him. But once he has been granted a favor from God, he forgets that for which he called Him before, and sets up rivals with God (Q 39:8).

This idea of a truthful inner devotion and sincerity that characterizes *ināba* is also found in Q 50:33, when the Qurʾān couples the externally unobservable fear of God with a heart marked by *ināba*:

> Who fears the Merciful One in secret (*khashiya al-Raḥmān bi al-ghayb*) and comes with a *munīb* heart (Q 50:33).

Like *tawba, ināba* is also closely paired with the idea of seeking forgiveness. In two instances, it is coupled immediately alongside the *istighfār* of the prophets David and Solomon:

> . . . so [David] *fastaghfara* his Lord and fell down on his knees and *anāba* (Q 38:24).

> . . . then [Solomon] *anāba*. He said, My Lord, *ighfirlī* . . . (Q 38:34–35).

In most Qur᾿ānic uses of *ināba,* however, the accent is not so much on "turning away from sin toward God" as in the case of *tawba,* but simply on "turning toward God." This may explain the general absence of any mention of *iṣlāḥ* insofar as such acts serve to rectify or set aright the consequences of a "past wrong." Such past wrongs are, more often than not, unmentioned in the *anāba* verses. *Ināba* therefore seems to represent a higher form of re/turning to God. This might also explain why prophets are the subjects of *ināba* in a little more than a quarter of its total occurrences, four of eighteen, as opposed to only two of fifty-three instances of human *tawba*. Besides David and Solomon, Abraham and Shuʿayb are also characterized by *ināba* (Q 11:75, 11:88). Shuʿayb's *ināba* is of particular interest because the Qur᾿ān explicitly states that it did not follow in the wake of a sin but the noble act of calling people to God. The Qur᾿ān has him returning to and putting his trust in God after pleading with his people to abandon their ungodly ways. While his own community is called to return through *tawba* and *istighfār* on account of their sins, he himself engages in *ināba* and *tawakkul.* This particular example illustrates that *ināba* is not, as in the case of *tawba,* necessarily from blatant sins or moral shortcomings. It may even follow a virtuous act whose consequences lie outside of one's hands, so that one sincerely returns to God by putting one's entire trust in Him.

The Root a-w-b

The last term we shall look at is *awba,* from the root **a-w-b**. Like *ināba,* it also expresses the basic ethical and directional sense of *tawba,* and functions therefore more or less as a synonym. The intensive *awwāb,* which is the only participial form of **a-w-b** the Qur᾿ān employs, refers, according to Iṣfahānī, to "the one who returns to God most High by abandoning sins and performing acts of obedience."[61] In the intensive form, it is almost identical in meaning to *tawwāb*. The Qur'ān also employs, along with *awwāb*, which occurs six times, the term *ma'āb* ("a place to which one returns") on nine occasions, *iyāb* ("return") once, and the second verbal form also once, giving us a total of seventeen **a-w-b** derivates in the text as a whole. As in the case of *ināba*, *awba* words never appear in the *tawba* verses. God is also never the subject of *awba*, so that the unique divine–human dialectic of *tawba* is once again absent.

Although the Qur'ān does pair the notion of *awba* with forgiveness, as in verse 17:25, which reads, "He is forgiving to the *awwābīn*," *awba* does not seem to be as closely tied to a preceding sin or moral lapse, as in the case of *tawba*. The prophet Job (Ayyūb), for example, is described as an *awwāb* after mention is made of his successful efforts to remain faithful to an oath he made, apparently in haste, to God (Q 38:44). It is also of some interest to observe that the Qur'ān describes the birds of David as *awwābs*: ". . . And the birds assembled. All were *awwāb* to him" (*kullun lahu awwāb*) (Q 38:19). The classical commentators differ over whether the Arabic means (1) "they returned to him (in praise)," that is to say, David, because of the power he was given over the earth, or (2) "they returned [with him] to God (in praise)."[62] This second interpretation finds support in other instances in which birds and mountains are ordered by God to "*awwibī* with him" (*ma'ahu*) (Q 34:10), typically taken to mean, "return to God with him (in praise)" or "echo his psalms of God's praise."[63] Insofar as even birds can participate in *awba*, we can assume that *awba* is not always necessarily from some form of sin, and that it bears, in this regard, yet another close relation to *ināba*. In this light, we can understand why, as in the case with *ināba*, prophets seem to be singled out as the subjects of this kind of return. Besides Job, the Qur'ān also associates the prophets David, Solomon, Abraham (Q 60:4), and Shu'ayb (Q 11:88) with *awba*.

Ma'āb, as noted above, is the most frequently used derivative of **a-w-b**. Unlike all of the Qur'ānic derivatives of **t-w-b** and **n-w-b**, this particular derivative of **a-w-b** is used both positively and negatively to describe the final abode of the human being. The Qur'ān promises, for the righteous, a splendid abode (*ḥusna ma'āb*) (Q 13:29, 38:25, 38:49), and for the transgressors (*ṭāghīn*), an evil abode (*sharra ma'āb*) (Q 38:55). In 88:25, the Qur'ān employs the word *iyāb* simply to describe the inevitable return of the human being, in this context, particularly the unrighteous, to God.

We should end our survey of **a-w-b** by drawing attention to a rather peculiar feature of the Qur'ān's use of the term. Unlike **t-w-b** and **n-w-b** words, which are more or less evenly spread out through the Qur'ān, eight of the **a-w-b** occurrences—almost half—appear in sūra 38, between verses 17 and 55. Moreover, as Yusuf Ali has astutely observed, the use of *awwāb* in verses 17 and 19 seems to provide the rhyme for the greater part of the sūra. Thus we find that most of the verses, from 10 to 55, end with such rhyming words as *wahhāb, asbāb, awtād, aḥzāb, ḥisāb, khiṭāb, miḥrāb, ma'āb, albāb, jiyād,* and *anāb*. It is in these same verses that the prophets Job, David, and Solomon, along with the birds, return to God through *awba*. According to Yusuf Ali, the rhythmic and rhyming pattern of this sūra echoes the main theme of these verses, which is "[t]urn to God in prayer and praise, for that is more than any worldly power or praise."[64]

As we bring our analysis of the internal structure and semantic field of *tawba* to a close, we may summarize some of the central findings of this chapter. We saw that the concept most closely associated to human *tawba* is that of *iṣlāḥ* and *al-ʿamal al-ṣāliḥ*. *Tawba* as it is presented in the Qur'ān is not simply a feeling of regret as we might understand from the etymological and theological connotations of the English "repentance," but closely tied to the notion of making amends and setting things aright. Moreover, for each of the ethico-religious sins or shortcomings the human being may fall prey to, there is, more often than not, a corresponding *iṣlāḥ* that should accompany one's *tawba* in order to ensure its completeness. Along with *iṣlāḥ,* promptness and sincerity are also presented as essential components of *tawba* in the Qur'ān.

We also saw that divine *tawba* has a particularly close relation to divine mercy. Not only is mercy tied in to the forgiveness that God grants those who re/turn to Him, it is also the *raison d'etre* for God's primary re/turn to the human being. Just as *iṣlāḥ* seems to be the closest concept to human *tawba,* divine mercy seems to be the closest concept to divine *tawba* considered in and of itself. We also saw in addition to this that the term typically employed by the Qur'ān as the opposite of human *tawba*—*tawallā*—has a causal relation to the Qur'ānic opposite of divine *tawba*: *ʿadhāb*. This divine punishment is the consequence of persistently "turning away" from God's call to re/turn. These four concepts thus stand in a somewhat symmetrical relation to each other, as our diagram illustrated.

We also found that the concept most closely related to divine and human *tawba* taken together is forgiveness. But despite this close relation, some key differences remain between *tawba* and *istighfār/maghfira,* and these are most discernable when the human dimensions of these ethical concepts are compared. We also learned that, although **gh-f-r** is the most commonly used root the Qur'ān employs for forgiveness, it also makes use of two other roots, besides **t-w-b**, to express this idea. Each of the four roots the Qur'ān uses for "forgiveness" conveys a different imagery or symbolism associated with the concept. In the case of **t-w-b**, this imagery is that of a "re/turning" or "turning toward in mercy"; with **gh-f-r**, it is of "concealing" and "protecting"; with **ʿ-f-w**, it is of "effacing" and "erasing"; and with **ṣ-f-ḥ**, it is of "turning away" in pardon. Of these roots, **gh-f-r** and **ʿ-f-w** are the only ones that can be applied to relations between God and the human being, or mutual relations between the latter. **T-w-b**, however, is the only root used exclusively for relations between God and the human being, and in this regard, inversely mirrors **ṣ-f-ḥ**, which is the only one used for human–human relations. **Gh-f-r** and **ʿ-f-w** are, moreover, closely related through their underlying imageries, which is that of the sin, in some form, being removed from sight. **T-w-b** and **ṣ-f-ḥ**, on the other hand, are both directional, spatial terms, but with opposite meanings, that of "turning toward" and "turning away," respectively. Insofar as these terms are used in the Qur'ān, **gh-f-r** is most frequently paired with **t-w-b**, and **ṣ-f-ḥ** with **ʿ-f-w**. Derivatives of **ṣ-f-ḥ** and **ʿ-f-w** are also much less common in the Qur'ān, in comparison to those of our other two roots.

We also saw that divine *tawba,* although it usually means "forgiveness," cannot be restricted to this narrow definition. There are instances in the Qur'ān when it becomes obvious that divine *tawba* refers to a form of divine guidance that leads, in some manner or another, to the first glimmerings of human *tawba,* whether this *tawba* be from minor sins or outright disbelief and/or hypocrisy. In this regard, divine *tawba* functions as a merciful catalyzing act that draws the human back to a state of surrender. "Forgiveness," as the response to human *tawba,* remains therefore an incomplete translation of divine *tawba* because it fails to adequately encapsulate the full range of meanings conveyed by the term.

Our inquiry into the root **n-d-m** also yielded some noteworthy results. We learned that despite *nadam*'s extremely close relation to *tawba* in the Islamic tradition, it is used in the Qur'ān almost entirely to describe not the response of the pious *tā'ibūn* to their ethical and moral shortcomings, but the psychological experience of the unrighteous in the wake of God's ultimate punishment, an *ʿadhāb* that is the consequence of repeatedly turning away from all opportunities to surrender. This *nadam* is the hopeless regret of the human being having now lost all chances to re/turn—it is the regret of the *khāsirīn* ("losers"). The one instance where it is used of the believers, of an injustice committed in ignorance, provides, however, a Qurʾānic basis for the relation to *tawba* it acquired in the wider Islamic tradition.

Finally, we saw that the Qurʾān employs, alongside *tawba*, two key words, *awba* and *ināba*, to express similar ideas of re/turn; these latter two, however, are never used of God. Moreover, *awba* and *ināba* appear to refer to higher forms of human re/turn, not necessarily from sin or disobedience, and this is why both of these concepts are so closely tied to the re/turn of prophets. *Rujūʿ* is another closely related term whose semantic field overlaps with the primary sense of *tawba*. But it is used in the Qurʾān in a variety of contexts: although it can refer to the virtuous return of the human being to faith and submission, it can also be used to express the negative idea of returning to disobedience, or the neutral one of returning from one place to another, or to another person. *Rujūʿ* thus does not carry the same ethical force as *awba, ināba,* and *tawba.*

Part II

Early Sufi Approaches to *Tawba*

Chapter 3

Tawba as Interior Conversion

In the opening chapter, we noted how the lexical authorities included the concept of "conversion" within the semantic field of *tawba*.[1] In the Sufi tradition, however, we find an emphasis on *tawba* not as a conversion to Islam, although this understanding of the term is also present, but an "interior conversion" that leads to a life entirely committed to God. Although the individual is in almost all cases already a Muslim prior to his *tawba*, the return marks an internal awakening in which a nominal or even relatively serious allegiance to one's religious identity is replaced by total submission to the dictates of the spiritual and mystical life. In many of the Sufi biographical tales this depiction of *tawba* as an "interior conversion" bears a striking resemblance to the onset of the spiritual journeys of saintly figures in other religious traditions. Leonard Hindsley's observation that conversion in the Christian Middle Ages "had more to do with the establishment of a setting that disposed the Christian to a deeper life in Christ" than "a change in religion from pagan to Christian or Muslim to Catholic"[2] could equally apply to *tawba* within the Sufi tradition, with the obvious qualification that this "deeper life" was rooted not in Christ but the spiritual message of Islam. Augustine remains perhaps one of our most famous examples of such a conversion. Although he was born a Christian and never formally left the religion of his birth, his repentance and conversion led him to devote himself entirely to God through Christ. It was a rebirth which, from his celebrated account in the *Confessions*, was preceded by a godless life spent in the pursuit of fleeting worldly pleasures—a conversion that brought him from the fringes of his religion of birth to its center.[3]

The early Sufi hagiographical literature provides us with some rather powerful and moving illustrations of the experience of *tawba* as "interior conversion"—the subject of the present chapter. Gerhard Böwering has noted that these conversion narratives tend to be quite similar and that recurring motifs appear in almost all of them. The usual pattern of the experience is of the sinner encountering, in the words of Böwering, "an unforeseeable, sudden event" that shocks him, so that "shaken by doubt or overcome by fear, he turns away from the world." He abruptly "abandons his accustomed way of life, repents and turns totally to God."[4] Sometimes the individual experiences a series of events, each of which serves to weaken, little by little, the attraction of a life immersed in heedless merriment. In other scenarios—and these are more common—it may simply be one single catalyzing event that initiates the rebirth. The incident, moreover, may appear rather trite and insignificant to an outsider. This is because it can be as simple as a penetrating insight into the meaning of life, or hearing, by chance, a recital of a Qur'ānic verse that, like an arrow, pierces the soul with regret and a desire for reformation. But for the individual himself, the event is powerful enough to force an existential reorientation that inaugurates the unfolding of a new destiny.

Another characteristic of these *tawba* narratives—but one Böwering does not note—is that in almost all of these accounts, the *tā'ib* is characterized by a degree of passivity. The catalyzing event that sparks the *tawba* is so powerful that it cannot be resisted, carrying with it a kind of cosmic force that impels the sinner to amend his life. The *tā'ib* does not turn to God of his own volition, but is compelled by circumstance to return, whether it be through a voice that will not go away, or an inescapable truth about the frivolity of his life. There are clear parallels between this characteristic of the *tawba*-conversions in Sufi literature and the prototypical model in Christianity, namely, Paul's repentance upon hearing the voice of Christ on his way to Damascus. Although his conversion is of his own choice, the choice is in effect forced upon him by the supernatural circumstances surrounding his experience. Interestingly, this "passivist paradigm" of conversion is found even in many scholarly explanations of the conversion experience—explanations that tend to minimize the agency of the convert, laying emphasis instead on the psychological and environmental factors that contribute to the conversion.[5] In the religious literature, however, causality tends to be retraced to God, and this view, as we saw in the second chapter, finds some basis in those Qur'ānic instances in which God is described as the initiator of *tawba* and guidance.

The pattern that Böwering describes for the life-transforming *tawba* in hagiographical literature dealing with the early Sufis is evident in some of the most famous and well known of the *tawba* narratives. Perhaps the most celebrated of these is that of Ibrāhīm b. Adham (d. 778–779), the prince of Balkh who renounced a life of worldly power and royal luxury for a higher calling, abandoning his kingdom to wander as a Sufi ascetic.[6] For understandable reasons, his conversion has often been compared in Western scholarship to that of the Buddha.[7] It is so celebrated in the Muslim tradition that we find mention of it in almost all the major Sufi biographical compendiums. Although these works do not always provide the *tawba* narratives of other Sufis, particularly in the shorter texts, we find the story of Ibrāhīm's *tawba* mentioned in almost all the major works, such as the *Ṭabaqāt al-ṣūfiyya* of ʿAbd al-Raḥmān al-Sulamī (d. 1021),[8] the *Ḥilyat al-awliyāʾ* of Abū Nuʿaym al-Iṣfahānī (d. 1037),[9] the *Kashf al-maḥjūb* of Hujwīrī (d. 1071),[10] and the *Risāla* of Abū al-Qāsim al-Qushayrī (d. 1074).[11] While the story also figures prominently in later sources such as the *Nafaḥāt al-uns* of ʿAbd al-Raḥmān Jāmī (d. 1492),[12] and in particularly elaborate and highly poetic form in the *Tadkhirat al-awliyāʾ* of Farīd al-Dīn ʿAṭṭār (d. 1220),[13] our following analysis shall focus, for the most part, on the earlier compositions in keeping with the aims of the present study, although some use will be made of later sources for relevant comparative purposes. The same approach will be followed in our study of the conversion stories of the remaining figures in the present chapter.

It should be stated at the outset of our analysis that our purpose is not to explore the embellishments of these narratives at the hands of clearly imaginative authors, but the depiction of *tawba* as a process of interior conversion that induces a radical reorientation in the person's life and a newfound sense of underlying purpose. Our intention is to observe how the Sufis have presented the various circumstances through which the process of *tawba* might be initiated, and to categorize the range of *tawba* types available in the hagiographical and biographical literature. In doing so, an attempt will be made to produce a taxonomy of conversion in early Sufism similar to that proposed by John Lofland and Norman Skonovd in their examination of the impetuses behind modern conversion, or what they call "conversion motifs,"[14] or Lewis Rambo in his categorization of "conversion types" in his own study of conversion.[15] The major difference is that the taxonomy proposed in this chapter is not based on a sociological or psychological analysis of early medieval Sufi converts. Instead, our purpose is to draw out undefined categories already present in the texts themselves.[16] The findings of the following survey shall be summarized at the end of the chapter.

Tawba through a Miraculous Call from On High

The richest and most elaborate account of Abū Isḥāq Ibrāhīm b. Adham's conversion from the early period is to be found in Iṣfahānī's *Ḥilyat al-awliyāʾ*. The account itself is narrated on the authority of his own personal servant (*khādim*) Ibrāhīm b. Bashshār.[17] One day he asks him, "O Abū Isḥāq, how were the beginnings of your affair (on this path), such that you became as you are today?" Sternly, the ascetic responds, "there are matters of more pressing concern for you." "Yes, it is indeed as you say. God bless you!" replies Ibrāhīm b. Bashshār, "but please do tell me so that perchance God may benefit us through it one day." Ibn Adham remains unmoved. "Woe unto you!" he admonishes, "preoccupy yourself with God!" "O Abū Isḥāq, please do tell me, if you would," beseeches the servant a third time. Abū Isḥāq finally concedes, and proceeds to tell the tale:

> My father was from the people of Balkh, from the kings of Khurasan, and a man of great wealth. Hunting was beloved to us. One day I set out on my horse with my dog, and as I was riding along, a rabbit or a fox sprung up. I spurred my horse and no sooner had I done this that I heard a voice call out from behind me, "You are not created for this! Nor for this have you been commanded!" I brought myself to a halt and looked around, to my right and left, but could not see a single person. "God curse Satan!" I exclaimed, and spurred my horse onwards. Then I heard a voice even louder than before, "O Ibrāhīm! You are not created for this, nor for this have you been commanded!" I brought myself to a halt again, looked to my right and left, but could not make out anyone in sight. "God curse Satan!" I exclaimed. I spurred my horse and heard the voice again, this time from the saddlebow of my saddle. "O Ibrāhīm! You were not created for this, nor for this were you commanded." I brought myself to a halt and exclaimed, "I have been awakened! I have been awakened! A warner (*nadhīr*) has come to me from the Lord of the worlds" [. . .] I then returned to my family, came off my horse and

made my way to my father's shepherd. I took from him his shirt and cloak and gave him my robe. Then I set out for Iraq.[18]

The basic elements of this narrative are also found, albeit in more concise form, in the accounts of Sulamī and Qushayrī, although in contrast to Iṣfahānī they note that in exchange for the personal belongings he gives to the shepherd, he receives a cloak of wool (*ṣūf*)—the coarse garment for which the early ascetics were known, and from which, according to most medieval and modern authorities, the term Sufi itself is known to derive.[19] Sulamī and Qushayrī also point out that the voice he hears is that of a *hātif*,[20] the mysterious, invisible caller who figures as a common trope in Islamic hagiographical literature to provide spiritual counsel and guidance. In the words of John Renard, the *hātif* is the source of the "ethereal voice [that] pipes up as an all-purpose revelatory source," whose teachings or admonitions serve as "the aural equivalent to dreams and visions."[21] In Hujwīrī's version, the source of the address is identified, no less miraculously, as the animal he is in chase of. "God caused the antelope to address him in elegant language," writes the author of the *Kashf*; "[H]e says: 'Were you created for this, or were you commanded to do this?' He repented, abandoning everything and entered the path of asceticism and abstinence."[22] Iṣfahānī, in keeping with the more comprehensive nature of his encyclopedic entries, provides an additional detail to the lengthy account cited above, on the authority not of Ibn Bashshār but a certain Yūnus b. Sulaymān al-Balkhī. Ibrāhīm, we are told, also receives a warning during the hunt in the form of a divine rebuke from above. "What is this play?" he is asked. "Did you think that We created you in play (*ʿabath*), and that to Us you will not return?" (Q 23:115). "Fear God! And gather provisions for the Day of Need (*yawm al-fāqa*)."[23] The Qurʾānic admonishment, not uncommon in conversion accounts, serves to weaken any lingering attachment the prince might have to the comforts of his life, and helps bring the story to its climax. The words, carrying the force of Scripture, have a power that cannot be resisted, so that the hunter, in the final scheme of things, ends up becoming the prey of divine *tawba* itself.

According to Iṣfahānī, immediately following his *tawba*, Ibrāhīm set out in search of lawful sustenance (*ḥalāl*). When he finally procured such employment, as an overseer and guardian of orchards and vineyards, he was so scrupulous in his duties that he would not allow himself to taste, let alone eat, of the fruit he was guarding or tending.[24] This characteristic is also highlighted by Qushayrī.[25] Likewise, Hujwīrī observes that "after his conversion he never ate any food except what he had earned from his own labor."[26] This aspect of the story suggests that Ibrāhīm's scrupulousness (*wara*ʿ) regarding matters of lawful sustenance may have been the result of a desire on his part to rectify past sins—part and parcel of his attempts at *iṣlāḥ* (recall our discussion in chapter 2). As a prince whose wealth would likely have been procured through highly questionable, if not outright unjust means, it is only natural for him to have sought to atone for his wrongs by becoming as meticulous as possible regarding the source of his livelihood.[27] This might also explain why, unlike other early ascetics, he insisted on earning his own living by "the sweat of his own brow" (to use a biblical expression).

As for the events surrounding Ibrāhīm's conversion, one of the characteristics that stands out in the story is its supernatural element. The prince is addressed by a mysterious *hātif*, experiences a revelation from the heavens above, and according to Hujwīrī, is spoken to by an animal. ʿAṭṭār provides a more embellished version that includes a number of highly dramatized encounters with Khiḍr.[28] (The meeting with the immortal guide, according to the earlier sources, takes place sometime after his conversion, when he is taught the Supreme Name.)[29] The magical and miraculous dimension, although central to Ibrāhīm's conversion, is absent in the majority of the early Sufi *tawba* narratives.[30]Although these other narratives may also appear miraculous in that a life-altering reorientation is triggered by a small and apparently trivial event, they tend to lack the extraordinary characteristics we encounter in Ibrāhīm's *tawba*. What we find, instead, are more or less mundane scenarios that any ordinary human being may encounter, as we shall see below.

What made Ibrāhīm's *tawba* unique in the eyes of later writers appears to have been not so much the miraculous nature of his calling, but the divine grace involved in his conversion as well as the level of his own sacrifice. He leaves an entire kingdom to tread the path of Sufi poverty and renunciation,[31] and this could not have been possible without a call from on high. In his *Laṭāʾif al-minan* (*The Subtle Blessings*), Ibn ʿAṭāʾ Allāh al-Iskandarī (d. 1309)[32] recounts the words of his spiritual master, Abū al-ʿAbbās al-Mursī (d. 1287), who informed him that the reason Qushayrī began the biographical section of his *Risāla* with the likes of Ibrāhīm b. Adham and Fuḍayl b. ʿIyāḍ (d. 803)[33] was to give hope to seekers turning to God from a life of vice and sin. Had he begun instead with the likes of Junayd and Sahl al-Tustarī—renowned for their scrupulous piety from childhood—aspirants would have despaired of ever joining their ranks.[34] ʿAbd al-Wahhāb al-Shaʿrānī (d. 1565) narrates a similar account of his own teacher, ʿAlī al-Khawwāṣ[35] in a short section on *tawba* in his *Lawāqiḥ al-anwār al-qudsiyya*.[36] Khawwāṣ informs him that by beginning the *Risāla* with the *tawba* of such men as Ibrāhīm b. Adham, Qushayrī intended to "strengthen the hearts of spiritual seekers." These examples prove, for ʿAlī al-Khawwāṣ, that "he for whom protection is preordained, is not harmed by sins."[37]

Tawba through an External Admonition or Word of Kindness

In many of the *tawba* narratives, as we have noted, a simple word of advice awakens the process of conversion. The advice or admonition may not even be intentional. The *tāʾib* who hears the words uttered may simply overhear them by chance, but they carry such a force so as to alter his life forever. Dāwūd al-Ṭāʾī (d. 781/782)[38] is one such example. According to one version, his *tawba* begins one day as he enters a cemetery and hears a woman leaning before a grave, reciting the couplet,

> In which of your two cheeks does decay appear?
> And which of your two eyes has begun to melt?[39]

The message of the transience of human life, and the ultimate end of the body that houses the soul, has a powerful effect on Dāwūd. Shortly after, the jurist Abū Ḥanīfa (d. 767) advises him to sit at the feet of the learned and patiently pay heed to their lessons. He follows the advice, well suited, according to his own account, for his particular state at that time. But knowledge of the formal precepts of religion can take him only so far. After learning the virtue of patience and self-mastery from silently attending such lessons for a year, and struggling to hold himself back from making an egotistical display of his own knowledge and mental prowess, he finally meets Ḥabīb al-Rāʿī,[40] who initiates him into the mystical life.[41]

Perhaps one of the most famous conversion accounts to fall into this category is that of Fuḍayl b. ʿIyāḍ,[42] of which Qushayrī provides a succinct version in the *Risāla*. The bandit is said to have been climbing over a wall one day to reach a woman he had fallen in love with when, unexpectedly, he heard someone recite the verse, "Is it not time that the hearts of those who believe should be humbled to the remembrance of God?" (Q 57:16). Moved by the enchanting power of the passage, he cried out in response, "O Lord! Indeed the time has come!" In Hujwīrī's account, which is more elaborate, the Persian author begins his entry by noting that as a highway bandit, Fuḍayl would not steal from women or the poorest folk in a caravan, and that he would even leave his victims with a portion of their belongings. One day as a merchant set out on a journey through a territory that Fuḍayl was known to rob travelers in, the merchant's friends advised him not to travel without a protective escort. The merchant replied that he knew Fuḍayl to be a God-fearing man, and that instead of guards he would travel with a Qurʾān reciter, one who would read aloud from the holy book for the duration of the journey. As the merchant approached the encampment where Fuḍayl was lying in wait, the reciter read aloud from Q 57:16. On hearing the verse, Fuḍayl's "heart was softened," writes Hujwīrī, so much so that he "repented of the business in which he was engaged, and having written a list of those whom he had robbed, he satisfied all their claims upon him."[43]

Fuḍayl would eventually become one of the most prominent Sufis of the early tradition. It is no surprise that, since his conversion took place through hearing a verse from the Qurʾān, he would be particularly sensitive to its recitation. According to Iṣfahānī, whenever he would hear or read the holy book, he would be overcome by fear and sadness.[44] He also said that he "who carries the Qurʾān (within himself) has no need to rely on creation."[45] His own son, ʿAlī, who according to an account in Sulamī was even more pious than Fuḍayl, is said to have died on account of an ecstatic trance that overcame him on hearing the verse, "On the Day of Judgment, you will see their faces turned black who lied against God" (Q 39:60).[46] Fuḍayl also acquired fame for his mastery of *ḥadīth* sciences, as well as his courage in addressing the Abbasid caliph Hārūn al-Rashīd.[47]

Qushayrī provides another conversion narrative that falls nicely into the present category. In his earlier days, Abū ʿAmr Ismāʾīl b. Nujayd (d. 977)[48] is said to have attended the gatherings of the Nishāpūrī Sufi Abū ʿUthmān al-Ḥīrī (d. 910),[49] whose words penetrated his heart and caused him to turn to God. Sometime later, he lapsed in his resolve, and not only left the company of Abū ʿUthmān, but avoided all contact with them. One day he accidentally stumbled across the *shaykh* on the street. No sooner did Abū ʿUthmān notice him than the young man quickly turned around and took another route. The *shaykh* gave chase and caught up. The man who had previously inspired his *tawba* addressed him with kindness. "O my son," he said, "you are not in the company of one who only loves you while you are sinless. Abū ʿUthmān can help you in this state."[50] Abū ʿAmr was touched by his compassion and renewed his *tawba*. Hujwīrī uses this story to press home the point that one's repentance can always be revived,[51] a theme explored in greater detail in chapter 6.

Sometimes the *tawba*-inducing admonition may even come from a non-Muslim. The beginning of Shaqīq al-Balkhī's (d. 809)[52] conversion took place through a chance encounter with an idolater on a trip to Turkestan for the purpose of trade. From the description found in the source material, the interlocutor is in fact a Theravadan Buddhist monk. Ironically, Shaqīq's conversion occurs after he attempts to enlighten the monk about the error of his ways. By the end of the short exchange, however, it is the monk who emerges as the teacher. His words trigger, according to Shaqīq's own confession, a profound inner spiritual awakening (*intibāh*). Qushayrī writes,

> The reason for his repentance was (as follows). He was of a wealthy background, and went on a trading expedition to the impure land of the Turks.[53] There he entered an idol-temple (*bayt li al-aṣnām*) and saw a caretaker of the idols (*khādim li al-aṣnām*) with a shaved head and clean shaven face, and dressed in a bright red robe. Shaqīq said to the caretaker, "You have a Maker who is Living, Knowing, and Powerful. Worship him and not these idols that can neither hurt nor benefit you." The man responded, "If things are as you say, then He is able to provide you sustenance in your own country. Why did you come all the way here for business?" Shaqīq awoke (*intabaha*), and took the path of renunciation (*zuhd*).[54]

It is also worth noting that it is a monk, an embodiment of detachment, who teaches him the true meaning of renunciation. In Iṣfahānī's version, Shaqīq is even more explicit: "the reason for my renunciation lay in the words of the Turk."[55] The encounter not only opens the way to his *tawba*, but also affects the quality of his subsequent spiritual life. It is no surprise that he eventually became a disciple of Ibrāhīm b. Adham, famous for his austerity. Shaqīq became well known himself for his discourses on total reliance on God.[56] Hujwīrī says that following his *tawba*, "he never troubled himself again about his daily bread."[57]

In ʿAṭṭār's version, Shaqīq also meets a Zoroastrian shortly after his encounter with the monk, whose advice intensifies his repentance. "If you are going in search of sustenance," he tells him, "that has not been preordained for you, you can travel till the resurrection and you will not attain it." He adds, "And if you are going after sustenance that has been foreordained for you, do not trouble to go, it will come to you of itself."[58] The words strengthen his desire to renounce the world. This encounter with the Zoroastrian is absent in the earliest accounts of Sulamī, Iṣfahānī, Qushayrī, and Hujwīrī, not to mention the later one of Jāmī. It may well have been a later embellishment added to dramatize the circumstances surrounding his conversion. But considering the multi-religious climate of Shaqīq's home province of Khurāsān, in which Manicheans, Buddhists, and Zoroastrians dwelt alongside Muslims, the meeting would not have been altogether impossible,[59] and ʿAṭṭār may well have relied on another source for this addition.

Tawba through an Internal Admonition

It is not always an external voice or admonition that sparks the repentance. In the case of ʿAbd Allāh b. al-Mubārak (d. 797),[60] the author of an extant early work on *zuhd*,[61] he is addressed by his own conscience one night as he stands outside the apartment of a woman with whom he has fallen passionately in love, hoping to catch a passing glimpse of the object of his affection. Despite the winter cold, Mubārak remains patiently outside her private quarters the entire night in the anticipation that she will at some point emerge. When the call for the morning prayer is made, he mistakes it for the night prayer. Realizing then that he has spent the entire time waiting for a human beloved, he castigates himself: "[S]hame on you, O son of Mubārak. Do you stand on foot all night for your own pleasure, yet become furious when the Imam reads a long chapter of the Qurʾān?"[62] Overtaken by remorse, he repents, devoting himself completely to worship.[63] Hujwīrī recounts that following his *tawba* "he attained such a high degree that once his mother found him asleep in the garden while a great snake was driving away the gnats from him with a spray of basil which it held in its mouth."[64]

Tawba Induced through an Act of Compassion toward Another

A recurring motif in the *tawba* narratives is of the *tawba* or spiritual transformation occurring because of an inadvertent act of piety or kindness by the individual. The gesture, typically small, draws such grace from heaven that the sinner is able to completely break free of previous heedlessness and give himself entirely to God. In the narratives cited so far, except perhaps in the case of Fuḍayl, there is nothing the repentant person does prior to his conversion through which he might deserve the gift of *tawba*. This aspect of the conversion stories was used by the Sufis to demonstrate the precedence of divine will in human guidance, as we gathered from al-Khawwāṣ's comments earlier. The human being, from this perspective, is not guided of his own volition, but through God's determination. But in the scenarios that follow we shall see that quite often the process of *tawba* is set in motion by a virtuous act, or series of acts, that ensue from the individual himself. Of course, from the viewpoint of an entirely deterministic theology, one would simply argue that these virtuous acts were themselves pre-eternally foreordained. But the intention behind the authors of these narratives is not to make such a theological point. Instead, it is to demonstrate that no act should be trivialized, that the slightest of deeds may indeed have the most far-reaching and unforeseeable of consequences. This view, we might add, is itself rooted in Muslim tradition. We have, for example, well-known *ḥadīths* in which the Prophet speaks of a prostitute who was admitted into Paradise over water she gave a thirsty dog suffering from the scorching heat. Another tradition teaches of a beggar who entered Paradise because she split a single date she received as charity to feed her two children, while remaining hungry herself. In the narratives below, the authors, as we shall see, are clearly encouraging the reader not to belittle any opportunity to carry out a charitable act or pious deed because one never knows what mercy it might draw. In some of these cases, the charitable act is met with a special prayer, either by the recipient of the charity or an onlooker, that miraculously transforms the heart of the person.

The *tawba* of the uncle of Junayd, Sarī al-Saqaṭī (d. 867) the "spice seller,"[65] falls into this category. According to Hujwīrī, the origins of his entry into the path are to be retracted to the day he gave Ḥabīb al-Rāʾī a crust of bread to distribute to the poor as he was passing by his shop. Al-Rāʾī simply responded with the words, "May God reward you." "From the day I heard this prayer," Sarī would later say, "my worldly affairs never prospered again."[66] The worldly loss was in fact a spiritual boon because through it his earthly attachments were broken off. Qushayrī relates a similar tale, but involving Maʿrūf al-Karkhī (d. 815).[67] One day he came to Sarī with an orphan by his side and asked him to procure some clothes for the young lad. Upon fulfilling his request,

Maʿrūf rejoiced and made a prayer, "May God make the world detestable to you. And may He free you from the state you are in [i.e., your business]." Immediately afterward, recounts Sarī, "there was nothing more detestable to me than the world."[68] He would eventually become Maʿrūf's disciple on the way, and transmit his teachings to the Baghdad Sufis through his nephew, Junayd, unanimously considered to be the head of the school. Sarī remarked that his entire spiritual standing was due to the blessing of Maʿrūf.[69]

A similar account of *tawba* induced through the performance of a charitable act can be found in the story of Abū al-Ḥārith al-Awlāsī (9th–10th century).[70] While Awlāsī is a relatively minor figure in the history of Sufism, at least in relation to others whose *tawba* narratives we are exploring, and even though the account itself derives from a slightly later source, that of Ibn Qudāma, the account's value lies in its illustration of the same theme one finds in Sarī's conversion tale above. Awlāsī explains to a fellow *zāhid* the beginning of his *tawba*, as follows:

> I was a handsome and comely youth. While in the midst of my heedlessness (*ghaflatī*) I saw a sick, homeless man lying in the middle of the road. I lowered myself before him and asked, "would you like something?" He replied, "yes, a pomegranate." So I went and fetched a pomegranate. When I placed it in his hands, he lifted his head towards me and said, "May God turn towards you" (*tāba allāhu ʿalayka*). Nightfall did not approach until (the state of) my heart was transformed with respect to all of the vanity in which I was immersed. I then set out desiring to perform the major pilgrimage . . .[71]

Neither he nor Ibn Qudāma comment on the identity of the man on the road. Perhaps he was one of those famous concealed saints, posing as a destitute beggar, and through the blessing of whose words God changed the life of the young man forever. Or he may have been a genuinely destitute soul, whose heartfelt prayer was met with the acceptance of God. In either case, a small act of charity followed by an apparently genuine prayer altered his destiny.

Tawba through an Act of Pious Devotion to God

The *tawba* of the famous Bishr b. al-Ḥārith al-Ḥāfī (d. 841) "the barefoot"[72] presents us with another example of a *tawba* that occurs as a result of a small act. In this case, it is not an act of compassion toward another human being, but a pious one of reverential devotion to God. According to Hujwīrī's version:

> His conversion began as follows. One day when he was drunk, he found on the road a piece of paper on which was written: "In the name of God, the Compassionate, the Merciful." He picked it up with reverence, perfumed it, and laid it in a clean place. The same night he had a dream that God said to him: "O Bishr as you have made my name sweet, I swear by my glory that I will make your name sweet both in this world and the next." Thereupon he repented and took the path of asceticism.[73]

In Iṣfahānī's account, Bishr recounts the story when he is asked about the beginnings of his conversion. The inquiry is made by a group of people curious over how his name has become as revered as that of a prophet. Bishr does not object to this veneration because, after all, it was promised to him by God. In this version, more dramatic, the oil he buys to perfume the divine name is with his last two dirhams.[74]

Bishr's *tawba* story is different from the others we have cited so far because in it we find an element of religious piety prior to his *tawba*. Bishr would not have shown such veneration to the divine Name had he not already harbored in his heart some devotion to God. The charitable act of Sarī al-Saqaṭī might be explained as a gesture of kindness that could just as easily have ensued from someone lacking religious sentiment. But Bishr's *tawba* is different because it is preceded by an act that reflects a deeply felt love for God.

A Final Consideration: Prophets and the Friends of God

Before proceeding to summarize our conclusions, one final point should be clarified insofar as *tawba* is conceived of as a process of "interior conversion." Such a process, for our authors, as it should be clear by now, applies only to those who are not prophets themselves. In other words, even though prophets engage in *tawba* (including *awba* and *ināba*), as our earlier analysis of the concept in the Qur'ān made clear, their repentance never takes on the form of an interior conversion—of a complete and total turn from sin and heedlessness to the consciousness of God. Ibrāhīm al-Daqqāq's[75] definition of *tawba* as a permanent state in which "you be unto God a face without a back, just as you were previously unto Him a back without a face,"[76] would, for our Sufi authorities, understandably apply only to those who stand outside the ranks of the *anbiyāʾ* and *rusul*. This is because such figures, even before their divine call, are marked by a relative degree of innocence and purity.[77] And as John Renard has shown, a comparison of the biographical and hagiographical accounts of the Sufis with the parallel *qiṣaṣ al-anbiyāʾ* literature dealing with the lives of "God's ambassadors" demonstrates that the experience of becoming a prophet is not only preceded by a morally edified state, but that prophets, even before their calling, usually exhibit a deep care and concern for God's creatures. After all, "every prophet began as a shepherd," and shepherds watch over their flock. With the friends of God, on the other hand, a sinfully self-absorbed life may precede one of virtue, compassion, and prayer, even acting as a catalyst of sorts for the latter.[78] What the friends of God and the prophets have in common, however, is the unique privilege of being chosen by divine providence to act as remarkable models of sanctity and holiness.

To summarize our analysis, we can say that, generally speaking, five kinds of *tawba* are presented in biographical/hagiographical Sufi literature. The interior conversion can be sparked by (1) an external admonition or invitation. This call can appear in the form of a Qurʾānic verse or line of poetry that awakens the soul to its own heedlessness, in the penetrating but harsh words of an outsider, or as a kind invitation, to name the most common examples. (2) The call to repent can also come from within, where the sinner or lackadaisical believer is admonished by his own conscience. In this category we may also include dreams. In other instances, the conversion is brought about through a response from heaven, a result either of (3) a charitable or generous act to another, or (4) a pious act of devotion to God. Sometimes in the case of an act of charity, the *tawba* is presented in the texts as the result of a prayer made either by the recipient of that charity or an onlooker. (5) Finally, there are those instances of a miraculous call from on high or through a supernatural experience. As noted, this type of catalyzing force is encountered less frequently in the texts. In all of these cases, however, the role of divine grace is paramount.

The five categories should not be seen as water tight. In many instances, more than one of the factors are clearly at work in inducing the interior conversion. The distinction between an external and internal admonition must also not be pushed too far. This is because the external admonition produces an internal call, just as an internal call is often the result of an external event. Also, although the supernatural element is vividly depicted in only a few of the conversion narratives, it is present in all of them, since God, for the authors of the hagiographical texts, was always understood to be the ultimate guide. In this larger sense, every conversion is the result of a miraculous call from on high.

What we have therefore attempted to do in our analysis is create general categories through which the conversion narratives can be loosely classified on the basis of those elements that seem to predominate in each of them. Although these categories should not be considered rigid and impermeable, they nevertheless provide us with an understanding of the various ways through which the Sufi authors understood how God's guidance may appear to spark a total and uncompromising commitment to the way. Thus the most significant contribution of this chapter is its taxonomy of *tawba* types in early Sufism, a taxonomy similar in some regards to those produced by contemporary social scientists in their own studies of conversion. The major difference is that the taxonomy proposed in this chapter is not the result of a sociological or psychological analysis of early Sufi converts, but of textual analyses that draw out and make explicit undefined categories of conversion already present in the literature.

Chapter 4

The States, Stations, and Early Sufi Apothegmata

The *Aḥwāl* and *Maqāmāt* in Early Sufi Writing

Now that we have looked at the *tawba* narratives of some of the most prominent early Sufis and the various ways through which these conversions were brought about, we are in a better position to explore the idea of *tawba* as the first stage of the Sufi journey to God. From the narratives analyzed in the previous chapter, we have seen how *tawba* marks an entry into the spiritual life, and how, in most cases, it is preceded by a negligible or minimal level of commitment to God. We are now in a better position to examine *tawba* from the perspective of what "interior conversion" entails, that is to say, the requirements of *tawba,* as well as its relation to the stages that come after it. Before we do this, however, we will situate repentance within the larger journey of the human soul by examining its relation to the ascending "stations" or *maqāmāt* of Sufi doctrine.

Early in the development of the tradition, the Sufis attempted to schematize the stages of the soul's return to its origin in God. This was accomplished by mapping out the psychological levels of the mystical journey from beginning to end. Each of these levels corresponded to a particular virtue—such as humility, trust in God, fear, hope, gratitude, and patience—which, arranged in a particular order, made up the rungs of the ladder leading up to the divine presence, or from another perspective, the concentric circles one centripetally traversed to the center and core of one's being to the divine secret embedded within the human self. The acquisition of the virtues was therefore seen as an indispensable part of the mystic life and not simply an accidental complement to the powerful experiences one encountered at the end of the path.

The levels of the Sufi path eventually came to be designated *maqāmāt*, though a few preferred to call them *manāzil* ("dwelling" or "alighting places").[1] Although both of these terms are of Qur'ānic origin, the word *maqām* came to predominate in the tradition. This word *maqām* appears fourteen times in Islam's Sacred Text, and the related *muqām* ("station," "time or place of abode"),[2] three times, with both terms occurring only in singular form. Sometimes *maqām* is used of humans, as when the Qur'ān says, "take as your abode of worship the *maqām* of Ibrāhīm" (Q 2:125); and sometimes it is used of God: "he who fears the *maqām* of his Lord shall have two gardens" (Q 55:46). It would not be surprising if some Sufis saw in this dual usage a Qur'ānic basis for the idea that it is God who ultimately stands in the station through the locus of the human being. The word *manzil*, on the other hand, appears only twice, and in both instances in plural form (*manāzil*). From its Qur'ānic usage, it is easy to see why some would have preferred this term. In Q 10:5 we read, "It is He who made the sun a radiance, and the moon a light, and measured for it [the moon] *manāzil* (stages/stations), that you might know the number of the years, and the reckoning;" and in Q 36:39, "And for the moon We have measured *manāzil* until it returns like an old-shriveled palm leaf." In both of its occurrences, *manāzil* is used to describe the stages of the moon's waxing and waning. This association with the stages in the movement and circulation of such a symbolic celestial body as the moon would, particularly in light of traditional cosmology, have appealed to those mystically inclined thinkers who saw the ascent of the soul as a journey through the inner universe of the soul. The moon's circular movement would also aptly represent this journey as a return to one's ontological origin in God. By opting for the term *manāzil* for the ascending levels of the soul, the Sufis who preferred it must also have been inversely counterposing it against the *tanzīl* or "descent" of the Qur'ān, which derives from the same **n-z-l** root.

Although the reasons *maqām* came to be preferred over *manzil* remain unclear, they might have to do with the fact that the idea of fixity or permanence which is associated with the levels of the ascent appears to be more strongly conveyed by the former term, whose root meaning is "to stand." This fixity or permanence of the virtue associated with the *maqām* is one of its key features in Sufi doctrine. The *maqām* is supposed to be a virtue that becomes embedded within the soul, typically following a rigorous process of spiritual and ethical training.[3] It is a virtue acquired through the effort and exertion of the *sālik*, the traveler. A subsequent *maqām* is obtained only after the conditions for the acquisition of the previous *maqām* have been met. Once acquired, the *maqām* remains. It is usually contrasted with the *ḥāl*, which, for most Sufis, represents the temporary, fleeting state that overcomes the seeker. In contrast to the acquired (*makāsib*) *maqāmāt*, the *aḥwāl* are bestowed (*mawāhib*) and considered gifts of grace.[4] Strictly speaking, however, all virtues are in the final scheme of things gifts of grace because of God's primal activity.

The word *ḥāl*, in its nominal form, does not appear in the Qur'ān. The verbs *ḥāla*, *yaḥūlu*, and *ḥīla* each occur once.[5] The closest instance in which the verbal form is used in its Sufi sense, to convey the idea of a transitory state, appears to be in Q 8:24: "Know that God *yaḥūlu bayna* (comes in between) a man and his own heart." Hujwīrī might have had this verse in mind when he defined the *ḥāl* as a state that "descends from God into a man's heart."[6] According to Massignon, however, the introduction of the word into Sufi vocabulary appears to have come primarily from the technical vocabulary of medicine, in which the *ḥāl* denoted the functional, physiological equilibrium of the body.[7] It is in the technical vocabulary of grammar, however, in which we find its closest correspondence to its use in Sufism. In grammar, the *ḥāl* is the state of the verb in relation to the agent, that is, its subjective and transitory state, its state of becoming.[8] This grammatical use most accurately captures the general Sufi idea of transience associated with the *ḥāl*. Whatever its origin may be, the *ḥāl* came to represent for almost all Sufis, as we have noted, the counterpart to the *maqām*.

Although the virtues associated with the *maqāmāt* are rooted in the Qur'ān, their systematization within the Sufi hierarchy of states and stations did not occur until later. It remains difficult to single out one particular figure to whom we can definitively trace the origin of this schematization. According to Shihāb al-Dīn Suhrawardī (d. 1234), the ascent was described by as early a figure as the fourth caliph, Imām ʿAlī (d. 661). "Ask me about the celestial paths (*ṭuruq al-samā'*)," he once told his listeners, "because I have greater knowledge of them than I do of the paths of the earth (*ṭuruq al-arḍ*)." He was alluding to the stations and states (*ashāra ilā al-maqāmāt wa al-aḥwāl*), noted Suhrawardī, and referred to them as celestial paths because through them the traveler's "heart becomes celestial."[9] Knysh, following Paul Nwyia, has suggested that Shaqīq al-Balkhī should be given credit for this development within the tradition. But that depends, Knysh adds, on whether the *Ādāb al-ʿibādāt* is correctly ascribed to him.[10] The text describes what its author considers to be the four *manāzil* of truthfulness (*ṣidq*), namely, renunciation (*zuhd*), fear (*khawf*), longing (*shawq*), and love (*maḥabba*). Surprisingly, there is no mention of *tawakkul*[11]—the virtue most closely associated with Shaqīq—in the entire text. This might be one reason to suspect its ascription.[12] According to Sulamī (d. 1021), Dhū al-Nūn (d. 860)[20] was the first to classify "the order of the states (*tartīb al-aḥwāl*) and the stations of the folk of sanctity (*maqāmāt ahl al-wilāya*)."[13] Although Massignon was also aware that earlier figures had produced outlines of the mystical path, such as Abū Sulaymān al-Dārānī (d. 830),[14] he accepted Sulamī's claim. "In Misrī," wrote Massignon, "it [the path] took the definitive form that would appear in Sufism's classical manuals."[15] The reason Massignon might have been persuaded by Sulamī's claim can be seen by a perusal through his aphorisms and sayings, which illustrate the lengths to which the Egyptian mystic went to address the nature of the *maqāmāt* and their relation to the wider *ṭarīqa*.[16] An elaborate description of the stages of the path does not seem to be present in earlier figures, at least not in their extant writings or aphorisms. Dhū al-Nūn's contemporary, Muḥāsibī, also played an important role in the theoretical development of the doctrine of states and stations, particularly through his psychological analysis of the states.[17] Hujwīrī examined the states and stations in his section on the "Muḥāsibīs" in the *Kashf al-maḥjūb*.[18] This suggests that Muḥāsibī was also associated, in the minds of later Sufis, with developing the theoretical stages of the spiritual journey.[19]

As noted earlier, the stations are arranged in such a way that, generally speaking, a subsequent station can be acquired only after the conditions for the previous one have been met. The logic of this is not hard to see. If someone wants to learn a language, she can proceed to study the more difficult grammatical rules only after the preliminary ones have been grasped. Similarly, quantum physics requires a comprehension of algebra, which itself requires basic arithmetic skills. The stages of the mystical path, according to our theoreticians, are not much different. A traveler uses what he has existentially learned to proceed to the next level of his journey. If a station becomes thoroughly existentiated, it enables the traveler to move toward the subsequent station. One might even say that the journey proceeds, in a sense, unconsciously, insofar as the internalization of one virtue naturally impels the individual to acquire and integrate other virtues. This organic unity of the levels of the way can be seen from an exemplary passage drawn from Dhū al-Nūn where he poetically describes the feelings of sadness and regret associated with *tawba*, and the precursory relation of *tawba* to the stations of patience (*ṣabr*), scrupulousness (*wara*ʿ), and renunciation (*zuhd*):

> There were some servants of God who, being faithful to God, planted the trees of their sins where they could see them, and then showered them with the water of their repentance (*tawba*). The trees bore the fruit of regret and sadness (*nadam wa ḥuzn*) [. . . and . . .] they inherited patience (*ṣabr*) on account of the length of their tribulation. Then their hearts began to burn for the Kingdom (*al-malakūt*), and their thoughts to wander among the places and under the veils of the [divine] Majesty (*ḥujub al-jabarūt*). They hid in shadows under the portico of regret, and read the book of [their] sins (*ṣaḥīfat al-khaṭāyā*). They made anxiety (*jaza*ʿ) their own legacy to themselves, until, through complete scrupulousness (*wara*ʿ), they attained the summit of renunciation (*zuhd*). That is how the bitterness of renouncing the world became so sweet for them, and the hard couch so soft, that they won love of salvation and the way to peace.[21]

The passage illustrates how *tawba* naturally leads to the stations of patience, scrupulousness, and then renunciation. But although this organic unity of the *maqāmāt* is found in almost all Sufi texts, in which the virtues grow out of each other, the Sufis disagree over the exact order and number of *maqāmāt*, as well as over whether particular virtues should be classified as states or stations. This produced from very early on quite a bit of diversity within the various systematizations of the mystic ascent. In fact, there is such a degree of diversity that it is rare to find two authors delineating the same schema of states and stations. Sarrāj in his *Kitāb al-luma*ʿ, one of the earliest comprehensive treatises of Sufi doctrine, lists seven *maqāmāt* in the following order: *tawba*, scrupulousness (*wara*ʿ), renunciation (*zuhd*), poverty (*faqr*), patience (*ṣabr*), trust in God (*tawakkul*), and contentment (*riḍā*ʾ).[22] Unlike the passage from Dhū al-Nūn above, he does not place patience immediately after repentance. Makkī lists nine in his *Qūt al-qulūb*, with patience, gratitude (*shukr*), and fear (*khawf*) following *tawba*, in that order.[23] In Kalābādhī's *Ta*ʿ*arruf*, patience, poverty, and humility (*tawāḍu*ʿ) follow *tawba*.[24] Kharrāz speaks of sixteen stations in his *Kitāb al-ṣidq*, with self-knowledge (*ma*ʿ*rifat al-nafs*) and knowledge of the Enemy (*ma*ʿ*rifat al-*ʿ*adūw*) coming after *tawba*, after which follows scrupulousness, concern for what is pure and lawful, renunciation, and trust in God.[25] Nūrī (d. 907) produces his own order,[26] while in Muḥāsibī's writings a definitive order seems to be lacking altogether.[27] This variety does not simply rest on the different number of stations which for each of these authors comprised the ascent, but also because a virtue that one author might have identified as a station was considered a state by another, such as love or fear, or because an author included both states and stations in his number of levels. In the later tradition, the levels of the path reached as many as forty, as we find in Abū Saʿīd's (b. Abī al-Khayr) *Maqāmāt al-ʿarbaʿīn* (d. 1049),[28] or a hundred, as in the case of Ansārī's *Manāzil al-sāʾirīn* (d. 1089).[29] Others enumerated up to three hundred or even a thousand stages.[30] The only occasion when a schema was replicated seems to be when one author consciously reproduced the order of another. In Ibn al-ʿArabī's *Futūḥāt* (d. 1240), for example, the *maqāmat al-yaqīn* are structured in a general sense according to the order found in Qushayrī's *Risāla,*[31] a text that we know the Spanish mystic read religiously as a youth.[32]

But despite this sheer range of schematizations—the result both of the authors' own experiences on the path and an attempt to impose some degree of structure and order to their treatments of the spiritual virtues—there are clear uniformities. In the case of *tawba* and its relation to the ascending *maqāmāt,* two of the most obviously shared features are the following. First of all, none of the Sufi figures classified repentance as a passing or transitory state, a fleeting *ḥāl*. If there are individuals who repent when they are overcome by feelings of intense religiosity, yet prove lax on other occasions, this simply means that they have not internalized the *maqām al-tawba*. It does not mean that *tawba,* as a Sufi virtue, is of itself a passing state,[33] such as "contraction" (*qabḍ*) or "expansion" (*basṭ*).[4] Second, *tawba* is considered to be the first stage of the journey in the eyes of almost all Sufis. This we find to be the case in such early figures as Tirmidhī (d. 932), Junayd, Kalābādhī, Makkī, and Sarrāj, to name but a few of the most important ones. Dhū al-Nūn is one exception (even though the passage cited above might suggest otherwise). A saying attributed to the Egyptian alchemist cites "wakefulness" instead of *tawba* as the first stage of the path. He likens repentance to a medicine that can be administered only to a sick and drunk man—the spiritually diseased, heedless sinner—after he has been brought to sobriety. The drunkard has to become fully conscious of his illness before he can begin to cure himself through *tawba,* and this requires *yaqẓa* or wakefulness.[35] But we should not be led to conclude from this persuasive explanation that others who placed *tawba* at the first stage of the journey did not also realize that wakefulness must precede repentance. They might simply have felt that wakefulness was subsumed within the initial phases of the process of repentance. Others, on the other hand, might not have considered a wakefulness that does not lead to *tawba* an actual stage of the journey, as the journey properly begins only once the individual takes concrete steps to heal the sickness of his soul. A wakefulness that does not produce repentance is like recognizing one's sickness without taking measures to alleviate it. We cannot say that one who is aware of his illness is on the way to recovery, just as we cannot consider a sinner to be on the way to God simply because he is cognizant of his lamentable state. He must repent to become a wayfarer or *sālik*. Only when he takes a step toward rectifying his condition does he enter the way. To reiterate, then, what we stated above: *tawba* was in almost all cases seen as the first stage of the soul's return to God. This is evidenced not only in the early tradition, but also in the most influential of Sufi manuals authored after the tenth century, such as Qushayrī's *Risāla*, Hujwīrī's *Kashf al-maḥjūb*, Ghazālī's *Iḥyā' 'ulūm al-dīn*, and Suhrawardī's *'Awārif al-ma'ārif*. Anṣārī's tremendously influential *Manāzil al-sā'irīn*, which begins with the *bāb al-yaqẓa*, remains a major exception.[36]

Tawba in Early Sufi Apothegmata

We shall now turn to examine the station of *tawba* with a particular focus, for the remainder of the chapter, on the sayings and aphorisms—often expressed in concise and poetic sententious form—found in early Sufi literature on the subject. Our purpose shall be to glean the most basic elements of repentance through a survey of these early sayings as we segue into a more comprehensive exploration of these themes in the following three chapters. Before proceeding, it should be clarified that the reason it is essential to provide a synopsis of the sayings, however brief, is because they offer us a window into some of the earliest conceptualizations of *tawba*. Taken as a whole, they allow us to form a relatively accurate, albeit limited, picture of the central ideas associated with the concept. Their value as source material, in this light, cannot be underestimated. It is also important to recognize, at least for purposes of the present study, that early Sufi works were often composed of various maxims and quotations thematically strung together through various degrees of creativity by the author or compiler—a characteristic of early Islamic Arabic literature as a whole. In the words of Dimitri

Gutas, "early Arabic prose literature is predominantly apothegmatic in nature."[37] This peculiar feature of the literature lies at least partly in the fact that these works marked something of a transition between an oral culture as it was developing into a more sophisticated written culture, part of a natural process of the codification and systematization of a fledging tradition concerned with transcribing and transmitting the views of earlier authorities, the most significant of whom was the Prophet himself.

The apothegmatic nature of which Gutas speaks is particularly discernable in mystical writings. "Sufi literature," he writes, "is by its very nature replete with maxims and anecdotes: terse and often paradoxical sayings are the major means of communication of Sufi ideas"[38]—an observation perhaps no more evident than in the early tradition. The reasons for the value ascribed in Sufi tradition to these sayings were manifold. For one thing, they were believed to carry a power that could catalyze or set in motion a metamorphosis in the listener or reader. As a *ḥadīth* states, "some poetry is *ḥikma* and some eloquent style is magic."[39] The magical force of this "eloquent style," when it had its origin in the tongue of a friend of God, could function, or so it was believed, as an elixir that alchemically transformed the substance of a soul from base metal to gold. This power is attested to in Abū al-Ḥasan al-Sīrjānī's (d. 1077) compilation of the words of the early Sufis in his *Kitāb al-bayāḍ wa al-sawād*, the opening chapter (*bāb al-ḥikma*) of which he dedicates to delineating their special value and significance, particularly for spiritual instruction. The impact poetically formulated apothegmata could have on their readers is illustrated by a story the author shares in his chapter on *tawakkul*. A man once set out in search of his sustenance, we are told, when after some time he was overcome by fatigue and sat down to rest. No sooner had he done this that he saw before him a poem inscribed on parchment, the opening two verses of which read, "Verily, I saw you seated facing Me, and realized how sorrowful you were / Let go of your concerns and have trust in your Lord, for it is in the nature of trust to ease one's burdens." Moved by these words, the man was aroused to a state of *tawakkul*, gave up anxiously searching for his sustenance, and eventually became, or so the story ends, wealthy and self-sufficient.[40] As we saw in the previous chapter, well-formulated words conveyed at the appropriate moment could, through a mysterious power, induce an abject sinner to repent and return to God.

Yet another reason these sayings were so prized was because of their quasi-revelatory status. It was commonly held that the meditations that the friends of God gave voice to were the result of a second order revelation of sorts, a privilege for which they were uniquely singled out as the "heirs of the prophets,"[41] and hence particularly worthy of transcription, transmission, and teaching. When the Qurʾān declares that "he who has been given *ḥikma* has received much good" (Q 2:269), where *ḥikma* may be understood, in line with pre-Islamic custom, not only as wisdom that is self-contained, but which instead flows out in the form of beautiful, ornate speech,[42] then we can better appreciate the value of these sayings. Indeed, a number of traditions ascribed to the Prophet underscore something of this notion, and were occasionally cited to highlight their divinely inspired origin. There is, for example, a *ḥadīth* that states, "no man can devote himself exclusively to the worship of God for forty days without the springs of maxims arising (*yanābīʿū l-ḥikma*) out of his heart and overwhelming his tongue."[43] Another reads: "As for the one who has renounced this world, God will have wisdom dwell in his heart and cause him to speak of that wisdom."[44] And yet another tradition, this time a *ḥadīth qudṣī*, has God declare, "No servant (of mine) renounces the world except that I send down rain out of which there sprouts that which affixes wisdom in his heart. And I cause his tongue to speak of that wisdom."[45]

Each of the traditions quoted above emphasize the passive role of the speaker. By detaching himself from all that is transient in this world and single-mindedly turning his gaze toward eternity, he becomes a mouthpiece of God, a channel for the outpouring of celestial knowledge. One is reminded of the verse that says of the Prophet, "he does not speak of his own desire. It is naught else but revelation by which he is inspired" (Q 53:3–4). Indeed, the same phenomenon was understood to be at work, albeit at much a lesser scale, in the pronouncements of God's friends, a point made explicitly by Hujwīrī when he states that they speak not out of volition but compulsion. "He who speaks hits the mark or misses it," he writes of the one who expresses his own opinion, "but he who is made to speak is preserved from transgression." "They prefer silence to speech so long as they are with themselves," he goes on to state, "but when they are beside themselves their words are written on the hearts of men."[46] The reason they are so inscribed, for Hujwīrī, is quite self-evident: they are divine words channelled through a human vessel that has become empty of itself.

Insofar as Sufi apothegmata deal with the virtues in the early tradition, they generally fall into any one of three overlapping categories. (1) They may define the station in question, sometimes through an explicit stipulation of its conditions (*shurūṭ*), or by enumerating the ethical qualities associated with the *maqām* but which are not conditions *sensu stricto*. (2) They may address the various levels at which the station can be realized. In this case they might contrast the difference between how the virtue is internalized by the friends of God and novices, or gnostics (*ʿārifūn*) and ascetics (*zuhhād*). Frequently, the comparison involves the tripartite division of commoners (*al-ʿawāmm*), the elect (*al-khawāṣṣ*), and the elect of the elect (*khāṣṣ al-khawāṣṣ*),[47] with the prophets sometimes included in a fourth category. (3) Finally, they may address the relation of one station to another. This is more often the case for virtues that are typically paired, either as opposites such as fear and hope (*al-khawf wa al-rajāʾ*), or complements, such as patience and gratitude (*al-ṣabr wa al-shukr*).[48] The sayings on *tawba* only on rare occasion fall into this third category. In Ghazālī's *Iḥyāʾ*, for example, half of the chapters on the virtues treat them in pairs, with repentance remaining one of the exceptions.

The aim of the survey below, as already noted, is to provide a cursory synopsis of early views of *tawba*. Here we will not explore the poetic, literary, or rhetorical features of these sayings, but instead extract from them the most essential elements of the concept. As one might expect, some of the sayings are rather germane and prosaic, addressing qualities that immediately come to mind when one thinks of repentance, and may be found in the theological discourses of most religions.[49] Others are witty, imaginative, and thought provoking, and reflect creative approaches to *tawba*, some of which are without precedent. Needless to say, many of the figures that will be cited may not have agreed with all of the characteristics associated with repentance in our survey. Our intention is not to highlight one particular individual's view, but of the early tradition as a whole, at least to the extent that is possible within the limits of our analysis.[50]

The Elements of *Tawba*

The most important aspect of *tawba* that our early authorities speak of is its absolute necessity, the idea that one's ultimate success and happiness is contingent on repentance and an all-embracing return to God. It is "the key to every good," says Abū ʿUthmān, citing the verse, "If you repent, it is better for you" (Q 9:3).[51] But such a course of action is not without its own challenges. Uprooting a sin, particularly one ingrained through habit, while not easy, is perhaps the most self-evident of *tawba*'s requisites. Repentance, insofar as it is accompanied by a desire for forgiveness, requires such an abandonment. In the words of Dhū al-Nūn, "seeking forgiveness (*al-istighfār*) without abandoning [the sin] (*min ghayr iqlāʿ*) is the repentance of liars."[52] The importance of leaving the sin for one's repentance to be sound is agreed upon by representatives of the various theological schools.[53]

Another salient characteristic of *tawba* is that it be accompanied by contrition and regret for past wrongs. Although this does not appear to have a deep Qurʾānic basis, as we saw in chapter 2, the central place that remorse acquires in the tradition derives from the famous *ḥadīth*, that "remorse (*nadam*) is (a sign of) repentance." And so we read in one saying that "repentance entails [. . .] holding on to remorse out of fear that the good fortune (of receiving the gift of repentance) will be lost,"[54] and in another, that "sincere repentance entails constant weeping (*idmān al-bakāʾ*),"[55] and in yet another, that "he who is not remorseful over a sin is incapable of leaving it."[56] Some of the early Sufis used Q 9:118[57] to describe the experience of grief and fear that should grip the *tāʾib*—the grief being over the past wrong and the fear being over the retribution that may lie ahead. "The reality of repentance," declared Dhū al-Nūn, "is that the earth, despite its vastness, becomes constrained for you so that you have no rest, and that your own soul becomes constrained, just as God most High says, 'And the earth, despite its vastness became constrained for them'" (Q 9:118).[58]

Along with the remorse, sadness, and fear associated with repentance, the *tāʾib* also must make efforts not to fall into the sin again. This does not mean simply abandoning the sin for the time being, but ensuring that it is not repeated again, neither in the near nor distant future. Typically, this means forming a firm resolve (*ʿazm*) not to return. Qushayrī states in the *Risāla* that such a resolve is one of the three conditions on which Sunni scholars have reached consensus.[59] Although the early Sufis generally consider *ʿazm* to be an essential ingredient of *tawba*, they disagree on the degree of its necessity. Some hold that repentance is only sound if the *tāʾib* never falls into the sin again; others, more aware of the frailties of human nature, contend that it is enough simply to intend not to repeat the sin, and that if one breaks his resolve, it is sufficient to renew it. In one saying we find that "the aspirant is not (considered) repentant until the angel on his left does not record a sin of his for twenty years,"[60] and in another, that "sincere repentance entails that its companion be remorseful over what has passed, and that he bring together his resolve (*ʿaqdahu wa ʿazmahu)* in what remains [of his life] not to return [to the sin] . . ."[61]

Repentance involves not only remorsefully abandoning the sin with a resolution never to return, but also in making concrete efforts to rectify the mistakes of the past. This concept of *iṣlāḥ,* as we saw in the second chapter, is deeply tied to repentance in the Qurʾān. Many of the early Sufis stipulated it as an essential condition of *tawba.* "The sign of sound repentance (*taṣḥīḥ al-tawba*) and its acceptance," in the words of one early figure, "is that it be followed by setting things aright (*iṣlāḥ*) [. . .] the repentance of one who does not follow it by the setting of things aright remains far from acceptance."[62] Along with *iṣlāh,* repentance should be followed by other unrelated acts of virtue and piety. Acknowledging the sin and turning away from it forms only a part of process. The other half requires turning away from the sin toward all that is good. As Ibn ʿAṭāʾ (d. 922)[63] said, "repentance is to turn from every blameworthy characteristic to every praiseworthy one."[64] *Iṣlāh* also includes compensating those who might have been adversely affected by one's own past wrongs.

Another component of *tawba* is to withdraw from foul company. In the words of Sarī al-Saqaṭī, "a necessary condition for repentance is that the penitent one (*al-tāʾib al-munīb*) begin with parting from people given to disobedience (*ahl al-maʿāsī*)."[65] Such a departure helps him eliminate those factors from his life through which he might be tempted to fall back into sin. The nature of the company one keeps, one's *ṣuḥba,* was given special attention in the early mystical tradition because of the influence others were believed to exercise over one's own inner state. When disciples would congregate under the direction of a master, it was not simply to benefit from his guidance but to participate in the companionship of likeminded seekers in whose longings for God one found inspiration. "You possess all that is good if you have a pious friend," said one figure, while another declared, "You should seek the company of one who, when you see him, makes you think of God." The divine grace that such companions could be instruments for, especially in the wake of one's own slips, was captured in a poignant remark of Abū Yazīd al-Bisṭāmī (d. 874): "A true brother in God is the one who does penance in your place, when you yourself commit a sin."[66] The companionship of such a friend, for Bāyazīd, was rooted in a self-sacrificing love of others, without which no real ascent to God could occur.

Repentance also requires abandoning the sin internally, a theme, as we shall see in chapters 6 and 7, Muḥāsibī and Makkī devote particular attention to. This is a subtler and more difficult requirement because a person cannot always exercise complete control over his inclinations or passing thoughts. The individual, for those who emphasize this feature of repentance, must fight against the inner inclination to repeat the offense by working to create an inner state in which one finds oneself repelled by the thought of the transgression. "If you remember the sin and do not find any sweetness upon its mention," declared Būshanjī (d. 959/960),[67] "[then know] that is repentance."[68] Another advised, "seek forgiveness of your Lord from your pretentious claims (*daʿāwī*) and turn in repentance to him from your blameworthy thoughts."[69] And yet another said, "sincere repentance (*al-tawba al-naṣūḥ*)[70] is that you leave the sin as you came to it, and that you detest it just as you [previously] loved it."[71]

Our authorities also note that the doors of *tawba* remain open until the moment of death, that, in the final order of things, it is never too late to return to God. Hujwīrī recounts the tale of an old man who approached Shaqīq al-Balkhī and inquired, "O Shaykh, I have sinned much and now wish to repent." To this the disciple of Ibrāhīm b. Adham replied, "you have come late." The old man retorted, "No I have come soon. Whoever comes before he is dead comes soon, though he may have been long in coming."[72] Yet even though it is never too late to return to God, at least while one is in this world, our authorities also stress the danger latent in delaying *tawba,* since such a deferral reflects an ignorance of one's mortality, of the possibility that one's end may lie closer than imagined. "He who thinks he can put off his repentance for a year," said one authority, "is as if he said, 'O Lord, I intend to sin after my death for a year,' because it may be that he has no more than an hour left of his life."[73] Another said, "the human being does not wish to repent until [the moment] of death. But if he dies [suddenly], when then shall he repent?"[74]

Finally, despite the illusion that repentance is the work of the human being, or that it proceeds of his own volition, human *tawba* is always the result of an act of divine *tawba*—the sinner's repentance is always preceded by heavenly grace. By realizing that the initial *tawba* is not his own, the *tāʾib* is thereby held back from feelings of spiritual hubris and self-righteousness. The idea is perhaps best encapsulated in a story of a man who came to Rābiʿa al-ʿAdawiyya (d. 801) and asked, "I have committed many sins. If I turn to God will He turn to me?" (*law tubtu hal yatūbu ʿalayya*). "No," she replied to the man's astonishment. "But if He turns towards you, you will turn towards Him" (*bal law tāba ʿalayka la tubta*).[75] The same teaching is found in the saying of Abū Ḥafṣ (d. 874)[76] when he states that "the servant has no share in repentance because the *tawba* is to him and not from him."[77] Along similar lines, Naṣrābādhī (d. 977)[78] would say, "you did not repent until God desired repentance for you. And were He not to have desired repentance for you, you would have been separated from it."[79] The seeming paradox—retraceable to the essentially contested[80] theological problem of predestination and free will—would be addressed in greater detail by Wāsiṭī, as we shall see in the following chapter.

The Levels of *Tawba*

Now that we have summarized the basic qualities associated with repentance, we are in a better position to analyze the second class of sayings that address the internal levels of this station. This is an important category to understand because it is very easy to mistakenly presume, through a cursory perusal of many of the Sufi sayings, that some of them concerning a given *maqām* contradict each other. In actual fact, they might simply be addressing different levels of the virtue, which is to say, the virtue as it should be embodied at different stages of the way. This is not to suggest that the early Sufis did not disagree with each other over the ethical or psychological qualities that must accompany any given station—an element we will explore in greater detail in the following chapters—but one cannot begin to examine these disagreements without ruling out the aforementioned possibility.[81]

A central ethical teaching found in the Sufi tradition is that almost any act considered virtuous in the eyes of common people can be viewed as a vice from a higher perspective. The Sufi maxim that most famously gave voice to this teaching was that "the good deeds of the pious are the sins of those brought near" (*ḥasanāt al-abrār dhunūb al-muqarrabīn*).[82] This is not because the spiritually advanced see common virtues as vices through a Nietzschean inversion or transvaluation of values, but because the common virtues, in relation to the loftier virtues that they aspire toward, appear incomplete. If a particular mystic criticizes a given act whose moral worth seems indisputable, it is simply because the act in relation to a more meritorious one is flawed or deficient, and therefore sinful. In this light, any embodiment of a virtue that is less perfect than another is a vice. Sufi discussions of the states and stations are grounded in what one might accurately describe as a philosophy of "relational ethics" or "ethical perspectivalism."[83]

In regard to *tawba,* the subdivisions of this *maqām* are stratified on the basis of the various sins of which individuals must repent. In the Sufi tradition, we find that as the traveler progresses on the way, his moral shortcomings become subtler, more ethereal and less perceptible. In many of the aphorisms, the authorities are clearly more concerned about heedlessness (*al-ghafla*) than actual Shariʿite sins (*al-maʿāṣī*). It is not that they belittle or trivialize the latter; rather, because of the rigor of their ascetic discipline—a basic requisite of the path, particularly in the early period—they are no longer tried by circumstances that would tempt others. Their sins of heedlessness involve those temporary, passing moments in which they may not be as acutely conscious of God as they could be. Hence the remark of Dhū al-Nūn: "[T]he repentance of the commoners (*al-ʿawāmm*) is from sins while the repentance of the elect (*al-khawāṣṣ*) is from heedlessness."[84] An almost identical apothegm is attributed to Bunnān al-Ḥammāl (d. 928),[85] that "repentance is of two kinds: the repentance of the commoners is from sins while the repentance of the elect is from heedlessness."[86] A story from the life of Jesus colorfully illustrates this teaching. The Israelite prophet is said to have once experienced a period of intimate communion with God that lasted sixty days. While in such a mode of intense prayer, the thought of bread crossed the Messiah's mind. No sooner did this happen than the sweetness of his intimacy was cut off, causing him to fall down and weep over what he had lost. A holy man walked by as this was unfolding. "O friend of God," cried Jesus, "pray to God for me, for while I was in a lofty state, the thought of bread crossed my mind and cut me off [from the intimacy I enjoyed with Him]." The friend of God then prayed, not in the manner Christ requested, but in admonishment to underscore the severity of his lapse. "O Lord," he spoke, "forgive me not if the thought of bread ever crossed my mind since the time I have known you."[87]

In some sayings, the contrast is not between sins and heedlessness but between the former and one's own good works (*al-ḥasanāt*). "The common people repent of their sins," said one gnostic, "while the Sufis (*al-ṣūfiyya*) repent of their good deeds (*min ḥasanātihim*)."[88] To repent of one's *ḥasanāt* may refer to shortcomings within virtuous deeds, such as the presence of some measure of insincerity, or as would more often be the case, laying claim to acts that are ultimately not one's own. Indeed, Sufi texts frequently speak of God's creation of acts, in line with what would become the position of Sunni orthodoxy in general. Since good deeds become manifest in the world through a divine creative fiat, to attribute them to one's own efforts requires repentance, since everything beautiful and wholesome is to be retraced to its origin in God, and not the means through which it appears in the world. To fail to recognize this metaphysical reality is to fall into the sin of "witnessing good deeds" (*ruʾyat al-ḥasanāt*),[89] which is to say, observing them as if they are of one's own making.[90] ʿAbd Allāh al-Tamīmī[91] captured this subtler kind of transgression when he remarked, "O what a difference there is between the *tāʾib* who repents of slips (*al-zallāt*), the one who repents of moments of heedlessness (*al-ghaflāt*), and the one who repents of witnessing his good deeds (*ruʾyat al-ḥasanāt*)."[92] Abū Yazīd al-Bisṭāmī may have had these blemishes in mind when he declared, "there is one only repentance [necessary] for a sin, but a thousand [are necessary] for a good deed."[93]

Finally, at the highest level of *tawba*, one repents of everything other than God (*mā siwa Allāh*). For the mystic absorbed in the contemplation of the One, all that distracts him, even for a passing moment, from his ultimate goal requires repentance. As one early figure states, "the masses (*al-ʿāmma*) seek forgiveness for sins, the elect (*al-khāṣṣa*) seek forgiveness for witnessing the acts, and for witnessing gifts and graces, while the great ones (*al-akābir*) seek forgiveness for witnessing everything other than the Real."[94] It was for this reason that Sahl al-Tustarī declared that "the *tāʾib* is in the grave," to which Sīrjānī added by way of commentary, "which is to say, he does not return [to the world of the senses]."[95] Another early authority stated that, in the final order of things, "repentance is to efface human qualities through an affirmation of divine qualities. It is to kill the self of all that is other than God."[96] This theme will be explored in greater detail in the following chapters.

To summarize our findings, the early Sufis speak of various levels of sins, with moral and spiritual deficiencies becoming more elusive and imperceptible the closer one draws to God. The subtleties of these transgressions eventually become as undetectable as the traces of darkness one encounters in approaching the blazing light of the sun. The levels of human imperfection, from the grossest to the most subtle, can be classified in the following order: (1) acts of outright disobedience (*al-maʿāṣī, al-mukhālafāt, al-dhunūb*), (2) slips (*al-zallāt*), (3) heedlessness (*al-ghafla*), (4) witnessing one's virtuous acts (*ruʾyat al-ḥasanāt*), and finally (5) witnessing anything other than God. *Tawba* marks a gradual movement toward human perfection through a spectrum that ranges from abject *kufr* on one end to a state of immersion in the pure unity of God (*al-tawḥīd*) on the other, where one is "alone with the alone" in the eternal now.

The Classification of Levels in the Sufi Manuals

By the late tenth and eleventh centuries, the Sufis more formally schematized the ascending levels of repentance. The teacher of Qushayrī, Abū ʿAlī al-Daqqāq (d. 1015 or 1021) said that "*tawba* has three levels: the first is *tawba*, the middle part is *ināba*, and its end is *awba*." Qushayrī traced the psychological origin of each of these three in his *Risāla*, respectively, to "fear of punishment," "desire for reward," and "guarding the divine command, neither out of desire for reward nor an escape from punishment."[97] A similar tripartite classification appears in Hujwīrī, for whom *tawba* is "to return from great sins to obedience," *ināba* "to return from minor sins to love," and *awba* "to return from one's self to God." *Tawba*, says Hujwīrī, is for the mass of believers, *ināba* for the friends of God (*awliyāʾ*) and those brought near (*muqarrabūn*), and *awba* for the prophets and messengers.[98]

Although I have not found this particular tripartite classification of *tawba-ināba-awba* in earlier sources,[99] the idea that *ināba* and *awba* represent higher levels of repentance has a Qurʾānic basis, where, as we saw in chapter 2, these terms are closely coupled with the return of prophets. Daqqāq was not the first to see this. We find *awba* and *ināba* used to describe higher levels of repentance in the early Sufi aphorisms. The only difference is that in none of these sayings does the triad appear as systematically formulated as in Daqqāq and later Sufis. There is, for example, a saying attributed to Ḥusayn,[100] that "*ināba* comes before gnosis (*maʿrifa*). The best of creation in their *ināba* towards God, and in their return to Him, are most advanced in their gnosis."[101] There is also a saying attributed to Qāsim,[102] that "[the heedful *awwāb* is] he who does not preoccupy himself with other than his Lord."[103]

Qāsim also spoke of the *ināba* of the self (*nafs*), the heart (*qalb*), and the spirit (*rūḥ*). "The *ināba* of the servant," he said, "is that he returns to his Lord from himself, his heart, and his spirit. The *ināba* of the self is that he preoccupy himself with His service and worship. The *ināba* of the heart is that it empty itself of other than Him. And the *ināba* of the spirit lies in the perpetuity of remembrance (of God) so that he does not remember anything other than Him, and does not contemplate anything except in Him (*illā fīhī*)."[104] Some of the Sufis even used *ināba* to describe God's return to Himself in a manner that would be expounded in greater detail by such luminaries as Ibn al-ʿArabī in later tradition. "*Ināba* is a return (*rujūʿ*) from Him to Him," said one authority, "not from something other than Him."[105] And another declared that once one's *ināba* is sound, "it becomes a return to Him from Him, so that he subsists, annihilated (*fa baqāʿ mustahlakan*) in witnessing the One to whom he returns. There [then] remains for him neither a return nor a perpetuation [in any affirmable quality (*thubūt*)]."[106]

To summarize the main findings of this chapter, we have seen that the early Sufis developed a complex theory of the virtues that underscored their relation to the levels of the mystical journey. Although there were considerable variations among them on the particular order in which these virtues had to be mastered, there were also clear cross-schematic features. The most significant of these for our purposes is that *tawba* was almost unanimously considered to be the first of the stations. The system of states and stations that developed in the ninth century through the influence of such figures as Dhū al-Nūn would become the foundation of Sufi psychology and ethical theory. By placing so much weight on the integration of virtues such as love, patience, and gratitude, the early Sufis underscored the role of the ethical component in the mystic quest. The tradition as represented by its founding figures was concerned not so much with supernatural or paranormal experiences, visions, or even higher states of consciousness (even though these often accompanied the mystic life), but with guiding the seeker into the presence of God through the internalization of certain key qualities. The ethical component was, in this respect, closely tied to the transformation that the aspirant underwent in his ascent. This was because the internalization of the virtues was in fact the process of becoming "God-like" insofar as the seeker was, through the actualization of these traits, taking on the qualities of God in a form and manner that was befitting to the human being.[107] By emphasizing the defining function of ethics, the Sufis were, from their own perspective, following the Prophetic injunction to "assume the character traits of God."[108] The gradual internalization of the virtues culminated in the extinction of human attributes and the (re)integration of the soul into its pre-eternal divine origin, although it was not until some time had elapsed that this phenomenon came to be described in more elaborate and systematic fashion. Nevertheless, there were enough references to it in the early period to allow one to recognize the later more systematic formulations as logical outgrowths of ideas already present.

Our analysis of many of the early sayings and aphorisms revealed that the early thinkers made it clear that certain conditions must be met in order for *tawba* to be accepted by God. Although they did not agree on which of these were essential, there appears to have been general agreement on the necessity of certain pivotal ones such as remorse for the sin, abandoning the sin, and resolving to remain upright afterward. We also saw that in many of the early sayings, *tawba* could be conceptualized through the lens of different levels of spiritual advancement, and that these levels were often stratified according to a dyadic division of the commoners and the elect, or a tripartite division comprising beginners, the elect, and the elect of the elect. For some masters, these levels of repentance corresponded to *tawba, ināba,* and *awba*. Moreover, as we saw, all the virtues associated with the path could, in like fashion, be stratified into multiple levels, with each level corresponding to a degree of spiritual realization. This "ethical perspectivalism" is one of the unique features of Sufi ethical philosophy, and it is present in the earliest sayings and aphorisms transmitted to us.

Chapter 5

Four Early Approaches to *Tawba*

Now that we have completed our survey of the various sayings and aphorisms about repentance in the early tradition, we shall move on to more closely examine the concept in the thought of four early figures: Kharrāz, Sahl al-Tustarī, Junayd, and Wāsiṭī. A certain degree of speculation will have to guide our analysis, as none of these individuals appear to have authored separate treatises on the subject—certainly, at least, none that have survived, nor of which there are any extant records. We shall examine the available material in an attempt to draw out whatever conclusions are possible. Due to the importance of these figures, and what we know of their larger mystical philosophies, an attempt will be made to situate their views of repentance within their larger theological systems, particularly in the case of the two towering figures of Junayd and Sahl.

Kharrāz (d. 899): The Requirements of *Tawba*

Abū Saʿīd Aḥmad al-Kharrāz was considered one of the leaders of the Sufis of Baghdad.[1] He was given the honorary title, the "tongue of Sufism" (*lisān al-taṣawwuf*) because, according to ʿAṭṭār, "no one in this community possessed a tongue of mystic truth such as he."[2] He was also credited with being among the first to explicate the Sufi doctrine of annihilation (*fanāʾ*) and subsistence (*baqāʾ*).[3] Despite his attempts to demonstrate the "orthodoxy" of mysticism, he was charged with unbelief by some of the *ʿulamāʾ* of Baghdad due to the purportedly heretical contents of his *Kitāb al-ṣirr* (*Book of Secrets*), and eventually took refuge in Bukhara.[4]

Kharrāz's views about *tawba* are to be drawn primarily from a treatise entitled the *Kitāb al-ṣidq* (*Book of Truthfulness*). The work is of particular value to us because it contains a chapter on repentance, which, despite its relative brevity, remains one of the most comprehensive treatments of the subject available from the formative period of Islamic mysticism. Arberry noted the importance of the *Kitāb al-ṣidq* when he observed that "apart from the writings of Muḥāsibī, it is the earliest systematic presentation of Sufi experience, written by a practicing Sufi."[5] Although Kharrāz authored a number of treatises, none of his other extant writings provide us with significant insight into his views on *tawba*.[6]

The purpose of the *Kitāb al-ṣidq*, as Kharrāz states, is to serve as a guide for novices. The work is not meant, as we might expect, to disclose inner mystical truths, even though this is what Kharrāz, along with other early Sufis like Dhū al-Nūn and Tirmidhī, is famous for in the eyes of posterity.[7] Instead, the intention behind the text is to address the outward meanings of the theory and practice of *ṣidq*.[8] It is thus not entirely surprising that Kharrāz's approach to *tawba* in this work does not seriously differ from that of other more ethically inclined Sufis, such as Muḥāsibī. We shall briefly look into some of the implications of this in our next chapter. Massignon's claim that the *Kitāb al-ṣidq* is a collection "of traditions (with *isnād*) on asceticism" is simply incorrect.[9]

Although the work is structured as an inquiry into the meaning and nature of *ṣidq*, each of its chapters deals with one of the stations of the Sufi path.[10] Kharrāz does this by drawing out the meanings of *ṣidq* insofar as they correspond to the stations. *Ṣidq* is therefore used as the starting point to explore the psychological and spiritual topography of the soul's ascent to God. After addressing the three principles (*uṣūl*) of sincerity (*ikhlāṣ*), patience (*ṣabr*), and truthfulness (*ṣidq*), which the aspirant must become familiar with at the onset of the spiritual journey, Kharrāz proceeds to examine the relation between truthfulness and the various stations. These latter are arranged in an order that suggests a linear hierarchy, although it remains unclear how dogmatic Kharrāz would have been about the order one encounters in this particular work.[11]

In general agreement with most of the Sufi tradition, Kharrāz maintains that repentance marks the beginning of the journey. "The first part of truthfulness," writes Kharrāz, "is truthfulness of the servant in turning to God in sincere repentance" (*ṣidq al-ʿabd fī ināba ilā Allāh taʿāla bi al-tawba al-naṣūḥ*). This is the "sincere repentance" spoken of in the verse, "O ye who believe! Turn to God in sincere repentance" (Q 66:8). According to Kharrāz, this sincere repentance has conditions, and it is through the fulfillment of these conditions that one becomes truthful in *tawba*. It requires first of all remorse (*nadam*) for one's violations, as well as a resolve to leave behind (*ʿazīma ʿalā tark al-ʿawd*) whatever displeases God. It also demands that one continuously seek divine forgiveness (*dawām al-istighfār*). One must also make efforts to appropriately recompense one's victims, whether through returning stolen wealth or other commensurate measures. It also requires acknowledging or confessing (*iʿtirāf*) one's wrong, either to God, if the sin is against Him, or the victim. Truthfulness in repentance also requires giving up the company of friends who assisted the *tāʾib* in his previous wrongs. The repentant one should in fact flee such friends as one flees enemies, because "friends on that Day will be foes one to another, except those who feared God" (Q 43:67). Finally, repentance goes beyond simply abandoning outward acts of transgression. The inner thoughts of sin, or sins of the heart (*maʾtham min al-qalb*), must also be expunged because of the Qurʾānic command: "And leave the outward part of sin, and the inward part thereof" (Q 6:120).[12] All the while, the *tāʾib* should be characterized by fear and sadness out of apprehension that he may have proven himself insincere, and that his repentance, as a consequence, has been rejected.[13]

In the next two chapters, Kharrāz addresses truthfulness concerning knowledge of the soul (*ṣidq fī maʿrifat al-nafs*) and of the enemy (*ṣidq fī maʿrifat al-ʿadūw*). In both of these, he stresses the importance of becoming conscious of the stratagems and machinations of the lower soul and Satan as they erect obstacles to the process of inner purification. These obstacles have to be dealt with in order for one's repentance to be sound. If ignored, the proclivities to sin will linger, causing one to continuously falter. "It is enough sin (*ithm*) for a man," Kharrāz quotes one of the learned as saying, "that he knows of a vice (*ʿayb*) in his soul, but does not amend it, nor is moved to repentance on its account."[14] If the aspirant is truthful in his quest for God, and yet finds that his soul resists conforming itself to what pleases God, then it should be tamed through a deprivation of lawful pleasures. As we shall see in the following chapter, Muḥāsibī offers the same advice. Satan must also be confronted with equal force because "he spares no effort to weaken your resolve, slacken your intention, and delay your repentance."[15] One must constantly take refuge in God because of Satan's vigilance. The aspirant must regularly watch over his soul through *murāqaba*, and not give attention to any incoming evil thought (*khaṭar*) lest it become a passion (*shahwa*),[16] the passion become an intention (*himma*),[17] and the intention become an act (*fiʿl*).[18]

At the end of his chapter on *tawba,* Kharrāz claims that the process of repentance is unending. As the inner lights of the aspirant become stronger, and he grows in faith and the knowledge of God, he becomes more vigilant in his repentance. This is because the purity of his heart allows him to detect the most subtle of its blemishes, so that, as soon as an internal defilement appears, he turns at once in *tawba* and *istighfār* to cleanse his soul. But near the very end of the *Kitāb al-ṣidq,* Kharrāz seems to qualify his earlier position. When the Sufi finally enters into the divine presence, he becomes so absorbed in his contemplation of God that he no longer needs to concern himself with the stations. Since he has by then already passed through and acquired them, the stations are firmly rooted in his nature. Once he beholds the awe-inspiring majesty of God, it defeats the purpose of his journey for him to turn his attention away from the Goal of his quest toward the stations through which he has arrived. This, however, does not mean that he is no longer qualified by these very virtues associated with the stations. Instead, he has become unconscious of them through his self-annihilation and subsistence in God. "What business do you have with remembering a station (*al-manzil*) in which you have dwelt," Kharrāz asks near the end of the treatise, "when it has brought (you) to your goal" (*ḥattā awṣala ilā baghiyyatika*)?[19] We can understand a saying of Kharrāz on weeping quoted by Qushayrī in the same light. He was once asked, "does the gnostic (*al-ʿārif*) ever reach a state where weeping becomes disliked?" He replied, "yes, for weeping pertains to the period of their journey towards God, most High. When, however, they descend into the realities of proximity (*ḥaqāʾiq al-qurb*) and taste the food of arrival (*dhāqū ṭaʿm al-wuṣūl*) from His holiness, it disappears from them."[20]

The tension between the two positions articulated by Kharrāz may simply reflect the difference in what is demanded of the mystic at different levels of the ascent. This, after all, is how later Sufis reconciled the two positions, as we shall see in other contexts.

Sahl al-Tustarī (d. 896): The Obligatory Nature of *Tawba*

Sahl al-Tustarī stands as another prominent Sufi of the early period. His influence on the later Sufi tradition came primarily through the *Qūt al-qulūb* of Makkī, who was affiliated with the Sālimiyya, a school of Sufism that retraced its mystical teachings back to Sahl through his close friend and disciple, Abū ʿAbd Allāh b. Sālim (d. 909).[21] Makkī studied under Ibn Sālim's son, Abū al-Ḥasan Aḥmad b. Sālim (d. 967), whom he refers to in the *Qūt* as "our master (*shaykhunā*)," as did Sarrāj, the author of that other notable work on early Sufism, the *Kitāb al-lumaʿ*. Sahl's wide-ranging influence on the later tradition can be discerned by the frequency with which he is quoted in both the practical manuals of Sufism (concerned with *al-ʿulūm al-muʿāmalāt*) as well in the more metaphysically inclined works (concerned with *al-ʿulūm al-mukāshafāt*).[22] Our knowledge of Sahl's doctrines is derived from the general Tustarī tradition consisting of his aphorisms, anecdotes about his life, as well a short Qurʾān commentary that was most likely compiled by his followers. Böwering, who studied the commentary in depth in his important study of Sahl, has convincingly argued for its authenticity.[23] This very commentary was used by later Sufi authors, such as Sulamī and Ruzbihān Baqlī (d. 1209), as a source for Sahl's interpretations of various Qurʾānic verses. Sahl authored nothing, however, by his own hand.

In our excavation of early notions of repentance, Sahl turns out to be a relatively important figure because of the emphasis he put on repentance in the religious life. The emphasis was rooted in a mystical psychology that appears to have developed early in his youth. When Sahl was a child, his uncle gave him the silent litany, "God is with me, God watches over me, and God witnesses me," to repeat every night before he went to sleep. He did this for years until, he says, "a sweetness for it entered my heart" (*fa waqaʿa fī qalbī lahu ḥalāwa*).[24] His uncle later advised him to continue the practice for the remainder of his life because it would profit him in both this world and the next. "When God is with someone, watches over him, and witnesses him," his uncle asked him, "will he sin against Him?"[25] This was the teaching his uncle presumably intended for him to internalize. According to Makkī, the *dhikr* became part of his *qūt* (nourishment). This is of particular importance considering the celebrated austerity of Sahl's diet.[26] It suggests he derived sustenance through a meditative act that emphasized God's witnessing of the human soul.[27] This orientation would later become one of the foundations of Sahl's spiritual method, according to which the individual must constantly watch over his own thoughts, inclinations, and shortcomings through a state of scrupulous self-examination. In such a state the soul is called to renew its repentance at the immediate sight of any moral or religious blemish because of its knowledge that God is a constant witness. For such a person, repentance is an essential, indispensable part of the religious life because of the natural human proclivity to fall, despite one's vigilance, into even the subtlest forms of disobedience.

Sahl described the human soul as a theater for the struggle between the luminous heart and the dense lower self. While the former is a positive force that inclines toward God, the latter is a negative force that turns man in the direction of his ego and disobedience.[28] Since the human being is pulled by these two opposing tendencies, the task of the spiritual seeker is to overcome the negative impulses of the lower soul and return constantly to God through the regenerative, transformative power of *tawba*. Through repentance, the soul reorients itself to God by means of a process of external and internal purification. The initial stages of this process in the Sufi's life were briefly described by Sahl in a commentary on Q 9:112, "the repentant ones, the ones who worship" (*al-tāʾibūn al-ʿābidūn*).[29]

> He [Sahl] said, the first thing that the novice (*al-mubtadīʾ*) is commanded to do is exchange blameworthy undertakings (*al-ḥarakāt al-madhmūma*) for praiseworthy ones, and this comprises repentance. Moreover repentance is not sound until he holds to silence; silence is not sound until he clings to solitary retreat (*khalwa*); solitary retreat is not sound until he clings to eating what is lawful; eating what is lawful is not sound until he holds to fulfilling the right of God, most High; and fulfilling the right of God, most High, is not sound until he holds to guarding the limbs and the heart. And all that we have described is not sound until he beseeches the help of God, glorious and majestic.[30]

Despite the concision of Sahl's words, they contain the essential requirements of the initial phases of the Sufi life as elaborated in the more detailed and comprehensive writings of figures such as Muḥāsibī and Makkī. These include, for example, the importance of silence, retreat, and concerning oneself with lawful food. In these longer treatises we find an explanation of the logic behind these requirements, and their effects on the growth of the spiritual aspirant. We shall see this more clearly in the following chapters.

We also have a number of much shorter sayings concerning repentance that have been transmitted by the Tustarī tradition. When he was once asked to define *tawba*, he replied that it is "to exchange ignorance for knowledge, forgetfulness for remembrance, and sin for obedience."[31] He also said that "repentance is not sound for anyone of you until he leaves much of what is [merely] licit (*al-kathīr min al-mubāḥ*) out of fear that he may [accidentally] fall into something else [i.e., the illicit],"[32] thereby underscoring the need for scrupulous piety. Sahl also encouraged the seeker to "strive against your lower soul with the sword of opposition, burden it with the weights of remorse, and drive it out into the deserts of fear (*sayyirhā fī mafāwiz al-khawf*). Perhaps you may drive it back to the way of *tawba* and *ināba*."[33]

Tawba as Never Forgetting the Sin

Although a number of Sahl's sayings about *tawba* have been transmitted by the Tustarī tradition, the most famous of these is that repentance "is that you not forget your sin" (*an lā tansā dhanbaka*).[34] What Sahl meant by this is that true repentance is marked by genuine regret over the past wrong, and one which the sinner never becomes unconscious of either out of heedlessness or self-satisfaction. The one who frequently recalls his sins will be characterized by a constant state of humility. This feeling of unworthiness before God will aid him in the religious life. By not forgetting his sins,[35] he will always strive to fulfill the conditions of repentance by experiencing remorse for past sins, exert himself to rectify mistakes, vigilantly guard himself against repeating offenses, and perform other similar commendable acts associated with *tawba*. Although the sins one turns away from will be subtler the further one advances on the path, the Sufi will never reach a state that might warrant forgetting them altogether. This is because human perfection, insofar as such perfection is defined as a freedom from sin, is not possible. Other Sufis who disagreed with Sahl's definition did not contest the definition itself, but its relevance to more advanced stages of the mystic life. We saw this earlier in the case of Kharrāz and will examine it in more detail when we come to Junayd's views of repentance shortly.

Sahl did not just stress the importance of repentance for both beginning and advanced Sufis, but made it a duty incumbent upon every Muslim. ʿAṭṭār relates an anecdote that illustrates Sahl's view on the inefficacy of prayers made for an unrepentant soul. When a certain ruler fell sick so that all of his physicians were unable to cure him, Sahl was invited to the royal court because his prayers were known to be answered. "Prayer," Sahl informed the ruler, "is only effective in the case of one who is repentant. In your prison there are men wrongfully detained." When the ruler realized the import of Sahl's words, he released the prisoners and repented. Sahl then beseeched the help of God with the following words: "[As] You have shown to him the abasement due to disobedience, so now display to him the glory gained by obedience. As You have clothed his inward parts with the garment of repentance, so now clothe his outward parts with the garment of health." ʿAṭṭār says the ruler immediately recovered his health following the prayer.[36] Whether or not the event actually occurred is secondary. What this incident as narrated by ʿAṭṭār demonstrates is the emphasis that the mystical tradition recognized Sahl placed on *tawba*. In this story, even such a simple, commonplace religious act as a prayer for someone depends on the completion of one's repentance.

Sahl's Expulsion from Tustar over the Question of Repentance

The rather uncompromising position Sahl took on the obligatory nature of *tawba* drew the ire of at least some of the *ʿulamāʾ*, according to our sources. A number of them point out that he was expelled from his home town of Tustar because of the unrest his theological views created. The campaign against Sahl was led by a man whose identity remains unknown, but who was considered to be learned and religious. Sarrāj presents the following account of the circumstance surrounding his expulsion:

> Despite his knowledge and the intensity of his exertion (*ma ʿa ʿilmihi wa shiddat ijtihādihi*)—he said, repentance is an obligation (*farīḍa*) imposed on every servant of God with every breath (*ma ʿa kulli nafas*). There was, in the district (*nāḥiya*), a man to whom knowledge and worship was attributed, who incited the public against him [Sahl], accused him of disbelief (*kaffarahu*), and attributed to him shameful acts (*qabāʾiḥ*) before the people, so that they fell upon him (*wathabūʿ ʿalayhi*). This was the reason for his departure (*khurūj*) from Tustar and his move (*intiqāl*) to Basra, God have mercy on him.[37]

In ʿAṭṭār's account, the event is even more dramatic:

> Sahl said, "repentance is a duty incumbent upon a man every moment, whether he be of the elect or the common folk, whether he be obedient to God or disobedient." There was a man in Tustar who laid claim to being learned and an ascetic. He protested against this saying of Sahl's [. . .] making him out to be a heretic and an infidel. All, commoners and

> nobles alike, took up this charge. Sahl refrained from disputing with them to correct their misunderstanding. Fired by the pure flame of religion, he wrote down on a paper a list of all his possessions, farms, houses, furniture, carpets, vessels, gold and silver. Then he gathered the people and scattered the pages over their head. He gave to every man all that was inscribed on the page that he picked up, as a token of gratitude for their relieving him of his worldly goods. Having given everything away, he set out for the Hijaz.[38]

Böwering has suggested that the theological reason seems to be an insufficient explanation for his departure from Tustar, and has sought to highlight some of the social and political factors that might have impelled Sahl to leave his hometown. While political factors may certainly have been at work—although the evidence Böwering presents appears, at best, rather speculative—the theological factor need not be dismissed as insufficient. The reason for this becomes clearer when we look at the boldness with which Sahl declared the obligation of repentance. In the Tustarī *tafsīr*, Sahl says, "there is nothing in the world more incumbent (*awjab*) upon creation, from the obligations [that are due God], than *tawba*. It is an obligation (*wājib*), at every moment (*lamḥa wa laḥẓa*). And there is no punishment more severe on them than a loss of the knowledge [of the law] of *tawba* (*min faqd al-ʿilm al-tawba*)."[39] Sarrāj's condensed version of the saying is very similar, except that in it Sahl declares repentance to be *farīḍa* rather than *wājib*.[40] In Makkī's *Qūt*, however, we encounter this obligatory nature presented in even stronger terms. He includes more or less the same words we find in the Tustarī *tafsīr*, but with a significant addition:

> Abū Muḥammad Sahl said, "there is nothing more obligatory (*awjab*) on creation (*hādha al-khalq*) than repentance. And there is no punishment more severe on them than a loss of the knowledge [of the law] of repentance (*min faqd al-ʿilm al-tawba*), and yet people have become ignorant of the knowledge [of the law] of repentance." And he [Sahl] said, "whoever says that repentance is not an obligation is a *kāfir*, and whoever is pleased by these words is also a *kāfir*."[41]

If Sahl did in fact take so strong a view in Tustar, it is understandable why his position would have evoked as severe a response as it did, particularly if the clerical establishment of Tustar was either Ḥanbalite or shared with Aḥmad b. Ḥanbal the position that repentance is advisable but not required for salvation.[42] If the clerical establishment had ties to the Ḥanbalites, Sahl would in effect have been accusing some of them of outright disbelief—certainly not a charge we can imagine they would have taken lightly. Although, as noted, none of the sources identifies the individual who spearheaded the expulsion of Sahl, it would not be surprising if he had ties to the traditionalist Ḥanbalite camp.

Although Sahl's view on the obligation of repentance may appear extreme, we must keep in mind that it was a question over which the community was genuinely divided. Abū al-Ḥasan al-Ashʿarī (d. 935) noted in his *Maqālāt* that the Muslims "disagreed over the obligation of repentance (*wujūb al-tawba*). One group said that repentance from sins is absolutely obligatory (*farīḍa*) while another group denied it."[43] Sahl clearly took the stricter view, and encountered the hostility of the Tustarians on its account. Although there is little evidence to suggest he engaged in *takfīr* over contested issues, he did take uncompromising positions on other religious matters besides repentance. As a result, his Sufi doctrine combined an extremely rich mystical theosophy with an unflinching stringency on particular issues over which the Sufis and community at large lacked consensus.[44] This characteristic of his philosophy was transmitted later to the Sālimiyya, and may partly explain Dhahabī's assertion about Sahl's spiritual heir, Aḥmad b. Sālim, that "he was opposed to fundamental principles (*uṣūl*) of the *sunna* in some respects though extremely orthodox in others."[45]

Junayd (d. 910): Repentance as the Forgetting of One's Sins

Honored by later writers by such titles as the "*shaykh* of *shaykhs*" (*shaykh al-mashāyikh*), "peacock of the dervishes" (*ṭāʾūs al-fuqarāʾ*), and "master of the tribe" (*sayyid al-ṭāʾifa*),[46] Junayd is considered a pivotal figure in early Sufism. As the head of the Baghdad Sufis, his influence extended to such prominent mystics as Nūrī, Abū Bakr al-Shiblī (d. 946),[47] Jaʿfar al-Khuldī (d. 959),[48] Sumnūn al-Muḥibb (d. 910),[49] and Ḥallāj.[50] His own spiritual training was inaugurated under the tutelage of his maternal uncle Sarī al-Saqaṭī, and a certain Muḥammad b. ʿAlī al-Qaṣṣāb (d. 888),[51] about whom we know very little, but whom he declared to be his real teacher.[52] He also studied under Muḥāsibī,[53] whose acute and penetrating analyses of the lower soul exercised a defining influence on the development of his own mystical psychology. Junayd disagreed with him, however, over the value of *kalām*. Junayd was also a leading *faqīh*, influenced by Sufyān al-Thawrī (d. 778 CE).[54] The recognition he received as a juridical authority established his credentials within the larger religious and clerical community so that Sulamī was able to say that he was accepted by everyone.[55] But it also appears to have created within him a genuine sensitivity to the parameters of "exoteric" Islam.[56] This respect for the laws of religion produced a cautious approach to the dissemination of mystical teachings. He is known within the Sufi tradition for his extensive, strategic use of *ishārāt* or "subtle allusions," a tactic he employed at least partly to safeguard or prevent the uninitiated from comprehending the full import of his teachings.[57]

The *ishārāt* of Junayd make it difficult to systematically explicate his larger Sufi doctrine, including his views of repentance, with confidence. Arberry has confessed that his manner of writing is "involved to the point of obscurity,"[58] while Sells has lamented that "even when we are fairly certain of what Junayd's words actually are, the style is often cryptic and contorted."[59] There are still, however, certain themes that are identifiable and that lie at the heart of his teaching, concerned first and foremost with *tawḥīd*. The two that stand out most distinctly seem to be his doctrine of *fanā*ʾ and the Covenant.[60] In what follows we shall briefly look at a few of his sayings on repentance in light of these themes. Although his sayings are few, we shall analyze them partly because of Junayd's pivotal role in the formation of the early tradition, and partly for their inherent interest.

Tawba and the Return to the Covenant

Junayd saw the goal of the religious life as ultimately an attempt to return to the state of the pre-eternal Covenant referred to in Q 7:172. In this pre-eternal state, human beings stood, according to Junayd, stranded between existence and nonexistence, in a "sense that no one can know but He and no one can find but He."[61] Junayd saw earthly existence as a kind of corporeal exile, but an exile that the human being could overcome through a life of prayer and ascetic self-discipline as well as an intense commitment to the laws of religion. We have numerous aphorisms in which he stressed the importance of a mystical journey defined by the practical dictates of the Qurʾān and *sunna*. If successful in his endeavor, Junayd argued that the human being could return to the divine presence before which he dwelt in the *akhdh al-mīthāq* or "taking of the Covenant." He saw the end of the path as a return to one's ontological origin, declaring on one occasion that "the end is a return to the beginning" (*al-nihāya hiya al-rujūʿ ilā al-bidāya*).[62] The beginning of this return, for Junayd, lay solely in repentance. When he was once asked about the initial stages of journey, he replied, "repentance that rules out persistence in sin, fear that destroys vain expectations, hope that keeps you on the road of righteousness, and contemplation of God that does not allow other ideas in the heart."[63]

According to Muslim scripture, in the verse of the Covenant human beings testified in their pre-earthly state to divine lordship (*rubūbiyya*) with the words "yes indeed!" (*balā*), in response to the divine interrogation, "Am I not your Lord?" Through a homonymic pun, Junayd understood this "yes indeed!" also as "trial!" (*balāʾ*),[64] with the implication that trials and tribulations would follow as a consequence of one's acquiescence to *rubūbiyya*. But the patriarch of Baghdadi Sufism was not the first to note this connection. Sahl al-Tustarī proposed it when he drew out the relation between *balā* and *ibtilāʿ* (trial) in his commentary on the same verse.[65] However, even though Sahl acknowledged the role that trials play in the spiritual life, he did not stress *balāʾ* to the extent of Junayd. This, without question, had to do with the central place the Covenant occupied in the latter's thought. In his *Kitāb al-fanāʾ*, for example, he devoted considerable attention to the theme of *balāʾ* which he saw as an essential element of the journey.[66] He explained in the short epistle how it is that trials persist even into the final stages of the ascent. As for the trials at the beginning of the journey, these would be encountered in the demanding exercises and practices of ascetic self-mortification that immediately follow *tawba*. Thus Junayd said, "repentance is a return from what your [lower] soul demands, natural inclinations (*al-ṭabʿ*) and caprice (*al-hawā*)."[67] And his student Wāsiṭī declared that "repentance is the lack of familiar comforts."[68] Although such sayings are commonplace in Sufi literature, Junayd seems to have been among the first to elaborate on the relation between *balāʾ* and the Covenant verse. In the subsequent Sufi tradition, this relation would be more explicitly highlighted. Some later Sufis, for example, argued that in the same way that grape juice is transformed into wine by the "tribulation" of fermentation, and wheat made into bread by the "tribulation" of grinding, kneading, and leavening, so too is the human soul purified through *balāʾ*.[69] The true onset of this *balāʾ*, as we have noted, comes through repentance and an entry into the mystical life.

Tawba as a Forgetting of One's Sin

Junayd's most frequently cited saying on repentance is "that you forget your sin" (*an tansā dhanbaka*).[70] In the early Sufi texts, this is almost always contrasted with Sahl's view, that repentance entails never forgetting your sin, as we saw earlier. Qushayrī mentions the incident through which this view came to be associated with Junayd:

> Junayd said, "one day I entered the presence of Sarī al-Saqaṭī, and found him to be baffled (*mutaghayyar*). I asked him what had happened. He replied, 'a youth entered and asked me about repentance. I told him that it is that you do not forget your sin. He differed, saying, "No. Instead repentance is that you forget your sin."' " Junayd continued, "[I told him that] the matter in my opinion is as the youth has said. 'How so?' inquired Sarī. I replied that if I was in a state of estrangement from God, and He transported me to a state of fidelity, then to remember estrangement in a state of purity is itself estrangement (*dhikr al-jafāʾ fī ḥāl al-ṣafāʾ jafāʾ*). Sarī remained silent."[71]

Slightly different interpretations of Junayd's explanation are offered in the early Sufi texts, none of them mutually exclusive. These differences, however, do not seem to be explicitly acknowledged in the texts. According to Kalābādhī, the meaning of forgetting your sin is that "the sweetness of that act so completely leaves your heart, there remains no trace of it whatsoever within your soul (*sirrika*), so that it is as if you never knew it."[72] In other words, the *tāʾib* so thoroughly abandons the sin, both externally through leaving the act and internally through eradicating the sense of pleasure he found in it, that it is as if the sin had never existed. The repentance is so total and complete that he has forgotten the act altogether. Note that Kalābādhī does not say that the *nisyān* is the result of a mystical annihilation in God. He simply says that because the *tāʾib* has so completely overcome the sin, presumably because of his moral and ethical transformation, that all of its traces have been wiped out from his soul so that it is as if he had never known it. This *nisyān*, in Kalābādhī's interpretation, seems to be an unconscious result or consequence of a natural process of growth.

Junayd's words do not exclude the possibility of an active, conscious forgetting of the sin either. From this perspective, rooted in an interpretation that ties, like Kalābādhī, Junayd's words to a feat of self-overcoming, we can draw out some further implications. Junayd's claim that "to remember estrangement in a state of purity is itself estrangement" might mean that if one has fulfilled the conditions of *tawba* then it is of little use to continue brooding over past wrongs. After properly repenting, one should forget the past and move on. Since it was through God's power and will that one was able to fulfill these conditions, to look back at the sin in prolonged regret is to display a discourtesy toward God who, through His grace, transported the sinner from a state of transgression to one of purity (*min ḥāl al-jafāʾ ilā ḥāl al-ṣafāʾ*). In this sense, forgetting the sin might even be viewed as a conscious psychological act of the *sālik* so as to enable him to continue his wayfaring without unnecessary impediments. But that, as we noted, can be done only once the conditions of repentance have been fulfilled. Junayd outlined these conditions when he said, "the *tāʾib* does not realize *tawba* until four qualities come together in him: firstly, regret; secondly, intense struggle [against sin] in what remains; thirdly, soundness of resolve in not returning [to the sin]; and fourthly, rectifying the wrong perpetrated against the victim."[73] Forgetting the sin (*nisyān al-dhanb*) can, in this light, be viewed as an act that signifies that one has fulfilled the conditions of repentance and brought to a close the act of atonement for the particular sin—even though repentance for other sins may still be in process. Although this interpretation is not explicitly offered in any of the early texts I have studied, Junayd's words certainly allow for it, and his Sufi doctrine does not, theoretically speaking, preclude this possibility. By "conscious forgetting" I simply mean that the aspirant intentionally does not look back at his sin.

The most common explanation of Junayd's words found in the Sufi tradition, however, is that the *nisyān* is a result of the soul's total absorption in its contemplation of God. This is an experience it undergoes at the final stages of the mystic journey. The all-consuming contemplation leads to forgetting everything other than God, including not only one's deficiencies but one's own being. The *nisyān*, from this perspective, is the result of existentially realizing *tawḥīd*, which, in Junayd's mystical theology entails returning to the moment of the primordial Covenant where the soul stood at the point of its ontological origin, between existence and nonexistence, immersed in the eternal and omnipresent unity of God.

The manner in which Junayd describes this primordial experience allows us to better understand why the repentance of the advanced mystic consists in forgetting one's sin. He says that during the experience of *tawḥīd,* the mystic dwells in an "existence without individuality before God" where he is "sunk in the flooding seas of His unity, completely obliterated both to himself and to God's call to him and his answer to God." It is here that he achieves "true realization of the Oneness of God in true proximity to Himself. He is lost to sense and action because God fulfills in him what He has willed of him." This is the moment of the Covenant because the mystic returns to the "first state where he was before he existed."[74] At this point, not only is the mystic annihilated in God, even his awareness of his annihilation is annihilated, so that his consciousness of God derives from God Himself. This consciousness is God's own because, according to Junayd, it was God Himself who responded with *balā* to His interrogation. The response came from God through the intermediary souls of human beings.[75]

The logic behind Junayd's position on repentance is not entirely different from that of Kharrāz, for whom, as we saw earlier, the mystic abandons his concern with the virtues associated with the stations once he reaches his goal. Kharrāz argues that after arriving in the presence of God, one should no longer concern himself with the stations he has traversed. This is possible, as we have noted, because the qualities associated with those stations are already, at this stage of the ascent, deeply ingrained in the human soul. Since Junayd also argued that "one cannot attain true gnosis and pure *tawḥīd* until one passes through the states and stations,"[76] his view that repentance is a forgetting of sins is tantamount to saying that, at the end of the path, one should forget repentance itself, or that the repentance one does engage in should entail forgetting residual traces of all that is other than God.

In this light, we can understand another one of his paradoxical sayings. In the *Iḥyāʾ*, Ghazālī quotes Junayd as stating that "humility in the eyes of the people of God is arrogance" (*al-tawāḍuʿ ʿinda ahl al-tawḥīd takabbur*).[77] Ghazālī suggests that the meaning of Junayd's words is that for those who have realized divine unity, to look upon their own souls in an attempt to subjugate and humble them, would, in effect, entail turning their attention away from God toward themselves. This simple act would amount to an act of arrogance because it would entail giving attention to the self at the expense of God, of arrogating something, that, at the highest level of *tawḥīd,* no longer exits. The most proper exercise of a virtue such as humility, which involves putting the self in its proper place, could, at the final stage of the path, mean only turning away from such a concern altogether. Although Ghazālī qualifies his explanation of

Junayd's words at the outset by stating that "[by this] he may have meant" (*la ʿalla murādahu*), there is little reason to contest his interpretation.[78]

The Difference between Sahl and Junayd on *Tawba*

As noted, the explanation for Junayd's words offered above is the one most commonly encountered in Sufi literature, and his view is typically contrasted with that of Sahl. Sarrāj compared these views in his chapter on *tawba* in the *Kitāb al-lumaʿ*, as follows:

> Al-Sūsī was asked about repentance and he said that "repentance is to return from everything which knowledge blames to what it praises." Sahl b. ʿAbd Allāh was asked about repentance and he said that "it is that you not forget your sin." Junayd, may God have mercy on him, was asked about repentance and said, "it is the forgetting of your sin." [. . .] As for Sūsī's response regarding repentance, may God have mercy on him, it was in reference to the repentance of the aspirants (*al-murīdīn*), embarkers (*al-mutaʿarriḍīn*), seekers (*al-ṭālibīn*), and intenders (*al-qāṣidīn*). They are sometimes in the right and sometimes in the wrong. The response of Sahl b. ʿAbd Allāh was similar. But as for the response of Junayd, may God have mercy on him, that one forget his sin, it refers to the repentance of the realized ones (*al-muḥaqqiqīn*) who do not recall their sins as a result of what has overcome their hearts of the Majesty of God, and of the persistence of their remembrance of Him.[79]

Qushayrī repeats this view, quoting Sarrāj (with acknowledgment).[80] The same explanation is more or less repeated by Makkī, in more elaborate form. He says that Junayd's position is applicable to an elect few who are completely immersed in their contemplation of God, whereas Sahl's applies to the majority of the travelers.

> Some of them have said that the reality of repentance is that you [always] place the sin before your two eyes. Another group has said that the reality of repentance is that you forget your sin. These are the approaches of the two groups, and the states of the folk of the two stations. As for the remembrance

of sins, the way of the aspirants and the state of the fearful ones bring forth for them, through the remembrance of sins, perpetual grief and an inescapable fear. As for the forgetting of sins because one is preoccupied with the remembrance of God and what one puts forward by way of an increase in acts of worship, this is the way of the gnostics and the state of the lovers [of God]. Their goal is witnessing divine unity, and this is a station of knowing. The goal of the first group on the other hand is observing the boundaries and limits, and this is a station of propriety (*taʿrīf*) [. . . but . . .] the station of witnessing divine unity is superior, in the eyes of the gnostics, to observing propriety.[81]

The question that immediately comes to mind, however, is whether Sahl intended his definition of *tawba* for novices, as Makkī, Sarrāj, and the others suppose. Nothing seems to have been transmitted from the Tustarī tradition to indicate this. On the contrary, all the available Tustarī aphorisms, anecdotes, and glosses on Qurʾānic verses suggest the opposite, that Sahl vigorously defended the relevance of his definition of repentance for all stages of the path.

Two reasons are possible for the explanation offered by Makkī and Sarrāj. One is that through their close contacts with Aḥmad b. Sālim, a disciple of Sahl, they had access to an oral Tustarī commentary tradition in which Sahl had qualified his well-known view on repentance. If this were the case, the earliest living representatives of the Tustarī tradition understood Sahl's view to be in harmony with Junayd's, and saw that the two mystics were in fact addressing different audiences in their definitions. The second possibility is that Sahl never proposed this view, and that Makkī and Sarrāj did so in his name with an understanding that it did not fundamentally conflict with his mystical psychology. Perhaps—as is also common in philosophical traditions—they corrected or qualified a view attributed to the master because they felt it was logically more consistent with his overall spiritual method. They might have felt that Sahl would have acknowledged—had the problem been posed to him—the superiority of a *tawba* in which one forgets sins of the past due to the intensity of one's contemplation of God.

Hujwīrī, however, unlike the authors we have mentioned, understood there to be a real difference between Sahl and Junayd, and reduced it to one of spiritual method. Whereas Sahl, in his eyes, stressed asceticism and spiritual struggle, Junayd, he contended, stressed contemplation and enlightenment. Hujwīrī provides this explanation in the *Kashf al-maḥjūb* in which he concludes by affirming the superiority of Junayd's view:

> As regards the nature and property of repentance, the sheikhs have diverse opinions. Sahl b. ʿAbd Allāh (al-Tustarī) and others believe that repentance consists in not forgetting your sins, but always regretting them, so that, although you have many good works to your credit, you will not be pleased with yourself on that account; since remorse for an evil action is superior to good works, and one who never forgets his sins will never become conceited. Junayd and others take the opposite view, that repentance consists in forgetting the sin. They argue that the penitent is a lover of God, and the lover of God is in contemplation of God, and in contemplation it is wrong to remember sin, for remembrance of sin is a veil between God and those who contemplate Him. This controversy goes back to the difference of opinion concerning self-mortification (*mujāhadat*) and contemplation (*mushāhadat*) [. . .] Those who hold the penitent to be self-dependent regard his forgetfulness of sin as heedlessness, while those who hold that he is dependent on God deem his remembrance of sin to be polytheism [. . .] Inasmuch as it behooves the penitent not to remember his own selfhood, how should he remember his sin? Indeed remembrance of sin is a sin, for sin is an occasion of turning away from God . . .[82]

Hujwīrī's explanation, however, cannot be taken without a grain of salt, particularly because his knowledge of Sahl al-Tustarī's school is questionable. In one place, he erroneously distinguishes the "Sahlīs" from the "Sālimīs." While he praises the former group, he identifies the latter as a "sect of anthropomorphists," an affiliate of the condemned sect of *Ḥulūlīs* (incarnationists).[83] Yet there appears to be little historical evidence for this claim.[84] (The only Sālimīs in the early Sufi literature that I have found are the followers of Sahl). Even the distinction he draws between the *mujāhada* of Sahl and the *mushāhada* of Junayd is problematic. The ascetic rigor that Junayd required of disciples is clearly evident from his sayings, perhaps the most famous of which is, "we did not take Sufism from talk (*al-qīl wa al-qāl*), but from hunger, abandoning the world, and cutting off [our] ties from things we were accustomed to and found pleasant."[85] It is true that extraordinary feats of fasting are associated with Sahl. But it would still be erroneous on the basis of this and other evidence we have to suggest he placed greater emphasis on *mujāhada* than Junayd.

Despite the importance of the *Kashf al-maḥjūb* as a source for early Sufism, we have more reason to accept the views of Makkī and Sarrāj regarding Sahl since both of them were direct heirs of the Tustarī tradition through Aḥmad b. Sālim. But despite their close ties to him, it still remains difficult to determine with confidence the true nature of Sahl's position on repentance, for reasons already outlined. What we can be certain of is that Junayd's view of *tawba* almost unanimously came to be acknowledged, in the subsequent Sufi tradition, as the more appropriate one for higher stages of the mystic journey. It fell to his disciple, Wāsiṭī, to elaborate in fuller detail the theological and philosophical implications of Junayd's understanding of *tawḥīd,* and its relation to repentance.

Wāsiṭī (d. 936): *Tawba* from the Claim to Act

Abū Bakr al-Wāsiṭī was a student of both Junayd and Nūrī.[86] Wāsiṭī is not as well known in the early Sufi tradition as the three other figures we have studied thus far, and had only one known close and constant disciple, Abū al-ʿAbbās al-Sayyārī (d. 953–954).[87] Although others also transmitted his teachings, Sayyārī was his most intimate student,[88] and transmitted his master's doctrines to his own disciples. Wāsiṭī's importance lies primarily in his metaphysical elaboration of *tawḥīd.* Sulamī praised him when he said that "no one spoke on the principles of Sufism (*uṣūl al-taṣawwuf*) as he did."[89] The refined theoretical orientation in Wāsiṭī's teaching is evident in Hujwīrī's section on the "Sayyārīs," the disciples of his student, in the *Kashf.*[90]

Like other Sufis of his time, Wāsiṭī was no stranger to controversy. Whereas Junayd only hinted at metaphysical doctrines through his abstruse *ishārat,* his student was less reticent. For this reason, Wāsiṭī drew the criticism of his master. It was not that Junayd disagreed with his doctrines, which after all were deeply indebted to his own. He criticized Wāsiṭī for his open and even careless disclosure of his views. In the eyes of his teacher, Wāsiṭī was guilty of revealing ideas that he and other likeminded Sufis had taken pains to conceal. Junayd once mildly rebuked him in a letter, "come out of your own state to their state, so that when you speak with them you speak in their state, measure, and capacity. And address them in that situation, in accordance with how you find them."[91] But Wāsiṭī seemed to show little consideration to the response his controversial sayings evoked, even acting, at times, as something of a gadfly.[92] Although Sarrāj admitted his admiration for Wāsiṭī when he wrote, "I find his goal to be sound and his aims are those found in the Principles [of the Religious Sciences]," he confessed that "his writings have only served as fodder for the people of contention," lamenting that "I find within his discourse an opening for the quarrelsome to defame and deny [the Sufis]."[93]

All that we now have of Wāsiṭī are sayings about the path and glosses on select Qur'ānic verses. These have been transmitted through the early Sufi texts,[94] with the largest concentration appearing in Sulamī's *Ḥaqā'iq*.[95] Kalābādhī includes Wāsiṭī's name in the introduction to his *Ta'arruf* in the section on those who authored books and epistles.[96] None of his writings, however, seem to have survived. Understandably, only a few of Wāsiṭī's sayings on repentance have come down to us. But those that are available are remarkable because of the extent to which they prefigure later mystical conceptualizations of *tawba,* most notably that of Ibn al-'Arabī.[97]

In highlighting Wāsiṭī's views about repentance, however, our focus shall remain on its relationship to his doctrine of the divine origin of human acts. We will not explore *tawba* from a more strictly nondualistic ontology—which he clearly espoused—simply because we do not have enough of his sayings addressing the subject from such a vantage point.

Wāsiṭī addresses the question of repentance from different levels. This must be kept in mind because the seemingly contradictory positions he takes are reconcilable when understood in light of the different audiences to whom he was speaking. For beginners, Wāsiṭī accepts the view that repentance requires regret for the sin as well as a resolve never to repeat it. At a higher level, repentance requires turning away not only from the sin, but also wrong intentions. This can be achieved only through a taxing and rigorous process of self-examination. Wāsiṭī most likely learned this process from Junayd, who acquired it from his own teacher, Muḥāsibī.[98] *Muḥāsaba* is a highly demanding spiritual exercise of introspection which, in ideal circumstances, should deprive the repentant one of familiar comforts. Thus Wāsiṭī says, "repentance is the absence of all that one is accustomed to" (*al-ma'lūfāt al-ajma'a*),[99] and "he whose repentance is sincere (*man kānat tawbatuhu naṣūḥ*) does not care how his evenings or mornings pass."[100] Wāsiṭī says that this *tawba naṣūḥ* is such that, "no trace (*athar*) of disobedient acts remain, either in secret or public."[101] In addressing the repentance of novices, Wāsiṭī's views would, as we can see, remain unobjectionable to even the most exoterically inclined of scholars. It is only when he begins to address *tawba* from the perspective of Sufi metaphysics that the more controversial nature of his views come to the forefront

At the highest level of repentance, Wāsiṭī argues that the *tā'ib* should turn away not from the sin but from looking at the act as though it were his own. This is because the act, for Wāsiṭī, belongs to God. He elaborates the view held by most of his peers that God is the creator of human acts (*khāliq al-afʿāl*). In this respect, his particular theological position is similar to the opponents of the Muʿtazilites who traced the creation of acts back to God. But whereas these opponents generally imputed responsibility to the servant for his sins, and in the later Ashʿarite tradition, were able to do this through a refined and elaborate doctrine of the soul's mental and volitional acquisition (*kasb*) of the deed,[102] Wāsiṭī takes the doctrine of predestination to its end: if the act truly emerges from God, then the mystic must properly reconcile himself with this underlying truth. Commenting on Q 10:23, "O people, your insolence (*baghyukum*) is against yourselves," Wāsiṭī says, "the insolence occurs from observing the self and looking at the mistakes it makes."[103] In other words, it becomes inappropriate for the advanced mystic to look at his sins in regret as though they were his own. Instead, he should turn his attention single-mindedly to the One through whose power the act became manifest, by way of a complete, total, and uncompromising return (*tawba*) to its Source.

The emphasis Wāsiṭī placed on turning one's attention away from the performance of sins is found in an incident that occurred with some of Abū ʿUthmān al-Ḥīrī's disciples while he was passing through Nishapur.

> When Wāsiṭī entered Nishapur, he asked the companions of Abū ʿUthmān, "What did your *shaykh* command you to do?" They replied, "He commanded us to adhere to acts of obedience and to look at how we fall short in them." Wāsiṭī said, "He commanded you with pure Magianism [i.e., dualism]. Why did he not command you to become absent from them by looking at their places of origination and flowing?"[104]

For Wāsiṭī, the divine command (*amr*) "flows" through the human heart and manifests itself in the act. The human heart is the primary locus through which God manifests Himself. Wāsiṭī says that when one engages in the *muḥāsaba* of repentance, one encounters God manifest in the heart. Through this encounter, one comes to understand the true nature of human actions, which is to say, their true divine origins. In this light, repentance entails turning away not so much from moral faults, but all claims to autonomy; it requires discarding the illusion that one has the power to act of one's own power.

In Wāsiṭī's thought, *tawba* therefore entails a radical shift from a view that we have the capacity to act to an affirmation of God's ultimate and all-embracing activity in and through us. This is an activity that precludes the possibility of a human will. From this perspective, it is more appropriate to say that God is not simply the creator of the act, but the Actor Himself. This was a position also held by his teacher, Junayd, who retraced the origins of this doctrine to the Covenant, as we noted earlier, where God responded to His interrogation through a human response that manifested His own Will.[105]

According to Wāsiṭī, since all acts have their origin in God, the human being is also not able to take credit for his obedience. Thus he says, "you do not act except by His power [and] you do not obey except by his bounty [. . .] why are you proud of your acts when nothing of your acts belong to you?" But this also means that one cannot properly lay claim to one's disobedience either, because, as Wāsiṭī provocatively asserts, "you do not disobey except by His abandoning."[106] To lay claim, then, either to good or evil works is essentially to associate a partner with God in His activity, and hence fall into the crime of *shirk*. Thus, in his commentary on Q 4:36, "Worship God and do not associate anything with Him," Wāsiṭī criticizes blaming the soul for its sins: "associating others with God is looking at the shortcomings and slips of his self and blaming it." Wāsiṭī asks, "does the blame adhere to Who is in charge of making it [the sin] stand up [i.e., God] or who the slip is decreed for?"[107] Elsewhere, Wāsiṭī says that "whoever observes anything of his own actions has made manifest his own baseness."[108]

Now since humans cannot lay claim to either their good or evil works, one might naturally ask, does this include repentance? Wāsiṭī remains consistent with his overall view. Since human *tawba* is ultimately a divine act that appears through the human locus, and was pre-eternally willed, the human being has no share in it. "The accepted repentance," says Wāsiṭī, "is accepted before the mistake (*qabl al-khaṭīya*) and before the intention of repentance [is made]."[109] For proof, he cites the Qur᾽ānic verse explored in chapter 2: "Then He turned (*tāba*) to them so that they might return (*li yatūbū*)" (Q 9:118).

Because of Wāsiṭī's radical doctrine of predestination, judgment is not determined by acts, since these acts are already foreordained in pre-eternity (*azal*). God does not punish or reward based on one's actions but His own decree.

> It was said to Wāsiṭī, "Does He permit the scales to be heavy with our works?" He said, "If He permitted that then everyone with numerous limpid works would be safe. Rather God makes heavy the scales of whomever He wills. Do you not see that the Prophet, peace be upon him, said, 'The scale is in the hand of God' [He lowers the just scale and raises it]? He lowers some people and He raises others. He raises them in pre-eternity and He lowers others in pre-eternity prior to the existence of each engendered thing."[110]

The underlying paradox we encounter in Wāsiṭī's conception of repentance is that if all acts have their origin in God, then even a proper orientation toward them, which Wāsiṭī demands at the more advanced stages of the path, comes from God. The human being is therefore called to do something for which he is ultimately powerless. Since everything flows from the divine command, a proper orientation toward works can emerge only through an act of God. Despite the penetrating insight of her scholarship on Wāsiṭī, Silvers does not seem to fully acknowledge this paradox. She writes that Wāsiṭī "does not negate the possibility of human agency. But human agency is dependent on turning one's perspective to view reality correctly [. . .] Human agency is gained when one gives up one's claim to it. Repentance is a fundamental part of this process."[111] But Wāsiṭī, it seems, is not so concerned in formulating a theoretically consistent view of repentance and human agency. There is nothing in his sayings that suggests he attempts to resolve this problem in the way the Ashʿarites did. The paradox in his doctrine is something that he, like so many other mystics, is willing to live with. Since he was neither a philosopher nor a theologian, we can presume with a fair degree of confidence that this was not a dilemma that he felt the need to resolve with logical rigor.

To summarize the central findings of this chapter, our study of the views of Kharrāz, Sahl, and Junayd allowed us to get a deeper sense of the nature of the discussions and debates regarding *tawba* that were taking place in early Sufism. Although many of these discussions centered on what was required of the aspirant in the preliminary stages of the journey, lively debates were also taking place on the nature of *tawba* from the vantage point of higher stages of mystic realization. Among the most well known of these was centered on whether the Sufi ever reaches a stage where he should turn away from the emotional experiences of regret and remorse that characterize the beginnings of the journey, and whether *tawba* can ever justify forgetting one's sins altogether. The Sufi tradition tended to present Sahl as an advocate for the continuous remembrance of past sins, and Junayd as an advocate for the opposite view, that the highest form of *tawba* eventually requires the forgetting of sins. But, as we also saw, it remains difficult to determine with any certainty the actual views of a figure like Sahl (as well as others) on such contentious issues since these views were often filtered through the lens of later Sufi writers (such as Kalābādhī, Sarrāj, Makkī, Sulamī, and Qushayrī). What is important to note is that the earliest debates set the stage for more elaborate inquiries into these themes by later Sufi writers.

Wāsiṭī's views of *tawba* as they have been transmitted to us primarily through Sulamī's Qur'ān commentary present us with one of the most sophisticated and creative attempts to conceptualize theoretically the ontology of *tawba* in the early period. Beginning with the premise that all human acts are ultimately divine acts, he developed a theory of *tawba* that drew out the implications of this principle. Though this premise was held in milder form by the Ash'arites (through their doctrine of *kasb*, in which the human being had a quasi-volitional share of the act, and in which God created but did not actually perform the act), Wāsiṭī did not shy away from taking this premise to its logical end. In the process, he proposed a somewhat counterintuitive perspective of human agency and divine justice, but one that was the logical outcome of a worldview in which God was not only transcendent but immanent through His Being and His Acts. For Wāsiṭī, this overriding divine omnipresence expressed the reality of *tawḥīd*. This perspective would find a much more comprehensive elaboration in the writings of Ibn al-'Arabī three centuries later.[112]

We shall now turn to two of the most elaborate treatments of *tawba* in the early period. The texts that we shall examine will serve to demonstrate Laury Silvers's observation (noted in the introduction of this study), that "the treatises and manuals that are the most visible face of early Sufism and the early institutional period tend to focus on the basics of the spiritual path and less so on theoretical questions."[113] Even though the texts that we will study concentrate on the "basics" of the path, they are, as we shall see, by no means simplistic primers consisting of a straightforward set of instructions.[114] It is hoped that through our analysis of these texts, we will be able to draw out something of the insights into human psychology that can be found in works authored more than a millennium ago.

Chapter 6

Tawba in the Writings of al-Ḥārith al-Muḥāsibī

For the remainder of our study we shall turn to examine repentance in the writings of two early figures who, unlike those whose views we have examined thus far, have left us key works on the subject. The first of these was the brilliant and prolific author al-Ḥārith b. Asad al-Muḥāsibī (d. 857), one of the most important writers to emerge out of the formative period of Sufism. Other than a few anecdotes, we know little about his life except that he was born in Basra and at a later age moved to Baghdad, where he died.[1] Although he encountered the hostility of the Ḥanbalites there for his use of dialectical theology (*kalām*), this did not seriously diminish his influence among the early Sufis. Hujwīrī said that "he was the chief shaikh of Baghdad in his time."[2] Among his students numbered some of the most important figures of the school of Baghdad, the most significant of whom, as noted in the previous chapter, was Junayd.[3] Credited by Louis Massignon for codifying the early tradition,[4] Muḥāsibī's influence was not confined to the formative period. As A.J. Arberry observed, he was "the first Sufi author of the foremost rank whose preserved writings may truly be said to have formed to a large extent the pattern of all subsequent thought."[5] Through his many treatises, particularly his *al-Riʿāya li ḥuqūq Allāh* (*Observing the Rights of God*),[6] his influence extended to such a range of towering personalities as Ghazālī,[7] Abū Madyan (d. 1126),[8] Ibn al-ʿArabī,[9] Ibn ʿAṭāʾ Allāh,[10] Afīf al-Dīn al-Yāfiʿī (d. 1367),[11] and Ibn ʿAbbād of Ronda (d. 1390),[12] to name but a few. But his influence was not confined exclusively to his own religious tradition. It has been suggested that through Ghazālī he may have indirectly exerted an influence on medieval Christian mystics and scholastics.[13] More recently, scholars in the field of Judeo-Arabic studies have drawn attention to some remarkable links with Jewish mysticism. Many of the central ideas of Baḥya b. Paqūda's (d. uncertain) famous and highly influential eleventh-century text, the *Farā'iḍ al-qulūb* (*Duties of Hearts*), for example, derive from Muḥāsibī, whose *al-Masā'il fī a'māl al-qulub wa al-jawāriḥ* (*Questions Concerning the Actions of the Heart and Limbs*)[14] may well have served as the basis for the title of this distinguished Jewish mystic's work.[15]

As for the formation of Muḥāsibī's own thought, it is to be traced to the Basran religious milieu. Above all he was influenced by the piety of Ḥasan al-Baṣrī (d. 728),[16] a man he never met but whose inward turn attracted him deeply,[17] and whose mode of spirituality, particularly his emphasis on "scrupulous abstinence," is evident in Muḥāsibī's writings. Considering this influence, it is not surprising that Muḥāsibī's primary fame within the Sufi tradition rests not on his elucidation of abstract mystical doctrines, but on the theoretical sophistication of his inquiries into the sciences of practical conduct[18] (*mu'āmalāt*).[19] He played such a central role in the development of the Sufi science of the soul that Michael Sells has gone so far as to declare that "he developed the most rigorous and influential moral psychology within the Islamic mystical tradition."[20]

Indeed, Muḥāsibī's writings are characterized by a penetrating psychological analysis of the various impulses of the soul, particularly the machinations and the stratagems of the lower ego. Acutely sensitive to the human proclivity for self-deception, Muḥāsibī constantly drew attention to the importance of becoming aware of one's true intentions and the maladies of the heart.[21] He did this by exhorting his reader to call himself to account through a perpetual and scrupulous examination of conscience. This practice of *muḥāsaba*—after which he was nicknamed[22]—is the most salient and recurring characteristic of his writings. Even modern scholars, separated from this medieval doctor of the soul by more than a millennium, have confessed their admiration for his subtle insights into the inner recesses of the human being. Joseph van Ess, who studied him in detail, admired his unprecedented "psychological finesse,"[23] while Massignon praised his "intense inner life" and the "translucence of his conscience."[24]

Muḥāsibī played a central role in the Islamic mystical tradition because he explained in remarkable detail the steps to the preliminary stages of the mystic ascent. Since it is only through mastering this aspect of the path that the soul is able to penetrate into the higher realms of mysticism, he played an indispensable role in the Sufi tradition. Julian Baldick's contention that "he was neither a Sufi nor a mystic, but a moralizing theologian"[25]—in line with the general revisionist thrust of his work on the early tradition—appears to reflect an ignorance of the nature and scope of medieval Sufi literature, most of which was concerned not with ecstatic, paranormal, and supernatural experiences, but with the everyday virtues that the mystics sought to perfect in order to ascend into the divine presence. Marshall Hodgson insightfully expressed this point in his historical analysis of the formation of the early tradition:

> [I]t is usual to think of the mystical as simply an extraordinary occasion in consciousness [. . . but the . . .] more striking events, at least as they appear in the classical Sufi tradition, are but peaks of a very widespread type of awareness. Mystics have almost always described a lengthy mystical "way," leading by innumerable small steps from the first glimmerings of devout *tawba* in the sinner up to the most ecstatic moments of the saint. Most mystical writers have spent far more time speaking of the everyday virtues of patience, courage and unselfishness, as they appear in the mystical perspective, than of ecstasies or even of the cosmic unity these ecstasies seem to bear witness to.[26]

Hodgson's observation is important because it enables us to appreciate Muḥāsibī's place within the Sufi tradition. It is precisely because of his penetrating psychological analysis "of the everyday virtues" that the Sufis attempted to embody in their fullness, that he wielded such a wide influence both during his time and in the later tradition. Baldick's view does not adequately account for or explain his place in the tradition, a fact evidenced by his inclusion in all the major biographical accounts of the early Sufis, ranging from those of Sulamī and Qushayrī to Hujwīrī and Iṣfahānī.[27] It is unlikely that the Sufis would have unanimously considered him a theoretical expositor of the way unless they felt an intrinsic quality within his writings indispensable for the purification, growth, and ultimately, mystic illumination of the soul. It is true that Muḥāsibī did not speak of his personal visionary or mystical experiences, but this general silence—not unlike that of other prominent Sufi psychologists, such as Ibn ʿAbbād—could very well have been the result of a desire to refrain from reveling in ostentatious displays of spiritual self-achievement, the danger of which he continuously brought attention to in his works.[28] The qualities of sobriety and personal modesty that he embodied and must have impressed on Junayd were later emphasized by the leading expositors of the Sufi tradition.

As for the style of Muḥāsibī's writing, although it is occasionally coarse and somewhat unpoetic,[29] it is also figuratively rich. His analyses are often couched in a question-and-answer format, a spiritual master responding to the probing inquiries of a student or disciple. The format serves as a useful didactic device since it serves to hold the attention of the reader, who feels as if he is privy to a dialogue in which his own queries or objections are sometimes voiced by the *shaykh*'s interlocutor. Indeed, we would not be off the mark in describing Muḥāsibī, as van Ess has done, as a born pedagogue.[30]

Muḥāsibī's writings represent some of the earliest extant Sufi works, thereby providing us with a window into the formative period of the tradition. We are fortunate to have a number of his works preserved in manuscript form, most of which have been published.[31] The most important of these in regards to the question of *tawba*—including his *Iḥkām al-tawba (The Establishing of Tawba)*[32]—shall be examined in the following analysis.

Tawba in Muḥāsibī

The nature of Muḥāsibī's moral psychology makes it difficult to conceptually isolate ethical concepts. Since repentance is connected to such a range of virtues as hope, fear, sincerity, preparedness (*isti'dād*),[33] and gratitude, an examination of the concept entails understanding, at the very least, something of its relation to these and other virtues. As we shall also see in the case of Makkī in the following chapter, Muḥāsibī's understanding of *tawba* can be grasped once one appreciates the unity and interdependence of the various qualities of the soul that he encourages the aspirant to acquire. This aspect of his thought will become clearer as our analysis of his particular understanding of the concept unfolds.

Like countless other Sufi writers, *tawba*, for Muḥāsibī, marks the first stage of the soul's return to God.[34] The soul is called to repent for its own salvation and ultimate felicity. Without *tawba* and the subsequent ascent to God through an acquisition of the virtues, the soul looms in a state of heedlessness in which death and the impending divine judgment can seize it unawares. The danger this presents for the individual is highlighted by Muḥāsibī when he writes,

> If we are neglectful in this world and do not seek to prepare for the meeting with Him, and death comes upon us suddenly, and we are summoned to a time of sorrow, then no complaint can be made, nor is any return (to this world) possible. He urges us to take the right course while repentance is still accepted, and we can make our plaint, and our prayers can be answered, so that we may be prepared to meet Him, and be found watching when death comes.[35]

Muḥāsibī explains some of the means through which the sinner can be inspired to turn in repentance. One is by reflecting on the proximity of death. As Luqmān[36] advised his son, "Do not delay repentance, for death comes all of a sudden."[37] The desire for *tawba* can also be strengthened by reflecting over one's previous transgressions, fear of God's anger, and hope in His forgiveness. A concern for the Promise (*al-waʿd*) and Threat (*al-waʿīd*) should, for Muḥāsibī, spark in the heart a genuinely felt need for *tawba,* setting in motion a process of interior conversion. As in many of his writings, Muḥāsibī attempts to make the final judgment present before the reader, to serve as a warning for him to reform his life while the opportunity remains available.[38] It "was an advanced realization of death," in the words of Paul Heck, that for Muḥāsibī "purified one's interior, purged it of selfish inclinations, not to mention devilish enticements, since such things had no hold in death, even a death that was not yet actual but only anticipated."[39]

The nature of the motivation that Muḥāsibī attempts to arouse might, on the surface, seem to conflict with that of other Sufis, such as Rābiʿa,[40] who denounced fear of divine punishment and a longing for divine reward, and who encouraged, instead, one to repent and worship God for His own sake. Muḥāsibī, however, embraces fear of Hellfire and desire of Paradise, and in the words of Sells, "makes them the ciphers for the opposition between those whose consciousness is rooted in the world and those whose consciousness is rooted in the Afterlife." There is no real contradiction here, Sells goes on to observe, as long as one keeps in mind that Muḥāsibī and others, such as Rābiʿa, were focused on different levels of spiritual development.[41] The tensions only arise when their words are taken to apply to all travelers without a consideration of spiritual rank or where they may stand on the journey, a theme we briefly explored in chapter 4.

Although Muḥāsibī addresses the question of how one should go about engaging in repentance for particular sins, his discussion of the topic is usually tied to the larger process of the soul's reorientation toward God. *Tawba* functions as a kind of regenerative and healing power, the purpose of which is to purify the self of the corrosive and debilitating effects of breaching the limits (*ḥudūd*) of God. It enables, ultimately, one to ascend into the divine presence and attain His good pleasure and final acceptance. For Muḥāsibī, *tawba* for sins should be included within the larger process of returning to God. Although He is not unable to accept the repentance of a person who turns away from one sin while remorselessly remaining immersed in others,[42] such a sinner is not a *tāʾib* in the true sense of the term insofar as *tawba* marks the first stage of the ascent to God. Before, however, we proceed to examine the central characteristics of this process of returning, we should begin by highlighting the most elemental requirements of *tawba* for individual sins.

Tawba for Individual Sins

The first requirement stipulated by Muḥāsibī is regret (*nadam*) for the previous wrong.[43] The sinner must feel the gravity of his offense by experiencing a contraction of his soul on account of the misdeed. Regret must be coupled with extended pleas for divine forgiveness (*ṭūl al-istighfār*),[44] sought through prolonged supplication and tears. Among the signs that one is deprived of genuine *tawba* is the inability to weep.[45] *Tawba* also requires the sinner to resolve (*ʿazm*) never to repeat the offense.[46] The sincerity of this is proven by the efforts he makes to avoid the causes that initially led to the slip. This might involve abandoning those whose presence might encourage one to repeat the offense, as well as avoiding those places where he feels more naturally disposed to sin. In short, he must flee everything that could lead to a lapse in his repentance. The Qurʾānic basis for this, according to Muḥāsibī, lies in the verse, "And those who when they do an evil thing or wrong themselves, remember God and implore forgiveness [. . .] and will not persist in what they did" (*lam yuṣirrū ʿalā mā faʿalū*) (Q 3:135). If however one slips and repeats the offense, he should quickly renew his *tawba* and resolve without delay.[47] Such a lapse however, is not free of consequences, the dangers of which will be explored below.

The *tāʾib* should also make efforts to amend his wrong, at least to the extent possible.[48] As we saw in the second chapter, *iṣlāḥ*, or the "setting of things aright," is, after forgiveness (*maghfira/istighfār*), the concept most frequently associated with *tawba* in the Qurʾān. By introducing rectification and the restitution of wrongs (*radd al-maẓālim*) into the process of repentance, Muḥāsibī echoes a recurring Qur'ānic motif regarding *tawba*. The scriptural roots of his analysis are further confirmed by the fact that for each sin Muḥāsibī stipulates a corresponding *iṣlāh*. This, as we saw, was also a feature of *tawba* in the Qur'ān. Muḥāsibī says, for example, that *iṣlāḥ* may involve repaying money that lawfully belongs to another, openly acknowledging a lie, or praising someone whom one has slandered.[49] If the nature of the sin makes rectification difficult, as in the case of a crime such as murder, then the guilty one should buy slaves and set them free. Similarly, for fornication or adultery, he should arrange marriages for the poor and help them with their livelihood.[50] For having drunk alcohol, he should freely distribute wholesome and pure drink (*sharāb ṭayyib ṭāhir*). Through such corresponding measures, the corruption that was introduced into the world by the sin can be undone through virtuous acts.

Muḥāsibī also states that in spite of his transgression the repentant one should think well of his Lord and not lose hope in divine forgiveness. He should remember that God provided the sinner with *tawba* as a way to escape the consequences of sin, and that it is from "the vastness of the mercy of God."[51] The *tā'ib*'s hope in divine mercy, however, should not allow him to become lackadaisical in fulfilling the conditions of *tawba*. "How many a repentant one," he writes, quoting Ibn ʿAbbās, will "come on the Day of Judgment unrepentant (*wa huwa ghayr tā'ib*) while he used to imagine himself repentant in the world."[52] The fear of appearing before God without properly having repented should keep him vigilant in observing its rights.

The Obligatory Nature of *Tawba*

What we have highlighted above are the most elemental requirements of *tawba*. But repentance, as just noted, is ultimately a process of healing and return. One cannot be characterized by *tawba* in its true sense if he simply repents of one or even a few sins. Muḥāsibī states that the characteristic of the repentant one is that he firmly resolves in his heart "never to return to those sins (of which he is repenting) as well as others."[53] If unchecked by *tawba*, the diseases of the soul will grow like a tumor, eventually leading to the death of the soul. The ultimate consequences of this death, however, will be fully experienced only in the next world. As Ghazālī states in his *Kitāb al-tawba* of the *Iḥyā'*, unless God decides to forgive the sinner who fails to repent, the cleansing of the impurities of his soul can take place only through the fires of the infernal realms. It behooves any person of intelligence, he says, to voluntarily cleanse himself of these impurities now through repentance and the tears of regret, before he is forced to experience a painful purification through the fires of hell in the other world.[54] Muḥāsibī would have little reason to disagree.

In the *Riʿāya*, Muḥāsibī explains the reasons for the obligatory nature of *tawba* by tying it to the importance of "preparedness." In order to be ready for death and the meeting with God, explains Muḥāsibī, one must turn from every sin.

> Preparedness is of two kinds. The first of these is obligatory (*wājib*). It is of the kind the remorseful ones (*nādimūn*) will feel sorry over at the moment of death, on account of it passing them by. It entails that the servant repent with a pure repentance (*tawba ṭāhira*) for sins and errors, so that if it were said to him, "you will die at this very hour," he would find no sin requiring repentance for which he would request a postponement (*al-nadhra*) [of death]. If he finds a sin with him which requires repentance he is not prepared to meet his Lord. [This is so because] if death came upon him, and that sin was with him, he would not be secure from divine anger. How can one be prepared to meet his Lord when he continues to abide in what angers God? [. . .] Death will come to him, without question. The fearful ones, on account of their fear of encountering God with what displeases Him, rush to repentance before death overtakes their spirits (*yusabbiqahum al-mawt ilā arwāḥihum*) and before they are unable to repent to their Lord and feel a remorse that is no longer accepted.[55] They rush to repentance out of caution and concern for the unexpected, sudden onset of death. This is the kind of preparedness that God most High made obligatory on his creation.[56]

The preparedness that Muḥāsibī makes obligatory can be realized only once the individual resolves to return to God wholeheartedly and surrender himself to the demands of the religious and spiritual life. Only through an unwavering devotion to God in this world can one be prepared to stand before Him in the next world. Without resolving to free oneself from the bondage of *all* sin, the sinner should expect to face the consequences of his transgressions, either in this world or the next. Since even the prophets could not escape divine chastisement, what right, asks Muḥāsibī, does anyone else have to feel secure? He adjures one to consider the example of Adam, who was banished from Paradise for eating from the forbidden tree. If there was any one, says Muḥāsibī, who could have been preserved from divine punishment on account of "his eminence and noble standing before God," it would have been Adam.[57] Yet his nobility did not protect him from the punishment of exile. The same can be said of Jonah, when he was swallowed by the whale, as well as "all (others) who were punished from among the prophets."[58] As long as there remain sins for which one has not repented, no one should ever feel safe from divine retribution. Muḥāsibī goes so far as to say that "you should expect punishment if you have not purified yourself of sins, nor disapprove of it [i.e., punishment] when it descends, for you are deserving of far greater than it."[59] We can see why he considers repentance for all sins obligatory (*farīḍa*).[60]

Tawba and the Return to God

As already noted, the only way for the individual to protect his own soul is by resolving to return to God wholeheartedly. Although intention and resolve are necessary foundations for the journey, the sinner must follow through with them by translating them into works. Otherwise, their relation to him is like that of food in the hands of a hungry man who makes no effort to eat.[61] "Be like one who quickens to perform good [deeds]," says Muḥāsibī, "and not like one who desires to love good [deeds]."[62]

Although all of Muḥāsibī's writings concern themselves in some form or another with the return to God, his views, particularly in relation to *tawba*, are perhaps most cogently expressed in *Badʾ man anāba ilā Allāh (The Beginning of the One Who Turns to God)*. In this short treatise, Muḥāsibī explains the topography of the initial stages of the journey and the means through which the aspirant can loosen the hold of previous sins. As the title of the work suggests, Muḥāsibi refers to this beginning as *ināba* rather than *tawba*. This choice of words might suggest that *ināba* refers to a broader and more encompassing concept for our author than *tawba*. Although this may be so in this particular work, one need not understand the two terms to refer, as a rule, to different stages of repentance. In other instances, Muḥāsibī speaks of *ināba* where, as the context makes clear, he could just as easily have spoken of *tawba*.[63] The two terms are often used synonymously by him, and refer to a turning away from sin toward God and obedience, in much the same way that medieval Jewish authorities defined the Hebrew *teshubah* in analogous contexts, as we saw in chapter 2.

One of the first requirements of the "*tawba* of return" is for the traveler to acquire "knowledge of God" (*maʿrifat Allāh*) and "knowledge of the soul" (*maʿrifat al-nafs*).[64] These two are juxtaposed together in a manner echoing the tradition that the Sufis have been fond of quoting, that "he who knows himself knows his Lord."[65] By *maʿrifa* of God and the self Muḥāsibī intends knowledge of the divine Promise and Threat, the scope of His pleasure and displeasure (*riḍāʾihi wa sakhaṭihi*), and an awareness of the true state of the soul as it begins to embark on the path.[66] For Muḥāsibī, when the seeker considers his actual condition, marred by the pleasures he previously derived from acts of disobedience and the weaknesses of his spiritual aspirations, he will be moved to strengthen his resolve to repent. The knowledge that arises in his soul will help create an internal state of turmoil and unrest, thereby catalyzing the process of repentance.[67] Through self-knowledge, the traveler will come to understand the guiles of the lower soul and thereby be saved from lapsing back into his sins. In the *Kitāb al-ṣidq*, Kharrāz defines this knowledge in terms that are not entirely different from Muḥāsibī's.[68]

Muḥāsibī states that the process of *tawba* and *ināba* also requires *taʾdīb*, or a disciplining of the soul. Among the first steps the aspirant should take is to practice external silence, that is, a silence of the tongue (*ṣamt*). This should produce, over time, an inner silence (*sukūt*), which will in turn allow the soul to perceive those slips and sins it was previously unconscious of due to its heedlessness. By bringing the soul's inner chatter to a halt, the *tāʾib* will be able discern with clarity his lamentable condition. Inner silence will help deepen the process of *tawba* as the aspirant awakens to the full extent of his past transgressions.[69] The attempt to unearth his previous wrongs is not unlike the work of a modern psychiatrist who helps his patient recollect painful memories pushed into the depths of the psyche. The difference is that in this case the psychiatrist is the aspirant himself, who through a prolonged process of self-examination (*muḥāsaba*) attempts to identify and treat the effect of past mistakes through the healing medicine of *tawba*.

In the *Qaṣd*, Muḥāsibī adds that the awareness of past sins should constrict the soul so it experiences the full weight and gravity of its sins. The soul's experience should be like that of the three men of Medina who were ostracized by the Muslim community on account of a misdeed, and whose experience the Qurʾān vividly describes in 9:118: "And the earth, despite its vastness, became constrained for them, and their [very] souls seemed constrained to them, until they perceived that there is no refuge from God except in God." For Muḥāsibī, the verse illustrates the ideal condition of the *tāʾib* insofar as he sincerely feels the magnitude of his offenses. Both the earth and his very soul should, for Muḥāsibī, contract so that he finds no rest or repose until he takes pains to fulfill the requirements of *tawba*.[70] Later Sufis would use the same verse to describe the state of the *tāʾib*. The characteristics described in this verse were for Abū ʿUthmān al-Ḥīrī "the initial proofs of sincere *tawba*" (*tawba naṣūḥ*),[71] with Dhū al-Nūn, as we saw in chapter 4, expressing a similar idea.[72]

By emphasizing the experience of inner grief and prolonged sadness that characterize the initial phases of *tawba*, Muḥāsibī underscores the place of *nadam* at the beginning of the return journey. To this *nadam* over past sins, Muḥāsibī adds the necessity of considering one's own previous good deeds to be of little significance.[73] "Making little (*istiqlāl*) of what one has done for God" is an essential component of sincere *tawba*.[74] By encouraging the aspirant to devalue his virtuous acts and simultaneously become more acutely conscious of past wrongs, Muḥāsibī attempts to safeguard the soul from a flawed sense of moral uprightness and self-worth. The intention behind this strategy is to protect the individual from a sense of religious pride (*kibr*) that might develop once he commits himself to the way, since such feelings would seriously impede the soul's journey.[75]

The purpose of becoming more conscious of one's past sins is not simply to accentuate the experience of remorse. If the aspirant is still embroiled in those sins, then he must exert himself to break their hold over him. This will require reflecting on their causes (*al-fikr bi al-asbāb*), and, once identified, uprooting them from his life. If the cause for certain sins lies in the company one keeps, then he should cut off all ties from them. The soul's *tawba*, Muḥāsibī contends, will never be successful except by parting from foul company.[76] If other causes are identified, they must be suitably dealt with. The aspirant must reflect over the origin of all of his sins until he determines, to the extent possible, their hidden sources.

Since the passions (*shahawāt*) remain one of the main sources of sin, Muḥāsibī bids the seeker to observe the supererogatory fast.[77] Depriving the passions of nourishment will, he argues, help weaken their power over the soul. If fasting remains insufficient, Muḥāsibī recommends continuous hunger (*jūʿ*), by which he means hunger beyond the times of the regular fast. The danger of satiation (*shabʿ*) lies in the fact that, among other things, it "arouses passion and produces hardness of heart" (*qaswa*).[78] By subjecting the body to prolonged deprivation of physical sustenance, the aspirant can help free himself from his bondage to carnal desires and appetites.[79] The lower passions can be subdued and tamed by limiting the means through which they derive their strength and power.[80] Since the seeker obviously cannot abstain from food altogether, he should take precautions to ensure that his nourishment, though meager, remain completely lawful[81] because of the corrosive effect of impure food. In laying such emphasis on its purity, Muḥāsibī encourages a scrupulousness common to early Sufis.

The seeker should also reflect over the immensity of the divine punishment during this process of self-mortification, thereby harnessing the capacity of the intellect (*ʿaql*) to help eradicate sinful inclinations.[82] By reflecting on the consequences of disobedient acts, he will be less inclined to pursue them. If he finds that the soul continues to take delight in its sinful cravings, then he should not stop short of making full-fledged war on his passions and caprice (*hawā*),[83] and fight them with the same vigor he would an enemy combatant in battle.[84] If necessary, he should even go to such an extent as to deprive the lower soul of permissible (*mubāḥ*) sources of pleasure as a form of punishment. Kharrāz, as we saw in previous chapter, would express a similar view in the *Kitāb al-ṣidq*.

The entire process of *tawba* and disciplining the soul can be strengthened by exchanging the causes that previously led one to sin with virtuous acts of opposing nature. If the *tāʾib* replaces evil friends and acquaintances with good ones, a preoccupation with worldly affairs with thoughts of the next world, and frivolous talk with silence and private conversation with God through the recitation of the Holy Book, "the lights of obedience will subjugate his passions," enabling him to overcome many of his remaining inclinations to sin.[85] The Qurʾān has a particular power in subjugating the forces that draw one back to sin because its preeminence over other speech is "like the preeminence (*faḍl*) of God over His creation."[86]

Although Muḥāsibī encourages one to pursue specific kinds of virtuous acts at the onset of *tawba*, the aspirant, as a general rule, should prioritize eliminating transparent sins over engaging in devotional acts of piety. When Muḥāsibī does prescribe such supererogatory works at an early stage of the soul's development, as in the few examples mentioned, the underlying purpose is to weaken the soul's propensity and desire to sin. But on the whole, Muḥāsibī considers it more meritorious for the seeker to be cleansed of vices, particularly those that have been cemented into nature by habit, than for him to embellish himself with pious acts. In the *Waṣāya*, Muḥāsibī advises the seeker to "draw close to God through *taqwā* and avoiding sins" (*mujānabat al-āthām*), because "the one who avoids sins enjoys a more favored position [in the eyes of] God, and has a higher rank than the mere worshipper."[87] One who is more vigilant of the divine prohibitions occupies a loftier station before God than the one who, though less vigilant, prays and fasts more often. Even when one does pursue good works (*ḥasanāt*), the intention, for Muḥāsibī, should be to wipe out evil deeds (*maḥw al-sayyiʾāt*) because it "is better and of higher rank."[88] A similar idea is underscored in the *Masāʾil*, where Muḥāsibī states that of the six aims of supererogatory forms of devotion (*nawāfil*), the first pertains to "the expiation of sins and the completion of religious obligations [regarding which one has fallen short]" (*takfīr al-dhunūb wa takmīl al-farāʾiḍ*).[89]

Insofar as the *tāʾib* finds himself successful in turning away from sins, Muḥāsibī requires of him to show gratitude to God, because "gratitude over the blessing (*niʿma*) of repentance is obligatory (*wājib*)."[90] The *tāʾib* should not, at any moment, become so deluded as to presume that his success in repentance was the result of his own power.[91] By succumbing to such a delusion, he could easily fall prey to feelings of pride (*kibr*) and conceit (*ʿujb*), thereby replacing his previous sins with more subtle ones. Muḥāsibī is acutely aware of this danger and so devotes a chapter in the *Riʿāya* entitled "the chapter on ascribing the act to the self" (*bāb iḍāfat al-ʿamal ilā al-nafs*),[92] in which he explains how one should psychologically orient himself to his good works. Although Muḥāsibī is known to have engaged in disputes with the Muʿtazilites, his chapter is not a theological critique of their position on free will, nor an alternative explanation of the nature of human activity. As the chapter is located in the *Riʿāya*'s *Kitāb al-ʿujb* (*Book of Conceit*), Muḥāsibī's intention behind his inquiry is principally pragmatic: to ensure that any good works a person accomplishes not become a source of hubris. And so he states that although a person should know that he is indeed the performer of a virtuous act, the act itself could not have been possible without the favor (*minna*) of God. The danger is not in realizing that one has performed a good deed—a fact that is, in any case, incontrovertible[93]—but to "ascribe (the deed) to the self with praise for it" and forget the divine favor that made the act possible to begin with.[94] In the *Masʾāil*, Muḥāsibī states that ascribing the origin of the act to divine favor is one of the obligations imposed on the heart.[95] Were it not for such favor, he would have inclined to its opposite (*khilāf dhālik*),[96] because the *nafs* in its natural state gravitates toward its passions and caprice. God, however, bestows upon the human being an intellect (*ʿaql*) which through His guidance enables him to overpower natural inclinations that pull him in the opposite direction of virtue.[97] The proper response to success in *tawba* is therefore not to feel a sense of personal accomplishment, but to instead express gratitude to God for enabling one to turn away from sin to begin with. By expressing thanks to the Creator, one opens himself up to receive the kind of grace through which he can pursue even greater works of piety.[98] This is partly based on an interpretation he cites of Q 14:7, "If you are grateful, I will certainly give you more" (*la azīdannakum*), where the *ziyāda* or *mazīd* (increase) refers to an increase in the worship of God (*la azīdannakum min ṭāʿatī*).[99] Just as gratitude leads to the showering of grace to pursue even more acts of virtue, ingratitude leads to a loss of that very *minna* through which one may remain faithful to the obligations of repentance.

Renewed Temptation and the Danger of Breaking One's Resolve

Even though the *tāʾib* will naturally be tempted to fall back into those very sins he is striving to leave, Muḥāsibī warns him of the danger of breaking his resolution. He gives particular attention to the weight of the resolve (*ʿazm*) in *tawba* insofar as it amounts, in his estimation, to an oath or promise (*waʿd*) to God.[100] By violating such an oath, the *tāʾib* potentially enters the ranks of those whom the Qurʾān condemns for failing to fulfill their vows.[101] Before the *tāʾib* allows himself to reoffend, he must therefore seriously reflect over the punishment that "becomes incumbent on one who makes a covenant (*ʿāhada*) and resolves (*ʿazama*) to be obedient yet fails to fulfill it."[102] For Muḥāsibī, the *tāʾib* faces a twofold danger if he returns to any of his sins. Not only will he have to face the consequence of the sin, but also, and perhaps more significantly, he will have to deal with the gravity of breaking his promise—an act that would require its own *tawba*. By returning to any one of his sins, he would therefore fall into greater peril than when he had committed it in the first place.

At least part of Muḥāsibī's strategy in bringing attention to this danger is no doubt to strengthen the *tāʾib*'s resolution to stay away from what he has left. Once he realizes the enormity of remaining unfaithful to a vow that accompanied his *tawba*, he will be less inclined to put his own soul in peril by repeating the offense. But this strategy, it seems, also has its drawbacks. It may be that the sinner, despite his feelings of remorse and his abandonment of the sin, will be less inclined to take on a vow in the first place, particularly when he reflects over his all-too-human frailty in the face of renewed temptation, as well as unforeseeable conditions that might draw him back to the sin with a force he cannot resist. Considering the danger that lies dormant in such a resolve, one might naturally wonder whether it might not be more prudent for the *tāʾib* to turn away from his sin but without resolution. After all, this way if he falters he will not have to repent for the added sin of a broken resolution. He can abandon his sin in regret, set aright any previous wrongs, and follow through with any number of righteous deeds to spiritually reinvigorate his soul, yet without jeopardizing his soul by taking on a potentially unrealizable vow. As much as this may appear to be a solution to the dilemma at hand, Muḥāsibī's understanding of *tawba* does not allow it. This is because, as noted earlier, he unconditionally stipulates resolve to be an essential ingredient of *tawba*. Insofar as the *tāʾib* fails to meet all of its requirements, his *tawba* will remain incomplete.

Muḥāsibī seems to be aware of the reticence one may have in resolving to give himself entirely to the way by abandoning his sins. His response to this dilemma is by encouraging the *tāʾib* to resolve with trust in God (*tawakkul*).[103] This trust is so essential that without it the seeker is not safeguarded from failure and humiliation (*khidhlān*). The reason Muḥāsibī places such an emphasis on trust is to remind the *tāʾib* never to become unmindful of the divine power and grace without which he cannot return to God. For Muḥāsibī, the *tāʾib* should have hope (*rajāʾ*) in success and see to it that he relies in his hope on God and not his own meager powers.[104] Through *tawakkul* he will receive the grace to remain true to his resolve. In short, one should not shy away from a resolve simply because of its weight, but rather resolve with trust in God. This is why, according to Muḥāsibī, the Prophet was told, "when you have resolved, then put your trust in God" (Q 3:159). And this is also why the prophet Shuʿayb said, "My success (*tawfīq*) lies only in the hands of God. In Him I trust and to Him I return" (*wa ilayhi unīb*) (Q 11:88).[105] Through these verses Muḥāsibī attempts to provide a scriptural basis for the manner in which he interlaces the concepts of *tawba*/*ināba*, *ʿazm*, and *tawakkul*. It should be clear that Muḥāsibī nowhere states that *tawakkul* on its own will protect one from reneging on his resolve. Instead, when the *tāʾib* struggles to break the nefarious power of sin by adopting a comprehensive spiritual regimen, it will be easier for him to leave his past wrongs. *Tawakkul* plays an essential part in this process.[106]

It is worth noting here that although the early Sufis almost unanimously considered resolve to be a condition of *tawba,* none of them, at least according to the sources that have been analyzed in this study, seem to equate the *ʿazm* with a promise to God. In fact, Muḥāsibī appears rather unique in his understanding of the gravity of the resolve as well as the danger the *tāʾib* faces in case he falls back into sin. Qushayrī, for example, relates an incident in his chapter on *tawba* in the *Risāla* that seems to illustrate the ease with which one could return to God after a breach of such resolve. He mentions how one of the disciples of his *shaykh,* Abū ʿAlī al-Daqqāq, once returned to a sin for which he had done *tawba.* He then asked himself, "What is the judgment concerning one who returns to his repentance?" only to hear the response of an invisible caller, a *hātif*: "You obeyed Us so We thanked you, then you left Us and We gave you respite. If you now return to Us, We will receive you."[107] Hujwīrī even devotes a short section in his chapter on *tawba* elaborating on the teaching found in Qushayrī's anecdote, in which he writes:

> Repentance does not necessarily continue after the resolution not to return to sin has been duly made. A penitent who in those circumstances returns to sin has in principle earned the divine reward for repentance. Many novices of this sect (the Sufis) have repented and gone back to wickedness and then once more, in consequence of an admonition, have returned to God. A certain sheikh relates that he repented seventy times and went back to sin on each occasion, until at the seventy-first time he became steadfast.[108]

The reason that these Sufis did not seem to consider the resolve to be as significant as Muḥāsibī did lies, it seems, in the fact that it was so difficult to maintain. "The Sufis knew," as Annemarie Schimmel writes, "how often *tawba* was broken."[109] It was such a recurring theme that in Persian Sufi poetry it came to be symbolized by the breaking of a wine glass. It was no doubt the frequency of such broken promises that led one authority to counsel the sinner never to lose hope, and to:

> Come back, come back, even if you have broken
> your repentance a thousand times.[110]

Ghazālī expressed a similar view:

> If you repented and then broke it by returning to the sin a second time, then rush back to repentance. Say to yourself: "it may be that I will die before I return to the sin this time." Similarly, [do this] a third and a fourth time. Just as you have made the sin and returning to it an occupation (*ḥirfa*), make repentance and returning to it an occupation. Do not be more incapable of repentance than you are of sin, nor despair,[111] nor let Satan prevent you from repentance on account of this reason.[112]

Among prominent Sufis, only Ibn al-ʿArabī seems to be in agreement with Muḥāsibī in equating the resolve with an oath to God. Unlike Muḥāsibī, however, he does not recommend resolve with *tawakkul*, but rather *tawba* with no resolve at all. In the *Futūḥāt* he states that a resolve constitutes "a tremendous danger," adding that "if there were to remain in the person something of disobedience, then he would, without doubt, be one who violated the oath (*ʿahd*), and enter among those condemned by His words, 'Those who break the oath of God, after having ratified it' " (Q 2:27).[113] Drawing on the example of Adam's repentance, Ibn al-ʿArabī writes, "one cannot see a more perfect gnosis (*maʿrifa*) than that of Adam, peace be upon him, when he acknowledged his sin (*iʿtarafa*), called upon God (*daʿā*), but did not make an oath with God involving a repentance of resolve (*tawba ʿazm*) in which he would not return to the sin."[114]

Whether or not Ibn al-ʿArabī was influenced by Muḥāsibī in equating the resolve with an oath or promise to God, we cannot be certain. What is clear is that both of these luminaries were in agreement on the weight of the resolve. Apart from the Qurʾānic verses they both cite to equate the resolve with a promise or oath to God, the reason behind their equation is understandable. If the resolve is not an oath to God, for which one is accountable, then what kind of binding power does it have? The resolve as understood by the others would be, for Muḥāsibī and Ibn al-ʿArabī, something like a semi-oath, a half-hearted promise without any real significance. If, on the other hand, it is to retain its force, it has to be an actual oath to God. But while Ibn al-ʿArabī understands the resolve to be much too dangerous, for Muḥāsibī it serves to solidify the *tāʾib*'s intention to abandon his previous sins.

The Renewal of *Tawba* and Turning Away from Sins of the Heart

Muḥāsibī makes it clear throughout his works that *tawba* is an ongoing process. He calls on the seeker to "renew repentance in every moment"[115] in order to aid the process of returning to God, stating that after faith (*īmān*), repentance is the most pressing obligation God has imposed on the heart.[116] Just as one must always have faith, one must always be in a state of repentance. Unlike those who argued (as we saw in the previous chapter, and as we shall see in greater detail in the following one) that one could reach a stage in the spiritual life where he could turn away from *tawba* altogether, Muḥāsibī makes no such claim. As long as the human being is stained by sin—and he will never free himself of it[117]—he is obliged to cleanse his transgressions with the waters of *tawba*. Sins for which one has not repented will lead potentially to his perdition, not necessarily of their own account, but through their effects. "Know my brother," admonishes Muḥāsibī, "that sins lead to heedlessness (*ghafla*),[118] heedlessness leads to hardness of heart (*qaswa*), hardness of heart leads to distance (*buʿd*) from God, and distance from God leads to the fire."[119] Muḥāsibī often compares the condition of the sinner before he turns in repentance to one of *jahl* (ignorance).[120] Knowledge of the shortcomings of the soul thus impels one to constantly turn in *tawba*.

Tawba is a gift of divine mercy, and one that is available to the human being until the moment of death.[121] Insofar as it is a mode of catharsis, the *tāʾib* is reborn into purity through the act of repentance, with the degree of his purity corresponding to the depth and extent of his *tawba*. The nature of *tawba* is such that there is no sin that cannot be cleansed through it.[122] This is why in the *Iḥkām al-tawba* Muḥāsibī goes so far as to claim that the one who repents of major sins (*kabāʾir*) stands in a safer position before God than one who persists in minor sins (*ṣaghāʾir*),[123] because all transgressions can be washed by *tawba*. If the conditions Muḥāsibī lays for its fulfillment appear difficult to attain, it is only because of the far-reaching consequences of its saving power.

For Muḥāsibī, as the traveler draws closer to God, the sins that he will have to turn away from in later stages of his growth will become rarified and less perceptible, a theme we explored briefly in chapter 4. After the external sins, the *tāʾib* will eventually have to confront the "sins of the heart," which he variously refers to as *dhunūb al-qulūb*, *maʿāṣī al-qulūb*, and *āthām al-qulūb*.[124] Although Muḥāsibī warns the spiritual traveler to be wary of all forms of sin, it is these to which, as a probing moral psychologist, he devotes the most extensive analysis. This is evident by the lengths to which he goes to address the inner transgressions. While the sins of the limbs (*jawāriḥ*) manifest themselves in such obvious acts of disobedience as theft and deceit, the sins of the heart are more difficult to detect, but no less dangerous. They include such corrosive qualities as pride, envy (*ḥasad*), prolonged hopes (*ṭūl al-amal*), hardness of heart (*qaswa*), scorning divine blessings (*iḥtiqār al-niʿam*), heedlessness, hypocrisy (*nifāq*), lacking mercy (*qillat al-raḥma*), covetousness (*hirṣ*) and ostentation (*riyāʾ*).[125] Just as the external sins vary in their degrees of severity, the internal sins vary in their degrees of subtlety.

The importance that Muḥāsibī lays on removing internal sins is highlighted by the advice he gives from one of the people of knowledge (*ahl al-ʿilm*): "seek medicine (*dawāʾ*) for them; their medicine is none other than your repentance and rectification of matters."[126] Since these sins are much more difficult to detect than external sins, Muḥāsibī reminds the *tāʾib* never to become unmindful of *muḥāsaba*. Through *muḥāsaba* he can recognize those vices that lie buried within his soul and that exercise a debilitating effect on his observance of the rights and duties (*ḥuqūq*)—both external and internal—owed to God. *Muḥāsaba* remains such an essential component of his moral psychology, and by extension, the entire process of *tawba*, that he goes so far as to assert that the very origin of the heart's corruption (*aṣl fasād al-qalb*) lies in abandoning self-examination.[127] The various spiritual exercises of fasting, prayer, silence, meditation, and reflection have as part of their objective the gradual introversion of the traveler so that he can come to a clearer understanding of the nature of his own heart and its illnesses. Muḥāsibī encourages these practices because of his overriding concern for *muḥāsaba*. He states that "he who is acquainted with the secret motions of the heart is better than he who acts with the motions of the limbs."[128] The reason it is so important to guard the heart is because, as the center of the human soul, in the final order of things the heart alone will bear the final consequences of sin.[129] A heart that is spiritually diseased is murky and dark, and "there is nothing more delightful (*aʿjab*) to Iblīs than the darkness of the heart (*ẓulmat al-qalb*)."[130]

Those who devote themselves to uprooting the poisonous weeds of the heart and to the worship of hearts (*ʿibādat al-qulūb*) will arrive, according to Muḥāsibī, to the highest of ranks in the Afterlife. In his *Kitāb al-ʿilm*[131]—a work that exercised a definitive influence on Ghazālī's own work of the same title—Muḥāsibī states that "the children of the Hereafter" (*abnāʾ*[132] *al-ākhira*) can be divided into two classes. The first of these consists of those who are content simply to turn away from external vices (*al-ʿuyūb al-ẓāhira*) and toward external acts of worship (*al-ṭāʿāt al-ẓāhira*). They are preoccupied principally with the *aʿmāl al-jawāriḥ*. Since they are concerned with the next world, their end will be good, but they will have to deal with the consequences of neglecting to turn in *tawba* from the inner sins.[133] To the extent that they fall short in meeting the demands of repentance—since *tawba* is an all-encompassing process—they will have to face divine judgment; and many of them, says Muḥāsibī, will be in for a rude awakening.

The second class comprises those who are concerned not only with everything the first class is, but also, in addition, with inner worship and weeding out the "internal vices" (*al-ʿūyub al-bāṭina*).[134] In addition to the *aʿmāl al-jawāriḥ*, they are also preoccupied with the *aʿmāl al-qulūb*.[135] But their attention is directed principally toward the interior life because they have managed to overcome their inclination toward external sins. Those who stand in this class will appear before God "pure, immaculate and repentant"[136] for having fulfilled the rights of *tawba*. Only they, in Muḥāsibī's eyes, are capable of entering into the ranks of the "inheritors of the prophets" and realizing that knowledge of God with which His elect alone are privileged—a knowledge that is "an ocean, the depth of which cannot be fathomed."[137]

We have seen that for Muḥāsibī repentance is an obligation imposed on every human being to protect him from the consequences of his own transgressions. The *tawba* that he calls for is an encompassing process that requires that one strive to break the hold of all sin. Since *tawba* demands a complete and total commitment to the path of self-purification, Muḥāsibī encourages the individual to reflect on the brevity of his life, the inevitability of death and the encounter with God, and the fact that he will eventually have to account for everything he has done during his short sojourn in the world. Muḥāsibī is confident that when any reasonable person reflects over the actual condition of his own soul, marred as it is by heedlessness and sin, as well as what awaits him upon death, that he will be impelled to turn to God completely. By harnessing the power of reflection—provided one accepts the premises of divine revelation—the individual will come to an awareness of the pitiful state of his soul and be inspired to return to God voluntarily through a commitment to the path. Insofar as *tawba* is all-encompassing, Muḥāsibī provides the individual with a comprehensive method that will enable him to slowly overcome his inclinations to sin as well as interiorize his consciousness so that his attention will turn toward the heart—the perceptual, moral, and cognitive center of the soul. Through this gradual interiorization, the *tāʾib* will become more acutely conscious of the less perceptible sins that afflict the interior regions of his being, and be moved to devote himself to eliminating subtler vices. For Muḥāsibī, only those who seriously undertake the task of eradicating both the external and internal sins attain the rank of the *tāʾibūn,* and only the *tāʾibūn* can reach the rank of the "knowers of God" and "inheritors of the prophets." Although the human being can never free himself of moral imperfections, in Muḥāsibī's view, God has provided him with repentance as a means through which he can protect himself from the corrosive proclivities of his own soul.

Chapter 7

Tawba in the *Nourishment of Hearts* of Abū Ṭālib al-Makkī

We shall bring our study of early Sufi approaches to *tawba* to a close with an analysis of repentance in the thought of Abū Ṭālib al-Makkī, one of the most influential authors of the early period. Dhahabī referred to him as a "leader (*imām*), ascetic (*zāhid*), and gnostic (*ʿārif*), the *shaykh* of the Sufis."[1] Unfortunately—as in the case of Muḥāsibī, who died a century and a half before him—little is known of Makkī's life. Richard Gramlich has lamented "the meager information that has come down to us with respect to the life of Abū Tālib."[2] Insofar as the details of his life are concerned, we can be more or less certain that he was born in the Persian province of Jibal and grew up in Mecca, where he studied under Ibn al-Aʿrābī (d. 952), a disciple of Junayd, as well as other Meccan masters.[3] According to Ibn Khallikān, it was because of his time in Mecca that he was given the attribution "al-Makkī."[4] He left Mecca for Basra sometime near the middle of the tenth century where, as noted earlier, he joined the Sālimiyya. It was here that he became heir to the spiritual teachings of Sahl al-Tustarī through the influence of Ibn Sālim's son, Abū al-Ḥasan Aḥmad b. Sālim. He later moved to Baghdad to study with Sarrāj,[5] and remained there until his death[6] in 996 CE. In his time, Makkī was known for his knowledge of *ḥadīth*, his public preaching, and his rigorous asceticism.[7] Although he is reported to have authored a number of works on *tawḥīd*,[8] none of them has survived. His most famous and influential treatise was the *Qūt al-qulūb*, a work widely read and studied to this day.

Makkī's most comprehensive discussion of *tawba* appears in the thirty-second chapter of the *Qūt*. Running twenty pages in the lithograph edition, the chapter represents the longest single sustained treatment of repentance, written from a Sufi perspective, currently available to us from the first four centuries of Islam.[9] Besides the length of Makkī's chapter on *tawba*, one of the main reasons it should be given prominence in a study of this topic in early Sufism lies in the overall significance of the treatise of which it is a part. The *Qūt* was one of the most influential and widely read Sufi manuals in the formative period of the tradition. As Arberry observed, Makkī's magnum opus was, along with Qushayrī's *Risāla*, among the most valuable works of early Sufi literature.[10] When Rūmī (d. 1273) spoke of the Prophet Noah's high spiritual standing, one he had attained without book learning, he singled out the works of Makkī and Qushayrī. "He had not read the *Risāla* nor the *Qūt*," he wrote in the *Mathnawī*.[11] Although clearly intended as a criticism of mere book learning, the Persian mystic made his point by acknowledging the status of the *Qūt* among Sufis. Ibn ʿAbbād recorded his own praise for Makkī's work when he observed that "nothing else of its scope is available and I know of no one who has produced the likes of it. In it he sets forth the erudite sciences of Sufism [in a manner] which defies explanation."[12] Makkī's most notable influence was undoubtedly on Ghazālī, in whose *Iḥyāʾ* appear pages taken straight out of the *Qūt*.[13]

Makkī's discussion of repentance falls within a lengthy section of the *Qūt* devoted to the Stations of Certainty (*maqāmat al-yaqīn*). As we noted earlier, the Sufis differ on the number of these stations, as well as whether some of them are to be included instead among the *aḥwāl* or states. These stations, which, in Makkī's mystical theology, are nine in number, function as the rungs of a ladder that the spiritual aspirant must climb in his ascending journey to God. The inner growth and purification of the soul is not possible without traversing each of these stations and realizing their corresponding virtues. For Makkī, these stations are, in ascending order, repentance, patience, gratitude, hope, fear, renunciation, trust in God, contentment, and love.[14] The elaborate analysis of these stations makes up nearly a quarter of the entire *Qūt*, with the section on *tawakkul* by far the longest.[15]

The reader who comes to Makkī's text on repentance expecting to find a metaphysical exploration of this concept will be disappointed. Although the *Qūt* remains one of the most important works in the history of Islamic mysticism, it was meant to serve as an instruction manual for spiritual novices and aspirants. Makkī's intention in his *bāb al-tawba* is not to elucidate the transcendental mysteries of repentance[16] but to invite the seeker to properly situate himself in relation to his own transgressions against God, thereby preparing himself to acquire the other virtues necessary for inner growth, illumination, and progress on the path. Although the work is primarily a practical work, it is also by no means simply a book of Sufi commandments. Like Muḥāsibī before him, Makkī minutely examines the workings of the human psyche and draws attention to the various maladies of the heart.[17] He explores, like an astute psychoanalyst, the inner promptings of the soul that impel it in the directions of virtue and vice. In this regard, the *Qūt* can be read as a work both of ethical philosophy and spiritual psychology, even though its primary purpose is pragmatic. Still, a perceptive reader will be able to draw out the universal relevance of many of his inquiries into human nature. John Renard has not inaccurately described him as an "extraordinarily shrewd observer of the human condition."[18]

The more universal appeal of the *Qūt*, however, can be difficult to discern considering the degree to which the work is steeped in the language of the Islamic revelation. The reader of the *Qūt* will not help but notice the extent to which the Qur'ān interlaces its fabric. Not only does Makkī open each chapter with the relevant thematic verses, he returns to scripture for every subject he broaches. So deeply is the Qur'ān interwoven into the text, one might argue that the work is something of a *tafsīr* in a different key. Makkī's claim that "the people of the Qur'ān [. . .] are the people of God, and His elect"[19] gives us a sense of the central role of scripture in his system of ascetic and moral psychology. But this extreme reverence for Islam's primary text is not a peculiar characteristic of his unique brand of Sufism. As Schimmel has observed, "the words of the Koran have formed the cornerstone of all mystical doctrines [in Islam]."[20] By integrating the Qur'ān so deeply into the substance of the *Qūt*, Makkī is also able to forcefully argue for the legitimacy of his views of repentance in particular, and Sufism in general, through Revelation itself.[21] This employment of the sacred text should not be viewed simply as a strategy to win converts to Sufism, but reflects, as well, a genuine reverence and veneration for the message given to the Prophet of Islam, as well as the depth to which the Qur'ān was internalized by Makkī.

Makkī also uses Prophetic traditions extensively, although some critics, such as Ibn al-Kathīr (d. 1372), accused him of employing weak *ḥadīths*[22]—unsurprisingly, the same charge he would also level against Ghazālī's *Iḥyā'*.[23] As we shall see in his discussion of repentance, Makkī frequently elaborates an idea using a *ḥadīth* as his starting point. He also heavily relies on Sufi sayings and anecdotes. This almost excessive use of quotations—from the Qurʾān, the Prophet, and the Sufis themselves—may be seen as a drawback, at least to the sensibilities of the modern reader accustomed to flowing, uninterrupted prose. One might get the impression that Makkī has simply strung together various sayings and divided them by subject headings. Knysh's contention that the *Qūt* "simply brims with long-winded quotations,"[24] is accurate, to a certain extent, and one can make a similar observation about other Sufi works composed around the same period. However, one should not forget that these compositions were among the first to systematically explicate Sufi ideas in Islamic history. Because the authors were transcribing teachings that were very often transmitted orally, it was only natural that some of these early works would be composed largely of the sayings of the earliest mystics and the Prophet insofar as they related to the path. Thus one will find that much of what Kalābādhī and Sarrāj have to say in the *Taʿarruf* and the *Kitāb al-lumaʿ*—texts authored around the same time period as the *Qūt* and that comprise, along with it, the first real "manuals" of Sufism—is quoted from earlier authorities. We must also recall, as we saw in chapter 4, the quasi-revelatory status that was assigned to many of the Sufi apothegmata, making later authorities more inclined to citing them.

Makkī's heavy reliance on quotations should not lead one to believe that the text is a haphazard string of Qurʾānic verses, prophetic traditions, and Sufi aphorisms. Although a superficial reading of the work might suggest that it is indeed, in the words of one scholar, "a rather unsystematic heap of quotations,"[25] a close analysis reveals that the quotations in fact serve as conceptual pegs that allow Makkī to ground and develop his own arguments. By basing his own views on those of his early predecessors, Makkī demonstrates to the reader that his positions are not simply personal opinions, but rooted in the Sufi tradition that he is representing. Although his treatment of material may appear to be unsystematic and even disorganized at times,[26] this does not mean that Makkī's various analyses in the *Qūt* lack, as a whole, a coherent structure. This becomes clear in Makkī's discussion of repentance, as the quotations that he employs serve to substantiate and legitimate a complex and psychological analysis of the soul as it undergoes a process of *tawba* and return to God. Makkī does not simply repeat the tradition to which he is heir, but engages it in a way that allows him to express his personal views. His own ideas can be unearthed by paying close attention to the progression of his discussions, and to the specific way he incorporates quotations into the chapter. This unearthing of Makkī's own views within the cluster of quotations, however, can often be difficult, and this difficulty is compounded by the fact that, in the lithograph edition, it is not always clear where a specific quotation ends.

The Obligatory Nature of *Tawba*

Makkī begins his discussion of *tawba* by highlighting its obligatory nature within the religious and spiritual life. "There is nothing more obligatory on creation," he writes, quoting Sahl, "than repentance."[27] *Tawba*, in Makkī's eyes, is not an optional act of religious devotion meant primarily for those who have committed themselves completely to God, but a requirement for the generality of believers. Unlike other expressions of religious piety, *tawba* is an essential and inescapable requirement for anyone who submits to Islam. Nor is repentance meant only for individual sins, but must, instead, be an all-embracing process of self-purification. Like Muḥāsibī and others, Makkī argues that the importance and value of *tawba* will be felt by the heedless soul only when the opportunity to repent is no more, and the soul is on the brink of final judgment. Makkī notes that according to one of the interpretations of the Qurʾānic verse, "a gulf is placed between them and what they desire" (Q 34:54), the object of desire is the repentance that is no longer possible at the moment of death. It is then that the soul will desire a *tawba* that it is incapable of attaining.[28] "*Tawba* is not for those who do wrong," he quotes the Qurʾān, "until when death attends one of them, he says, 'lo! I repent now!' " (Q 4:18). The soul's regret will be for neglecting to repent and reform itself while the opportunity was still present. Makkī writes, "He, most High, has decreed that repentance is not accepted after the signs of the next-world are made manifest (*ẓuhūr iʿlām al-ākhira*)."[29] Among the first of these signs is the appearance of the angel of death, the first epiphanic eruption from the world of the unseen.[30]

The Process and Conditions of *Tawba*

Makkī's analysis of the inner process of repentance yields significant insights into the inter-relation of the virtues within his psychological system. In this respect, his ideas bear a resemblance to Muḥāsibī's moral psychology. Ultimately, for Makkī, *tawba* cannot be separated from the other *maqāmāt* that the aspirant must go through in his journey to God.

Although, as we shall see, it is most deeply connected to the virtues of patience and spiritual combat or inner struggle (*mujāhada*), there are other positive qualities that the soul will necessarily acquire, or be forced to acquire, in order for its process of repentance to be sound, just as there are vices above and beyond the particular sin or sins it is leaving that it will be necessary to abandon. *Tawba* is an all-consuming process that impels the soul in the direction of a fuller and more complete religious life.

Near the opening of his chapter, Makkī stipulates ten requirements for the repentance of individual sins. For much of his analysis of *tawba*, he elaborates, in one form or another, the implications of these requirements. An examination of the chapter reveals that many of his discussions can be drawn back to one or more of these conditions. Makkī emphasizes the importance of these conditions when he says that a close reading of the sayings of the earliest members of the Muslim community about repentance that have been transmitted to us will yield these ten conditions, and that the ones who came after them elaborated on these conditions. Only near the end of the chapter, when he begins to probe some of the higher levels of *tawba*, does Makkī go beyond these requirements. We will explore these further requirements at the end of our inquiry.

The ten conditions that Makkī states are incumbent upon the *tāʾib* are (1) not to repeat the sin, and (2) if tried by it, to avoid, at all costs, from falling back. There must be no persistence in the sin. The *tāʾib* must (3) return to God from the sin, as well as (4) feel regret (*nadam*) for what has been lost. (5) He must then vow or resolve to remain upright for the remainder of his life, (6) fear the punishment that is his due, but also (7) have hope in divine forgiveness. (8) He must acknowledge (*iʿtirāf*) that he has sinned, but also that (9) God has decreed the sin for him (*qaddara dhālika ʿalayhi*) and that this decree does not detract from His justice (*ʿadl*). (10) Finally, he must follow the sin with a righteous act as a penance or atonement (*kaffāra*) for his previous wrong.[31]

Although Makkī's discussion of repentance remains, as just noted, to a large extent an elaboration of these conditions, he does not set up or structure his discussion so that the reader can see that he is in fact expanding these conditions. Makkī's discussion lacks the relatively neat structure one finds, for example, in a work such as Ghazālī's *Iḥyāʾ*. The format of Makkī's analyses may be one reason why so few modern scholars have attempted to study the *Qūt*.[32] Only a diligent and patient reader can begin to appreciate the full import of the work. Because of the efforts Makkī takes to demonstrate the "orthodox" nature of Sufism, it is not surprising that he opens his analysis of *tawba* by stipulating the conditions outlined by the earliest generation of Muslims and then using them to develop his subsequent inquiry.

The Predetermination of the Sin

Makkī does not devote equal space to all of the conditions outlined above. He has next to nothing, for example, to say about the ninth condition, even though it remains one of the most problematic and disputed issues in Islamic theology and a serious point of contention between the Ashʿarites and Muʿtazilites.[33] The significance of this condition is moreover underscored by the fact that both Ghazālī and Ibn al-ʿArabī, in their chapters on *tawba* in the *Iḥyāʾ* and the *Futūḥāt*, devote significant attention to resolving the ethical dilemma raised by the religious imperative to repent for predetermined and divinely created sins.[34] One might even say that this question becomes the central problem in their respective analyses. We can only speculate as to why Makkī decides to overlook this issue altogether, with the exception of acknowledging in principle God's decree of the act. The reason seems to lie in the "*praxis*-oriented" or *ʿamalī* nature of the work, which holds Makkī back from plunging into theological debates that have very little bearing on the immediate needs of the spiritual seeker. Makkī's silence might be no different from that of the Buddha when he was confronted by metaphysical questions. The Buddha explained that for a man struck by an arrow, it is of little use for him to know trivial details about the archer and the arrow, details that would not alleviate his suffering or attend to the real problem at hand. The focus of an intelligent man would be on removing the arrow and treating the wound. For Makkī as well, theological inquiries in a chapter concerned fundamentally with *how to repent* may ultimately be seen as of little use for one trying to pull out the arrows of sin from his soul and healing the wound with the medicine of *tawba*.

Another related reason for his silence may have to do with a certain disdain for *kalām* altogether, which we know of on the basis of remarks he makes about partisans of scholastic theology in other parts of the *Qūt*. He quotes, for example, Aḥmad b. Ḥanbal approvingly in his criticisms of the *mutakallimūn*.[35] Although Ghazālī could also be critical of *kalām*, he did not shy away from deeply probing into such philosophical matters when occasion demanded it, even in his later post-conversion years. In the case of Makkī, he appears to have had an aversion to such debates altogether, and the rational methods employed to resolve them.

Tawba and Resolve

The fifth condition Makkī highlights is particularly important in understanding the view he takes toward this *maqām*. Makkī stipulates that the repentant one must vow or resolve to remain upright until his death. In other words, he cannot truly be characterized by *tawba* as long as an effort is not made on his part to loosen the shackles of all sin and make a total commitment to obey God in all future matters. It would betray his sincerity if he were to repent of one sin while recklessly indulging in others. This is why Makkī says that the "reality of uprightness" demands of the *tāʾib* to "follow the path of the one who penitently turns (*sabīl man anāba*) to God."[36] This *ināba* must be complete and total, requiring the full commitment of the seeker. It is in this condition that we find what seems to be the most explicit requirement for the all-embracing character of repentance. Although Makkī nowhere states that God rejects the *tawba* of the sinner who repents of one sin but not others—as theologians such as the Muʿtazilite Abū Hāshim and Mānakdīm held[37]—he does appear to come close to this position by requiring a complete change in the person's life as part of the repentance process. This is reflected in the words of an anonymous *ʿālim* he quotes: "he who repented of ninety-nine sins while there remained a single sin for which he did not repent is not from among the repentant ones in our estimation."[38] Makkī's view of the all-consuming character of *tawba* is similar to that of Muḥāsibī, as we saw in the previous chapter.

Tawba and Regret

In his fourth condition of regret (*nadam*), Makkī is in agreement not only with the Sufis but with virtually the entire spectrum of theologians, from the Ashʿarites to the Muʿtazilites. If there is one condition about which there is consensus, it is regret. This consensus is no doubt rooted in one of the oft-repeated *ḥadīth*s about *tawba*, that regret is the sign of repentance. Makkī says the reality of the regret is that the sinner never returns to the likes of the sin that caused the regret. The regret, moreover, must be a deeply felt and perpetual sadness (*dawām al-ḥuzn*). "Among the signs of the sincerity [or truth] of repentance," he says, "are tenderness of heart and abundance of tears."[39]

For Makkī, the feeling of regret is made deeper by what the *tāʾib* should see as the magnitude of the offense, even though it may appear trite to others. Trivializing a sin is, according to one authority he cites, itself a major sin (*istiṣghār al-dhanb kabīra*). Although Makkī does not consider all sins to be major, as some held,[40] he does encourage the repenting one to see the weight of the misdeed insofar as it is an act of disobedience against God. By considering the sin to be trite, one in fact magnifies it on the scales, and conversely, by magnifying it in one's own eyes, one diminishes its weight on the scales.[41] Despite the subjectivity of this approach to sin, Makkī still divides sins into the major and minor, a classification that, in his view, remains independent of one's orientation toward sin. Nevertheless, Makkī does seriously warn the *tā'ib* against belittling his offense, as small as it may be in the eyes of the Law, because, as God warned one of his friends, "do not look at the insignificance of the wrong, but the magnificence of the One you face on its account."[42] This emphasis is not dissimilar, as we saw in the previous chapter, to Muḥāsibī's exhortation for the *tā'ib* to consider his previous good deeds to be insignificant.[43]

Tawba and Overcoming the Inclination to Repeat the Sin

One of the ways to ensure the feeling of regret does not subside is for the aspirant to continuously remember his sins. This will create a feeling of humility before God. But Makkī also sees the need to occasionally turn away from the memory of the sin if such a memory has an adverse effect on the *tā'ib*. If he finds that by calling the sin to mind he feeds a renewed desire for it, Makkī suggests abstaining from the recollection altogether. This is because such a remembrance defeats its intended purpose, which is to deepen the experience of *tawba* by intensifying the regret. Makkī does not dogmatically take the position that repentance requires of the beginner to remember his sin in all circumstances. Instead, like a true doctor of the soul, he administers medicine according to the illness of the *tā'ib*. Acknowledging the danger in remembering one's sins, Makkī writes:

> Know that the one who is weak in certainty and of strong lower soul (*nafs*), is not safe, when he remembers his sins, from feeling a passion (*shahwa*) for them when he looks at them with his heart, or to incline towards them with his lower soul, experiencing a sense of sweetness (*ḥalāwa*). And this can become the cause for his [renewed] temptation.[44]

An individual of this kind should therefore avoid remembering past wrongs, because "cutting off the causes of sin is safer, and what is safer for the aspirant is better for him."[45] Since the desire for the sin and the sweetness the individual derives from it are sources of the sin, the *tā'ib* must make it a priority to eliminate such internal forces that draw him back to the direction he is turning away from, even if it requires adopting a course of action that might diminish the experience of regret and humility.

Although Makkī's concern with eliminating the soul's passionate desire (*shahwa* and *hawā*) for the sin, along with the sweetness (*ḥalāwa*) it experiences upon thinking about it, is guided by a desire to protect the sinner from repeating the offense, he also sees intrinsic value in their elimination. The presence of these qualities within the individual signifies a level of incompleteness within the *tawba* process. If *shahwa, hawā,* and *ḥalāwa* are present, the aspirant has only outwardly turned away from the sin. But since *tawba*—insofar as it is a return to God and obedience from disobedience—must encompass both the outward and inward dimensions of the human being, the inward inclination to sin must also be cut off. The traces of the passion for the sin, as well as the sweetness the unregenerate soul feels when it considers it, must be eradicated. To highlight this point, Makkī cites the sayings of some of the earlier Sufis: "The *tawba* of the servant [of God] is not sound until he forgets his passions [for sin];"[46] "One of the signs of the sincerity of the *tā'ib* is that the sweetness of passion (*hawā*) be replaced by the sweetness of obedience;"[47] "The servant [of God] is not a *tā'ib* until the sweetness of conforming to the lower self is replaced by the bitterness of opposing it."[48]

But Makkī also understands how difficult it can be to eliminate these internal inclinations. The difficulty in self-purification is compounded by the fact that such urges and inclinations are rooted in human nature, within the very elemental makeup of the human being. Makkī recounts Sahl al-Tustarī's response upon being asked about the man who repents and leaves a particular sin, but who then experiences a sense of sweetness when the thought of it crosses his mind, or when he sees or hears about it. "The sweetness [he finds] is a natural disposition of the human being" (*al-ḥalāwa ṭabʿ al-bashariyya*), Sahl responds, adding:

> There is no escape from it, except if he lifts his heart towards his Lord in complaint, by rejecting it within his heart, holding fast to the rejection (*inkār*) and not parting from it, and praying to God that He make him forget it and that He preoccupy him with His own remembrance and worship.[49]

Although Makkī acknowledges, in conformity with Sahl, that the inner inclination is a part of human nature, the *tāʾib* is still obliged to strive against it. "Repentance is not sound," writes Makkī, "as long as passion [for it] remains" (*maʿa baqāʾ al-shahwa*).[50] The *tāʾib* is called to subjugate those impulses which, though part of his nature, draw him to sin. Though Makkī does not explicitly state it, the elimination of these traits help to ensure the *tāʾib* will remain true to the first, second, third, and fifth conditions stipulated earlier, namely that (1) he not repeat the sin; (2) that if tried by the sin, he avoids it at all costs; and (3) that he return to his Lord completely. Eradicating the root cause of the sin helps him fulfill (5) his resolve to remain upright afterward.

The way to strive against these inclinations is through struggle (*mujāhada*) and patience (*ṣabr*), the second station on Makkī's schema of *maqāmāt*. By tying in the qualities of struggle and patience to the process of repentance, Makkī illustrates the unity and inter-relation of the virtues in his mystical psychology. In the passage below, he argues that the eradication of the passions that attract one to the sin is essential for the completion of *tawba*. As long as these passions remain, there remains a latent danger of the *tāʾib* falling back into the sin. Makkī writes:

> The best thing that a servant can do is cut off the passions of the lower soul. This is sweeter to him than what desire (*hawā*) offers because its passions (*shahawāt*) have nothing in truth to offer that one might anticipate later, just like they have nothing in the beginning that can be traced [i.e., because they are fleeting]. If he does not cut them off there will be for him no end to them. If on the other hand he preoccupies himself with what he dislikes by more deeply immersing himself in acts of obedience (*mazīd al-ṭāʿāt*), he will find a sweetness in his worship. But if he does not, he should adhere to patience and struggle. This is the way of the truthful ones (*ṣādiqīn*) from among the aspirants (*murīdīn*). It has been said, about His words, Most High, "Seek help from God and be patient" (Q 7:128), that they mean, seek help from Him in your worship and be patient in your struggle against disobedience.[51]

Struggle and patience are therefore necessary components for the completion of *tawba* insofar as they help the *tāʾib* eliminate lingering inclinations to repeat the offense. By diligently submitting himself to religious acts of worship and self-denial, he will eventually come to find his obedience to God, which he previously abhorred, sweet. Even if the signs of this sweetness remain nowhere in sight, he must nevertheless persist in *ṣabr* and *mujāhada* until his persistence bears fruit.

One of the ways to prevent the inclination to sin from arising within the heart is by cutting off its internal sources. For Makkī, the stages that lead one to the sin begin with the "incoming evil thought" of the act (*khāṭir al-sūʾ*).[52] This is the first step toward transgression. The safest course is for the *tāʾib* to block it as soon as it appears, before it grows into an "[evil] whispering of the soul" (*waswās al-nafs*), and the whispering into a more powerful and potentially irresistible source of seduction:

> The aspirant should work to eliminate the whisperings of the soul (*waswās al-nafs*) which prompt him to sins (*khaṭāyā*),[53] otherwise he will fall into them. This is because the [errant] thoughts (*khawāṭir*) grow strong and become whisperings. And if the whisperings multiply, they become inroads (*ṭuruq*) for the Enemy through the embellishment and seduction of sin. The most harmful thing for the *tāʾib* is to establish the evil thought in his heart by paying attention to it, since it leads him to his own destruction. Every cause that induces one to disobedience, or calls one's attention to disobedience, is itself an act of disobedience. And every cause that eventually leads one to carry out the sin is itself a sin, even if it is legally permissible (*mubāḥ*). Cutting off the permissible act in such a case is an act of worship. This is from among the subtleties of acts (*daqāʾiq al-aʿmāl*).[54]

Makkī traces the inception of the sin back to its first thought. Although the *khāṭir* is weak and insignificant in its own right, it is the seed for the transgression. If watered by the attention of the heart, it will grow into a passion until the passion eventually manifests itself externally in the form of an act.[55] The seed must therefore be unearthed from the heart as soon as it is planted by the winds of fate, so no possibility of disobedience remains.[56] Unlike the *wārid*, the *khāṭir* can be either a source of good or evil.[57]

The last part of the passage is reminiscent of Muḥāsibī's injunction to abandon even permissible enjoyments in order to safeguard one from lapsing in his resolve. Like Muḥāsibī before him, Makkī is acutely aware of the potential of permissible acts or sources of pleasure to change, under certain circumstances, into causes of sin.[58] If the *tā'ib* becomes aware of this danger, what is typically allowed by the Law becomes, in his particular case, objectionable.[59] Through a process of *murāqaba* and self-reflection, the *tā'ib* should strain to identify the subtlest causes for his disobedience to God and then strive to uproot them from his soul.[60] Insofar as the intention behind this effort remains to overcome the propensity and inclination to sin, the entire process of self-examination and taming the lower soul becomes a form of *ʿibāda*.

On Effortlessly Abandoning the Sin

Even though Makkī considers struggling against the inclination to sin to be laudable, and a proof of the *tā'ib*'s sincerity, the penitent soul who is able to renounce the sin without much exertion, has, in his eyes, a loftier standing before God.[61] This is because the absence of such struggle (*tanāzuʿ/mujāhada*) on his part reflects a higher level of purity and the presence of a submissive lower soul, at least in relation to the particular sin in question. The position Makkī takes on this particular matter was not, however, as he points out, shared by all of the early Sufis. He notes that they were divided over the question of whether the individual who had to struggle against a particular sin held a loftier position, in the eyes of God, or the one who was able to leave the sin without much effort.[62] Ibn Abī al-Ḥawārī (d. 844–845)[63] and the companions of Abū Sulaymān al-Dārānī held that the former held a higher position because he would be rewarded both for his *tawba* and his *mujāhada*. The one who did not have to struggle, on the other hand, received only the reward for abandoning the sin. In their eyes, the temptation to sin was not itself blameworthy. Rabāḥ b. ʿAmr al-Qaysī (d. 767),[64] however, as Makkī notes, and with whom he agrees, argued that the one whose lower soul puts up no resistance because "of a sign from the signs of certainty and repose" (*shāhid min shawāhid al-yaqīn wa al-ṭuma'nīna*[65]) has a higher standing. He is less likely to fall back into the sin considering the temptation to return is, in his case, altogether absent. The one who has to struggle against his inclination is not safeguarded from returning.[66] This debate was similar to another one, notes Makkī, regarding whether the individual who had to struggle to give charity in the way of God was more virtuous than the one who was generous without effort.[67] Ibn ʿAṭā' and his companions held that the former was in a better position since he would receive two rewards, one for his efforts and the other for his charity. Junayd, on the other hand, argued that the latter held a higher station because his effortless generosity (*sakhāwa*) was the fruit of *zuhd*. His generosity meant that he had already acquired a positive character trait that was wanting in the case of the former, whose struggle against worldly attachments signified he had not yet attained the same rank.[68]

For Makkī, although the struggle in the case of both individuals in the examples above is commendable, the one who is able to perform virtuous acts without internal impediments is more spiritually advanced, more secure from the sin, and therefore closer to God. We can presume that for Makkī such a person has already gone through, at some earlier stage in his life, the struggle that has brought him to the station at which he now stands. This remains merely speculative, however, because Makkī does not explicitly state it. Although Makkī's stance in this debate is, on the whole, persuasive, he does not address the question of the person who is able to renounce the sin, not because he has reached a level of self-mastery as a consequence of subjecting himself to a regimen of ascetic training and spiritual exercise (*riyāḍa*), but because of a peculiar God-given temperament. In this case, the position of Ḥawārī and Dārānī's companions would appear more convincing. It would make little sense for God to deprive the *tā'ib* who struggles to overcome a certain sin of a reward, while He rewards the one who does not have to struggle simply because he is born with an innate disinterest in the vice, or a weaker passion for it. In fact, he might, one could argue, be more accountable for falling into the sin to begin with. A person who has a strong appetite for food, for example, a characteristic he is born with, should not receive, one would think, a lesser reward for keeping a gluttonous impulse in check than the one who eats little because he lacks such cravings to begin with. Although it is unclear how Makkī would respond to these particular scenarios, because he does not address them, at least in his chapter on *tawba*, his general position, as already mentioned, is to privilege abandoning a sin or vice without exertion and inner resistance.

What is perhaps most interesting about this aspect of Makkī's discussion, as brief as it is, is that it reflects the more universal significance of some of the issues being addressed in early Sufism. A similar question as the one touched on in the *Qūt* was dealt with by some of the leading philosophers in the West,[69] starting primarily with Aristotle. In the *Nicomachean Ethics*, Aristotle argued that a person could not be characterized by a particular virtue if the performance of that virtue did not come easily to him. In order to possess the virtue in question, the individual had to genuinely enjoy and find pleasure in it. There had to be an inner attraction for the virtue and a corresponding repulsion from the opposing vice for him to be qualified by the exemplary character trait.[70] For Aristotle, a man could not be called courageous if he felt fear in the face of circumstances that required bravery, or did not delight in acts of courage. Generosity, likewise, required that one found selflessness and munificence enjoyable. Thus he wrote that "moral excellence is concerned with pleasures and pains."[71] If one did not experience joy in a particular virtue, he would be required to train himself, in Aristotle's view, until he found it enjoyable. A virtue had to be learned in the same way as a craft or a particular art, through practice and repetition. He argued that just as men become builders by practicing the craft of building, or lyre players by continuously playing the lyre, "so too we become just by doing just acts, temperate by doing temperate acts, brave by doing brave acts."[72] The learning of virtues, however, did not consist of acquiring a theoretical knowledge of them, or mastering their external forms, but of habituating the soul to find them pleasurable. Virtue was therefore something that had to be acquired through practice and repetition. It would be inappropriate to characterize someone as virtuous who was undergoing a process of habituation just as one could not be a called a craftsman until he learned the particular craft in question.

Aristotle's understanding of the ideal virtuous man is not entirely different from the realized Sufi in Makkī's thought, at least in relation to the question of the soul's inclination and attraction to what is virtuous. Just as for Aristotle the ethically accomplished man finds it pleasurable to do all that is good, the advanced Sufi, for Makkī, finds obedience to God pleasant. His soul is so trained through *mujāhada* that what he may have found to be difficult at the onset of his spiritual journey comes effortlessly near the end, and becomes a source of inner joy. The "spiritual athleticism" that he has undergone, and that has brought him to his present state, is, in many ways, similar to the habituation Aristotle speaks of. Both the virtuous man and the ideal Sufi possess a purity of soul actualized through laborious practice. The performance of good deeds, and the avoidance of evil ones, is second nature to both of them, ingrained into the substance of their beings. For both Makkī and Aristotle, it is not enough simply to know a virtue, or to practice it with a heart that delights in its exact opposite. The one who strives to attain ethical or spiritual perfection must actualize the latent goodness of his soul, so that it comes to find all that is morally good to be sweet, and all that is evil to be repugnant.

Despite these similarities, however, for Makkī the performance of a good act without struggle does not mean that the act itself cannot be considered virtuous or good. If someone is grudgingly generous, he is still generous because of the effort he makes to do what is commendable. Aristotle, we know, would have disagreed. In his view, such a man would simply be on his way to acquiring the virtue. He was habituating himself—as he should—to eventually find it pleasant, even though he could not yet be properly qualified by it. Insofar as they both consider the one who does what is good without struggle to stand at a higher rank of ethical and spiritual development, Aristotle and Makkī are in agreement, just as they are about the thoroughly lamentable state of the one who is repelled by virtue and makes no effort to pursue it.

A slightly different perspective on this question of inner inclination and virtue was articulated in the Western philosophical tradition by Immanuel Kant.[73] He presents the case of a man who on account of some personal sorrow "which extinguishes all sympathy for the plight of others"[74] manages to show them benevolence out of duty to the good. This act, in Kant's eyes, has more moral worth than the kindness shown by a man naturally disposed to such sympathetic conduct, who acts simply on account of a good tempered and congenial predilection. For the German philosopher, it is not the inclination and feeling to do what is good that makes an act morally commendable, but carrying it out solely out of a sense of duty to the "categorical imperatives" of the universal moral law.[75] The ideal scenario is of a man who carries it out against inner resistance with no personal benefit. For Kant only then can one know that it is accomplished out of a sense of duty and not mere feeling.[76] Insofar as Kant presents the man who struggles against his own urge to do what is right as a model of virtue, his view comes close to the one that Makkī attributes to Ḥawārī and Dārānī's disciples, when they argue that the *tā'ib* who leaves a sin with struggle is superior to the one who leaves it without exertion. The struggle to do what is right signals for both Kant and this group of Sufis the seriousness of the agent's commitment to what is morally right.

What we can gather from this comparison is the universal significance of many of the debates that were taking place in early Sufism and that are addressed in the *Qūt*. The Sufis were not simply concerned with issues unique to their own community but with ethical questions that had broad relevance and could be intelligible to those outside of Muslim civilization. Even though the vocabulary of these debates was, for the most part, derived from Islamic Revelation, it is not impossible to extrapolate the universal import of these debates from their specific religious and cultural context.

Tawba Followed by Righteous Deeds

In the tenth condition, as we saw earlier, Makkī stipulates that the *tā'ib* must follow the sin with a righteous act as a penance or expiation (*kaffāra*) for his previous wrong. His general discussion of this theme centers on the broader concept of *iṣlāḥ* (setting things aright). As we saw in the second chapter, this concept is deeply tied to *tawba* in the Qur'ān. It should not come as a surprise, then, considering the scriptural roots of Makkī's analysis, that he should devote considerable attention to the theme of rectification and following the sin with pious acts.

The regret for the sin, in Makkī's eyes, if it is genuine, will naturally lead the *tā'ib* not only to turn away from it, but to pursue good works in its wake.[77] The most important of these works is for him to preoccupy himself with amending wrongs (*al-ishtighāl bi al-iṣlāḥ*).[78] Like Muḥāsibī before him, Makkī argues that the rectification should correspond to the sin.[79] Thus, for theft—to use a straightforward example—*tawba* requires returning the stolen property; for *nifāq* (hypocrisy), it requires *ikhlāṣ* (sincerity). Each group of sinners has conditions unique to its repentance: "it is necessary," writes Makkī, "that the *tawba* of the servant be the [moral] opposite of his disobedience" (*'an ḍidd ma'āṣīhi*) and "contrary to the corruption he was responsible for."[80] The *fasād* introduced by the transgression must be corrected by an *iṣlāḥ* peculiar to the nature of the sin. The corresponding rectification, moreover, is not only qualitative, since *tawba* requires "some [good] deeds for some [evil] deeds, and many [good] deeds for many [evil] deeds."[81]

The hope of the *tā'ib* in performing good works following his sin should be that God include him in the category of those lauded in Q 25:70: "Except for him who repents and believes and does right, as for such, God will transmute (*yubaddilu*) their evil deeds into good deeds."[82] This transmutation (*tabdīl*) is, for Makkī, the fruit of genuine *tawba*. When the *tā'ib* exerts to change his state, keeping in mind that "God does not change the condition of a people until they change what is within themselves" (Q 13:11), he will receive divine succor in the form of *tabdīl*. The transmutation the verse speaks of takes place in the world as a consequence of the efforts on his part. Although some exegetical authorities understood this transmutation to be a reward that the *tā'ib* receives in the next world for *tawba* in this world, Makkī explicitly denies this interpretation. Following the opinion of Ibn ʿAbbās, Mujāhid, Qatāda, and Ḥasan, Makkī writes that "the transmutation occurs in this world."[83] This interpretation underscores the importance of good works that must immediately follow the sin.

One of the reasons Makkī places so much emphasis on following evil deeds with good deeds (*tabdīl*) is that in his view the initial sin was itself a perversion of a divine blessing (*niʿma*) into something reprehensible. The sinner employed divine gifts such as health, wealth, or prosperity to commit an offense against God.[84] By transmuting the *niʿma* into a source of disobedience against the Benefactor, the sin represents an act of supreme ingratitude, or what Makkī calls *kufr al-niʿma*.[85] The blessing was bestowed on the servant so that through it he may seek to acquire greater bounties. But "if he used these blessings to disobey God, he transmuted them in ingratitude" (*qad baddalahā kufran*). Makkī bases his view on two Qurʾānic verses: "They transmuted (*baddalū*) the blessing of God in ingratitude" (Q 14:28); and "He who transmutes (*yubaddil*) the blessing of God, after it has come to him. (For him) Lo! God is severe in punishment" (Q 2:211). The *tabdīl* of which these verses speak, argues Makkī, is of transforming the gifts of God into sources of sin and corruption. This explains the severity of divine punishment.[86]

Insofar as every sin is at root a transmutation of good into evil—a *fasād*, the very opposite of *iṣlāḥ*—*tawba* cannot be complete without a *tabdīl* through *iṣlāḥ*, a rectifying inversion that restores the moral order ruptured by the act of disobedience. This is why Makkī says that "the servant is not a *tāʾib* until he is a *muṣliḥ*."[87] Moreover, just as all sin is a *tabdīl* of good into evil, all good works that follow the sin, even those that are not directly related to it, can be considered, in a more general sense, as forms of *iṣlāḥ*. Although the *tāʾib* needs to give the particular rectification for the sin priority, *iṣlāḥ* need not to be restricted to the narrow meaning or idea of correcting the wrong most directly and immediately related to the offense. It can refer to any range of good works that he strives to perform after the sin, to set aright the process he initiated when he turned good into evil. In this light, all of his good work can be subsumed under the larger effort to amend wrongs. Since every sin is a *fasād*, every good deed ensuing from *tawba* is an *iṣlāḥ*. This idea, as we saw in chapter 2, is deeply Qurʾānic. Iṣfahānī observes this when he notes that the opposite of *iṣlāḥ* in the Qurʾān tends to be either *fasād*, or *sayyiʾa*—sin itself.[88]

The Categories of *Tā᾿ibūn*

At the end of his chapter, Makkī turns his attention to the various classes or levels of *tā᾿ibūn*. As we saw in the fourth chapter, these levels are often divided in Sufi literature into the triadic scheme of commoners (*al-ʿawāmm*), the elect (*al-khawāṣṣ*), and the elect of the elect (*khāṣṣ al-khawāṣṣ*). In this hierarchy, everyday believers stand at the lowest rung of the ladder, and the gnostics and the most realized of Sufis at the summit.[89] Sometimes the contrast is simply between two groups of the *khawāṣṣ* and the *ʿawāmm*, the Sufis and the common lot of Muslims. The purpose behind these comparisons is typically to demonstrate the difference between a virtue understood at the level of average religious experience and through the lens of mystical annihilation in God. The contrast is usually striking because it presents a conceptualization of the virtue based on a mystical awareness that subverts or at the very least goes beyond commonsense notions of the virtue in question. When more than one class is compared, the intermediary class or classes represent an embodiment of the virtue standing somewhere in between the pietistic and the mystical. Some examples of these classifications in relation to *tawba* are expressed in the following sayings, some of which we cited earlier: "the common people repent of their sins while the Sufis repent of their good deeds;"[90] "what a difference there is between the *tā᾿ib* who repents of slips, the one who repents of moments of heedlessness, and the one who repents of witnessing his good deeds;"[91] and, "the masses (*al-ʿāmma*) seek forgiveness for sins, the elect (*al-khāṣṣa*) seek forgiveness for witnessing the acts, and for witnessing the gifts and graces, while the great ones (*al-akābir*) seek forgiveness for witnessing everything other than the Real."[92] One of the most famous of these sayings on the question of the sins of the commoners and the elect is attributed to Rābiʿa. A man once came to her and said, "I have not sinned for so many years," to which she replied "your existence is a sin the like of which there is no other" (*wujūduka dhanb lā yuqās bihā dhanb*).[93]

Although sayings of this kind are occasionally encountered in the *Qūt*, Makkī does not explore them in much detail, and certainly not to the extent one would find in those works that have as their principle goal the explication of the most advanced of mystical teachings. For the most part, the *Qūt* examines the Sufi virtues from a religious and psychological perspective in a manner that is not much different from that of the writings of Muḥāsibī or other Sufi primers. It should come as no surprise, then, that in his categorization of *tāʾibūn*, his analysis does not extend beyond the moral and religious plane. Even those most vehemently opposed to all forms of mysticism would have little reason to object to Makkī's four levels, each of which corresponds, in the eyes of the author, to a soul described or at least alluded to in the Qurʾān.

The Four Levels

The first kind of person, for Makkī, is the one who turns away from sins immediately after he falls into them. He does not incline toward them afterward because of the uprightness of his *tawba* and purity of his character, and he replaces his previous transgressions with righteous acts. Because of the fullness of his return to God in the wake of each slip, his repentance is always *tawba naṣūḥ*. Although Makkī does not describe the nature of the sins this person falls into, his soul stands at the level of the *al-nafs al-muṭmaʾinna* or *al-nafs al-rāḍiya* praised in Q 89:27.[94]

The second kind of individual is the one who returns to God after his sins, resolves to remain upright, and does not concern or preoccupy himself with thinking about his transgressions either with the purpose of lapsing in his repentance or because of a sweetness he finds in them. Despite the merit of his *tawba*, he is nevertheless tried by sins that he may occasionally fall into but without intending them beforehand (*ʿan ghayr qaṣad*). The sins that he is tried by, argues Makkī, are in a sense inevitable because their origin lies in the specific constitution of the human being, a unique makeup that derives from the range of elements found in the earth. The tests faced by the faithful who occupy this class are directly the result of the human constitution. This truth, for Makkī, is evinced by the thematic sequence of Q 76:2—"Lo! We created man from a drop of mingled fluid to try him (*nabtalīhi*)"—which addresses the inevitability of trial (*ibtilāʾ*) immediately after calling to mind the heterogonous nature of the human constitution. It is for this reason Makkī argues that the Qurʾān says "do not ascribe purity to yourselves" (Q 53:32), and the Prophet said, "the believer is tried and oft-repenting" (*al-muʾmin muftan tawwāb*),[95] without ascribing complete purity to the believers. Although the first group of *tāʾibūn* are also invariably tested by the sins that have their origin in the human composition, we can presume that in the eyes of Makkī they are less likely to fall into them than this group, and that if they do, they return to God with a *tawba* that is more perfect.

For Makkī, the sins that this second group falls into are the "small faults" that the Qur'ān speaks of in 53:32: "Those who avoid the enormities of sin and the abominations (*kabā'ir al-ithm wa al-fawāḥish*), except the unwilled offenses/small faults (*al-lamam*)." There seems to be some ambiguity, however, regarding whether this group can fall into *fawāḥish* because he quotes another verse that for him speaks of their ideal response to these sins: "And those who when they fall into an abomination (*fāḥisha*), or wrong themselves, remember God and seek forgiveness for their sins" (Q 3:135). Despite this ambiguity, what does seem clear is those who stand at this level of spiritual development avoid the major sins, and the slips that they fall into are not preceded by resolution or *mens rea*, a premeditated intention. Their *tawba*, though commendable, falls short in relation to the first group but surpasses the third group. The soul of the *tā'ib* who stands at this level is the *nafs al-lawwāma*, the self-reproaching soul of Q 75:2.

The third kind of person "sins, then repents, then returns to the sin, then is saddened on account of his intention to sin, his striving toward it, and his choosing it over obedience."[96] Although he has a propensity to postpone *tawba*, he nevertheless desires it but fails because of the strength of his lower soul. He admires the ranks of *tawwābīn* and the *ṣiddiqīn*, but his passion tends to get the better of him. Since the strength of his sinful habits holds him back from freeing himself from them, his *tawba* is lost from time to time. For Makkī, "he has mixed a good deed with an evil deed. It may be that God will forgive him."[97] The sinner of this class is stranded between two potential states: he may incline toward *tawba* out of his reverence for God, or he may fall prey to the inclinations of his entrenched habits and passions. Because of his inability to consistently return in *tawba*, his soul is self-deceived and beguiled (*wa nafs hādhā hiya al-musawwala*). Although the Qur'ān does not speak of a *nafs al-musawwala*, it does use the second form of the verbal root **s-w-l** on four occasions, and in each one to describe either Satan's wiles or self-deception.[98] The idea of a *nafs al-musawwala* therefore has scriptural basis, even though it is not as explicitly singled out in the Qur'ān in the same way as the other three well-known souls (of the first, second, and fourth groups).

The fourth kind of person is the most lackadaisical in matters pertaining to *tawba*. He "sins, then follows his sin with a similar or even greater one, persists in it, and resolves to commit it to the extent he is able. He does not intend repentance nor uphold uprightness." Such an individual does not even "hope for the Promise of reward (*al-wa'd*) by thinking good [of his Lord], nor does he fear the Threat of punishment (*al-wa'īd*)."[99] The soul of this person commands it to evil (*wa nafs hādhā hiya al-ammāra*). One should fear for this person an evil end (*sū' al-khātima*). Though a believer, his ultimate fate lies in the hands of God. He belongs to the class of "profligate sinners" (*fāsiqūn*) and is to be included, for Makkī, among those who "await God's decree" (Q 9:106).

A Comparison with the Classifications of Muḥāsibī and Ghazālī

Makkī's fourfold classification of *tā'ibūn* bears a few resemblances to the threefold classification of the believers in their "quest for godfearingness" (*ṭalab al-ṭaqwā*) that appears in the *Ri'āya*,[100] and which 'Abd al-Ḥalīm Maḥmūd used to classify the levels of the *tā'ibūn* in Muḥāsibī's thought.[101] While we cannot be certain that Makkī was directly influenced by Muḥāsibī in the construction of his fourfold scheme, we cannot entirely discount the possibility. It is not out of the question that in his tetradic classificatory scheme Makkī was simply expanding Muḥāsibī's triadic one found in the *Ri'āya*. As far as similarities go, the first and last groups for both Makkī and Muḥāsibī are virtually identical: the first in the promptness, purity, and completeness of their *tawba*, and the last in their total neglect of it. The only difference is that, for Muḥāsibī, those who belong to this group entertain the delusion of a good end, while for Makkī they are not much concerned, despite a nominal profession of faith, with their final state. The second class of pious believers in both schemes is also very similar: they constantly strive to ward off sin, promptly return to God in the aftermath of each slip, and struggle in their efforts to obey Him in all circumstances. Makkī and Muḥāsibī both cite the words of the Prophet to describe the believer who stands at this level, that he is "tried and oft-repenting" (*muftan tawwāb*).[102] If Makkī was employing Muḥāsibī's classification, he simply added another level to accommodate believers who, although of good intention, were less devout in their religious commitments. Muḥāsibīs's threefold division could have appeared, for Makkī, too restrictive to encompass the range of potential believer types.[103] Although a Muḥāsibīan influence insofar as the unique and peculiar features of his scheme are concerned is absent in Makkī (none of the nine Qur'ānic verses and *ḥadīth*s he uses to describe the levels of believers, for example, is quoted by Makkī, with the exception of the one cited above), when we consider the conceptual overlaps between the two schemes, as well as Makkī's incorporation of elements of the *Riʿāya* into the *Qūt* in other places,[104] at least some measure of Mūḥāsibīan influence cannot be entirely ruled out.

What is indisputable, however, is that Ghazālī's fourfold classification of *tāʾibūn* in his *Kitāb al-tawba* of the *Iḥyāʾ* is virtually a replication of Makkī's scheme.[105] Not only are most of the Qurʾānic verses and *ḥadīth*s Makkī brings to his discussion cited by Ghazālī, he even integrates Makkī's peculiar expressions into what becomes a slightly expanded—and clearer—analysis of the various groups, structured as a running commentary on Makkī's analysis. Some of the ambiguities in Makkī's schema are clarified by Ghazālī, such as the relation of the second group to "abominations." Ghazālī says that they avoid the "major sins from among the abominations (*kabāʾir al-fawāḥish*)" even though they may fall into minor forms of *fawāḥish*. The transition from the first to the second group is also clearer in Ghazālī. (In Makkī it is a bit difficult to determine where his description of the first class ends and the second begins.) Ghazālī's extension of Makkī's fourfold schema demonstrates, as a case in point, that he was able to do for his Sufi predecessor what he is widely credited with doing for the philosophers: articulate their doctrines with a clarity and lucidity they were unable to do themselves.

Does *Tawba* Ever Come to an End?

Despite the practical concerns of the *Qūt*, a feature of the text we have repeatedly drawn attention to in the course of this chapter, a few of Makkī's analyses broach areas typically explored in greater detail in more advanced mystical texts. Near the end of his chapter, shortly before his classification of the seven sins that the aspirant must avoid, or, if committed, immediately repent of, he goes into a short discussion of the requirements of *tawba naṣūḥ*, the "sincere repentance" of Q 66:8. One cannot, for Makkī, stand among the ranks of the *tawwābīn* loved by God[106] without fulfilling these requirements. The ten conditions with which Makkī opened his chapter lead up to and in a sense culminate in this complementary list, the first nine of which summarize many of the themes he has explored in the chapter. The main intention behind these conditions is to ensure that the *tāʾib*'s abandonment of what he has left for God be total and uncompromising. The *tawbāt* or "repentances" for *tawba naṣūḥ*, after the *tāʾib* (1) abandons the sin, are that he must turn away from (2) speaking of the sin, (3) all of its causes, (4) whatever is similar to the sin, (5) thinking about what he has left, (6) listening to those who speak of it, (7) his aspiration for it (*al-himma bihi*), (8) his deficiencies in fulfilling the rights of repentance,[107] and (9) not completely desiring the face of God in his *tawba*.[108] These nine requirements are confined to the themes that he has explored, in greater and lesser detail, over the course of the chapter. Makkī in a sense reiterates the steps the *tā'ib* must take to turn away from the sin both externally and internally, outwardly and inwardly.

It is in the tenth condition however that he introduces a new theme—central to many Sufi explorations—of the never-ending cycle of *tawba*. Makkī states that the final requirement of the aspiring *tawwāb* is that he should repent of bringing his repentance to a close.[109] According to this last stipulation, the process of *tawba* should never reach an end. The reason for this, argues Makkī, is that even after the aspirant is able to turn away from the particular sin, or sins, he is still tainted by deficiencies and less perceptible faults in his return to God. Following his abandonment of the sin or vice, he should repent of his shortcomings in fulfilling what is demanded by the right of divine Lordship (*min taqṣīrihi ʿan al-qiyām bi ḥaqq al-rubūbiyya*), and then, of what is demanded by the reality of his vision or witnessing of God (*min taqṣīrihi ʿan al-qiyām bi ḥaqīqat mushāhadatihi*).[110] To put it less opaquely, let us recall that *tawba* has two dimensions: turning away from the sin, on the one hand, and turning toward God, on the other. It comprises an "aversion" and a complementary "conversion," or spiritual "inversion," in which one labors to shift his focus from the created realm to his Origin. Makkī states that even when one succeeds in turning away from his sin, he will still fall short in the second half of *tawba*, in his turn toward God and in his *mushāhada* of His magnificence. This is a higher stage of *tawba*, and one that can be realistically pursued only by one who is not tried by the more elementary sins that afflict the common lot of believers. But for those who have already left them, their focus should be on perfecting *tawba*, and this perfection is possible only when the *tā'ib* realizes that since *tawba* is an unending process, he can never fulfill the conditions of *tawba naṣūḥ*. Paradoxically, only when he realizes this fact, that he is never free of its demands, does he fulfill its requirements and become a *tawwāb*.

The underlying reason that the return to God through repentance is never ending, at least in this world, is because of the inability of the human being to attain moral and spiritual perfection. Although the sins that one turns away from become subtler and more difficult to detect as the aspirant matures on the path, they never disappear. No one is ever free of faults, not even the most advanced of Sufis. "For everything he witnesses other than God," says Makkī, "there is a sin, and in every rest he finds in other than Him, there is blame."[111] Even the mystic who is absorbed in his contemplation of God will have to turn in *tawba* from a contemplation that is less perfect to one that is more perfect. This is why Makkī says that ultimately "there is no end for the *tawba* of the gnostic" (*lā nihāya li tawbat al-ʿārif*).[112] Since even the prophets did not shy away from *tawba*, how, asks Makkī, can those who do not stand at the prophetic rank feel absolved of the obligation to repent? He writes:

> For every station there is a repentance, and for every state from among a station there is a repentance, and for every act of witnessing (*mushāhada*) and unveiling (*mukāshafa*) there is a repentance. This is the state of the *tā'ib munīb* who is drawn close (*muqarrab*) to God and loved by Him (*ʿindahu ḥabīb*). This is the station of the one who is tried and oft-repenting (*muftan tawwāb*), meaning, tried and tested by things and yet oft-repenting (*tawwāb*) to God most High.[113]

On the basis of this passage, Makkī's position on the obligation to repent in all circumstances seems uncompromising. However, earlier in the chapter Makkī broaches a related subject, which we explored in some detail in chapter 5, where he takes a view that might appear to conflict, at least on the surface, with the position he takes above. In the debate that occurred in early Sufism as to whether *tawba* should entail never forgetting one's sin, or never remembering it, recall that Makkī acknowledged that the latter view represented a position more appropriate for advanced Sufis. He saw turning away from the remembrance of sins to engage in the remembrance of God to be a higher form of *tawba*, but not necessarily appropriate for novices. Thus, he argued (to return to an earlier passage):

> Some of them have said that the reality of repentance is that you [always] place the sin before your two eyes. Another group has said that the reality of repentance is that you forget your sin. These are the approaches of the two groups, and the states of the folk of the two stations. As for the remembrance of sins, the way of the aspirants and the state of the fearful

> ones bring forth for them, through the remembrance of sins, perpetual grief and an inescapable fear. As for the forgetting of sins because one is preoccupied with the remembrance of God and what one puts forward by way of an increase in acts of worship, this is the way of the gnostics and the state of the lovers [of God]. Their goal is witnessing divine unity, and this is a station of knowing. The goal of the first group on the other hand is observing the boundaries and limits, and this is a station of propriety [. . . but . . .] the station of witnessing divine unity is superior, in the eyes of the gnostics, to observing propriety.[114]

If Makkī sees immersing oneself in the contemplation of God to be superior to remembering one's sins, then does his view that one must always strive to eliminate his shortcomings, regardless of the level of his mystical standing, lead to a contradiction, or at least a tension, in his views? It might, if we understand the second position to amount to an abandoning of repentance altogether, as many of the Sufis did who used Junayd's position to develop the concept of "repenting of repentance" (*tark al-tawba*). For these Sufis, forgetting one's sins because of one's absorption in the contemplation of God meant, essentially, that one had reached a stage at which he was no longer preoccupied either with himself or his faults. Since repentance necessitated giving attention to one's faults in order to turn away from them, forgetting one's faults meant, for these Sufis, also to forget one's *tawba*, or to abandon *tawba* altogether. Ibn al-ʿArabī argued that the *tāʾib* is in a state of distance from his divine origin because he is preoccupied with a return through *tawba*.[115] The *tāʾibūn*, he said, are the exiled ones because only those in a state of exile (*ḥāl al-ghurba*) strive to come back to their home. "There is no exile for the one who has returned to his family," wrote Ibn al-ʿArabī, "except for the absent one (*al-ghāʾib*), and the absent one is in exile, and the exiled ones are the *tāʾibūn*."[116] Sometimes this concept of *tark al-tawba* was also expressed through the idea of repenting of repentance, of *tawba al-tawba* or *al-tawba min al-tawba*, as in the case of the Andalusian Ibn al-ʿArīf (d. 1141), when he poetically declared, "many have repented, but no one has repented of repentance but I" (*qad tāba aqwām kathīr, wa mā tāba min al-tawba illā anā*).[117] Ruwaym (d. 915)[118] was perhaps one of the earliest Sufi figures to speak in such terms. For Sarrāj, his expression conveyed the fundamental import of Junayd's definition:

> As for the response of Junayd, may God have mercy on him, that [*tawba* entails] one forget his sin, it refers to the *tawba* of the realized ones (*al-muḥaqqiqīn*) who do not recall their sins as a result of what has overcome their hearts of the Majesty of God, and of the persistence of their remembrance of Him. This is similar to [the response of] Ruwaym b. Ahmad, may God have mercy on him, when he was asked about *tawba* and said that it is *tawba* from *tawba* (*al-tawba min al-tawba*).[119]

Since to repent of something is to leave it, by drawing a parallel between Ruwaym's words and those of Junayd, Sarrāj saw that Junayd's definition of *tawba* could imply turning away from *tawba* altogether. It is true that many authorities, including Sarrāj, understand that *al-tawba min al-tawba* could also mean repenting of the deficiencies in one's repentance, which is to say, repenting of falling short in fulfilling its requirements. This, for example, is how Kalābādhī explained Ruwaym's words. He wrote that what Ruwaym meant was no different from Rābiʿa al-ʿAdawiyya when she said, "I seek forgiveness from my little sincerity in my saying, 'I seek forgiveness from God.' "[120] But although this later interpretation of *al-tawba min al-tawba* was common,[121] it did not necessarily preclude the first one. One could understand the expression in both senses, commensurate with the level of the mystic. There were figures who objected to the first interpretation, such as Ibn Qayyim al-Jawziyya (d. 1350) who vehemently opposed the idea of abandoning *tawba* altogether in his commentary on Anṣārī's own advice in the *Manāzil al-sāʾirīn* to "repent of repentance." "Repentance is among the greatest of good deeds," wrote Ibn al-Qayyim, "and to repent of good deeds is of the greatest of evil deeds, nay it is [outright] disbelief" (*bal huwa al-kufr*). Although he accepted the idea of *tawba min al-tawba,* what it meant for him is that the individual "repents from the shortcoming of repentance" (*nuqṣān al-tawba*).[122] What is significant for our purposes, however, is that numerous Sufi authorities interpreted Junayd's words to imply the possibility of leaving *tawba* at a certain level of mystic realization.

Despite these interpretations of Junayd, he himself did not explicitly speak of turning away from or abandoning *tawba* based on our sources. When he said that *tawba* is to forget one's sin, he simply defined the *tawba* of advanced mystics, but without stipulating that the mystic should ever leave *tawba* altogether. By preferring Junayd's definition of *tawba* for more realized individuals, Makkī does not necessarily contradict himself. The apparent inconsistency is based on an interpretation of Junayd's definition that is not necessarily forced upon us by his own words. It is not surprising that Makkī does not quote Ruwaym anywhere in his chapter on *tawba*. Since both Kalābādhī and Sarrāj in their own works, authored around the same time as the *Qūt*, cite Ruwaym's words in their much shorter chapters on *tawba*, we can presume that Makkī, though familiar with his expression, wished to avoid any confusion quoting him might create in the minds of his readers.

Finally, Makkī's insistence on the never-ending process of *tawba* should not be seen as a pietistic attempt to defend a scriptural and prophetic mandate. It is also rooted in a particular conception of the mystic journey that understands the journey to God as infinite, without a terminal point. As long as the path is understood in such terms, the need for constant *tawba* makes complete sense. It is only when one presumes that the journey can be completed in this world, in a state of permanent mystical annihilation or "arrival" (*wuṣūl*), can one see the rationale behind turning away from repentance altogether. The origin of the problem of whether *tawba* can ever come to an end thus rests on how one understands the nature of the mystic goal.

To summarize the results of our analysis of Makkī's treatment of *tawba*, it is, as we have seen, first and foremost directed at the practical needs of the spiritual aspirant. To this end he stipulates a number of requirements necessary in order for repentance to be sound and therefore acceptable to God. *Tawba* is obligatory for all sins because without it the sinner stands in the perilous state of potentially facing the consequences of his misdeeds in the form of divine punishment. Unless God decides to forgive his offenses through an act of Mercy, *tawba* remains the only way to escape such a consequence. The requirements of *tawba*, as we have also seen, are both external and internal. Externally, the *tā'ib* is called to avoid those circumstances that might tempt him to repeat the offense, while internally he must strive to eradicate the impulses that attract him to the sin. Moreover, he must feel regret for his wrong, strive to rectify his past mistake, and follow the misdeed with pious acts as a display of the seriousness of his commitment to *tawba*. The entire process is taxing and laborious, and calls for patience, struggle, and beseeching divine help. We can better appreciate how Makkī unifies and inter-relates the virtues within his mystical psychology by observing how the process of repentance integrates these other key virtues. Although Makkī briefly touches on themes dealt with in greater detail in more advanced mystical texts, his primary focus, as we have seen, is to provide the aspirant with a manual through which he can take concrete steps to return to his own origin in God.

Conclusion

ʿAṭṭār recounts a story in the *Tadhkirat* from the life of al-Ḥakīm al-Tirmidhī. When he was a young man, it so happened that a woman of great beauty once offered herself to him. Fearing for his soul, he refused, with the rejection only serving to inflame the woman's passion even more. Learning of his whereabouts in a garden not long afterward, she sought to seduce him yet again, with her advances refused a second time. Intent this time around on vengeance, she decided to make a public spectacle by openly accusing him of unwarranted advances. Immediately, Tirmidhī fled, managing to escape from the scene by jumping over a wall. Later in old age, as he was recounting the deeds of his life, the episode crossed his mind. "What would it have mattered," he thought, "if I gratified the woman's need? After all, I was young and could afterward have repented." No sooner had the idea occurred to him that he fell into a state of penitent remorse. "Foul and rebellious soul," he reproached himself. "Forty years ago, in the first flush of youth, this thought did not occur. Now in old age, after so many struggles, from where has come this repining over a sin not committed?" For three days he remained in a state of contrition, until the Prophet finally appeared to him in a dream. "Do not grieve," he consoled him. "What happened was not due to a lapse on your part. This thought occurred to you because forty years more had passed since my death. What you experienced was due to the long extension of the period of my departure from the world, not any deficiency in your character."[1]

While the story does not seem to be present in the early sources, at least not in the material that has been examined in our study, and while it remains absent in Tirmidhī's own autobiography, its moral is not incongruous with what can be found in the early textual tradition. ʿAṭṭār uses the tale to illustrate the loss of divine grace that gradually set in after the Prophet's departure from the world. No less important, however, is its message of the power of *tawba*, attested to by Tirmidhī's passing thought that, had he succumbed to temptation, all that would have been required of him was to repent. *Tawba,* he recognized, can wash the slate clean—a belief, as we have seen in our study, that permeates Islamic revelation. "Despair not of the Mercy of God," says the Qur᾿ān to those "who have been prodigal against their own souls," for "verily God forgives all sins" (Q 39:53). And "God desires to turn to you [in *tawba*]," we read elsewhere (Q 4:27). Similarly, the *ḥadīth* literature is replete with such traditions as "he who repents is as if he never sinned,"[2] and "all of the children of Adam are sinners, and the best of sinners are the *tawwābūn*."[3]

It is true that, unlike the Mu῾tazilites, the vast majority of Sunni theologians did not hold that God is technically obliged to forgive the *tā᾿ib*.[4] While such a view rested primarily on a desire to preserve divine omnipotence—a characteristic feature of mainstream Sunni *kalām*—it also brought with it certain psychological and spiritual benefits that those who advocated it were certainly not unaware of. By freeing God from the fetters of necessity and obligation, it prevented the *tā᾿ib* from ever feeling secure in his repentance, thereby confining him to a state of fear and hope. At the same time, the doctrine could not eclipse the overwhelming reality of God's Mercy and Forgiveness, affirmed repeatedly throughout the scriptural sources of Islam, and which virtually guaranteed the acceptance of the sinner's repentance—provided he earnestly sought to fulfill its conditions. *Tawba,* in this light, offered a mechanism for the atonement of past wrongs through which the sinner could come, as close as possible, to freeing himself from the consequences of his own transgressions. If the blood of Christ washed away sins in Christian theology, the tears of the *tā᾿ibūn*, coupled with moral rectification (*iṣlāḥ*) and hope in divine Mercy, washed them away in Islam. Tirmidhī's confidence that had he slipped *tawba* would have been sufficient reflected a knowledge of its saving grace.

Throughout the course of this work we have seen how *tawba* was understood in the early Sufi tradition not only as repentance for individual sins, but as an entire process of returning to God. To the extent that it marked the beginning of the journey, it signified death and rebirth, an "interior conversion" in which a nominal allegiance to the religion of one's birth was replaced by a complete and unwavering commitment to the spiritual life, one that brought with it an "aversion" or "turning away" from everything that stood in the way to God. Since it marked the first stage of the spiritual ascent, it was only natural that the most extensive treatments of the concept would focus on practical considerations, or *muʿāmalāt*, in aiding and abetting the seeker to overcome the seductive power of vice and sin. To this end, the early masters provided specific methods that would help the traveler in his efforts, all the way from encouraging him to part from foul company and suspect food to practicing silence and consciously redirecting his thoughts to nobler ends. Since repentance was believed to be an all-encompassing process of catharsis and inner-purification, the authorities required of the *tāʾib*, particularly as we saw in the case of Muḥāsibī, to uproot not only the "sins of the limbs" but also "sins of the heart"—such weeds as envy, pride, and insincerity, through a "turning inward," or interiorization of conscience. Yet, despite the overwhelming focus on *praxis* in the early tradition, the spiritual authorities did not entirely shy away from exploring more abstract theoretical or esoteric questions related to sin and repentance, particularly when it came to addressing the higher stages of the path where the line became blurred between *praxis* and gnosis, between *muʿāmala* and *mukāshafa*. We saw this in the case of Junayd, when he explained the nature of *tawba* in light of the primordial Covenant, as well as Wāsiṭī, in his disquisitions on the effect of divine determination of acts on human agency, sinfulness, and repentance.

A number of central questions related to *tawba* would be explored in much greater detail in later tradition, even though their seeds were planted earlier on. Among the most important of these revolved around the relation between the one who had managed to remain free from a given sin, and the one who fell into it and repented. Which of these two was superior in the eyes of God? Makkī had very briefly touched on this question, partly by drawing on the Qurʾānic verse, "They will be given their rewards twice over because they are patient and overcome evil with good" (Q 28:54). Interpreting the passage as a reference to the penitent, he claimed that because the *tāʾib* received two rewards—one for his patience in turning away from sin, and the other for the *iṣlāḥ* that accompanied repentance—the state of *tawba* was superior to that of undefiled purity. But he did not explore the question in any depth, nor draw out its broader implications, only addressing it in passing within the context of a larger discussion on the eminence of repentance.[5] It would be left up to a figure such as Ibn al-ʿArabī more than two centuries later to explain perhaps more comprehensively than anyone before him exactly why it was the *tāʾib* stood at a rank above that of the undefiled believer.

Drawing on the figure of Adam, the Andalusian mystic argued that Adam's "perfection" (*kamāl*) was in fact a "completeness," one that brought together not only the luminosity of the angels, but also the bestial qualities of animals, as well as the darker, rebellious capacities of demons. Adam's sin and repentance—transhistorical mythical events central to Muslim consciousness—signified for him not an imperfection in his constitution, but a wholeness, one through which his own rank surpassed even that of the angels. Moreover, because Adam's configuration contained both the exalted and degenerate qualities of existence, he had within himself the capacity to function as a microcosm for *wujūd*. Michael Sells drew attention to this feature of Ibn al-ʿArabi's thought with respect to Adam when he observed that the "strongly ascetic tendency of much of early Sufism was spiritualist in character. The goal of the Sufi path was to shed one's humanity and to become as 'perfect' (*kāmil*) as possible. Although Ibn al-ʿArabī maintained the ethical seriousness of the early Sufis, he placed the Sufi life [. . .] in a new context." "Adam's central place in the cosmos," he went on to state, was due not so much to his moral perfection as much as it was to his completeness, "in the sense of embracing all realities of existence."[6] In this light, Adam's sin and repentance served only to raise his standing before God. Ibn al-ʿArabī was not unaware of the scriptural objection that would be raised by those who might contest such an interpretation of the first man. How would he respond to the fact that his sin occasioned a banishment from Paradise, attested to by the famous verse in which God apparently castigates him and Eve by ordering them to "go down!" (*fahbiṭ*) (Q 7:13) as a seeming punishment for their transgression? His response was that the *hubūṭ* or "descent" was a "descent of rulership (*wilāya*) and vicegerency (*istikhlāf*) not a descent of banishment"—it was "a descent from place and not from level."[7] The expulsion from Paradise, coupled by *tawba*, allowed Adam to realize his own latent capacity for wholeness and completion, and thereby rise above all created beings to become a perfect theophany of God.

A similar view regarding the superiority of the *tāʾib* was supported by Rūmī, but along more practical lines. He likened the *tāʾib* to a thief who reformed himself and became a policeman. "All the tricks of thievery that he used to practice now become powers on behalf of good and justice," he declared. "Indeed, he is superior to policemen who were not formerly thieves because a policeman who has committed theft knows the ways of the thieves—that is, the habits of thieves are not unknown to him." Rūmī felt that if such a man were to become a *shaykh*, his counsel and instruction would be unmatched. Aware of the psychological intricacies that keep a soul entangled in vice, he would be able to guide novices with greater mastery and skill than anyone else on how to repent and return to God.[8]

Yet another issue that would be explored in greater detail would be the value that sinfulness followed by repentance could have on the spiritual life. As Ibn ʿAṭāʾ Allāh declared in one of his aphorisms, "it may be that He will decree for you a sin and make it a means of arrival;"[9] or as he declared in another, "a sin which bequeaths humiliation and need is better than obedience which bequeaths hubris and pride."[10] While such teachings were certainly not absent in the earlier texts, as we saw in the conversion accounts of Fuḍayl b. ʿIyāḍ and Ibrāhīm b. Adham, they were not emphasized. In keeping with the more ascetic impulses of the earlier tradition, the Sufi authorities generally did not draw attention to the benefits of sin. Such a theme, however, would become more prominent in the later tradition, where the Sufi masters would take an approach that seemed to reflect a greater awareness of the frailties of human nature.

An engaging didactic tale centered on this very theme is to be found in Rūmī's *Mathnawī*. One early morning, the caliph Muʿāwiya was awoken in his chambers by a mysterious figure who turned out to be Iblīs. "The time for prayer has all but come to an end," the devil informs him, "you must run quickly to the mosque." Sensing a ruse, Muʿāwiya pressed him to reveal his real intentions. After all, why would Iblīs, whose job is to ensure that human beings fall short of fulfilling the obligations of faith, wake up the caliph for this very end? "If a thief were to come into my dwelling place and inform me that 'I am keeping watch,'" declared Muʿāwiya, "why would I believe the thief?" Following a lengthy debate between the two, the devil finally confessed his true motives:

> If the time for prayer had passed, this world would have become dark to you and without a gleam of light. And then from disappointment and grief tears would have flowed from your eyes in the fashion of water from water skins. Since everyone takes delight in some act of devotion and cannot bear to miss it even for a short while, that disappointment and grief would have been as a hundred prayers. What is ritual prayer in comparison to the spiritual glow of humble supplication?[11]

Iblīs feared that the sincerity of his repentance for having missed the morning canonical prayer would have drawn him closer to God than the prayer itself. Far from conceiving of *tawba* simply as a method of atoning for sins, Rūmī saw it as a means through which the soul could be catapulted into the divine presence, like an arrow pulled backward on a bow, away from its goal, only to be swiftly propelled toward its target. It was for this reason that the Persian mystic stressed that the doors of repentance remain open so long as the angel of death does not make his appearance, since as long as one is alive, it is never too late to repent and return to God. *Tawba,* he declared, is

> A door from the West until the day
> When the sun rises in the West.[12]

Notes

Introduction

1. For a brief analysis of the universal human experience of sin, see Christoph von Furer-Haimendorf, "The Sense of Sin in Cross-Cultural Perspective," *Man* 9, no. 4 (1974): 539–556. See also Edward L. Schaub, "The Consciousness of Sin," *Harvard Theological Review* 5, no. 1 (1912): 121–138. For the idea of sin in some of the major world religions, see Eric J. Sharpe and John R. Hinnells, eds., *Man and His Salvation: Studies in Memory of S.G.F. Brandon* (New Jersey, 1973). See also *Encyclopedia of Religion*, s.v. "Sin and Guilt;" *Routledge Encyclopedia of Philosophy*, s.v. "Sin." For a more popular but insightful treatment of the history of sin from a progressive Christian theological perspective, see John Portman, *A History of Sin: Its Evolution to Today and Beyond* (Lanham, MD: Rowman and Littlefield, 2007).

2. For an excellent comparative survey of this concept in Judaism, Christianity, Islam, Hinduism, and Buddhism, see the essays in Amitai Etzioni and David E. Carney, eds., *Repentance: A Comparative Perspective* (Lanham, MD: Rowman and Littlefied, 1997). For a focus on repentance in the Abrahamic traditions, see Adriana Destro and Mauro Pesce, eds., *Rituals and Ethics: Patterns of Repentance in Judaism, Christianity, Islam* (Paris-Louvain: Peeters, 2004). See also Meir Dan-Cohen, *Revising the Past: on the Metaphysics of Repentance, Forgiveness, and Pardon* (Toronto: University of Toronto, 2006).

3. A.J. Wensinck, *Concordance et indices de la tradition musulmane* (1943; repr., Leiden: Brill, 1992), 1:284.

4. The best general survey of *tawba* in the Islamic tradition is to be found in Mahmoud Ayoub's "Repentance in the Islamic Tradition," in *Repentance: A Comparative Perspective*, 96–121. To this we should also add Ida Zilio-Grandi's recent "Return, Repentance, Amendment, Reform, Reconversion: A Contribution to the Study of *Tawba* in the Context of Islamic Ethics," *Islamochristiana* 39 (2013): 71–91.

5. See Frederick Denny, "The Qur'anic Vocabulary of Repentance: Orientations and Attitudes," *Journal of the American Academy of Religion* (Thematic Issue

S) 47, no. 4 (1980): 649–664. Uri Rubin's short piece on *tawba* in the *Encyclopedia of the Qur'ān* is also useful. See *EQ*, s.v. "Repentance."

6. Syed Muʿazzam has looked at the jurisprudence of *tawba* based on a study of the Qur'ān in his short article, "Effect of *Tauba* (Repentance) on Penalty in Islam," *Islamic Studies* 8 (1969): 189–198.

7. Joseph van Ess provides a theological overview of *tawba* in *Theologie und Gesellshaft im 2. und 3. Jahrhundert Hidschra. Eine Geschichte des religiösen Denkens in frühen Islam* (Berlin: Walter de Gruyter, 1991–1997), 4:579–590. Chawkat Moucarry presents the theological positions in a clear and remarkably structured way in *The Search for Forgiveness: Pardon and Punishment in Islam and Christianity* (England: Inter-Varsity Press, 2004). But the overall scholarly merit of the work is marred by the evangelical spirit that guides it, evidenced by the author's effort to demonstrate the superiority of the Protestant Christian position at the end of each chapter. See also Mokdad Arfa Mensia, "Théories du repentir chez théologiens musulmans classiques," in *Rituals and Ethics: Patterns of Repentance in Judaism, Christianity, Islam*, 107–123; Mongia Arfa Mensia, "L'acte expiatoire en Islam: 'Al-Kaffāra,'" in idem, 125–139; Maurice A. Pomerantz, "Muʿtazilī Theory in Practice: The Repentance (*tawba*) of Government Officials in the 4th/10th century," in *A Common Rationality: Muʿtazilism in Islam and Judaism*, eds. Camilla Adang, Sabine Schmidtke and David Sklare (Würzburg: Ergon Verlag, 2007), 463–493.

8. See G.R. Hawting, "The Tawwābūn, Atonement and ʿAshūrā'," *Jerusalem Studies in Arabic and Islam* 17 (1994): 166–181; Ayoub, "Repentance in the Islamic Tradition," 114–117. Imām Zayn al-ʿĀbidīn's prayer of *tawba* (*munājāt al-tā'ibīn*) can be found in *Saḥīfat al-sajjādiyya al-kāmila: The Psalms of Islam*, trans. William C. Chittick (repr., Qum: Ansariyan Publications, 2006), 481–485.

9. See Philip F. Kennedy, *The Wine Song in Classical Arabic Poetry: Abū Nuwās and the Literary Tradition* (Oxford: Oxford University Press, 1997), 194–240. Mention should also be made of the English translation of a work that some consider to be the first major Urdu novel, Maulana Nazīr Ahmad's (1836–1912) *Tawbat al-naṣūḥ*. See Nazir Ahmad, *The Repentance of Nussooh (Taubat al-Nasuh)*, trans. M. Kempson (1884; repr., Delhi: Permanent Black, 2004). For a critical analysis of this work based on the original Urdu, see Christina Oesterheld, "Nazir Ahmad and the Early Urdu Novel: Some Observations," *Annual of Urdu Studies* 16 (2001): 27–41, especially 31–39. See also Francis Robinson's review of the English edition in the *Journal of the Royal Asiatic Society* 14, no. 3 (2004): 285. Both of these reviewers seem to miss the word play in the title: Nussooh is both the name of the novel's protagonist as the well as the "sincere" *tawba* the Qur'ān demands in 66:8.

10. See Montgomery Watt, "Conversion in Islam at the Time of the Prophet," *Journal of the American Academy of Religion* (Thematic Issue S) 47, no. 4 (1980): 726. Yohanan Friedmann has explored the requirements of conversion from a classical legal perspective in "Conditions of Conversion in Early Islam," in *Rituals and Ethics: Patterns of Repentance in Judaism, Christianity, Islam*, 95–106.

11. See Hava Lazarus-Yafeh, "Is There a Concept of Redemption in Islam?" in *Some Religious Aspects of Islam* (Leiden: Brill, 1981), 48–57; and Muzammil Husain Siddiqui, "The Doctrine of Redemption: A Critical Study," in *Islamic Perspectives: Studies in Honor of Mawlānā Sayyid Abul A'lā Mawdūdī*, eds. Khurshid Ahmad and Zafar Ansari (United Kingdom: Islamic Foundation, 1979), 91–102.

12. The specialized academic literature on *tawba* in Sufism is scarce. Gerhard Böwering has briefly explored some aspects of *tawba* in the early period in his excellent essay, "Early Sufism Between Persecution and Heresy," in *Islamic Mysticism: Thirteen Centuries of Controversies and Polemics*, eds. Frederick De Jong and Bernd Radtke (Leiden: Brill, 1999), 45–67. Laury Silvers has done a fine job in examining *tawba* in Wāsiṭī's thought in "Theoretical Sufism in the Early Period: With an Introduction to the Thought of Abū Bakr al-Wāsiṭī (d. ca 320/928) on the Interrelationship between Theoretical and Practical Sufism," *Studia Islamica* 98/99 (2004): 71–94. Ayoub has a few remarks on Sufi approaches to *tawba* in "Repentance in the Islamic Tradition," 111–114. There have been a few works on *tawba* in Ghazālī. The *Kitāb al-tawba* of the *Iḥyā' 'ulūm al-dīn* was translated by Martin Stern in *Al-Ghazzali on Repentance* (New Delhi: Sterling Publishers, 1990). See also Martin Stern, "Notes on the Theology of Ghazzali's Concept of Repentance," *The Islamic Quarterly* 23, no. 2 (1979): 82–98; Susan Wilzer, "Untersuchungen zu Ġazzālis Kitāb al-Tauba," *Der Islam* 32 (1957): 237–309; idem, 33 (1958): 51–120; idem, 34 (1959): 128–137. For a comparative study of *tawba* in the thought of Ghazālī and two important medieval Jewish thinkers, a philosopher and a mystic, see M.S. Stern, "Al-Ghazzālī, Maimonides, and Ibn Paqūda on Repentance: A Comparative Model," *Journal of the American Academy of Religion* 47, no. 4 (1979): 589–607. For the Qur'ānic language of *tawba* within a Sufi context, see Hussein Ali Akash, *Die sufische Koranauslegung: Semantik und Deutungsmechanismen der išārī-Exegese* (Berlin: Klaus Schwarz Verlag, 2006), 183–190. There was also a doctoral dissertation completed at the University of Edinburgh in 1991 by W. Amin, entitled "An Evaluation of the Qūt al-Qulūb of al-Makkī with an Annotated Translation of his Kitāb al-Tawba," which remains unpublished. Works with very general observations on *tawba* in Sufism are too numerous to cite, as well as those with a few passing cursory remarks on *tawba* in the thought of individual Sufi figures.

13. Michael Sells, *Early Islamic Mysticism: Sufi, Qur'an, Mi'raj, Poetic, and Theological Writings* (New York: Paulist Press, 1996), 17–26; cf. idem. "Heart-Secret, Intimacy, and Awe in Formative Sufism," in *The Shaping of an American Islamic Discourse: A Memorial to Fazlur Rahman*, eds. Earle H. Waugh and Frederick M. Denny (Atlanta: Scholars Press for the University of South Florida, University of Rochester, and Saint Louis University, 1998), 165–166.

14. Sells, *Early Islamic Mysticism*, 18; cf. Ahmet Karamustafa, *Sufism: The Formative Period* (Berkeley: University of California Press, 2007), 83.

15. Some important scholarly contributions to our knowledge of early Sufism, particularly of the first phase of the founders, can be found in the

following works: Ali Hasan Abdel Kader, *The Life, Personality, and Writings of Junayd* (London: E.W.J Gibb Memorial, 1976); Kenneth Avery, *Shiblī: His Life and Thought in the Sufi Tradition* (Albany: State University of New York Press, 2014); Gerhard Böwering, *The Mystical Vision of Existence in Classical Islam: The Qur'ānic Hermeneutics of the Sufi Sahl al-Tustarī* (Berlin: Walter De Gruyter, 1980); Richard Gramlich, *Abu l-ʿAbbās b. ʿAṭāʾ: Sufi und Koranausleger* (Stuggart: F. Steiner, 1995); *Alte Vorbilder des Sufitums*, 2 vols. (Wiesbaden: Harrasowitz Verlag, 1995–1996); Ahmet Karamustafa's excellent historical overview, *Sufism: The Formative Period*, is one of the best contributions to our knowledge of the early period; Louis Massignon, *Essay on the Origins of the Technical Language of Islamic Mysticism*, trans. Benjamin Clark (Notre Dame, IN: University of Notre Dame Press, 1997); idem, *The Passion of Ḥallāj*, 4 vols., trans. Herbert Mason (Princeton, NJ: Princeton University Press, 1982); Paul Nwyia, *Exégèse coranique et langage mystique* (Beirut: Dār el-Machreq, 1970); Gavin Picken, *Spiritual Purification in Islam: The Life and Works of al-Muḥāsibī* (London: Routledge, 2011); Bernd Radtke, *The Concept of Sainthood in Early Islamic Mysticism: Two Works by al-Ḥakīm al-Tirmidhī* (Surrey: Curzon Press, 1996); John Renard, *Knowledge of God in Classical Sufism* (New York: Paulist Press, 2004), 19–26; Sells, *Early Islamic Mysticism*, 75–96, 151–303; Laury Silvers, *A Soaring Minaret: Abu Bakr al-Wasiti and the Rise of Baghdadi Sufism* (Albany: State University of New York Press, 2010); Margaret Smith, *An Early Mystic of Baghdad: A Study of the Life and Teaching of Ḥārith B. Asad al-Muḥāsibī A.D. 781–857* (1935; repr., London: Sheldon Press, 1977); idem, *Rābiʿa the Mystic, A.D. 717–801, and Her Fellow Saints in Islam* (Cambridge: Cambridge University Press, 1928); Joseph van Ess, *Die Gedankenwelt des Ḥārith al-Muḥāsibī* (Bonn: Selbstverlag des Orientalischen Seminars der Universität Bonn, 1961); Saeko Yazaki, *Islamic Mysticism and Abū Ṭālib al-Makkī: The Role of the Heart* (London: Routledge, 2013). The following surveys of the historical development of Sufism also contain useful sections on the formative period: A.J. Arberry, *Sufism: An Account of the Mystics of Islam* (repr., New York: Dover Publications, 2002); Nile Green, *Sufism: A Global History* (West Sussex, UK: Wiley-Blackwell, 2012); Alexander Knysh, *Islamic Mysticism: A Short History* (Leiden: Brill, 2000); Marijan Molé, *Les mystiques musulmane* (Paris: Presses Universitaires de France, 1965); Annemarie Schimmel, *Mystical Dimensions of Islam* (Chapel Hill: University of North Carolina Press, 1975). Margaret Smith's study of Christian and Muslim mysticism, though dated, is also helpful in attempting to reconstruct the social and religious context of early Sufism: *Studies in Early Mysticism in the Near East* (1931; repr., Amsterdam: Philo Press, 1973), 103–143.

16. Victor Danner, "The Necessity for the Rise of the Term Sufi," *Studies in Comparative Religion* 6, no. 2 (1973): 71–77; Paul Heck, "Sufism—What Is It Exactly?" *Religion Compass* 1, no. 1 (2007): 152; Fritz Meier, "The Mystic Path," in *The World of Islam: Faith, People, Culture*, ed. Bernard Lewis (London: Thames and Hudson, 1976), 118. See also Green's useful discussion in *Sufism: A Global History*, 16–23.

17. Knysh, *Islamic Mysticism*, 6; Sells, *Early Islamic Mysticism*, 20. See also Christopher Melchert, "The transition from asceticism to mysticism at the middle of the ninth century," *Studia Islamica* 83, no. 1 (1996): 51–70.

18. There is also the issue when dealing with important historical figures of the authenticity of their transmitted sayings, particularly on highly contentious theological issues. Ḥasan al-Baṣrī, for example, was presented in later tradition as both a proponent and opponent of the doctrine of free will.

19. Laury Silvers, "Theoretical Sufism in the Early Period," 71.

20. It must be kept in mind that any single definition of Sufism cannot embrace all of its facets nor do justice to its multifarious expressions. Within Sufi discourse itself, this problem was acutely felt. See Tamar Frank, "'*Taṣawwuf* is . . .': On a Type of Mystical Aphorism," *Journal of the American Oriental Society* 104, no. 1 (1984): 73–80.

21. By speaking of "practical Sufism" I do not wish to artificially polarize it against "theoretical Sufism." As the principal figures of theoretical Sufism made it very clear, one could only properly grasp the perspective of theoretical Sufism after fully putting into practice and internalizing the precepts of practical Sufism. Theoretical and practical Sufism are therefore organically related. We can, however, make a useful hermeneutic distinction, and speak of two genres of Sufi texts, one concerned with *praxis* (*muʿāmala*), and the other with theoretically describing the nature of reality on the basis of mystical experience (*dhawq*) and unveiling (*mukāshafa*). For a brief discussion of these two kinds of texts within Sufi discourse, see Chittick, *Faith and Practice of Islam: Three Thirteenth Century Sufi Texts* (Albany: State University of New York Press, 1992), 16–21. We can describe the latter texts as "esoteric" even though some scholars (such as Chittick) eschew the term due to its often misleading occultist connotations. But if we understand that these texts also describe the inner life of the soul, then the word, to the extent that it is understood etymologically, is not entirely inappropriate. These texts can also be described as "theosophical," since they are concerned with knowledge and wisdom (*sophia*) of God (*theos*). But once again, the term has to be used with the same caution as "esoteric" for similar reasons. We can also speak of them as "metaphysical" insofar as they describe what lies beyond (*meta*) the sensory, physical world, or even more importantly, insofar as they describe Being *qua* Being.

22. Fritz Meier, "The Mystic Path," in *The World of Islam: Faith, People, Culture*, ed. Bernard Lewis (London: Thames and Hudson, 1976), 118.

23. *Mujāhada* can also be translated as "spiritual combat," "ascetic self-discipline," "self-mortification," or "devotional exercise." The more literal sense of the term ("struggle") highlights the place of effort and exertion in the *tawba* process, particularly in relation to overcoming the renewed temptation to sin. This sense of the term is also conveyed in the Qurʾān, in such verses as, "Those, who strive (*jāhadū*) in Us, We shall surely guide them to Our paths" (Q 29:69).

24. See Jawid A. Mojaddedi, *The Biographical Tradition in Sufism: The* ṭabaqāt *genre from al-Sulamī to Jāmī* (Surrey: Curzon, 2001), 1.

Chapter 1

1. *The Century Dictionary and Cyclopedia,* 2nd ed., s.v. "Repentance;" *Oxford English Dictionary,* 2nd ed., s.v. "Repentance."

2. T.G. Tucker, *A Concise Etymological Dictionary of Latin* (Halle: Maz Niemeyer Verlag, 1931), 177; F.E.J. Valpy, *An Etymological Dictionary of the Latin Language* (London: Baldwin and Co., 1838), 349.

3. Some have argued that repentance is etymologically related to *punishment, pen-ality, pun-itive, pain,* and *pen-ance,* all of which derive from the Latin *poena* (punishment, penalty), which, according to these scholars, is related to *paenitēre* (Eric Partridge, *A Short Etymological Dictionary of Modern English* [London: Routledge, 1961], 463; Walter W. Skeat, *An Etymological Dictionary of the English Language* [Oxford: Oxford University Press, 1924], 423; Valpy, 349). It is no doubt on the basis of this etymological connection that Valpy asserts that *paenitēre* may also refer to that "after concern and pain which acts as a retribution and punishment for offences" (349). This etymological link, if true, potentially broadens the semantic field of repentance to include notions of punishment, pain, and penalty. This etymological relation between *poena* and *paenitēre,* however, has been explicitly denied by others, such as Tucker and Klien, the latter of whom writes that "the spelling poenitet [a variant of *paenitet,* third person singular of the infinitive *paenitēre*], etc., is due to the influence of L. poena, to which, however, paenitet is not related" (Ernest Klien, *A Comprehensive Etymological Dictionary of the English Language* [London: Elsevier Publishing Company, 1967], 2:1152; Tucker, 177). *The Oxford English Dictionary* and *Oxford Latin Dictionary* do not connect the two terms, and neither do Ernout and Melliot (*Oxford English Dictionary,* 2nd ed., s.v. "Pain," "Penal," "Penitence," "Repent," and "Repentance;" *Oxford Latin Dictionary,* s.v. "Paene," "Paenitentia [and 'Poen-']," "Paeniteō," and "Poena;" A. Ernout, and A. Meillet, *Dictionnaire Etymologique de la Langue Latin,* 3rd edition [Paris: Librairie C. Klincksieck, 1951], 840, 917). The tendency to link *paenitēre* and *poena,* according to Klein, Tucker and the *OED,* is rooted in the Medieval Latin practice of spelling *paenitēre* as *poenitēre,* even though the two terms are unrelated. *Poena* derives from the Greek *poinē,* meaning punishment or penalty, whereas the origin of *paenitēre* is unclear. According to the *OED,* it is unknown. Klein opines that it ultimately derives from the Indo-European base pe-, pĕ-, "to damage, injure, or hurt" (Klein, 1:1152; see also Norman Bird, *The Roots and Non-Roots of Indo-European: A Lexicostatistical Survey* [Weisbaden, Harrowssowitz Verlal, 1993], 38). The Persian word for repentance, *pashīmānī* (the other being *tawbat,* from Arabic), may very well derive from this base. If so, this would reveal a distant etymological relation with the English term, provided, of course, Klein's speculation is true. Although the philological arguments against linking *poena* and *paenitēre* appear strong, those who employ these arguments disagree over the English derivatives of the Latin terms, suggesting by this disagreement

that the question of etymological origins remains ultimately unresolved. For our purposes, it is enough to note the principle lexical sense of repentance, indisputably a derivative of the Latin *paenitēre,* which is that of grief, sorrow, contrition, dissatisfaction, or regret for a past wrong.

4. Ibn Fāris writes *al-tā' wa al-wāw wa al-bā' kalima wāḥida tadullu ʿalā al-rujūʿ* ("*tā'*, *wāw* and *bā'* are [when joined] a single word that refers to 'return'"). See *Muʿjam maqāyīs al-lugha,* ed. ʿAbd al-Salām Muḥammad Hārūn (Egypt: Maktabat al-Bābī, 1969), 1:357.

5. Fīrūzābādī, *al-Qāmūs al-muḥīṭ* (Damascus: Maktabat al-Nūrī, n.d.), 1:40; Ibn Fāris, 1:357; Ibn Manẓūr, *Lisān al-ʿarab,* ed. Muḥammad ʿAbd al-Wahhāb (Beirut: Dār al-Iḥyā' al-Turāth al-ʿArabī, 1997), 2:21–22; Ibn Sīda, *al-Muḥkam wa al-muḥīṭ,* ed. ʿAbd al-Ḥamīd Handāwī (Beirut: Dār al-Kutub al-ʿIlmiyya, 2000), 9:541–542; Jawharī, *al-Ṣiḥāḥ,* eds. Amīl Yaʿqūb and Nabīl Ṭarīfī (Beirut: Dār al-Kutub al-ʿIlmiyya, n.d.), 1:139; Edward Lane, *Arabic-English Lexicon* (repr., Cambridge: Islamic Texts Society, 1984), 1:321; Ṣaghānī, *al-Takmila wa al-dhayl wa al-ṣila,* eds. ʿAbd al-ʿAlīm al-Ṭaḥāwī and ʿAbd al-Ḥamīd Ḥasan (Cairo: Maṭbaʿat Dār al-Kutub, 1970), 1:75; Zabīdī, *Tāj al-ʿarūs* (Kuwait: al-Turāth al-ʿArabī, 1966), 2:161; Zamakhsharī, *Asās al-balāgha,* eds. Mazīd Naʿīm and Shawqī al-Maʿarrī (Lebanon: Maktaba Nāshirūn, n.d), 80.

6. Ibn Manẓūr, *Lisān,* 2:21.

7. Fīrūzābādī, *Qāmūs,* 1:40; Ibn Manẓūr, *Lisān,* 2:21; Ibn Sīda, *Muḥkam,* 9:541–542; Jawharī, *Ṣiḥāḥ,* 1:139; Lane, *Lexicon,* 1:321; Ṣaghānī, *Takmila,* 1:75; Zabīdī, *Tāj,* 2:161; Zamakhsharī, *Asās,* 70.

8. Citing an example from Zamakhsharī's commentary on the Qur'ān, Mustansir Mir writes, "it would not be wrong to use *tāba ʿalayhi* with a human being as a subject of the verb." See his *Verbal Idioms of the Qur'ān* (Ann Arbor: University of Michigan, 1989), 67–68.

9. Zabīdī, *Tāj,* 2:161.

10. This sense of *tābūt* can even take on a metaphorical form, as highlighted in an expression cited by Zamakhsharī: "I have not deposited anything within my *tābūt* [of knowledge] that I have lost." See *Asās,* 62. However Zamakhsharī does not—and in this he is a minority—consider *tābūt* a derivative of **t-w-b** but **t-b-t**. Virtually all of the major lexicographers who include *tābūt* in their entries under **t-w-b** highlight this disagreement, which boils down to a question of whether the word is of the *faʿalūt* or *fāʿūl* pattern. If it is of the former, it derives from **t-w-b**; if of the latter, it derives from **t-b-t**. Jawharī, Zabīdī, Fīrūzābādī, Ibn Manẓūr, and others who trace it to **t-w-b** mention that the origin of the word is *tābuwa,* of the *faʿluwa* pattern, like *tarquwa*. But when the *sukūn* replaces the *fatḥa* of و, the ة is transformed into a ت, thus rendering it تابوت (*tābūt* → فعلوت). See Zabīdī, *Tāj,* 2:161; Jawharī, *Ṣiḥāḥ,* 1:92; Ibn Manẓūr, *Lisān,* 1:21; and Fīrūzābādī, *Qāmūs,* 1:40. For our purposes it is enough simply to reiterate that most of the lexicographers who include this word in their dictionaries trace it to **t-w-b.**

Although Ibn Manẓūr includes it under his entries for both **t-w-b** and **t-b-t**, he justifies including it under **t-b-t** simply on grounds of "caution" for the view of Ibn Barrī for whom *tābūt* was a derivative of **t-b-t.** See Ibn Manẓūr, *Lisān*, 2:12.

11. In the Jewish tradition the divine immanence or *shekhinah* (*sakīna*) is most perfectly manifest in God's revelation to Moses at Sinai.

12. It is also possible that *tābūt* is of Hebrew origin, from *tēbāh*, meaning "box" or even "ark." The word is used in the Bible to refer both to the "small ark" in which Moses is placed as a child to escape death, as well as the "great ark" of Noah. See Douglas K. Stuart, *The New American Commentary, An Exegetical and Theological Exposition of Holy Scripture: Exodus* (Nashville, TN: B&H Publishing, 2006), 88.

13. Jawharī, *Ṣiḥāḥ*, 1:91; Ibn Manẓūr, *Lisān*, 1:21; Lane, *Lexicon*, 1:321. Kafāwī indirectly cites this *ḥadīth* through another one: "Hajj is *ʿarafa*." This second *ḥadīth* is frequently mentioned in Sufi texts alongside the one on regret to illustrate the central place of *nadam* in the religious sense of *tawba*. Regret is to *tawba* what *ʿarafa* is to the major pilgrimage, for just as hajj remains incomplete without *ʿarafa*, so too does *tawba* remain incomplete without regret or contrition. See his *al-Kulliyyāt: muʿjam fī musṭalaḥāt wa al-furūq al-lughawiyya*, eds. Muḥammad al-Miṣrī and ʿAdnān Darwīsh (Beirut: Muʾassasat al-Risāla, 1996), 307.

14. Ibn Māja, *Sunan* (Arabic-English edition), trans. M.T. Ansari (New Delhi: Kitab Bhavan, 1994), 5:491.

15. Ibn Manẓūr, *Lisān*, 14:94–95.

16. Al-Rāghib al-Iṣfahānī, *Mufradāt alfāẓ al-qurʾān*, ed. Ṣafwān ʿAdnān Dāʾūdī (Beirut: Dār al-Shāmiyya, 1997), 169. See also T.H. Weir's entry on *tawba* in the *Encyclopedia of Religion and Ethics*, s.v. "Repentance (Muhammadan)."

17. Zamakhsharī, *Asās*, 70.

18. See the opening endnote of chapter three.

19. On the basis of Helmer Ringren's research, in pre-Islamic Arabia *aslama* would have meant "to abandon something, to give something up, to let loose entirely." With the coming of Islam, it came to acquire the meaning of surrendering the self to God. See Watt, "Conversion in Islam," 726.

20. Ibn ʿAbbād, *al-Muḥīṭ fī al-lugha* (Beirut: ʿĀlim al-Kutub, n.d.), 9:473.

21. Ibn Manẓūr, *Lisān*, 2:21; Ibn Sīda, *Muḥkam*, 9:541–542; Zabīdī, *Tāj*, 2:161.

22. Ibn Manẓūr, *Lisān*, 2:21.

23. John Penrice, *A Dictionary and Glossary of the Qurʾān: With Copious References and Explanations of the Text*, rev. ed. (1873; repr., Surrey: Gresham Press, 1985), 102.

24. Lane, *Lexicon*, 1:124.

25. Ibn Manẓūr, *Lisān*, 1:257.

26. Ibn Manẓūr, *Lisān*, 14:318; Lane, *Lexicon*, 1:2862.

27. Ibn Manẓur, *Lisān*, 14:318.

28. Ibn Manẓūr, *Lisān*, 14:318.

29. Ibn Manẓur, *Lisān*, 14:318; Lane, *Lexicon*, 1:2863.

30. Ibn Manẓūr, *Lisān*, 1:144; Khalīl b. ʿAyn, *Kitāb al-ʿayn* (Beirut: Dār Hayāʾ al-Turāth al-ʿArabī, n.d.), 12; Lane, *Lexicon*, 1:361; Zabīdī, *Tāj*, 1:103.

31. Ibn Manẓūr, *Lisān*, 1:144; Lane, *Lexicon*, 1:361; Zabīdī, *Tāj*, 1:103.

32. Q 3:145, 3:148, 4:134, 18:31 and 28:80.

33. Ibn Durayd, *Jamharat al-lugha*, ed. Ramzī Munīr Baʿalbakī (Beirut: Dār al-ʿIlm, 1987), 2:1016.

34. "And We have made the House a *mathāba* for people, and a sanctuary" (Q 2:125).

35. Ibn ʿAbbād, *Muḥīṭ*, 10:188; Khalīl b. ʿAyn, *Kitāb al-ʿayn*, 121; Lane, *Lexicon*, 1:363.

36. Lane attributes this latter interpretation to Bayḍāwī's *Tafsīr*. See *Lexicon* 1:363.

37. Jawharī, *Ṣiḥāḥ*, 1:47.

38. Ibn Manẓūr, *Lisān*, 1:144.

39. A comprehensiveness that does not, however, match that of Zabīdī's *Tāj* or Ibn Manẓūr's *Lisān*.

40. *The New Schaff-Herzog Encyclopedia of Religious Knowledge*, s.v. "Repentance."

41. Francis Brown, S.R. Driver and Charles A. Briggs, *A Hebrew and English Lexicon of the Old Testament: Based on the Lexicon of William Gesenius as Translated by Edward Robinson* (Oxford: Claredon, 1907), 996. See also Montefiore, "Rabbinic Conceptions," 212–213.

42. William L. Holladay, *The Root Shub in the Old Testament* (Leiden: Brill, 1958), 4.

43. Brown, Driver and Briggs, *A Hebrew and English Lexicon*, 996.

44. Martin Zammit, *A Comparative Lexical Study of Qurʾānic Arabic* (Leiden: Brill, 2002), 114.

45. C.G. Montefiore, "Rabbinic Conceptions of Repentance," *The Jewish Quarterly Review* 16 (1904): 211–212.

46. *The Jewish Encyclopedia*, s.v. "Repentance;" *Encyclopedia of Religion and Ethics*, s.v. "Repentance;" Montefiore, "Rabbinic Conceptions," 213.

47. Montefiore, "Rabbinic Conceptions," 211–212. When Montefiore wrote his piece, he confessed that the period when *teshubah* acquired this particular religious meaning remained unknown to him. In a more recent article, Richard Bell traces *teshubah*'s first use in the sense of a technical religious term to the Qumran literature, which is part of the Dead Sea Scrolls and dated roughly to the 1st century BCE. In this literature, the few occurrences of *teshubah* indicate that it involves "turning from sins [. . .] to the law of Moses." See Bell, "*Teshubah*: The Idea of Repentance in Ancient Judaism," *Journal of Progressive Judaism* 5 (1995): 23.

48. Sanders has argued that *teshubah* came to become a "status-maintaining" concept in Judaism, the purpose of which was to allow Jews to remain bound to the Covenant, despite their human breaches. In Islam *tawba* plays no such role. See E.P. Sanders, *Paul and Palestinian Judaism* (London: SCM Press, 1977), 175–182.

49. Jacob J. Petuchowski, "The Concept of 'Teshuvah' in the Bible and Talmud," *Judaism: A Quarterly Journal* 17 (1978): 180.

50. According to Brown, Driver and Briggs, the cognate Arabic root of the Hebrew is **n-ḥ-m**, which refers to the panting or breathing of a horse. See *A Hebrew and English Lexicon*, 636; cf. David Clines, *The Dictionary of Classical Hebrew* (Sheffield, UK: Sheffield Academic Press, 2001), 5:663. Although it is not a direct cognate, *naham* remains a close synonym of the Arabic *nadam*.

51. Montefiore, "Rabbinic Conceptions," 212. See also Brown, Driver and Briggs, *A Hebrew and English Lexicon*, 636–637.

52. Montefiore, "Rabbinic Conceptions," 212.

53. James Crossley, "The Semitic Background to Repentance in the Teaching of John the Baptist and Jesus," *Journal for the Study of the Historical Jesus* 2 (2004): 139.

54. Henry George Liddell and Robert Scott, *A Greek-English Lexicon*, 9th ed., revised by Henry Stuart Jones et al. (1940; repr., Oxford: Clarendon Press, 1961), 661.

55. Crossley, "The Semitic Background," 139.

56. Guy Nave, *The Role and Function of* Repentance *in Luke-Acts* (Atlanta: Society of Biblical Literature, 2002), 52. See also *ER*, s.v. "Repentance."

57. Liddell and Scott, *A Greek-English Lexicon*, 1115.

58. Nave, *Role and Function*, 48–66.

59. Geza Vermes writes in the *Religion of Jesus the Jew*, that in the "Semitic mentality of Jesus the Jew, it [i.e., repentance] implied not a change of mind as the *metanoia* of the Greek Gospels would suggest, but a complete reversal of direction away from sin, in accordance with the biblical and post-biblical dual Hebrew concept of 'turning,' viz. 'turning away from' or 'returning to' conveyed by the verb *shuv* and the noun *teshuvah*." Cited in Crossley, "The Semitic Background," 138.

60. Nave writes that "the Jewish translators of the Hebrew Scriptures never once used μετάνοέω [*metanoia*] to translate [*shūb*]." See *Role and Function*, 119 ff 383. The same observation is made by Thomas Finn, when he notes that the Greek-speaking Jews who translated the Hebrew Bible into Greek "chose forms of *[s]trephein* [. . .] to render the Hebrew *shub*." See his *From Death to Rebirth: Ritual and Conversion in Antiquity* (Mahwah, NJ: Paulist Press, 1997), 22–23.

61. For a treatment of this question, see Crossley, "The Semitic Background," 138–157; and E.P. Sanders, *Paul and Palestinian Judaism* (London: SCM Press Ltd., 1977), 174–182.

62. God may feel *naham* from a Biblical perspective, but in the Qur᾿ān and the Islamic tradition, God never experiences *nadam*.

Chapter 2

1. Toshihiko Izutsu, *God and Man in the Qur᾿an: Semantics of the Qur᾿anic Weltanschauung* (Kuala Lumpur: Islamic Book Trust, 2002); idem, *Ethico-Religious*

Concepts of the Koran, 2nd ed. (Montreal: McGill-Queen University Press, 2005).

2. For a historical survey of Sufi exegesis, see Kristen Z. Sands, *Ṣūfī Commentaries on the Qur'ān in Classical Islam* (London: Routledge, 2006); cf. Todd Lawson's review of this work in the *Journal of the American Oriental Society* 127, no. 4 (2007): 543–545. For a succinct overview of Sufi *tafsīr*, see Alexander Knysh's entry on "Ṣūfism and the Qur'ān" in *EQ*. See also Seyyed H. Nasr, "The Qur'ān as the Foundation of Islamic Spirituality," in *Islamic Spirituality: Foundations*, ed. S.H. Nasr (New York: Crossroad, 1987), 3–10; Abdurrahman Habil, "Traditional Esoteric Commentaries on the Qur'ān," idem, 24–47.

3. Izutsu, *God and Man in the Qur'an*, 18–24.

4. Izutsu, *God and Man in the Qur'an*, 19–20.

5. Izutsu, *God and Man in the Qur'an*, 34.

6. The most significant criticism leveled against Izutsu's semantic method is that it does not sufficiently take into consideration the historical chronology of the Qur'ān, that is, the manner in which the relational meanings of terms may have changed over the course of the Prophet's experience of revelation. See Harry B. Partin, "Semantics of the Qur'an: A Consideration of Izutsu's Studies," *History of Religions* 9, no. 4 (1970): 360; Joseph Schacht, Review of *Ethico-Religious Concepts in the Qur'an*, by Toshihiko Izutsu, *Journal of the American Oriental Society* 83, no. 3 (1963): 360; W. Montgomery Watt, Review of *God and Man in the Koran* and *The Concept of Belief in Islamic Theology*, by Toshihiko Izutsu, *Journal of Semitic Studies* 12 n. 1 (1967): 156. While Izutsu's method prevents us from appreciating the semantic development of Qur'ānic terms, it does allow us to approach the Qur'ānic text in a manner similar to that found in the Islamic mystical tradition. This is because Sufi hermeneutics tends to be ahistorical; it does not focus extensively on the historical or "horizontal" context of Qur'ānic verses. Were, on the other hand, our analysis of *tawba* legal or juridical in nature, Izutsu's method would have presented greater drawbacks. In the domain of *fiqh* one must, in an effort to derive specific legal rulings, take historical context and "occasions of revelation" (*asbāb al-nuzūl*) into serious consideration. Other criticisms have also been leveled against Izutsu's studies of the Qur'ān, but since these pertain not to his method but his actual findings, there is little reason to explore them in detail here. There is one criticism, however, that is worth noting, and that is that there is a strong subjective element present in what Izutsu has identified as the "key concepts" of the Qur'ān. But this is only a real problem if one presumes, through an "essentialist" reading, that the Qur'ān is a univocal text with one meaning. As Angelika Neuwirth has recently noted, "what scholars should be looking for is not a particular 'right' understanding of the text, that polarizes another understanding as wrong but rather the text itself as a medium of transport, as reflecting a communication process." See Angelika Neuwirth, "Orientalism in Oriental Studies," *Journal of Qur'ānic Studies* 9, no. 2 (2007): 357. For critical appraisals of Izutsu's works on the Qur'ān, see John Burton, Review of *Ethico-Religious Concepts in the Qur'an*, by Toshihiko Izutsu, *Bulletin of the School of African Studies* 31, no. 2 (1968): 391–392; Partin, idem, 358–362; Schacht, idem, 359–360; Watt, idem, 155–157.

7. For my translations I have freely consulted the ones of M.A.S. Abdel Haleem, A.J. Arberry, Abdullah Yusuf Ali, Muhammad Asad, and Marmaduke Pickthall.

8. Iṣfahānī does not give a definition of *iṣlāḥ* insofar as it applies to the human being in his *Mufradāt*. But he does define *ṣalāḥ*—the state that *iṣlāḥ* attempts to realize—as the "opposite of corruption" (*ḍidd al-fasād*). A clumsy but technical translation might, in this light, be "decorrupting." Iṣfahānī adds that *iṣlāḥ* is contrasted in the Qur'ān sometimes with *fasād* and other times with *sayyi'a* (evil or wrong). See Iṣfahānī, *Mufradāt*, 469. See also Izutsu's short discussion of this concept in *Ethico-Religious Concepts*, 204–207.

9. But there is certainly more to divine *iṣlāḥ* than this. Iṣfahānī says that divine *iṣlāh* can refer to three things: (1) God's creation of the human being as a *ṣāliḥ* from childhood; (2) God's removal of an element of *fasād* in his life; or (3) God's bestowing on the human being some form of prosperity. See Iṣfahānī, *Mufradāt*, 490.

10. In Q 46:15, where it appears immediately before the human being's *tawba*: "And [O God] be gracious to me with respect to my posterity (*waṣliḥ lī fī dhurriyyatī*). Verily I turn to you (*innī tubtu ilayka*)." In none of verses in which divine *tawba* appears is there any mention of divine *iṣlāḥ*

11. This is excluding the number of times it does not appear immediately alongside *tawba*, or its appearance in a surrounding verse.

12. The close relation between *al-'amal al-ṣāliḥ* and *tawba* is also confirmed by occasional references in the Qur'ān to *tawba* on account of *al-'amal al-sū'*, an act that stands at the opposite end of *'amal ṣāliḥ*; cf. Izutsu, *Ethico-Religious Concepts*, 206–207.

13. Iṣfahānī, *Mufradāt*, 169.

14. Pickthall translates *Tawwāb* here as "Forgiving." Although Arberry opts for a more literal translation of the phrase, "they would have found God turns," the turning here is still clearly one of forgiveness.

15. In other contexts this word can take on different meanings. It is used, for example, of God as well as of humans in a positive sense, where it means to "take as a friend" (Q 5:51). See also note below on *barā'a*.

16. It should be noted that *tawba* is not the only opposite of *tawallā* in the Qur'ān.

17. An observation should be made here of divine *barā'a* ("release, exemption"), which is closely associated with turning away (*tawallā*) from God and the Prophet in at least one instance in the Qur'ān. In the opening of sūra *al-Tawba*, the Qur'ān asserts that God and the Prophet are no longer obliged to remain faithful to the treaty made with the polytheists because they have reneged on its terms (Q 9:3). Unless the polytheists turn in *tawba*, God and the Prophet are *barī'* (free, exempt) from all obligations of peace. The verse ends with the polytheists being warned of God's *'adhāb* if the polytheists persist in their *tawallā*. The severe consequences of this *barā'a* explain, according to some classical Muslim commentators, the absence of the customary *basmala*, with its mention of God's

overriding mercy, at the beginning of the sūra. This view can be traced back to ʿAlī, who is reported to have said that the reason sūra *al-Tawba* does not open with the *basmala* is because the *basmala* "is a protection (*amān*), whereas this sūra was revealed with the sword (*bi al-sayf*) and [it] flung away the covenants (*nabadha al-ʿuhūd*), so there is no protection in it (*laysa fīhā amān*)." See Fakhr al-Dīn al-Rāzī, *al-Tafsīr al-kabīr* (Beirut: Dār al-Kutub al-ʿIlmiyya, 1990), 15:173. This employment of *barāʾa* in the Qurʾān allows us to better understand the negative sense of *tabarruʾ* (which derives from the same trilateral root as *barāʾa*) in Shiʿite theology, in which the term signifies dissociating oneself from or repudiating the opponents of ʿAlī, the subsequent Imams, and their families. As a technical term, it is juxtaposed against *tawallā* (understood in its positive sense [see note 15]) and *walāya/wilāya*, which denote its exact opposite: one's devotion and loyalty to the Imam. See Meir M. Bar-Asher, *Scripture and Exegesis in Early Imāmī Shiism* (Leiden: Brill, 1999), 102–103, 19–202; EI^2, s.v. "Barāʾa," "Tabarruʾ," and "Wilāya;" Etan Kohlberg, "Barāʾa in Shīʿī doctrine," *Jerusalem Studies in Arabic and Islam* 7 (1986): 139–175. For the positive use of *tawallā* in Sufism, see Hermann Landolt's excellent article, "Walāyah," in *ER*.

18. Izutsu, *Ethico-Religious Concepts*, 110.

19. One may argue that the concept of repentance, as a feeling of regret and remorse for a past wrong, can exist, like forgiveness, within a "nontheistic" worldview—at least insofar as the basic semantic meaning of the term is concerned. Within this worldview a criminal may repent of his crime (i.e., experience *nadam*), seek the forgiveness of his victim, and even desire to engage in some form of penance and rectification, but he cannot do *tawba* insofar as the concept entails, in the *Weltanschauung* of the Qurʾān, a return to God. This does not preclude the possibility of the secularization of the Qurʾānic concept, insofar as one simply returns from wrong action to right action. For some insightful comparative observations about the role and function of repentance in religious and secular worldviews, see Etziono and Carvey, eds., *Repentance: A Comparative Perspective*, 1–20.

20. Thus Ibn al-ʿArabī (d. 1240) says that an individual may be qualified by *tawba* until the "moment of death," while he may be qualified by the virtues associated with other "stations" (*maqāms*) in the next world. See William Chittick, *Sufi Path of Knowledge* (Albany: State University of New York Press, 1989), 279–280; cf. ʿAbd al-Razzāq al-Kāshānī (d. 1330), *Rashḥ al-zulāl*, ed. Saʿīd ʿAbd al-Fattāḥ (Cairo: Maktabat al-Azharī li al-Turāth, 1995), 48. This view is also premised on a number of Prophetic traditions that explicitly state that the doors of *tawba* close at death.

21. Izutsu, *Ethico-Religious Concepts*, 110.

22. Denny, "The Qurʾanic Vocabulary of Repentance," 650.

23. Iṣfahānī, *Mufradāt*, 609.

24. Iṣfahānī, *Mufradāt*, 609.

25. One may note here the phonetic similarity between the roots **k-f-r** and **gh-f-r**, both of which are separated by radicals whose vocalizations originate in

the same region of the throat. When these roots are paired, the ensuing phonetic consonance serves to enhance the overall rhythmic and aural aesthetic of the Qur'ān. Neal Robinson has explored the relation between sound and meaning in the Qur'ān. See *Discovering the Qur'ān: A Contemporary Approach to a Veiled Text* (Washington, DC: Georgetown University Press, 2003), 162–188. See also Michael Sells, "Sound, Spirit, and Gender in *Sūrat al-Qadr*," *Journal of the American Oriental Society* 11, no. 2 (1990): 101–139; idem, "Sound and Meaning in *Sūrat al-Qāri'a*," *Arabica* 40 (1993): 403–430; idem, "A Literary Approach to the Hymnic Sūras of the Qur'ān: Spirit, Gender, and Aural Intertextuality," in *Literary Structures of Religious Meaning in the Qur'ān*, ed. Issa J. Boullata (London: Curzon, 1999), 3–25.

26. I stress "in relation to forgiveness" because derivatives of **ʿ-f-w** can also take on meanings that are, for the most part, unrelated to forgiveness. One such example is 2:219: "They will ask you about what they ought to spend. Say, *al-ʿafwa*." *Al-ʿafwa* in this context can refer to anything abundant or superfluous. This is how Pickthall and Arberry translate this term.

27. Iṣfahānī, *Mufradāt*, 574. See also Penrice, *Glossary of the Qur'ān*, 98.

28. Abū Ḥāmid al-Ghazālī, *The Ninety-Nine Beautiful Names of God: al-Maqṣad al-asnā fī sharḥ asmā Allāh al-ḥusna*, trans. with notes by David B. Burrell and Nazih Daher (Cambridge: Islamic texts Society, 1995), 138–139.

29. Arberry tends to consistently translate it as "Pardoning" and *Ghafūr* as "Forgiving." Pickthall translates it as "Forgiving" but also as "Clement," "Mild," and "Benign." Ali is the only one who consistently expresses the more literal sense with his rendition of *ʿAfūw* as "one who blots out sins." But he also occasionally translates **ʿ-f-w**, when applied to the human being, as "forgiveness."

30. But this is not always the case. There are two instances in which other terms are employed as opposites. In the first, the 4th form of **w-b-q**, "to cause to perish" or "destroy," is used: "Or He *yu'biqhunna* (destroys them) on account of what they have earned. And He *yaʿfu* much" (Q 42:34). In the second instance, it is the 8th form of **n-q-m**, "to take vengeance." The verse reads, "God *ʿafā* what is past. But whoever returns [to offend], God will *yantaqim* [take vengeance] on him" (Q 5:95). These examples do not diminish the semantic affinity between divine *ʿafw* and the other two terms under consideration, because it is not uncommon for a Qur'ānic word to have more than one opposite. *Kufr*, for example, is sometimes counterposed against *īmān* (Q 3:86, 3:90, 32:29, 34:31), and sometimes against *shukr* (Q 2:152, 27:40, 31:12, 76:3).

31. According to Fakhr al-Dīn al-Rāzī, *ʿafw* involves forgoing a right that one is due (*ḥaqīqat al-ʿafw isqāṭ al-ḥaqq*). Insofar as both God and one's fellow human beings have such rights over an individual, they can exercise *ʿafw*. See Rāzī, *al-Tafsīr al-kabīr*, 5:46.

32. We should draw attention, before closing our remarks about *ʿafw*, to that one instance where the word is paired with *iṣlāḥ* in the same way that the latter is so often paired with *tawba*: "the recompense of an ugly deed is an ugly deed the like of it, but whoever *ʿafā* and *aṣlaḥa*, his wage falls upon God" (Q 42:40). The structure of this pairing illustrates yet another point of intersection between the two concepts.

33. Daniel C. Peterson's article on "Forgiveness" in *EQ* overlooks **ṣ-f-h** entirely, and fails to draw attention to the contrasting imagery conveyed by the other three roots.

34. Lane, *Lexicon*, 2:1694.

35. See also Lane, *Lexicon*, 2:1694.

36. He writes, *safḥ shay' ʿurḍuhu wa jānibuhu ka ṣafḥ al-wajh*. See Iṣfahānī, *Mufradāt*, 486.

37. *afanaḍribu ʿankum al-dhikra ṣafḥan an kuntum qawman musrifūn.*

38. "Shall We utterly ignore you because you are a wanton folk" (Pickthall); "Shall We turn away the Remembrance from you, for that you are a prodigal people" (Arberry); "Shall We then take away the message from you and repel (you) For that you are a people transgressing beyond bounds" (Yusuf Ali); "Should We quietly slip the Reminder away from you since you have been such dissipated folk" (Irving).

39. See, for example, Ibn Kathīr, *Tafsīr al-qur'ān al-ʿaẓīm* (Riyadh: Dār Ṭayyiba li al-Nashr wa al-Tawzīʿ, 1997), 7:218–219; Muḥammad b. ʿAlī al-Shawkānī, *Fatḥ al-qadīr* (Damascus: Dār Ibn Kathīr, 1998), 4:627; Rāzī, *al-Tafsīr al-kabīr*, 27:167–168; Muḥammad b. Aḥmad al-Qurṭubī, *al-Jāmiʿ li aḥkām al-qur'ān* (Cairo: al-Maktaba al-ʿArabiyya, 1967), 16:62–63; Jalāl al-Dīn al-Suyūṭī and Jalāl al-Dīn al-Maḥallī, *Tafsīr al-jalālayn*, eds. ʿAbd al-Qādir al-Arnā'ūṭ and Aḥmad Khālid Shukrī (Damascus: Dār Ibn Kathīr, 1998), 489; Muḥammad b. Jarīr al-Ṭabarī, *Jāmiʿ al-bayān ʿan tafsīr al-qur'ān* (Beirut: Dār al-Maʿrifa, 1992), 25:30–31; Maḥmūd b. ʿUmar al-Zamakhsharī, *al-Kashshāf* (Riyadh: Maktaba al-ʿAbīkān, 1998), 5:425–426. Although Muḥammad b. Aḥmad al-Gharnāṭi says that *ṣafḥan* can mean *iʿrāḍan ʿankum* ("turning away from you" or "shunning you"), he is the only commentator I have encountered who argues that it can also mean, in this context, *ʿafwa* and *ghufrān*. See *Tashīl al-ʿulūm al-tanzīl* (Beirut: Dār al-Arqam, n.d.), 2:254. The other commentators do not even present this as a weaker opinion. The main point of disagreement among the commentators rests on the nature of the *dhikr* mentioned in the verse, and what God's "turning away" entails.

40. The historical context of this verse surrounds three men of Medina who were ostracized by the Muslim community as well as their own families for not participating in the *ghazwa* of Tabūk. See Ṭabarī, *Jāmiʿ*, 11:40–45.

41. This "initiative" is confirmed in the commentary literature. See Gharnāṭī, *Tashīl*, 1:349–350; Ibn al-Jawzī, *Zād al-tafsīr* (Beirut: Maktabat al-Islāmī, 1965), 3:513; Rāzī, *al-Tafsīr al-kabīr*, 16:174–175; Ṭabarī, *Jāmiʿ*, 11:40–45. Elsewhere Rāzī says that "*tawba* is not obtained by the servant except by the creation of God most high." See *al-Tafsīr al-kabīr*, 8:192. See below for further analysis of the commentary literature on divine *tawba*.

42. Ṭabarī, *Jāmiʿ*, 21:94.

43. Ibn al-Jawzī says the Qur'ānic expression "Or *yatūbu* towards them" means that God "takes them out of hypocrisy into faith (*yukhrijuhum min al-nifāq ilā al-īmān*) and [then] forgives them" (Q 33:24). For Ibn Kathīr, God turns in *tawba* toward the hypocrites "by guiding them to discard hypocrisy for faith" (*al-nuzūʿ ʿan al-nifāq ilā al-īmān*). See *Tafsīr al-qur'ān al-ʿaẓīm* (Riyadh: Dār Ṭayyiba li al-

Nashr wa al-Tawzīʿ, 1997), 6:395. Suyūṭī quotes Qatāda as saying the following about God's *tawba* in this context: "He takes them out from hypocrisy through *tawba*." See *al-Durr al-manthūr* (Beirut: Dār al-Kutub al-ʿIlmiyya, 2000), 5:397. This of course can occur only through faith. Bayḍāwī suggests God's *tawba* might be aimed at furnishing the servant with the ability to perform *tawba* (*al-murād bihā al-tawfīq li al-tawba*). This *tawfīq*, implies, of course, being guided. See *Tafsīr al-bayḍāwī* (Cairo: 1926), 585. A similar interpretation appears in Qurṭubī, *Jāmiʿ*, 14:160. According to Rāzī, the reason God says He might punish them "if He so wills (*in shāʾa*)" is because it had not yet become clear to the Prophet whether some of them might actually acquire faith, as indeed some of them later did. This reception of faith is, in Rāzī's commentary, implicitly tied to God's *tawba*. See *al-Tafsīr al-kabīr*, 25:176–177.

44. Zamakhsharī, *Kashshāf*, 5:61.

45. For some brief observations on the Muʿtazilite underpinnings of Zamakhsharī's Qurʾān commentary, see Jane McAuliffe, *Qurʾānic Christians: An Analysis of Classical and Modern Exegesis* (New York: Cambridge University Press, 1991), 53; Andrew Lane, *A Traditional Muʿtazilite Qurʾān Commentary: The Kashshāf of Jār Allāh al-Zamakhsharī (d. 538/1144)* (Leiden: Brill, 2006), 104–113; Walid Saleh, *The Formation of the Classical Tafsīr Tradition: the Qurʾān Commentary of al-Thaʿlabī* (Leiden: Brill, 2004), 127–129.

46. The interpretation offered by Zamakhsharī is found in the earlier exegesis of the Shīʿite Muʿtazilite scholar, Muḥammad ibn al-Ḥasan al-Ṭūsī (d. 1067). His commentary reads, "[As for] His saying, 'Or *yatūba* towards them,' its meaning is that if He wills He [will] accept their *tawba* and remove their punishment if they *tābū*." See *al-Tibyān fī tafsīr al-qurʾān* (Iraq, 1963), 8:369.

47. Rāzī, *al-Tafsīr al-kabīr*, 8:192. For more on the Muʿtazilite understanding of God's "benevolence" (*luṭf/alṭāf*), also translated as "assistance," see Khalid Blankinship, "The Early Creed," in *Classical Islamic Theology*, ed. Tim Winter (Cambridge: Cambridge University Press, 2008), 47, 50; Sajjad Rizvi, "The Developed Kalām Tradition (Part 2)," idem, 94.

48. We should also note here that the late Shīʿite Muʿtazilite, ʿAllāma Ṭabaṭabāʾī, in his commentary on verse 9:118, explains that God is *Tawwāb* because He is "frequent to return (*kathīr al-rujūʿ*) towards his servants. He returns to them through guidance (*hidāya*) and grace (*tawfīq*) to allow them to perform *tawba* towards Him, and then [returns to them also] by accepting [their] *tawba*." See *Mīzān fī al-tafsīr* (Beirut, 1971), 9:400.

49. Denny, "Qurʾanic Vocabulary," 654.

50. The Qurʾān uses the first form of the verbal root, *radda/yaruddu* (lit. "to cause to turn back"), to describe the process of causing one to apostasize. See for example Q 2:217 ("They will not stop fighting you until they *yaruddukum* [cause you to turn away] from your religion") and Q 3:100 ("They will *yaruddukum* [cause you to turn away], disbelievers, after your faith"). For definitions of *ridda* (apostasy) among Muslim jurists, see Rudolph Peters and Gert J.J. Vries, "Apostasy in Islam," *Die Welt des Islams* 17, no. 1 (1976–1977): 2–4.

51. Denny, "Qur'anic Vocabulary," 654.
52. Iṣfahānī, *Mufradāt*, 509; see also Ibn Manẓūr, *Lisān*, 8:78–79.
53. Iṣfahānī, *Mufradāt*, 281.
54. Denny, "Qur'anic Vocabulary," 653.
55. Iṣfahānī, *Mufradāt*, 281–282.
56. Denny, "Qur'anic Vocabulary," 661; see also *EQ*, s.v. "Repentance."
57. Iṣfahānī, *Mufradāt*, 343.
58. Iṣfahānī, *Mufradāt*, 828.
59. See also Izutsu, *Ethico-Religious Concepts*, 110–111.
60. *al-rujūʿ ilayhi bi al-tawba wa ikhlāṣ al-ʿamal*. See Iṣfahānī, *Mufradāt* 828.
61. *al-rājiʿ ilā Allāh taʿāla bi tark al-maʿāṣī wa fiʿl al-ṭāʿāt*. See Iṣfahānī, *Mufradāt*, 97.

62. According to Shawkānī, exceptional for the attention he gives to grammatical detail, *kullun lahu awwāb* means that "every one of them—from David, the mountains, and the birds—were returning to the obedience of God and His command. The pronoun in *lahu* [toward him] returns to God most High." But he also notes the opinion, which he considers weaker, according to which the pronoun goes back to David (*wa qīl al-ḍamīr li dāwūd*), thus making the Israelite prophet the object of *awba*. See *Fatḥ*, 4:488. For the different interpretations proffered by the commentators, see Gharnāṭī, *Tashīl*, 2:204; Rāzī, *al-Tafsīr al-kabīr*, 26:162–163; Suyūṭī and Maḥallī, *Jalālayn*, 454; Ṭabarī, *Jāmiʿ*, 23:87. These interpretations are reflected in modern translations of the Qur'ān.

63. The contexts of these verses make it clear that the "returning" is one of praise (*tasbīḥ*). According to Ibn ʿAbbās, the birds and the mountains would join David in singing the praises of God. This was one of the particular miracles given to him. See Rāzī, *al-Tafsīr al-kabīr*, 26:163. Qushayrī points out even more explicitly that David's miraculous powers included the ability to understand the praise. See *Laṭā'if al-ishārāt*, ed. ʿAbd al-Laṭīf Ḥasan ʿAbd al-Raḥmān (Beirut: Dār al-Kutub al-ʿIlmiyya, 2000), 3:100.

64. Abdullah Yusuf Ali, *The Holy Qur'ān: Text, Translation, and Commentary* (Washington DC: American International Printing Company, 1946), 1221.

Chapter 3

1. The English "conversion" bears some interesting parallels with the Arabic, especially insofar as spatial metaphors are concerned. Etymologically, conversion has the same root meaning as *tawba*, namely, to turn. Conversion implies turning from one thing to another, in that with every "conversion" there is, as noted earlier, a concomitant "aversion." See Frederick H. Russell, "Augustine: Conversion by the Book," in *Varieties of Religious Conversion in the Middle Ages*, ed. James Muldoon (Gainesville: University of Florida Press, 1997), 13. Conversion, however, is usually not used to describe repentance for a single sin, whereas with *tawba* this remains a possibility, even though, as this chapter

will demonstrate, it is not the ideal. We can also not speak of the "conversion of God" in the way we can of divine *tawba*, hence its limitations as a translation of the Arabic term. *Tawba* can include the idea of conversion within its semantic field whereas the opposite is not possible.

2. Leonard P. Hindsley, "Monastic Conversion: The Case of Margaret Ebner," in *Varieties of Religious Conversion in the Middle Ages*, 31. See also Smith, *Studies in Early Mysticism in the Near and Middle East*, 170–171.

3. Russell, 13–30. He writes that Augustine "was never far from the outward life of the Church, thanks to his mother, and he never—even during the violent swings of sentiment and conviction—expressly renounced the Christian faith. So in effect his conversion in the garden at Milan (*Confessions* 8) can actually be seen as a *re*conversion." See Russel, "Conversion by the Book," 14; and James Muldoon, "Introduction: The Conversion of Europe," in *Varieties of Religious Conversion in the Middle Ages*, 4.

4. Gerhard Böwering, "Early Sufism Between Persecution and Heresy," in *Islamic Mysticism: Thirteen Centuries of Controversies and Polemics*, eds. Frederick De Jong and Bernd Radtke (Leiden: Brill, 1999), 45–67.

5. This view is best summed by the sociologist, Roger Straus, when he writes, "sociologists have conventionally approached religious conversion as something that happens to a person who is destabilized by external or internal forces [. . .] This stands in contrast to the individual *seeker* striving and strategizing to achieve meaningful change in his or her life experience." See "Religious Conversion as a Personal and Collective Accomplishment," *Sociological Analysis* 40, no. 2 (1979): 158–165. See also Brock Kilbourne and James T. Richardson, "Paradigm Conflict, Types of Conversion, and Conversion Theories," *Sociological Analysis* 50, no. 1 (1988):1–21. The prototypical model of passive conversion in the West, the authors point out, is Paul's conversion to Christianity.

6. The most comprehensive survey of the source material on Ibrāhīm b. Adham is to be found in Richard Gramlich's *Alte Vorbilder des Sufitums*, 1:135–279.

7. Ignaz Goldziher, *Introduction to Islamic Theology and Law*, trans. Andras and Ruth Hamori (Princeton, NJ: Princeton University Press, 1981), 143. See also Arberry, *Sufism*, 36.

8. ʿAbd al-Raḥmān Muḥammad b. Ḥusayn al-Sulamī, *Ṭabaqāt al-ṣūfiyya*, ed. ʿAbd al-Qādir ʿAṭāʾ (Beirut: Dār al-Kutub al-ʿIlmiyya, 2003), 35. For full entry, see 35–42.

9. Abū Nuʿaym Aḥmad b. ʿAbd Allāh al-Iṣfahānī, ed. ʿAbd al-Qādir ʿAṭāʾ, *Ḥilyat al-awliyāʾ wa ṭabaqāt al-aṣfiyāʾ* (Beirut: Dār al-Kutub al-ʿIlmiyya, 2002), 7:426–427. For the full biographical entry on Ibrāhīm, see 7:426–452.

10. ʿAlī b. ʿUthmān al-Jullābī Hujwīrī, *Kashf al-maḥjūb: The Oldest Persian Treatise on Sufism*, trans. Reynold A. Nicholson (1911; repr., Lahore: Islamic Book Service, 1992), 103. For the full biographical entry, see 103–105.

11. Abū al-Qāsim al-Qushayrī, *al-Risāla*, ed. ʿAbd al-Ḥalīm Maḥmūd and Maḥmūd b. Sharīf (Damascus: Dār al-Farfūr, 2002), 52–54. For the full entry on him, see 52–57.

12. ʿAbd al-Raḥmān b. Aḥmad al-Jāmī, ed. Muḥammad ʿAdīb, *Nafaḥāt al-uns* (Beirut: Dār al-Kutub al-ʿIlmiyya, 2003), 1:60–61. For full entry on him, see 1:60–62.

13. Farīd al-Dīn ʿAṭṭār, *Muslim Saints and Mystics: Episodes from the Tadhkirat al-auliyā'*, trans. A.J. Arberry, (1966; repr., London: Penguin Books, 1990), 63–66. For full entry, see 62–79. Since Arberry's translation is not a complete version of the text, subsequent references to the work will appear in the form *Tadkhirat* (abridged).

14. They propose six such causal factors behind conversion: (1) *intellectual* (the result of extended personal investigation); (2) *mystical* (the result of a supernatural experience); (3) *experiential* (the consequence of participating, for a given trial period, in the lifestyle of a religious group); (4) *affectional* (the result of receiving some form of emotional affection, love, or care from members of a given religious group); (5) *revivalist* (the consequence of emotionally aroused crowd conformity); and (6) *coercive* (the result of brainwashing, mind control, or coercive persuasion). See John Lofland and Norman Skonovd, "Conversion Motifs," *Journal for the Scientific Study of Religion* 20, no. 4 (1981):373–384. What shall be proposed in this chapter are, as expected, subcategories of the second aforementioned category. In some scenarios (as in the case of Ghazālī's famous conversion), *tawba* be can also be rooted in an intellectual quest. I have not, however, come across any such conversion narrative in early Sufism in the hagiographical literature.

15. These are the different modes or forms of conversion. Lewis Rambo reduces them to five category-types: (1) *apostasy* or *defection* (repudiating or leaving a given religious community or tradition); (2) *intensification* (a deepening of involvement in a community or tradition of which one is already a part); (3) *affiliation* (transition from minimal or no religious commitment to a faith community); (4) *institutional transition* (transition or movement from one subtradition or community to another within a given religion; also called "denominational switching"); *tradition transition* (conversion from one religion to another). See Lewis Rambo, *Understanding Religious Conversion* (New Haven, CT: Yale, 1993), 12–14. Each of the aforementioned types can be the result of any of the six "conversion motifs" outlined by Lofland and Skonovd. "Interior conversion" within Sufism coincides most closely to Rambo's second category of "intensification," though it may exhibit some characteristics of "institutional transition" insofar as one may enter the Sufi path after having previously been committed to an intellectual subtradition such as *fiqh* or *kalām*.

16. In Munʿim Sirry's article, "Pious Muslims in the Making: A Closer Look at Narratives of Ascetic Conversion" (*Arabica* 57 [2010]: 437–454), he attempted to produce a classification of conversion in early Sufism. A close examination of his treatment, however, raises some serious concerns surrounding scholarly ethics. The lengthy translation from the *Ḥilyat* on pp. 444–445, for example, is a direct replication of Michael Cooperson's translation ("Ibn Ḥanbal and Bishr al-Ḥāfī: A Case Study in Biographical Traditions," *Studia Islamica* 86, no. 2 [1997]:89), with no mention of Cooperson's study in the entire article. The passage from

the *Ḥilyat* on p. 441 is taken from Leah Kinberg and once again, without reference to the original piece (except in a different context, earlier on); see "What is Meant by Zuhd?" *Studia Islamica* 61 (1985): 36. The Sulamī passage on the same page is also from Kinberg, p. 31, also without any mention of her original study. The Ibn al-ʿArabi passage from the *Fuṣūṣ* on p. 453 is taken directly from Ralph Austin's famous translation, p. 45, but cited directly to the Arabic without an acknowledgment of Austin. There are also passages from secondary sources quoted verbatim without appropriate quotation marks. Compare, for example, (1) the first paragraph on p. 440 with Renard, *Friends of God*, p. 43; (2) the third paragraph on p. 452, also with Renard, *Friends*, 251; and (3) the second paragraph, lines 7–11, p. 439, with Denny, "Qurʾanic Vocabulary," 650. These examples, just a few of many, serve to undermine the integrity of Sirry's study and call into serious question its scholarly value.

17. Sirry is mistaken in his claim that according to Sulamī the source in the story is not Ibn Bashshār but Abū ʿAbd Allāh al-Sakhāwī. "Pious Muslims in the Making," 444. Compare with Sulamī, *Ṭabaqāt*, 36–37.

18. Iṣfahānī, *Ḥilyat*, 7:426–427.

19. Schimmel, *Mystical*, 14.

20. *fa hatafa bihi hātif*. Sulamī, *Ṭabaqāt*, 45.

21. John Renard, *Friends of God: Islamic Images of Piety, Commitment, and Servanthood* (Berkeley: University of California Press, 2008), 83, 68.

22. Hujwīrī, *Kashf*, 103. I have slightly modified the language of Nicholson's 1911 translation to render it more idiomatic in modern English.

23. Iṣfahānī, *Ḥilyat*, 7:427.

24. Iṣfahānī, *Ḥilyat*, 7:427–428.

25. Qushayrī, for example, relates a saying of Ibrāhīm in which he states that if one's food is pure, then there is no need for night vigils and daily fasts. The author of the *Treatise* also presents a story in which the ascetic refuses to acquiesce to the demands of a passing soldier for grapes from a vineyard he is supervising because the owner has not given him explicit permission to distribute or consume its produce. When the solider begins to beat Ibrāhīm for his refusal, he penitently lowers his head and offers it to the solider, overcome as he is by regret over his many sins against God. By then, however, the solider is too overcome with fatigue to continue. *Risāla*, 53–54.

26. Hujwīrī, *Kashf*, 103. In his entry on Ibrāhīm, Shaʿrānī wrote that "if he did not find lawful food, he would eat the dirt (*turāb*)." *Al-Ṭabaqāt al-kubrā*, ed. Khalīl Manṣūr (Beirut: Dār al-Kutub al-ʿIlmiyya, 1997), 101.

27. It was common practice for the Sufis and pious scholars in the medieval Islamic world to avoid accepting food offered by royalty or government officials due to suspicions surrounding their legal status. See Schimmel, *Mystical*, 111.

28. ʿAṭṭār, *Tadhkirat* (abridged), 63–64.

29. Sulamī, *Ṭabaqāt*, 37–40; Qushayrī, *Risāla*, 53.

30. That is to say, in most but not all of the narratives. Mālik b. Dīnār's (d. 748) *tawba* is induced after he is addressed by a lute. Dhū al-Nūn's (d. 861)

tawba also has like Ibrāhīm's *tawba* many supernatural components. See Qushayrī, *Risāla,* 56.

31. Rodney Stark has written a penetrating article exploring the phenomenon of what he calls "upper class asceticism." By exploring some of the accounts of the privileged and "well-to-do" that embraced lives of holy poverty, particularly among medieval Catholics, he argues against the common presumption in the social sciences that "faith is rooted in want and misery" and that it draws its most fervent adherents from the impoverished and the lower classes. This view, notes Stark, was most famously expressed by Marx when he said that "religion is the sigh of the oppressed creature." Although Stark does not examine any figures from the history of Islamic mysticism, Ibrāhīm's story (and those of countless others) might serve to augment his criticisms of what is known as the "deprivation thesis," and substantiate his broader conclusions about the factors that might draw one to religious forms of worldly renunciation. The only problem Ibrāhīm's *tawba* story might present is the extent to which it is steeped in legend. See Rodney Stark, "Upper Class Asceticism: Social Origins of Ascetic Movements and Medieval Saints," *Review of Religious Research* 45, no. 1 (2003): 5–19. A succinct formulation of the "deprivation thesis" can be found in Charles Y. Glock, "The Role of Deprivation in the Origin and Evolution of Religious Groups," in *Religion and Social Conflict,* eds. Robert Lee and Martin Marty (New York: Oxford University Press, 1964), 24–36.

32. For more on this important Shādhilī figure, see Paul Nwyia, *Ibn ʿAṭāʾ Allāh et la naissance de la confrèrie šadilite* (Beirut, 1973).

33. He is third in the order of Qushayrī's biographical section; Ibrāhīm is first. Fuḍayl's *tawba* is discussed below.

34. *La qāla al-qāʾil wa man yadruku hāʾulāʾi.* See Ibn ʿAṭāʾ Allāh al-Iskandarī, *Laṭāʾif al-minan,* ed. Khālid ʿAbd al-Raḥmān al-ʿAkk (Damascus: Dār al-Bashāʾir, 1992), 205; *The Sutble Blessings in the Saintly Lives of Abū al-ʿAbbās al-Mursī and His Master Abū al-Ḥasan al-Shādhilī,* trans. Nancy Roberts (Louisville, KY: Fons Vitae, 2005), 244–245.

35. Al-Shaʿrānī considered Khawwāṣ to be the spiritual "pole" (*qutb*) of the time. See Margaret Smith, "Al-Shaʿrānī the Mystic," *The Muslim World* 29, no. 3 (1930): 241. For more on Shaʿrānī, his teachers, and his works, see Leila Hudson, "The Sufi Genealogy of Islamic Modernism in Late Ottoman Damascus," *Journal of Islamic Studies* 15, no. 1 (2004): 45–53; Michael Winter, *Society and Religion in Early Ottoman Egypt* (Piscataway, NJ: Transaction Books, 1982), 31–69.

36. ʿAbd al-Wahhāb al-Shaʿrānī, *Lawāqiḥ al-anwār al-qudsiyya fī bayān al-ʿuhūd al-muḥammadiyya,* ed. Muḥammad ʿAbd al-Raḥmān (Beirut: Dār Iḥyāʾ al-Turāth al-ʿArabī, 1996), 299.

37. Shaʿrānī, *Lawāqiḥ al-anwār,* 299.

38. For some of the biographical entries on him, see Hujwīrī, *Kashf,* 109–110; Iṣfahānī, *Ḥilyat,* 7:392–425; Qushayrī, *Risāla,* 70–72. For the most comprehensive survey of the source material, see Gramlich, *Alte Vorbilder des Sufitums,* 1: 283–319.

39. Qushayrī, *Risāla,* 71. It is worth noting that Qushayrī provides two accounts for the reason behind Dāwūd's entry into the path. As for the couplet, Ibn Qudāma (d. 1291) cites an alternative version that runs, "You lie here until God raises His creation. There is no hope in meeting you, though you are close. You increase in decay, day and night. Yet, as you deteriorate, you are gradually forgotten, though you are beloved." *Kitāb al-tawwābīn,* ed. ʿAbd al-Qādir al-Arnāʾūṭ (Damascus: Dār al-Bayān, 1969), 206. Although Ibn Qudāma's work does not fall into the typical category of Sufi hagiographies, the Ḥanbalite author gathered together the *tawba*-narratives of angels, prophets, and the pious folk of both the Islamic and the pre-Islamic communities. The work contains a significant section on the conversion narratives of prominent Sufis.

40. For biographical data, see Hujwīrī, *Kashf,* 90–91. Qushayrī and Sulamī do not have an entry on him.

41. Hujwīrī, *Kashf,* 109; Qushayrī, *Risāla,* 71; Iṣfahānī, *Ṭabaqāt,* 7:392–393. See also ʿAṭṭār, in Arberry, *Muslim Saints,* 139.

42. For biographical entries on him, see Hujwīrī, *Kashf,* 97–100; Iṣfahānī, *Ḥilyat,* 8:87–148; Qushayrī, *Risāla,* 57–59; Sulamī, *Ṭabaqāt,* 22–27. For the accounts of his *tawba,* see Hujwīrī, *Kashf,* 97–98; Ibn Qudāma presents two versions, *Tawwābīn,* 207–208; Qushayrī, *Risāla,* 57–58. The conversion narrative is absent in Iṣfahānī as well as Jāmī (*Nafaḥāt,* 1:53–55). For more on Fuḍayl, particularly his relation to the early Ḥanbalī movement, see Jacqueline Chabbi, "Fuḍayl b. ʿIyaḍ, un précurseur du ḥanbalisme," *Bulletin d'études orientales* 30 (1978): 37–55.

43. Hujwīrī, *Kashf,* 97.

44. Iṣfahānī, *Ḥilyat,* 87.

45. Sulamī, *Ṭabaqāt,* 24. For more on Fuḍayl's devotionional reverence for the Qurʾān, see Saleh, *Formation,* 91–92.

46. Jāmī, *Nafaḥāt,* 1:55. According to Ibn Qudāma, who describes his death in a chapter entitled, "The *Tawba* of ʿAlī b. al-Fuḍayl b. ʿIyaḍ," the verse that caused his death was Q 39:47: "there will appear to them from God what they had never reckoned." Ibn Qudāma notes that Fuḍayl, who was aware of his son's sensitivity to Scripture, would exercise self-restraint when reciting the Qurʾān in his company. One day, however, unaware of his son's presence, he read it with his usual intensity, upon which ʿAlī fell into a swoon and died. See Ibn Qudāma, *Tawwābīn,* 209. A companion of Fuḍayl who spent thirty years with him never saw him laugh or smile until the demise of his son. When asked about this, Fuḍayl replied that God "loved this matter, and I have loved what God loved." Fuḍayl's joy was obviously not over the loss of his son, with whom he had a close relation, but over the manner of his death. See Christopher Melchert, "The transition from asceticism to mysticism at the middle of the ninth century," *Studia Islamica* 83, no. 1 (1996): 54. For more on ʿAlī b. Fuḍayl, see Iṣfahānī, *Ḥilyat,* 8:330–333. For an analysis of Thaʿlabī's (d. 1035) *Kitāb yudhkar fīhi qatlā al-qurʾān,* a work which explored early accounts of those "slain by the Qurʾān," see Saleh, *Formation,* 59–64. In the treatise Thaʿlabī argues that those who die in such a manner are to be numbered among martyrs.

47. Hujwīrī, *Kashf*, 98–100.

48. For biographical entries on Abū ʿAmr, see Qushayrī, *Risāla*, 140–141; Sulamī, *Ṭabaqāt*, 339–341.

49. For biographical entries on him, see Hujwīrī, *Kashf*, 132–134; Iṣfahānī, *Ḥilyat*, 10:261–264; Qushayrī, *Risāla*, 97–99; Sulamī, *Ṭabaqāt*, 140–144. For a survey of the source material on him, see Gramlich, *Alte Vorbilder des Sufitums*, 2:113–241.

50. Qushayrī, *Risāla*, 210. I closely follow here the translation of Rabia Harris, 113.

51. Hujwīrī, *Kashf*, 298. ʿAṭṭār provides what appears to be an alternate version of the same story in the *Tadhkirat*, but without identifying the youth whose conversion Abū ʿUthmān inspires, nor with any details about the lapse and subsequent renewal of his *tawba*: "A dissolute young fellow was strolling along with a lute in his hand, completely drunk. Suddenly catching sight of Abū ʿUthmān, he tucked his curls under his cap and drew the lute in his sleeve, thinking that he would denounce him to the authorities. Abū ʿUthmān approached him in the kindest manner. 'Do not be afraid, Brothers are all one,' he said. When the young man saw that, he repented and became a disciple of the shaykh. Abū ʿUthmān instructed him to be washed and invested him, and then raised his head to heaven. 'O God,' he cried, 'I have done my part. The rest Thou must do.' Immediately the youth was visited by such mystical experience that Abū ʿUthmān himself was amazed." Abū ʿUthmān al-Ḥīrī would then later confess to a friend that all which he sought in a lifetime was freely given to a youth "from whose belly the odor of wine still proceeds." ʿAṭṭār, *Tadhkirat* (abridged), 234–235.

52. For some of the biographical entries on him, see Hujwīrī, *Kashf*, 111–112; Iṣfahānī, *Ḥilyat*, 8:62–72; Qushayrī, *Risāla*, 73–84; Sulamī, *Ṭabaqāt*, 63–67. For a comprehensive survey of the source material, see Gramlich, *Alte Vorbilder des Sufitums*, 2:13–62.

53. *arḍ al-turk wa huwa ḥadath*. The "Turks" mentioned here would be the Uighurs of Eastern Turkestan.

54. Qushayrī, *Risāla*, 73.

55. Iṣfahānī, *Ḥilyat*, 8:63; cf. Ibn Qudāma, *Tawwābīn*, 161.

56. Qushayrī, *Risāla*, 73; Sulamī, *Ṭabaqāt*, 63.

57. Hujwīrī, *Kashf*, 112. Alexander Knysh observes that "Shaqīq is often described as the earliest exponent, if not the founder, of *tawakkul*." See *Islamic Mysticism*, 33. He acquired a reputation for his views on the "repudiation of normal gain" (*inkār al-kasb*). According to Muḥāsibī, he claimed that any effort (*ḥaraka*) in its direction was a sin. This meant that one had to live on what was provided by circumstance. See Christopher Melchert, "Baṣran Origins of Classical Sufism," *Der Islam* 82 (2005): 231. It is worth noting the contrast between Shaqīq's own views on the question of earning a livelihood and those of his own teacher Ibrāhīm b. Adham. The latter's position, as noted earlier, may have had to do with the peculiar circumstances of his own *tawba*, along with his desire to atone for past wrongs.

58. ʿAṭṭār, *Tadhkirat* (abridged), 134.

59. *EI*², s.v. "Balkh," "Khurāsān."

60. For biographical entries, see Hujwīrī, *Kashf*, 95–97; Iṣfahānī, *Ḥilyat*, 9:172–206. Qushayrī and Sulamī do not have entries on him.

61. Knysh, *Mysticism*, 21.

62. Hujwīrī, *Kashf*, 96.

63. Hujwīrī, *Kashf*, 96. There is no entry on him in Qushayrī's *Risāla* and Sulamī's *Ṭabaqāt*; nor is his *tawba* included in Ibn Qudāma's work. Iṣfahānī also does not mention the circumstances of his *tawba* in the *Ḥilyat*.

64. Hujwīrī, *Kashf*, 96.

65. For biographical entries on Sarī al-Saqaṭī, see Hujwīrī, *Kashf*, 110–111; Iṣfahānī, *Ḥilyat*, 10:119–132; Qushayrī, *Risāla*, 62–65; Sulamī, *Ṭabaqāt*, 51–58.

66. Hujwīrī, *Kashf*, 110–111. The entries on Saqaṭī in Jāmī, Iṣfahānī, and Sulamī do not mention his conversion.

67. For biographical entries on him, see Hujwīrī, *Kashf*, 113–115; Iṣfahānī, *Ḥilyat*, 8:404–412; Qurayshī, *Risāla*, 59–61; Sulamī, *Ṭabaqāt*, 80–86.

68. Qushayrī, *Risāla*, 62. See also ʿAṭṭār, *Muslim Saints*, 163–164.

69. Qushayrī, *Risāla*, 62.

70. I have been unable to determine the exact date of his death. Jāmī has an entry on him immediately after his *shaykh*, Ibrāhīm b. Saʿd al-ʿAlawī. See *Nafaḥāt*, 1:63. He would have lived sometime between the ninth and tenth centuries since his *shaykh* was a contemporary of Abū Saʿīd al-Kharrāz (d. 899). Hujwīrī, *Kashf*, 374. His conversion would have occurred in the ninth century. According to Jāmī, he set out to visit Dhū al-Nūn (d. 861) in Egypt to find an answer to a particular question, but arrived on the day following his death. After being overcome by sleep after a prayer over his gravesite, he beholds him in a dream, whereupon the Egyptian Sufi answers his query. Jāmī, *Nafaḥāt*, 1:64. There is no biographical entry on Awlāsī in Sulamī, Iṣfahānī, Hujwīrī, and Qushayrī. Iṣfahānī includes a few anecdotes about him and Ibrāhīm b. Saʿd in an entry on the latter, *Ḥilyat*, 10:163–165.

71. Ibn Qudāma, *Tawwābīn*, 230.

72. For biographical entries on him, see Hujwīrī, *Kashf*, 105–106; Iṣfahānī, *Ḥilyat*, 8:378–403; Qushayrī, *Risāla*, 65–69. For a study of his representation in the source literature, see Michael Cooperson, "Ibn Ḥanbal and Bishr al-Ḥāfī," 85–91.

73. Hujwīrī, *Kashf*, 105. The same account is found in Qushayrī, without mention of his drunkenness. Qushayrī writes, "The reason for his *tawba* [was as follows]: He found on the road a slip of paper on which was inscribed the name of God, most High, and which had been trodden over, under foot. He took it and bought, with a dirham in his possession, some perfume made of musk and ambergris (*ghāliya*) and perfumed it, putting it in the crevice of a wall. Then, later when he was asleep, he saw in a dream (*fa raʾā fīmā yarā al-nāʾim*) as if a caller were saying to him, 'O Bishr, you perfumed My name, I will perfume your name in this world and the next.'" Qushayrī, *Risāla*, 66.

74. Iṣfahānī, *Ḥilyat*, 8:378; cf. Ibn Qudāma, *Tawwābīn*, 210.

75. I have been unable to determine more about the identity of this figure on the basis of a survey of the biographical literature. He is not to be confused with Abū ʿAlī al-Daqqāq, the teacher of Qushayrī.

76. Kalābādhī, *Taʿarruf,* 65; Sulamī, *Ḥaqāʾiq,* 1:183. Sulamī attributes the saying simply to Daqqāq.

77. This is not withstanding the debate over exactly how sinless prophets may be even before their divine callings. Kalābādhī has a concise discussion on the "slips" of the prophets. See *Taʿarruf,* 46–47.

78. Renard, *Friends,* 44.

Chapter 4

1. The term *mawāqif* or "halting places" was also employed, most notably by Niffarī (d. 965), but it was not used in the same sense as *maqām* or *manzil* to designate the ascending hierarchy of virtues beginning with repentance. See *EI*[2], s.v. "Al-Niffarī;" Muḥammad b. ʿAbd al-Jabbār al-Niffarī, *Al-Mawāqif wa al-mukhāṭabāt,* ed. and trans. A.J. Arberry (London: Cambridge University Press, 1935). Derivates of the root **w-q-f** appear in the Qurʾān on four occasions (Q 6:27; 6:30; 34:31; 37:24), but in none of these as *mawāqif* or its singular *mawqif.* The term never gained the degree of circulation as *maqāmāt* or *manāzil* in the Sufi tradition. The entry on "*Mawqif*" in *EI*[2], for example, makes no mention of its use in Sufism.

2. Penrice, *Dictionary and Glossary of the Koran,* 122.

3. Qushayrī, *Risāla,* 156; ʿAbd Allāh b. ʿAlī al-Sarrāj, *Kitāb al-lumaʿ fī al-taṣawwuf,* ed. Reynold Nicholson (Leiden: Brill, 1914), 41–42. The use of *maqām* may also have been influenced by the popularity of powerful eschatological terms derived from the same root, such as *qiyāma* ("resurrection"), which appears in the Qurʾān no less than seventy times. It is worth noting in this context that in the early Syriac speaking churches of the Syria-Mesopotamia region (where Sufism would have flourished after the coming of Islam) those who were baptized and surrendered themselves to the ascetic and celibate demands of the religious life were known as the *benai qeyāmā* ("sons of the Qeyāmā"). While most scholars understand the expression to mean "sons of the covenant," in which the covenant is taken to be that of the baptismal vow, some such as Peter Nagel understand it to mean "sons of the resurrection." In Nagel's reading, the *benai qeyāma* are those who anticipate through their monastic otherworldliness the final resurrection while still in this world. See S.P. Brock, "Early Syrian Asceticism," *Numen* 20 (1973): 6–8. If Nagel is correct, the expression seems to have its origin in the Old Syriac translation of Luke 35–36, which runs (in Brock's translation), "Those who become worthy to receive that world [i.e., the kingdom] and that resurrection from the dead, do not marry, nor can they die, for they have been made equal with the angels, [and being] the sons of the resurrection [they are] like the sons of God." See Brock, 6. Most of the *benai qeyāmā* are now considered to be part of the community of the early Desert Fathers.

4. Qushayrī, *Risāla,* 157.

5. See Q 8:24, 11:43, and 34:54.

6. Hujwīrī, *Kashf,* 181.

7. Massignon, *Passion,* 3:67. According to Massignon, this is where Muḥāsibī most likely integrated the term into his own Sufi psychology.

8. *EI²*, s.v. "Ḥāl;" Massignon, *Passion,* 3:67–68.

9. Abū Ḥafṣ Shihāb al-Dīn Suhrawardī, *ʿAwārif al-maʿārif,* ed. Sayyid Aḥmad, Adīb al-Kimrānī, and Maḥmūd Muṣṭafā (Saudi Arabia: Al-Maktaba al-Makkiyya, 2001), 2:812–813.

10. Knysh, *Islamic Mysticism,* 34. Paul Nwyia has argued for the authenticity of this attribution in *Exégèse coranique et langage mystique,* 213–216.

11. For an analysis of *tawakkul* in Sufism, see Benedikt Reinert, *Die Lehre vom tawakkul in der klassischen Sufik* (Berlin: Walter de Gruyter, 1968).

12. *Ādāb al-ʿibādāt,* in *Nuṣūṣ al-ṣūfiyya ghayr manshūra,* ed. Paul Nwyia (Beirut: Dār el-Mashreq, 1972), 17–22. For more on this text and Shaqīq's views on the growth of the the soul, see Sarah Sviri's "The Self and its Transformation in Ṣūfism," in *Self and Self-Transformation in the History of Religions,* eds. David Shulman and Guy G. Stroumsa (Oxford: Oxford University Press, 2002): 199–200.

13. Massignon, *Essay,* 145. I have made some slight modifications in the translation on the basis of the Arabic citation within brackets.

14. For some of the early biographical entries on Abū Sulaymān al-Dārānī, see Hujwīrī, *Kashf,* 112–113; Iṣfahānī, *Ḥilyat,* 9: 267–292; Qushayrī, *Risāla,* 80–81; Sulamī, *Ṭabaqāt,* 74–80. For a survey of the source material, see Richard Gramlich, "Abū Sulaymān ad-Dārānī," *Oriens* 33 (1992): 22–85.

15. Massignon, *Essay,* 145.

16. See, for example, some of the standard collections, where he speaks extensively of such virtues as *tawakkul, rajāʾ, maḥabba,* and *khawf,* and their relation to each other and the larger journey; Iṣfahānī, *Ḥilyat,* 9:345–410; Jāmī, *Nafaḥāt,* 1:46–50; Sulamī, *Ṭabaqāt,* 27–34.

17. *EI²*, s.v. "Ḥāl."

18. Hujwīrī, *Kashf,* 180–182. Muḥāsibī was one of those few figures for whom the *ḥāl* could be permanent, 181.

19. Although Dhū al-Nūn, and to a lesser extent, Muḥāsibī, stand out as the most likely candidates to whom we can trace the origins of this schematization, we should keep in mind the difficulty in drawing crisp chronological or conceptual lines that do injustice to the "process of the organic, gradual growth of mystical ideas from the simple piety of Islam's first devotees." See Knysh, *Mysticism,* 34.

20. For some of the biographical entries on him, see Hujwīrī, *Kashf,* 100–103; Iṣfahānī, *Ḥilyat,* 9:345–419; Qushayrī, *Risāla,* 54–57; Sulamī, *Ṭabaqāt,* 27–34. See also Mohammed Rustom, "The Sufi Teachings of Dhuʾl Nun," *Sacred Web* (2009): 69–79.

21. Massignon, *Essay,* 146. I have modified Mason's English translation of Massignon's original French based directly on the Arabic as it appears in Abū Ḥāmid al-Ghazālī, *Iḥyāʾ ʿulūm al-dīn* (Aleppo: Dār al-Waʿi, 1998), 4:23.

22. Sarrāj, *Lumaʿ,* 43–54.

23. Abū Ṭālib al-Makkī, *Qūt al-qulūb fī muʿāmalat al-maḥbūb wa waṣf ṭarīq al-murīd ilā maqām al-tawḥīd*, ed. Saʿīd Nasīb Mukārim (Beirut: Dār al-Ṣādir, 1995), 1:361.

24. Abū Bakr b. Muḥammad al-Kalābādhī, *al-Taʿarruf li madhhab ahl al-taṣawwuf*, ed. Yuḥannā Ḥabīb Ṣādir (Beirut: Dār Ṣādir, 2001), 65–66.

25. Abū Saʿīd al-Kharrāz, *The Book of Truthfulness (Kitāb al-Ṣidq) by Abū Saʿīd al-Kharrāz* [with Arabic text], ed. and trans. by A.J. Arberry (Oxford: Oxford University Press, 1937), 7–27; Arabic, 9–41.

26. See the *Risāla maqāmāt al-qulūb* of Nūrī in Paul Nwyia, "Textes Mystiques Inédits D'Abū-l Ḥasan al-Nūrī (m. 295/907)," *Mélanges de l'Université Saint Joseph* 43 (1968): 131–132. Nūrī does not explore in any detail the order of the *maqāmāt* in this short treatise, which is concerned first and foremost with the various kinds of spiritual hearts. See Nwyia, ibid, 117–127. For some of the early biographical entries on Nūrī, see Hujwīrī, *Kashf*, 189–195; Iṣfahānī, *Ḥilyat*, 10:267–273; Qushayrī, *Risāla*, 99–100; Sulamī, *Ṭabaqāt*, 135–139. See also Gramlich's study of Nūrī and his *Maqāmāt al-qulūb* in *Alte Vorbilder des Sufitums*, 1:381–445, and Schimmel's excellent article, "Abu'l Ḥusayn al-Nūrī: 'Qibla of the Lights,'" in *Classical Persian Sufism from Its Origins to Rumi*, ed. Leonard Lewisohn (London: Nimatullahi Publications, 1993), 59–64.

27. Although Muḥāsibī does place some virtues before others, as we shall see in chapter 5, he does not produce a fixed order.

28. For more on Abū Saʿīd, see Fritz Meier, *Abū Saʿīd-i Abū l-Ḫayr (357–440/967–1049): Wirklichkeit und Legende* (Tehran: Bibliothèque Pahlavi, 1976).

29. Kamāl al-Dīn ʿAbd al-Razzāq al-Kāshānī, *Sharḥ manāzil al-sāʾirīn*, ed. Muḥsin Bidārfur, 2nd edition (Qum: Shariʿat, 1381 AH Solar). The levels begin with wakefulness and end with *tawḥīd*.

30. William Chittick, *Sufism: An Introduction* (Oxford: Oneworld, 2000), 93.

31. I say "general sense" because technically speaking Ibn al-ʿArabī does not simply repeat Qushayrī's order of chapters. Most of them are followed by chapters on leaving (*tark*) the very *maqām* in question. The chapter on *tawba*, for example, is followed by a chapter on "abandoning repentance" (*tark al-tawba*). The general order of the *maqāmāt*, however, remains the same as found in the *Risāla*. For more on the relationship between the *Futūḥāt* and the *Risāla*, see Michel Chodkiewicz, "*Miʿrāj al-kalima*: de la *Risāla Qushayriyya* aux *Futūḥāt Makkiyya*," in *Reason and Inspiration in Islam: Theology, Philosophy, and Mysticism in Muslim Thought*, ed. Todd Lawson (London: I.B. Tauris & Institute of Ismaili Studies, 2005), 248–261.

32. Ibn al-ʿArabī's first exposure to the technical language of Sufism came through the influence of one of his teachers, Yūsuf al-Kūmī, who introduced him to the *Risāla*. According to the historian Ibn ʿAbd al-Mālik al-Marrākushī (d. 1303), Ibn al-ʿArabī was so committed to reading this work that he was given the surname "al-Qushayrī." See Claude Addas, *Quest for the Red Sulphur: The Life of Ibn ʿArabi*, trans. Peter Kingsley (Cambridge: The Islamic Texts Society, 1993), 102–103.

33. Ibn ʿAjība, the eighteenth-century Shādhilī figure—admittedly a much later author—notes that a station may be experienced temporarily as a state before it becomes fixed. In other words, a person may lapse in and out of *tawba* before it finally becomes rooted as a station. See his *Book of Ascension to the Essential Truths of Sufism: Miʿrāj al-tashawwuf ilā ḥaqāʾiq al-taṣawwuf*, trans. Mohamed Aresmouk and Michael Fitzgerald (Louisville, KY: Fons Vitae, 2011), 30.

34. For brief discussions of *qabḍ* and *basṭ*, see Hujwīrī, *Kashf*, 374–375; Qushayrī, *Risāla*, 159–161; Sells has translated Qushayrī's short section in *Early Islamic Mysticism*, 105–108. See also ʿAbd al-Razzāq al-Kāshānī, *Iṣṭilāḥāt al-ṣūfiyya*, ed. ʿAbd al-ʿĀl Shāhīn (Cairo: Dār al-ʿInār, 1992), 352–354; idem, *Rashḥ al-zulāl*, 70–72.

35. Sulamī, *Ṭabaqāt*, 30.

36. Interestingly, however, in his Persian treatise, *Kitāb-i ṣad maydān*, also a study of various stages of the way, he begins with repentance. See Anṣārī, *Chemin de Dieu: Trois traités spirituels (Les Cent Terrains / Les Etapes des Itinérants vers Dieu / Les Déficiences des Demeures)*, ed. and trans. Serge de Laugier de Beaurecueil (Paris: Sinbad, 1985), 86. A.G. Ravan Farhadi has compared the order of the stations in three of Anṣārī's texts in his *Abdullah Ansari of Herat: An Early Sufi Master* (Surrey: Curzon, 1996), 147–150.

37. Gutas, "Classical Arabic Wisdom Literature: Nature and Scope," *Journal of the American Oriental Society*, 101, no. 1 (1981): 49–86. See 60.

38. Gutas, "Classical Arabic Wisdom Literature," 60.

39. Cited in Gutas, "Classical Arabic Wisdom Literature," 50.

40. Sīrjānī, *Bayāḍ*, 286 [#623]. The translation is a slightly modified version of that provided by the editors in their introduction, 12–13.

41. See my discussion of this theme in "Abū Ṭālib al-Makkī and the *Nourishment of Hearts* (*Qūt al-qulūb*) in the Context of Early Sufism," *Muslim World* 122, no. 2 (2012): 335–356.

42. This at least is Gutas's argument. He notes that the *ḥakīm* in pre-Islamic Arabia was distinguished not only for his knowledge, but his ability to express it with the right choice of words. This was unlike simply the *ʿālim*, whose words on occasion did not arise above "prattle." This understanding of *ḥikma*, for Gutas, is also assumed by the Qurʾān. See "Classical Arabic Wisdom Literature," 49–55, especially 54.

43. Cited in Gutas, "Classical Arabic Wisdom Literature," 52.

44. Cited in Sīrjānī, *Bayāḍ*, 7 [#4]. The translation is a slightly modified version of that provided by the editors in their introduction, 18.

45. Cited in Sīrjānī, *Bayāḍ*, 7 [#4]. I offer here a slightly modified version of the saying offered by the editors in their introduction, 18.

46. Hujwīrī, *Kashf*, 356–357.

47. This tripartite division is not unique to Sufism. Fārābī (d. 950) employs it in his political philosophy to describe the three classes of citizens: the common lot of believers, the theologians, and the philosophers. Ibn Rushd (d. 1198) elaborates this scheme in his *Faṣl al-maqāl*, where he argues that each of these

three classes of people comes to understand God, respectively, through rhetoric (*al-aqāwīl al-khiṭābiyya*), dialectic (*al-aqāwīl al-jadaliyya*), and demonstration (*al-aqāwīl al-burhāniyya*). See *The Decisive Treatise and Epistle Dedicatory*, trans. Charles E. Butterworth (Provo, UT: Brigham Young University Press, 2001), 8. For the Sufis, the division is typically between average religious people, novice Sufis, and advanced Sufis, each of whom possess, in ascending order, *ʿilm al-yaqīn* (knowledge of certainty), *ʿayn al-yaqīn* (essence of certainty), and *ḥaqq al-yaqīn* (truth or reality of certainty). Sometimes the tripartite schema is among the general class of Sufis (novices, advanced mystics, and realized mystics). See Spencer Trimingham, *The Sufi Orders of Islam*, reprint (Oxford: Oxford University Press, 1998), 264–265. For a treatment of these three levels of knowledge by a modern Sufi writer, see Abū Bakr Sirāj al-Dīn (Martin Lings), *The Book of Certainty: The Sufi Doctrine of Faith, Vision, and Gnosis* (Cambridge: The Islamic Texts Society, 1992). Jonathan Brown has explored the origins of this tripartite division in "The Last Days of al-Ghazzālī and the Tripartite Division of the Sufi World," *Muslim World* 96, no. 1 (2006): 97–106.

48. The pairing is not always consistent. As it has been shown in the case of *zuhd*, the virtue is variously defined in the early literature in relation to *tawakkul* or *riḍāʾ*, as well as through the quality of *qiṣar al-ʾamal* ("shortened hopes"). See Leah Kinberg, "What is meant by Zuhd," *Studia Islamica* 61 (1985): 31–36.

49. Etziono and Carvey draw out a few of the universal features of repentance in the introduction to *Repentance: A Comparative Perspective*, 1–20.

50. Since these sayings tend to become redundant in the sources, the citations will be limited in our inquiry to limit repetition.

51. Sulamī, *Ḥaqāʾiq*, 1:281. The saying is ascribed to Abū ʿUthmān. This is most likely the well-known Sufi, Abū ʿUthmān al-Ḥīrī. For more on him see note 49 in chapter 3. It could also be Saʿīd b. Salām (d. 983), also known as Abū ʿUthmān al-Maghribī (d. 983), and on whom Sulamī also has an entry, *Ṭabaqāt*, 359–362; see also Hujwīrī, *Kashf*, 158–159; Qushayrī, *Risāla*, 112–113. Of the latter, Sulamī quotes the following saying: "the sinner (*al-ʿāṣī*) is better than the one who makes claims (*al-muddaʿī*) because the sinner is constantly looking for a way to his repentance (*ṭarīq tawbatihi*) while the one who makes claims fumbles about [entangled] in the cords of his pretensions." See *Ṭabaqāt*, 359. Ḥīrī is more often quoted by Sulamī than Maghribī.

52. Qushayrī, *Risāla*, 214. The saying appears anonymously in Sulamī, *Ḥaqāʾiq*, 1:312.

53. Moucarry, *Search for Forgiveness*, 106–116.

54. Sulamī, *Ḥaqāʾiq*, 2:44.

55. Sulamī, *Ḥaqāʾiq*, 2:337. Attributed to Dhū al-Nūn. Another early figure said, "from among the signs of the sincerity of the repentant one in his repentance is that he exchange [. . .] for the enjoyment [found] in committing the sin, sadness on its account (*al-ḥuzn ʿalayh*)." Makkī, *Qūt*, 1:366.

56. Sīrjānī, *Bayāḍ*, 90 [#195].

57. The verse reads, "And to the three also who were left behind, the earth, despite its vastness became constrained for them, and their own souls were

constrained for them, until they thought there is no refuge from God except toward Him. Then He turned to them that they might re/turn."

58. Qushayrī, *Risāla*, 214. Compare with Abū ʿUthmān al-Ḥīrī, "He who returns to God and His path (*sabīlihi*), let the description [found] in this verse [apply to him], that the earth constrains itself for him to the extent that he does not find a firm place to step without fear that God might avenge him in that [very] place. And that his breaths become constrained so that he awaits destruction with every breath (*nafas*). These are the initial proofs of sincere repentance." Sulamī, *Ḥaqāʾiq*, 1:291.

59. Qushayrī, *Risāla*, 208.

60. Makkī attributes the saying to an anonymous figure from Shām. *Qūt*, 1:366. Khargūshī identifies the individual as a certain Abū ʿAbd Allāh b. al-Jallāʾ. See *Tahdhīb*, 80.

61. Sulamī, *Ḥaqāʾiq*, 2:337. Attributed to Abū Sulaymān al-Dārānī.

62. Sulamī, *Ḥaqāʾiq*, 2:42.

63. For more on Abū al-ʿAbbās b. ʿAṭāʾ, see Sulamī, *Ṭabaqāt*, 207–212. See also Qushayrī, *Risāla*, 115–116. Sulamī frequently quotes him in the *tafsīr*. See also Richard Gramlich, *Abu l-ʿAbbās b. ʿAṭāʾ: Sufi und Koranausleger* (Stuggart: F. Steiner, 1995).

64. Sulamī, *Ḥaqāʾiq*, 2:69. Ibn ʿAṭāʾ also states that "he who makes sound his repentance through righteous deeds has his repentance accepted." Sulamī, *Ḥaqāʾiq*, 2:69.

65. Makkī, *Qūt*, 1:366.

66. The last three sayings are cited in Tor Andrae's chapter on "Solitude and Fellowship" from *In the Garden of Myrtles: Studies in Early Islamic Mysticism*, trans. Birgitta Sharpe (Albany: State University of New York Press, 1987), 59–60. His work, originally published in Swedish in 1947 shortly after his death, offers one of the most sensitive insights into the early tradition.

67. His full name was Abū al-Ḥasan ʿAlī Aḥmad b. Sahl al-Bushanjī; he was a disciple of the famous Ibn ʿAṭāʾ (d. 922) and Jurayrī (d. 923–924). See Qushayrī, *Risāla*, 141–142. See also Sulamī, *Ṭabaqāt*, 342–344.

68. Qushayrī, *Risāla*, 214.

69. Sulamī, *Ḥaqāʾiq*, 1:312.

70. This is the "sincere repentance" referred to in the famous *tawba* verse, Q 66:8.

71. Sulamī, *Ḥaqāʾiq*, 2:337.

72. Hujwīrī, *Kashf*, 112.

73. Sīrjānī, *Bayāḍ*, 90–91 [#196].

74. Khargūshī, *Tahdhīb*, 78.

75. Qushayrī, *Risāla*, 215. The author most likely had in mind Rābiʿa al-ʿAdawiyya (d. 801). Although there were others of the same namesake who preceded Qushayrī, she was the most famous and oft-quoted of them. Qushayrī does not have an entry on her in the biographical section of the *Risāla* for the simple reason that his entries are on men. Sulamī has an entry on her, not in

the *Ṭabaqāt*, also dedicated to the biographies of men, but in an appendix to the work on distinguished female Sufis, the *Dhikr al-niswa al-muta'abbidāt al-ṣūfiyyāt*. See *Early Sufi Women*, trans. Rkia E. Cornell (Louisville, KY: Fonz Vitae, 1999), 74–81. Rābi'a al-'Adawiyya's prominence among female mystics is attested to by Sulamī's decision to begin his entries with her. If the Rābi'a in question is not al-Adawiyya, it may be Rābi'a al-Azdiyya (d. uncertain) or Rābi'a b. Ismā'īl (d. 9th century), on both of whom Sulamī also has entries. See *Early Sufi Women*, 128; 138–141. It is not out of the question that although Qushayrī thought he was quoting al-'Adawiyya the account is that of another. Karamustafa notes "a certain degree of confusion between her and other Rābi'as" in the hagiographical literature, "most notably her contemporary Rābi'a bint Ismā'īl of Syria." In many of these cases, sayings and anecdotes of the other Rābi'as were ascribed to her. See Karamustafa, *Sufism*, 3; Sells, *Early Islamic Mysticism*, 152. For more on Rābi'a al-'Adawiyya, see 'Abd al-Wahhāb al-Sha'rānī, *al-Ṭabaqāt al-kubrā*, ed. Khalīl Manṣūr (Beirut: Dār al-Kutub al-'Ilmiyya, 1997), 95; Smith, *Rabi'a the Mystic*. An excellent translation of 'Aṭṭār's account of her in the *Tadhkirat al-awliyā'* appears in Sells, *Early Islamic Mysticism*, 151–170. For her life story presented in the form of a novel, see Widad el Sakkakini *First Among Sufis: The Life and Thought of Rabia al-Adawiyya, the Woman Saint of Basra*, trans. Nabil Safwat (1982; repr., London: Octagon Press, 1995). For more on Rābi'a b. Ismā'īl, wife of Aḥmad al-Ḥawārī (d. 845), see Massignon, *Essay*, 154; Sha'rānī, *Ṭabaqāt*, 96; Schimmel, *Mystical*, 427; Smith, *Rabi'a the Mystic*, 170–173. For some insightful scholarly treatments of women in Sufism in general, see Saadia Khawar Khan Chishti, "Female Spirituality in Islam," in *Islamic Spirituality: Foundations*, ed. Seyyed Hossein Nasr (New York: Crossroad, 1987), 199–219; Maria Massi Dakake, "'Walking the Path of God like Men?' Women and the Feminine in the Islamic Mystical Tradition," in *Sufism: Love and Wisdom*, ed. Jean-Louis Michon (Bloomington, IN: World Wisdom Books, 2006), 131–152; Annemarie Schimmel, *My Soul is a Woman: The Feminine in Islam*, trans. Susan H. Ray (New York: Continuum, 1995), 34–54; Timothy Winter, "The Chador of God on Earth: The Metaphysics of the Muslim Veil," *New Blackfriars* (2004): 144–157. Sachiko Murata's *Tao of Islam* (Albany: State University of New York Press, 1992) remains the most thorough study of the cosmology and ontology of the feminine in Sufism and the wider sapiential tradition of Islam.

76. This is Abū Ḥafṣ Nīshābūrī. See Sulamī, *Ṭabaqāt*, 103–109. See also Hujwīrī, *Kashf*, 123–125; Qushayrī, *Risāla*, 87–88. The year 874, according to Qushayrī, is the approximate date of his death. Also known as Abū Ḥafs al-Ḥaddād, he was the teacher of Abū 'Uthmān al-Ḥīrī and one of the *shaykh*s of those affiliated with the *malāmatiyya* or "Path of Blame." See Karamustafa, *Sufism*, 48–49.

77. Qushayrī, *Risāla*, 215; Sulamī, *Ḥaqā'iq*, 1:290.

78. This is Abū al-Qāsim al-Naṣrābādhī. See Sulamī, *Ṭabaqāt*, 362–365. See also Hujwīrī, *Kashf*, 159–160; Qushayrī, *Risāla*, 147–148. Sulamī is said to have received a *khirqa* of initiation from him. See Karamustafa, *Sufism*, 62–63.

79. Sulamī, *Ḥaqāʾiq*, 1:114.

80. For an excellent discussion of the nature of "essentially contested" problems in the history of philosophy and theology, see Peter Coates, *Ibn ʿArabī and Modern Thought: The History of Taking Metaphysics Seriously* (Oxford: Anqa Publishing, 2002).

81. Indeed, as Ghazālī would argue in his *Kitāb al-ṣabr wa al-shukr*, some of the sayings of the early Sufis were articulated in response to a particular questioner, whose capacity for comprehension and whose state (*ḥāl al-sāʾil*) the respondent had in mind when he gave his answer. Others were uttered in a particular state that had overcome the Sufi himself, and may have been different had he been experiencing another state. These considerations, for Ghazālī, cannot be ignored when attempting to understand the sayings of the Sufis. *Iḥyāʾ*, 4:131.

82. Sometimes the order is inverted so the saying runs, "the sins of those brought near are the good deeds of the pious." The teaching remains the same. The saying is attributed to Dhū al-Nūn in many of the early sources. For one citation, see Sarrāj, *Lumaʿ*, 44. He also cites another saying illustrative of what Dhū al-Nūn had in mind, that "the ostentation of the gnostics is the sincerity of the aspirants." Ibid.

83. This reaches an extreme in mystical thinkers like Wāsiṭī and Ibn al-ʿArabī, who speak of the intrinsic goodness of even morally reprehensible acts on account of their ultimate divine origins. But this, again, is not an inversion of values because all acts from this perspective are seen as beautiful. Sells briefly addresses the question of "perspectivalism" in Sufi texts, and although his observations are not directed at Sufi ethics, they are just as relevant. See Sells, *Early Islamic Mysticism*, 98, as well as my essay, "The Interplay of Divine-Human Gratitude in the Non-Dualism of Ibn al-ʿArabī," in *Remembrance, Discourse, and Beauty in Islamicate Civilization*, edited by Omid Ghaemmaghami and Sebastian Günther (Leiden: Brill [forthcoming]).

84. Qushayrī, *Risāla*, 117–118.

85. The text has Nubbān, but this is a typo involving the placing of the dots as the individual is clearly Bunnān al-Ḥammāl, on whom Sulamī has an entry. See *Ṭabaqāt*, 224–227. Cf. Khargūshī, *Tahdhīb*, 78.

86. Sulamī, *Ḥaqāʾiq*, 2:68–69.

87. Ṭabarī, *Salwat*, 112. The author does not comment about the *walī*'s seemingly superior rank before a prophet as great as Christ, at least with respect to his detachment from food.

88. Makkī, *Qūt*, 1:380.

89. We shall see how Wāsiṭī draws out the wider implications of this theological view in relation to repentance later in this chapter.

90. Even if the particular Sufi was, in those rarer cases, of Muʿtazilite persuasion, and traced the origin of the act back to himself, he could still very well accept the notion of repenting of *ruʾyat al-ḥasanāt*. In his case it would simply entail striving to eradicate whatever traces of pride might be felt on account of his moral and spiritual accomplishments. For more on Sufi Muʿtazilites, see

Osman Aydinli, "Ascetic and Devotional Elements in the Muʿtazilite Tradition: The Sufi Muʿtazilites," *The Muslim World* 97 (2007): 174–189; Florian Sobieroj, "The Muʿtazila and Sufism," in *Islamic Mysticism Contested: Thirteen Centuries of Controversies and Polemics*, ed. Frederick De Jong and Bernd Radtke (Leiden: Brill, 1992), 68–92.

91. I have been unable to find any reference to him in the biographical literature.

92. Qushayrī, *Risāla*, 213. This saying is attributed to Bunnān al-Ḥammāl in Sulamī, *Ḥaqāʾiq*, 2:69, and Khargūshī, *Tahdhīb*, 78. See also Sīrjānī (who cites two variants), *Bayāḍ*, 90 [#193, 195].

93. Sīrjānī, *Bayāḍ*, 90 [#193]. There is also the saying of Shiblī (d. 945), "the [common] people repent of their sins, but God has servants who repent of defects (*ʿuyūb*) in acts of obedience (*ṭāʾāt*)." Sīrjānī, *Bayāḍ*, 91 [#197]. For more on Shiblī, see note 47 in chapter 5.

94. Sulamī, *Ḥaqāʾiq*, 1:312. Similarly, Nūrī describes *tawba* as turning away from "everything other than God most High"; see Sarrāj, *Lumaʿ*, 44.

95. Sīrjānī, *Bayāḍ*, 89 [#192].

96. *maḥw al-bashariyya bi ithbāt al-ilāhiyya wa qatl al-nafs ʿammā dūn Allāh.* Sīrjānī, *Kitāb al-bayāḍ wa-l sawād*, 89.

97. Qushayrī, *Risāla*, 212. Elsewhere Daqqāq produces a somewhat analogous tripartite division of prayer: "There are three degrees: to ask, to pray, to praise. Asking belongs to those who wish this world, praying to those who wish the other world, and praising to those who wish the Lord" (cited in *Schimmel, Mystical*, 161–162). For more on Daqqāq, see Hujwīrī, *Kashf*, 162–163; Jāmī, *Nafaḥāt*, 418–421.

98. Hujwīrī, *Kashf*, 294–296. See also Böwering, "Early Sufism," 50.

99. It is absent from my inquiry into a wide range of extant works, including the writings of Kharrāz, Muḥāsibī, Kalābādhī, Makkī, Sarrāj, Sulamī, Sīrjānī, Khargūshī, and Ṭabarī. According to Schimmel, Hujwīrī's "tripartition is not found elsewhere." See *Mystical*, 110.

100. This is most likely Ḥallāj (d. 922), whom Sulamī refers to in other places of the *tafsīr* by his full name Ḥusayn b. Manṣūr. In Sulamī's entry on him in the *Ṭabaqāt* (236–239), some of his sayings are introduced by someone reporting, "I heard Husayn say," or "Ḥusayn was asked," indicating that he was, on occasion, simply referred to by his first name. The individual in question could also be al-Ḥusayn b. ʿAbd Allāh (no death date given), on whom Sulamī also has an entry, but this seems unlikely considering how little we know of him, and how frequently "Ḥusayn" is quoted in the *tafsīr*. See *Ṭabaqāt*, 252–254. Ḥallāj is also quoted simply by his first name in Sulamī's *Laṭāʾif al-miʿrāj*. See *Subtleties of the Ascension*, trans. Frederick Colby (Louisville, KY: Fons Vitae, 2006), 53, 217. For other biographical entries on Ḥallāj, see Hujwīrī, *Kashf*, 150–153; Jāmī, *Nafaḥāt*, 1:225–227. That Qushayrī excluded him from the biographical section of the *Risāla* is not surprising considering his intention to present, in the words of Jawid Mojaddedi, "the diachronic Sufi community stemming from the time of

the Prophet without any 'weak links.'" Although Ḥallāj's sayings are included in the main text of the *Risāla*, which indicates that he did not reject him, to have included an entry on him would have defeated one of the purposes of the work, which was to legitimize Sufism. See Jawid Mojaddedi, "Legitimizing Sufism in al-Qushayrī's *Risala*," *Studia Islamica* 90 (2000): 42.

101. Sulamī, *Ḥaqā'iq*, 2:202.

102. This is most likely the famous Abū al-ʿAbbās al-Sayyārī (d. 953–954), whose name was Qāsim b. al-Qāsim b. al-Mahdī, and the only one by that name on whom Sulamī has an entry. See *Ṭabaqāt* 330–335. See also Hujwīrī, *Kashf*, 157–158; Iṣfahānī lists him as Qāsim al-Sayyārī, *Ḥilyat*, 10:410–411; Qushayrī, *Risāla*, 138–139.

103. Sulamī, *Ḥaqā'iq*, 2:268.

104. Sulamī, *Ḥaqā'iq*, 2:184.

105. Sulamī, *Ḥaqā'iq*, 2:125.

106. Sulamī, *Ḥaqā'iq*, 1:325.

107. Both God and the human being, for example, engage in *tawba*, but the nature of this embodiment must necessarily differ.

108. Cited in Chittick, *Sufi Path of Knowledge*, 283.

Chapter 5

1. Nwyia, *Exégèse coranique et langage mystique*, 231.

2. ʿAṭṭār, *Tadhkirat* (abridged), 218–219. See also Knysh, *Islamic Mysticism*, 56–60.

3. Hujwīrī, *Kashf*, 143; Iṣfahānī, *Ḥilyat*, 10:264; Sulamī, *Ṭabaqāt*, 183. Though, as Madelung notes, "these concepts had been used by earlier Sufis and were commonplace among his contemporaries." See *EI*[2], s.v. "al-Kharrāz."

4. Böwering, "Early Sufism," 58; Knysh, *Islamic Mysticism*, 57; Massignon, *Essay*, 204; *EI*[2], s.v. "al-Kharrāz."

5. Arberry, "Preface," ed. and trans., *The Book of Truthfulness (Kitāb al-Ṣidq) by Abū Saʿīd al-Kharrāz* (Oxford: Oxford University Press, 1937), vi.

6. See Fuat Sezgin, *Geschichte des Arabischen Schrifttums* (Leiden: Brill, 1967–2000), 1:646. Some of his short treatises were edited by Qāsim Samarrā'ī and published as *al-Rasā'il* (Baghdad, 1967). Nada A. Saab translated them in her dissertation, "Sufi Theory and Language in the Writings of Abū Saʿīd al-Kharrāz (d. 286/899)" (PhD diss., Yale, 2005), 142–182.

7. Massignon, *Essay*, 203–204; Nwyia, *Exégèse coranique et langage mystique*, 231–311; Renard, *Knowledge of God*, 22–26.

8. Kharrāz, *Kitāb al-ṣidq*, 60.

9. Massignon, *Essay*, 204.

10. Kharrāz refers to them as *maqāmāt*, *manāzil*, or *manāzil al-ṭālibīn* ("levels of the seekers"). See *Kitāb al-ṣidq*, 75.

11. In the *Kitāb al-ṣidq* the order runs: repentance, self-knowledge, knowledge of the enemy, godliness, knowledge of the lawful, abstinence, trust, fear,

shame, gratitude and the knowledge of God's blessings, love, contentment, longing, intimacy. But in the *Ḥilyat* Kharrāz offers what appears to be a different sequence. Iṣfahānī recounts the following incident, narrated by al-Kattānī and al-Ramlī: "We said (to Kharrāz), 'Inform us of the initial (stages) of the way to God.' He replied, 'repentance,' then he described its conditions. He went from the station of repentance to the station of fear, from the station of fear to the station of hope, from the station of hope to the station of the righteous (*ṣāliḥīn*), from the station of the righteous to the station of the aspirants, from the station of the aspirants to the station of the obedient (*muṭīʿīn*), from the station of the obedient to the station of the lovers, from the station of the lovers to the station of the yearning ones (*mushtāqqīn*), from the station of the yearning ones to the station of the friends of God (*awliyāʾ*), and [finally] from the station of the friends of God to the station of those brought near (*muqarrabīn*). For every station he described ten conditions." See Iṣfahānī, *Ḥilyat*, 10:265–266.

12. Muḥāsibī uses this verse to prove that one can be taken to account for evil intentions. See chapter 6.

13. Kharrāz, *Kitāb al-ṣidq*, 9–10; Arberry, 8–9. The translations are my own based on the Arabic text provided in the edition, although I have frequently consulted Arberry.

14. Kharrāz, *Kitāb al-ṣidq*, 12–13; Arberry, 10.

15. Kharrāz, *Kitāb al-ṣidq*, 15; Arberry, 12.

16. The term may also be translated as "carnal appetite," "sensual desire," or "concupiscence." It is usually paired with *hawā* ("passion" or "caprice").

17. *Himma* in this context may also mean "effort" or "determination." The Qurʾān, employing the verbal root of this word, says that Zulaykha "desired" or "aspired for him [Joseph]" (*hammat bihi*) and that he would have likewise "desired her" (*hamma bihā*) had he not seen "the argument of his Lord" (Q 12:24). As a technical term in Sufism, however, *himma* usually carries a positive connotation, referring to the "aspiration," "resolve," or "high spiritual ambition" of the spiritual traveler. Kāshānī defines three levels of *himma*, the lowest of which is "the incentive to seek what remains [i.e., God and the Next World] and abandon what perishes" (*al-bāʿitha ʿalā ṭalab al-bāqī wa tark al-fānī*). *Iṣṭilāḥāt al-ṣūfiyya*, 71. The term is also used to refer to the spiritual powers of a Sufi *shaykh*. Ibn al-ʿArabī speaks of *al-fiʿl bi al-himma* ("acting through resolve"), which is the ability to produce effects in the physical world simply through one's power of concentration. See Chittick, *Sufi Path of Knowledge*, 265; Schimmel, *Mystical*, 79.

18. Kharrāz, *Kitāb al-ṣidq*, 15; Arberry, 12.

19. Kharrāz, *Kitāb al-ṣidq*, 75; Arberry, 60.

20. Qushayrī, *Risāla*, 533.

21. Böwering, *Mystical*, 110–128; Knysh, *Islamic Mysticism*, 121–122. For biographical entries on him, see Iṣfahānī, *Ḥilyat*, 10:408; Sulamī, *Ṭabaqāt*, 312–314. See also Renard, *Knowledge of God*, 34.

22. Sahl is quoted almost two hundred times in the *Qūt*, and frequently in Ghazālī's *Iḥyāʾ*. Most of these aphorisms pertain to the importance of self-mortification. Ibn al-ʿArabī also referred to Sahl al-Tustarī on a number of

occasions, particularly to his more esoteric doctrines, such as belief in a pre-existent column of Muḥammadan light, the "secret of Divine Lordship" (*sirr al-rubūbiyya*), and the "prostration of the heart" (*sujūd al-qalb*). See Gerhard Böwering, *Mystical*, 39; William Chittick, *Sufi Path of Knowledge*, 149, 185, 407.

23. Böwering, *Mystical*, 110–128.

24. Qushayrī, *Risāla*, 76.

25. Qushayrī, *Risāla*, 76.

26. According to Ghazālī, "Sahl b. ʿAbd Allāh used to go some twenty days or so without eating. Food [purchased by] one dirham would suffice him for a year. He used to exalt hunger and go to great lengths in it" (*yubālighu fīhi*). He is reported to have said, "I don't know of anything more harmful to the seekers of the next world than food," and "wisdom and knowledge (*hikma wa ʿilm*) lie in hunger whereas rebellion and ignorance (*maʿṣiya wa jahl*) lie in satiation." *Iḥyāʾ*, 3:132. He also said that "the origin of every form of godliness that exists between the heavens and earth lies in hunger, and the origin of every form of debauchery that exists between the heavens and the earth lies in satiety." Sīrjānī, *Bayāḍ*, 149 [#312]. Sarrāj recounts how Sahl was weakened by eating and strengthened by hunger. *Lumaʿ*, 330. There was perhaps no early figure who developed such a reputation for fasting as Sahl al-Tustarī. In his eyes, to abstain from unnecessary food would count for more in the eyes of God on the Day of Judgment than all other pious works and devotions. See Andrae, *Garden of Myrtles*, 53.

27. Sahl's austerity regarding food, it is clear, was not simply rooted in asceticism for its own sake but in a mystical vision that identified spiritual practice as the real source of nourishment. Makkī, *Qūt*, 2:325. The author of the *Qūt* adopted this view, and this would explain Ibn Khallikān's rather peculiar observation that "he left food [altogether] for a while and resorted simply to the eating of lawful herbs (*al-ḥashāʾish al-mubāḥa*). Because of this his complexion [lit. "skin," *jald*] turned green." *Wafayāt al-aʿyān*, ed. Iḥsān ʿAbbās (Beirut: Dār al-Thaqāfa, 1968–1973), 4:303; cf. Dhahabī, *Siyar aʿlām al-nubulāʾ*, ed. Shuʿayb Arnāʾūṭ (Beirut: Muʾassasat al-Risāla, 1996), 16:536–537; Renard, *Knowledge of God*, 35. For Makkī's discussion of the virtues of hunger and eating little, see *Qūt*, 2:324–344. Ibn al-ʿArabī has a remarkable but brief discussion on God as the ultimate source of nourishment in a chapter of the *Futūḥāt* entitled *The Presence of the Food Giver* (*Ḥadrat al-muqīt*), in which he recounts a telling anecdote about Sahl. See *al-Futūḥāt al-makkiyya*, ed. Aḥmad Shams al-Dīn (Beirut: Dār al-Kutub ʿIlmiyya, 1999), 7:365–366. The account is a slightly modified version of the incident as it originally appears in Makkī; cf. *Qūt*, 2:325.

28. Böwering, *Mystical*, 253.

29. In Sulamī's *Ḥaqāʾiq*, virtually the exact saying appears, but as a commentary instead on Q 25:70, "except for the one who repents, believes, and does right." See 2:68–69.

30. Tustarī, *Tafsīr al-qurʾān al-karīm*, eds. Ṭāhā ʿAbd al-Raʾūd Saʿd and Saʿd Ḥasan Muḥammad ʿAlī (Cairo: Dār al-Ḥaram li al-Turāth, 2004), 160.

31. Tustarī, *Tafsīr al-qurʾān*, 206.

32. Tustarī, *Tafsīr al-qur'ān*, 209.

33. Tustarī, *Tafsīr al-qur'ān*, 160.

34. Kalābādhī, *Ta'arruf*, 64; Makkī, *Qūt*, 1:368; Qushayrī, *Risāla*, 212–213; Sarrāj, *Luma'*, 43.

35. Sahl's position seems to echo that of St. Augustine, when he writes that if "you want him [God] to turn his face from your sins, then turn your face away from yourself and do not turn your face away from your sins. You are yourself indignant over your sins if you do not turn your face away from them. But if you do not turn your face away from your sins, you acknowledge them and he forgets them." See Augustine, *Augustine of Hippo: Selected Writings*, trans. Mary T. Clark (New Jersey: Paulist Press, 1988), 251.

36. 'Aṭṭār, *Tadhkirat* (abridged), 156–157. See also my article, "Is God Obliged to Answer Prayers of Petition (*Du'a*)? The Response of Classical Sufis and Qur'anic Exegetes," *Journal of Medieval Religious Cultures*, 37, no. 2 (2011): 97–98.

37. There is a lacuna in Nicholson's edition of the *Kitāb al-luma'*, from where this passage is extracted. For this particular passage I consulted Kāmil Muṣtafā al-Hindāwī's edition of the text (Beirūt: Dār al-Kutub al-'Ilmiyya, 2001), 356. Böwering also cites this passage in his study of Sahl but translates the final words, *wa intiqālihi ilā al-baṣra*, as "and his demise in Basra." The choice of translation may be because it is followed by the common prayer of blessing over the deceased. See *Mystical*, 61. The Nicholson edition has been consulted for all other passages from the *Kitāb al-luma'*.

38. 'Aṭṭār, *Tadhkirat* (abridged), 155–156.

39. Tustarī, *Tafsīr al-qur'ān*, 160.

40. An act that is *farīḍa* is typically considered to be more religiously binding than one that is simply *wājib*.

41. Makkī, *Qūt*, 1:362. Sahl of course may have simply directed his *takfīr* against those who are lackadaisical in repentance. As the context of Makkī's discussion makes it clear, *hādha al-khalq* refers to all humans.

42. Massignon, *Passion*, 3:148. This view is also reflected in the *Sharḥ al-sunna* of Sahl's contemporary, Ghulām Khalīl (d. 888) (ibid.), a popular preacher whom Carl Ernst has argued was Ḥanbalite. See Ernst, *Words of Ecstasy in Sufism* (Albany: State University of New York Press, 1985), 97. Van Ess, however, contests this juridical affiliation. See his "Sufism and its Opponents: Reflections on Topoi, Tribulations, and Transformation," in *Islamic Mysticism Contested: Thirteen Centuries of Controversies and Polemics*, eds. Frederick De Jong and Bernd Radtke (Leiden: Brill, 1999), 26. Khalīl is most notorious for the inquisition he led against the Baghdad Sufis in 885 CE on charges of heresy (*zandaqa*).

43. Abū al-Ḥasan al-Ash'arī, *Maqālat al-islāmiyyīn*, ed. Helmut Ritter (Wiesbaden: Franz Steiner, 1980), 476.

44. Makkī, for example was also critical of those who were guilty of *shaṭaḥāt*, such as Bisṭāmī. He says, "the ones who exceed proper bounds are those guilty of ecstatic utterances (*shāṭiḥūn*)." He puts them in the same ranks as the innovators (*mubtadi'ūn*) and people of ignorance (*ahl al-jahāla*). See my article, "Abū Ṭālib

al-Makkī and the *Qūt al-Qulūb* (*Nourishment of Hearts*) in the Context of Early Sufism," *Muslim World* 122, no. 2 (2012): 335–356, especially 351.

45. Böwering, *Mystical Vision*, 97; Nicholson, "editor's introduction," *Kitāb al-luma*ʿ, x. Nicholson notes that Dhahabī's observation might refer instead to the father since "Muhammadan writers fail to distinguish between the father and son."

46. *EI*², s.v. "Djunayd."

47. For biographical entries, see Hujwīrī, *Kashf*, 155–156; Qushayrī, *Risāla*, 123–125; Sulamī, *Ṭabaqāt*, 257–265. See also Kenneth Avery's recent study, *Shiblī: His Life and Thought*.

48. For biographical entries, see Hujwīrī, *Kashf*, 156–157; Qushayrī, *Risāla*, 137–138; Sulamī, *Ṭabaqāt*, 326–330.

49. For biographical entries, see Hujwīrī, *Kashf*, 136–138; Qushayrī, *Risāla*, 106–107; Sulamī, *Ṭabaqāt*, 158–162.

50. See note 100 in chapter 4 on Ḥusayn.

51. Qushayrī, *Risāla*, 95; Sulamī, *Ṭabaqāt*, 129.

52. Abdel Kader, *Writings of Junayd*, 26.

53. Qushayrī, *Risāla*, 95; Sulamī, *Ṭabaqāt*, 129.

54. Qushayrī, *Risāla*, 95; Sulamī, *Ṭabaqāt*, 129. Thawrī was the founder of a legal school that did not survive. Massignon, *Essay*, 116. According to Hujwīrī, though a jurist he wore the patched woolen frock of Sufis. *Kashf*, 46. Iṣfahānī has a lengthy biographical entry on him in the *Ḥilyat*, 6:393–436, 7:3–165.

55. *maqbūl ʿalā jamīʿ al-alsina*. See Sulamī, *Ṭabaqāt*, 129.

56. Junayd also remained free from the censure of the wider religious establishment, no doubt because of his emphasis on self-control and "sobriety." For an analysis of the contrasting representations of Junayd and the famous "drunken" Sufi Abū Yazīd al-Bisṭāmī (d. 874), particularly in the works of Hujwīrī, Kalābādhī, Qushayrī, and Sarrāj, see Jawid A. Mojaddedi, "Getting drunk with Abū Yazīd or staying sober with Junayd: The creation of a popular typology of Sufism," *Bulletin of the School of Oriental Studies* 66, no. 1 (2003): 1–13.

57. We must not overlook the spiritual hermeneutic involved in the use of such allusive and even cryptic language by mystics. Apart from guarding the uninitiated from doctrines that can prove harmful if misunderstood, this hermeneutic can also be employed to reveal truths that cannot, by their very nature, be disclosed through normal, discursive means.

58. *EI*², s.v. "Djunayd."

59. Sells, *Early Islamic Mysticism*, 251.

60. Abdel Kader, *Writings of Junayd*, 75; Julian Baldick, *Mystical Islam* (London: I.B. Tauris, 1989) 44; Ahmet Karamustafa, "Walāya According to Junayd," in *Reason and Inspiration in Islam*, 65.

61. Junayd, *The Book of Fanā*ʿ, trans. in Sells, *Early Islamic Mysticism*, 260.

62. Quoted in Ṣadra, *Elixir of the Gnostic* (*Iksīr al-ʿārifīn*) [with facing Arabic text], trans. William C. Chittick (Provo UT: Brigham Young University Press, 2003), 54.

63. Muhammad Abdul Haq Ansari, "The Doctrine of One Actor: Junayd's View of *Tawḥīd*," *Muslim World* 63:1 (1983): 44.

64. *Balā*, an affirmative response to a negative interrogation, or an affirmation of a negative proposition, is simply a combination of the Arabic ب + لا = بلى , while *balā*ʾ is a derivative of a triliteral root.

65. Tustarī said, "He ended with their words *balā* since it lies in the province of *ibtilā*ʾ" (*idh huwa ʿalā jihat al-ibtilā*ʾ). See Tustarī, *Tafsīr al-qur*ʾ*ān*, 151; cf. Sells, *Early Islamic Mysticism*, 92. It should be noted in passing that given the propensity for word play among Arabs in general it is quite possible that Sahl was not the first to draw attention to this relation.

66. Abdel Kader, *Writings of Junayd*, 156–159.

67. Sulamī, *Ḥaqā*ʾ*iq*, 164.

68. Laury Silvers, "Theoretical Sufism in the Early Period," 73.

69. Schimmel, *Mystical*, 136–137.

70. Sometimes it is defined simply as "forgetting of your sin" (*nisyān dhanbaka*); cf. Kalābādhī, *Ta*ʿ*arruf*, 64; Makkī, *Qūt*, 1:368; Qushayrī, *Risāla*, 213; Sarrāj, *Luma*ʿ, 43.

71. Qushayrī, *Risāla*, 213. A slightly different version of this incident appears in Iṣfahānī, 10:292. Mojaddedi has looked at the different narratives of this event and argued that the biographical authors sought to present Junayd's superiority over Sarī. See Mojaddedi, *The Biographical Tradition*, 50–52.

72. Kalābādhī, *Ta*ʿ*arruf*, 64.

73. Sulamī, *Ḥaqā*ʾ*iq*, 1:281. In Qushayrī's *Risāla* Junayd leaves out "inner struggle" in his three requirements for *tawba*. 212.

74. Abdel Kader, *Writings of Junayd*, 177.

75. Ansari, "Doctrine of One Actor," 53.

76. Ansari, "Doctrine of One Actor," 48.

77. Ghazālī, *Iḥyā*ʾ, 3:538–539.

78. Ghazālī, *Iḥyā*ʾ, 3:539.

79. Sarrāj, *Luma*ʿ, 43; cf. Sells, *Early Islamic Mysticism*, 199–200.

80. Qushayrī, *Risāla*, 213.

81. Makkī, *Qūt*, 1:368.

82. Hujwīrī, *Kashf*, 297. Although he ends the passage by saying the highest position is to turn away from both remembering and forgetting the sin, he still sees Junayd's view as higher.

83. Hujwīrī, *Kashf*, 131.

84. Although the Sālimiyya were subject to the criticisms of Ibn Khafīf (d. 982) and others, there is little evidence to suggest they were guilty of espousing the heretical doctrines of which they were accused. This is particularly because of the wide scale acceptance and circulation of Sarrāj's *Kitab al-luma*ʿ and Makkī's *Qūt*, texts authored by individuals who had intimate ties with Ahmad b. Sālim and whose contents posed no serious, lasting doctrinal problems for the Sufi community (although some Ḥanbalites did raise a few objec-

tions, based on misinterpretations of their doctrines; cf. Ibn Taymiyya (d. 1328), *al-Risāla al-ṣafadiyya* [Beirut: Dār Ibn Ḥazm, 2002], 264–265). The first mention of the Sālimiyya appears in Muqaddasī's (d. 990) *Aḥsan al-taqāsīm*, where he defines them as popular preachers, ascetics, and Sufi theologians of Basra. For more on the Sālimiyya, including the debates over their (supposedly) heretical doctrines, see Böwering, *Mystical*, 89–99; ʿAbd al-Qāhir al-Baghdādī, *Al-Farq bayn al-firaq*, ed. Muḥammad al-Hamīd (Beirut: Al-Maktaba Al-ʿAṣriyya, 1998), 261; Hujwīrī, *Kashf*, 131; ʿAbd al-Qādir al-Jīlānī, *al-Ghunya*, ed. Yūsuf Maḥmūd al-Ḥājj Aḥmad (Damascus: Maktabat al-ʿIlm al-Ḥadīth, 2001), 172–173; Nicholson, "editor's introduction," *Kitāb al-lumaʿ*, x–xi; Massignon, *Essay*, 199–203; EI^2, s.v. "Sālimiyya."

85. Qushayrī, *Risāla*, 95.

86. Qushayrī, *Risāla*, 119; Sulamī, *Ṭabaqāt*, 232.

87. Silvers, *A Soaring Minaret*, 4, 13. For biographical entries on Sayyārī, see note 102 on Qāsim in the previous chapter.

88. Qushayrī, *Risāla*, 138.

89. Sulamī, *Ṭabaqāt*, 232.

90. Hujwīrī, *Kashf*, 251–261.

91. Silvers, *Soaring Minaret*, 49.

92. Silvers, *Soaring Minaret*, 49.

93. In openly speaking about matters that other Sufis had made efforts to guard, Wāsiṭī was not entirely unlike Junayd's other student, Ḥallāj. Unlike the famous martyr of Baghdad, however, Wāsiṭī's sayings, though provocative, were presented in a relatively tempered style. It is significant that Sarrāj and other later Sufis did not classify them as *shaṭaḥāt*. The comparisons with Ḥallāj can therefore be pushed only so far. While Massignon considered Wāsiṭī to be a student and disciple of Ḥallāj (*Essay*, 213), recent scholarship has shown otherwise. Silvers unequivocally states that Massignon was mistaken in his view, while conceding that the two figures may have at least met. See *Soaring Minaret*, 11–12. I have not found any substantial links between Ḥallāj and Wāsiṭī to corroborate Massignon's position.

94. Richard Gramlich has translated Wāsiṭī's sayings in *Alte Vorbilder des Sufitums*, 2:267–410.

95. Laury Silvers, "Theoretical Sufism," 73.

96. Kalābādhī, *Taʿarruf*, 18.

97. In drawing out the mystical implications of *tawḥīd*, Wāsiṭī proposed ideas about repentance that are strikingly similar to the foremost representative of what later came to be called the "unity of being." In this regard, Wāsiṭī can be seen as a theoretical link between Junayd's allusive esoteric intimations and Ibn Arabi's full-fledged non-dualism. It is no surprise that Massignon said Wāsiṭī should be assigned the role of "precursor, in the fourth century A.H. to Ibn ʿArabi's monism." See *Essay*, 213. For a treatment of Ibn al-ʿArabī's view of *tawba*, see my article, "Ibn al-ʿArabī (d. 1240) on the Three Conditions of *Tawba*," *Journal of Islam and Christian-Muslim Relations*, 17 (2006): 403–416.

98. Silvers, "Theoretical Sufism," 76.

99. Sulamī, *Ḥaqāʾiq*, 2:44.

100. Silvers, "Theoretical Sufism," 77; Qushayrī, *Risāla*, 213.

101. Silvers, "Theoretical Sufism," 77; Qushayrī, *Risāla*, 213.

102. For approaches to *kasb* in Ashʿarite theology, see Majid Fakhry, *History of Islamic Philosophy* (New York: Columbia, 1983), 208–209; Harry A. Wolfson, *Philosophy of the Kalam* (Cambridge, MA: Harvard University Press, 1976), 684–710. For "pre-Ashʿarite" notions of *kasb* in Islamic theology, see Wolfson, *Kalam*, 663–683. For *kasb* in Māturīdī thought, see J. Meric Pessagno, "*Irāda, Ikhtiyār, Qudra, Kasb* the View of Abū Manṣūr al-Māturīdī," *Journal of the American Oriental Society* 104, no. 1 (1984): 177–191; Wolfson, *Kalam*, 711–719. For Abū al-Ḥasan al-Ashʿarī's own treatment of this issue, see *al-Ibāna ʿan ʿuṣūl al-dīyāna* (Damascus: Dār al-Bayān, 1999), 122–131.

103. Sulamī, *Ḥaqāʾiq*, 1:299; cf. Silvers, "Theoretical Sufism," 77.

104. Qushayrī, *Risāla*, 156–157; cf. Silvers, *Soaring Minaret*, 36; cf. Qushayrī, *Risāla*, 156–157.

105. Some of the later Sufi writers referred to this doctrine as *waḥdat al-fiʿl* (unity of action). See Ansari, "Doctrine of One Actor," 56.

106. Silvers, "Theoretical Sufism," 87.

107. Silvers, "Theoretical Sufism," 88.

108. Silvers, "Theoretical Sufism," 91. Ibn al-ʿArabī would express a remarkably similar perspective three centuries later, but qualify it by demanding of the *tāʾib* to take ownership of the wrongful act out of courtesy (*adab*) before God. Even though the Andalusian mystic argues that the act is retraceable to God and thus intrinsically beautiful, it is, for him, still relatively evil when viewed in light of the religious law. Since it would be inappropriate or disrespectful to ascribe anything evil to God, the *tāʾib* must take ownership of the act. Ibn al-ʿArabī uses the example of Adam and Eve, who cried out to God that "we have wronged ourselves" (Q 7:23), even though they knew, for the mystic, that their act of disobedience was ultimately a divine act. He contrasts this with Satan's argument for refusing to bow before Adam, when he complained to God that it was "because You have led me astray" (Q 15:39). While Adam and Eve showed courtesy, Satan used his knowledge to dispute with God. See *al-Futūḥāt al-makkiyya*, 3:208–213. This same perspective would be echoed by Rūmī: "When Adam sinned, God exiled him from Paradise. God said to him, 'Oh Adam! Since I have held you responsible and punished you for that sin you committed, why did you not dispute with Me? After all, you had an argument. You could have said, "All is from Thee, and Thou makest all. Whatever Thou desirest in the world comes to pass, and whatever Thou doest not desire will never come to pass." After all, you had such a clear, correct and patent argument. Why did you not give expression to it?' Adam replied, 'I knew that, but I did not abandon courtesy in Thy Presence; love for Thee did not allow me to reproach Thee.'" Cited in William Chittick, *Sufi Path of Love: The Spirtual Teachings of Rumi* (Albany: State University of New York Press, 1983), 84–85. Traces of this perspective can also

be found in the early Sufi tradition. See my article, "Contentment, Satisfaction and Good Pleasure: *Rida* in Early Sufi Moral Psychology," *Studies in Religion/Sciences Religieuses*, 43, no. 3 (2014): 17–19.

109. Sulamī, *Ḥaqā'iq*, 1:291.

110. Silvers, "Theoretical Sufism," 90.

111. Silvers, "Theoretical Sufism," 92.

112. Massignon, *Essay*, 213.

113. Silvers, "Theoretical Sufism," 71.

114. In describing the circumstances of his own "interior conversion," Ghazālī gives some of the credit to the influence of these early Sufi texts. In the *Munqidh min al-dalāl* (*Deliverance from Error*) he writes, "I began to acquaint myself with their belief by reading their books, such as the Food of Hearts (*Qūt al-Qulūb*) by Abū Ṭālib al-Makkī (may God have mercy on him), the works of al-Ḥārith al-Mūḥāsibī [. . .] and other discourses of their leading men." Cited in Mohamed Ahmed Sherif, *Ghazali's Theory of Virtue* (Albany: State University of New York Press, 1975), 105.

Chapter 6

1. *EI*², s.v. "Muḥāsibī." For an excellent overview of the source material on Muḥāsibī's life, see Gavin Picken's recent study, *Spiritual Purification in Islam*, 46–66. See also my review of this work in the *Journal of Medieval Religious Cultures* 42, no. 2 (2016): 278–280.

2. Hujwīrī, *Kashf*, 108–109.

3. For a list of his disciples and the transmitters of an early "Muḥāsibīan tradition," see Smith, *Early Mystic*, 27–44. See also Massignon, *Essay*, 170–171; Picken, *Spiritual Purification in Islam*, 53.

4. Massignon, *Essay*, 164–169.

5. Arberry, *Sufism*, 46.

6. Muḥāsibī, *al-Ri'āya li ḥuqūq Allāh*, ed. 'Abd al-Qādir 'Aṭā' (Cairo: Dār al-Kutub al-Ḥadītha, 1970).

7. Margaret Smith, "The Forerunner of Ghazālī," *Journal of the Royal Asiatic Society* (1936):65–78. See also Sherif's observations in *Ghazali's Theory of Virtue*, 105; cf. Smith, *Early Mystic*, 269–281.

8. Knysh, *Islamic Mysticism*, 45.

9. Knysh, *Islamic Mysticism*, 45; Smith, *Early Mystic*, 283–284.

10. Smith, *Early Mystic* 266–267.

11. Smith, *Early Mystic*, 266–267.

12. Ibn 'Abbād encouraged seekers to read the writings of Muḥāsibī. See *Ibn 'Abbād of Ronda: Letters on the Sufi Path*, trans. and with an introduction by John Renard (New York: Paulist Press, 1986), 125. See also Knysh, *Islamic Mysticism*, 45. Massignon notes that Muḥāsibī had a particularly strong influence on the Shādhilīs of North Africa. See *Essay*, 167; cf., Renard, "introduction," *Ibn 'Abbād of Ronda*, 46.

13. Smith, *Early Mystic*, 287.

14. Muḥāsibī, *al-Masāʾil fī aʿmāl al-qulūb wa al-jawāriḥ*, ed. Khalīl ʿImrān (Beirut: Dār al-Kutub al-ʿIlmiyya, 2000).

15. Diana Lobel, *Between Mysticism and Philosophy: Sufi Language and Religious Experiences in Judah Ha Levi's Kuzari* (Albany: State University of New York Press, 2000), 182–183. Lobel relies for this link on the research of Amos Goldreich who "has argued cogently for this possible influence." See Lobel, 183. Goldreich presents his findings in a Hebrew article (which I have not consulted), "Possible Arabic Sources for the Distinction between 'Duties of the Heart' and 'Duties of the Limbs'," *Teʿudah* 6 (1988): 179–208. The expression *farāʾiḍ al-qulūb* may also derive from a passage in Muḥāsibī's *Waṣāya* (which Lobel does not draw attention to), where he speaks of "the knowledge of confirmed duties [placed] on the hearts and limbs" (*maʿrifa al-farāʾiḍ al-muʿakkada ʿalā al-qulūb wa al-jawāriḥ*). See Muḥaṣibī, *al-Waṣāya*, ed. ʿAbd al-Qādir ʿAṭāʾ (Beirut: Dār al-Kutub al-ʿIlmiyya, 2003), 75. For more on Baḥya's Sufi sources, see Paul Fenton, "Judaeo-Arabic Mystical Writings in the XIII–XIV Centuries," in *Studies in Muslim-Jewish Relations: Judaeo-Arabic Studies*, ed. Normal Golb (Oxford: Harwood Academic Publishers, 1997), 87–103; idem, "Judaism and Sufism," in *History of Islamic Philosophy*, eds. Oliver Leaman and Seyyed Hossein Nasr (London: Routledge, 1996), 1:756–757. See also Diana Lobel's more recent study, *A Sufi-Jewish Dialogue: Philosophy and Mysticism in Baḥya ibn Paqūda's* Duties of the Heart (Philadelphia: University of Pennsylvania Press, 2007). The work examines in detail the Islamic philosophical, theological, and mystical origins of many of Baḥya's central views.

16. For more on Ḥasan al-Baṣrī, considered to be the patriarch of Islamic mysticism, see Massignon, *Essay*, 119–138. See also Suleiman Ali Mourad, *Early Islam Between Myth and History: al-Ḥasan al-Baṣrī (d. 110 H/728 CE) and the Formation of His Legacy in Classical Islamic Scholarship* (Leiden: Brill, 2005).

17. Joseph van Ess, *Theologie und Gesellshaft im 2. und 3. Jahrhundert Hidschra* (Berlin: Walter de Gruyter, 1997), 4:196–197.

18. According to Sulamī, he was "from among the learned masters of the outward sciences and the sciences of practical conduct and intimations." And Qushayrī said that "he was peerless in his time in knowledge, watchfulness, practical conduct (*muʿāmala*) and state." See Sulamī, *Ṭabaqāt*, 58; Qushayrī, *Risāla*, 69; cf., Iṣfahānī, *Ḥilyat*, 10:79; Jāmī, *Nafaḥāt*, 1:75, Shaʿrānī, *Ṭabaqāt al-kubra*, 108–109.

19. For more on the *ʿulūm al-muʿāmalāt*, see Chittick, *Faith and Practice*, 17–18.

20. Sells, *Early Islamic Mysticism*, 171.

21. For more on the nature of the heart (*qalb*) in Muḥāsibī, see van Ess, *Die Gedankenwelt*, 139–143.

22. Picken, *Spiritual Purification*, 47. According to a less common view, he was given the appellation in question because of the practice of "counting" or "enumerating" (*yaḥsubuhā*) litanies in remembrance of God on small pebbles. Ibid, 47.

23. Van Ess, *Theologie*, 197.

24. Massignon, *Essay*, 169.

25. Baldick, *Mystical*, 34.

26. Marshall Hodgson, *The Venture of Islam: Conscience and History in a World Civilization* (repr., Chicago: The University of Chicago Press, 1974), 1:396.

27. See note 19 of this chapter.

28. According to Schimmel, Muḥāsibī claimed to have a vein in his finger that would throb whenever it approached food that was illicit. See Schimmel, *Mystical Dimensions,* 54. She traces this interesting fact to Jāmī's *Nafaḥāt,* but I was unable to find it in his entry on Muḥāsibī; 1:108–109. Qushayrī mentions a story in which he informed Junayd of his inability to swallow food of doubtful status. See Qushayrī, *Risāla,* 70.

29. Sells, *Early Islamic Mysticism,* 171.

30. Van Ess, *Theologie,* 198.

31. For a list of extant manuscripts and published works see Picken, *Spiritual Purification,* 67–122. See also Yolande de Crussol, *Le rôle de la raison dans la réflexion éthique d'Al-Muḥāsībī: ʿAql et conversion chez al-Muḥāsībī* (Paris: Consep, 2002), 373–376, 450–458.

32. The full title of the work is *Iḥkām al-tawba wa radd maẓālim al-ʿibād wa khāliṣ minhā qabl al-maʿād (The Establishing of Tawba and the Restitution of Wrongs Done to the Servants [of God] and Deliverance from them before the Resurrection),* MS. Berlin, 1435. This work is not to be confused with Muḥāsibī's *Badʾ man anāba ilā Allāh* published somewhat misleadingly under the title *al-Tawba li Ḥārith b. Asad al-*Muḥāsibī, ed. ʿAbd al-Qādir Aḥmad ʿAṭā, (Egypt: Dār al-Iʿtisām, 1984). This latter text includes as an appendix the *Aḥkām al-tawba* of ʿAbd al-Ghanī b. Ismāʿīl al-Nābalūsī (d. 1731), the contents of which have very little to do with the treatise alongside which it is published. In the *Aḥkām* Nābalūsī engages not Muḥāsibī's ideas of *tawba* but those of Ibn al-ʿArabī as they are articulated principally in his two chapters on *tawba* in the *Futūḥāt al-makkiyya,* 3:208–214. Nābalūsī voices his disagreement, for example, with some of the views set forth in Ibn al-ʿArabī's discussion, such as his belief in the intrinsic, ontological goodness of evil acts. See *al-Tawba,* 90.

33. This can also be translated as "capacity."

34. Muḥāsibī, *al-Qaṣd wa al-rujūʿ ilā Allāh,* ed. ʿAbd al-Qādir ʿAṭāʾ (Beirut: Dār al-Kutub al-ʿIlmiyya, 2003), 145.

35. Cited in Smith, *An Early Mystic,* 151.

36. For more on this Qurʾānic figure (Q 31:12–19), considered by some to have been a prophet, see Brannon M. Wheeler, *Prophets in the Quran: An Introduction to the Quran and Muslim Exegesis* (London: Continuum International Publishing Group, 2002), 72–73; *EI*^{2}, s.v. "Luqmān."

37. Muḥāsibī, *Qaṣd,* 147.

38. Van Ess, *Theologie,* 198. This is particularly noticeable in a short treatise entitled *al-Tawahhum,* which presents a graphic description of the Afterlife. See *al-Tawahhum,* in *al-Waṣāya aw al-naṣāʾiḥ al-dīniyya wa nafaḥāt al-qudsiyya,* ed. ʿAbd al-Qādir ʿAṭāʾ (Beirut: Dār al-Kutub al-ʿIlmiyya, 2003), 241–279. According to Smith, "its lurid pictures of the Hell destined for the unrepentant sinner, is calculated to rouse the emotion of fear to its highest pitch," See Smith, *Early Mystic,* 96.

39. Paul Heck, "Sufism—What Is It Exactly?" *Religion Compass* 1, no. 1 (2007):152.

40. See note on Rābiʿa in earlier chapter.

41. Sells, *Early Islamic Mysticism*, 173.

42. This is because Muḥāsibī, in his critique of the Muʿtazilite position, states that if God wills He can forgive even major sins (*kabāʾir*) without the *tawba* of the sinner. Only those who do not repent of *shirk* face inevitable punishment. Muḥāsibī's proof text for this view is Q 4:48: "Verily God does not forgive that a partner be ascribed to Him, but He forgives all else to whom He wills." See Muḥāsibī, *Fahm al-qurʾān*, in *al-Aql wa fahm al-qurʾān*, ed. Ḥusayn al-Quwwatī (n.p.: Dār al-Fikr, 1978), 372–373; cf. idem, *Iḥkām al-tawba*, fol. 8b. According to the Muʿtazilite position, major sins for which the sinner does not repent cannot go unpunished. For more on Muʿtazilite views of *tawba*, see Mānakdīm Aḥmad b. Abī Hāshim al-Qazwīnī, *Sharḥ al-uṣūl al-khamsa* (incorrectly attributed to ʿAbd al-Jabbār b. Aḥmad), ed. ʿAbd al-Karīm ʿUthmān (Cairo: Maktabat Wahba, 1965), 789–804. See also Moucarry, *Search for Forgivenes*, 82–89, 108–116, 133–139, 153–158; Pomerantz, "Muʿtazili Theory in Practice," 463–493. The work of Mānakdīm (d. 1034, Persian = Māng Dīm, "moon faced" for his beauty, also vocalized Mānkdīm, Mānkadīm, Mānkedīm) is in fact a running exegesis of ʿAbd al-Jabbār's lost *Sharḥ*, which the latter dictated between the years 970 and 990 as a commentary on his own *Kitāb al-uṣūl al-khamsa*.

43. Muḥāsibī, *Iḥkām al-tawba*, fol. 8a; idem, *Mustarshidīn*, 113; idem, *Qaṣd*, 147.

44. Muḥāsibī, *Iḥkām al-tawba*, fol. 8a.

45. Muḥāsibī, *Iḥkām al-tawba*, fol. 8a.

46. Muḥāsibī, *Iḥkām al-tawba*, fol. 8b; idem, *Qaṣd*, 147.

47. Muḥāsibī, *Riʿāya*, 361.

48. Muḥāsibī, *Iḥkām al-tawba*, fols. 8b–9a; cf. idem, *Mustarshidīn*, 113; idem, *Qaṣd*, 146; idem, *Riʿāya*, 609.

49. Muḥāsibī, *Iḥkām al-tawba*, fols. 8b–9a.

50. Muḥāsibī, *Iḥkām al-tawba*, fol. 9a.

51. Muḥāsibī, *Iḥkām al-tawba*, fol. 8a.

52. Muḥāsibī, *Iḥkām al-tawba*, fol. 9a.

53. Muḥāsibī, *Iḥkām al-tawba*, fol. 8b.

54. Ghazālī, *Iḥyāʾ*, 4:20.

55. As we saw in the second chapter, the hopeless *nadam* one experiences in the next world must be contrasted with the hopeful *nadam* that accompanies *tawba* in the world.

56. Muḥāsibī, *Riʿāya*, 154. See also Sells, *Early Islamic Mysticism*, 180.

57. Muḥāsibī, *Badʾ man anāba*, 45.

58. Muḥāsibī, *Badʾ man anāba*, 45.

59. Muḥāsibī, *Badʾ man anāba*, 45.

60. Muḥāsibī, *Iḥkām al-tawba*, fol. 8a; idem, *Risālat al-mustarshidīn*, ed. ʿAbd al-Fattāḥ Abū Ghudda (Aleppo: Maktab al-Matbūʿāt al-Islāmiyya, 1964), 64. In the *Iḥkām* Muḥāsibī cites two verses to justify his view that it is *farīḍa*: Q 24:31

("And turn [*tūbū*] towards God altogether, O believers, so that you may prosper"), and Q 49:11 ("And he who does not repent, such are the wrong doers [*ẓālimūn*]"). Although neither of these explicitly delineates the obligatory nature of *tawba*, Muḥāsibī uses them as evidence for his position (*dalīl ʿalā dhālik*). In the *Mustarshidīn* Muḥāsibī states that both God and his Prophet have made *tawba farīḍa*, using as his proof text Q 66:8 ("O believers, turn [*tūbūʾ*] to God with a sincere *tawba* [*tawba naṣūḥa*]"), and a *ḥadīth* where the Prophet states, "O people, turn (*tūbūʾ*) towards your Lord before you die, and draw near to God through righteous works before you become preoccupied." The *ḥadīth* appears in a slightly different form in Ibn Mājah's *Sunan* in his section on the obligation of the Friday congregational prayer. See *Sunan*, 1:583. It remains difficult to determine to what extent Sahl's own view regarding the obligatory status of *tawba* may have been influenced by Muḥāsibī.

61. Muḥāsibī, *Ādāb al-nufūs*, 129–130.

62. Muḥāsibī, *Ādāb al-nufūs*, 119.

63. For some examples of the synonymous use of these terms, see Muḥāsibī, *Riʿāya*, 88, 90; idem, *Waṣāya*, 95, 126.

64. Muḥāsibī, *Badʾ man anāba*, 21–22.

65. The tradition, which calls to mind the Delphic maxim, is not found in the six canonical Sunni sources. For a brief but illuminating discussion of how Sufis justify their reliance on traditions that fail to meet the rigorous standards of *ḥadīth* specialists, see Chittick, *The Sufi Path of Knowledge*, 250–251.

66. For more on *maʿrifat al-nafs* in Muḥāsibī, see his *Iḥkām al-tawba*, fol. 9b; idem, *Masāʾil*, 97–103.

67. Muḥāsibī, *Riʿāya*, 68.

68. Kharrāz, *Kitāb al-ṣidq*, 9–41; Arberry (translation), 7–27.

69. *Badʾ man anāba*, 25. Muḥāsibī qualifies this by stating that although silence is preferable with others, with God private conversation is to be preferred. See *Masāʾil*, 83. For more on Muḥāsibī's views on the importance of controlling one's speech, see *Iḥkām al-tawba*, fols. 10a–11a; idem, *Masāʾil*, 83–91. See also Picken, *Spiritual Purification*, 83–84; Smith, *Early Mystic*, 55, 101, 157–158, 165; van Ess, *Die Gedankenwelt*, 112.

70. Muḥāsibī, *Qaṣd*, 147; cf. idem, *Ādāb al-nufūs*, 95.

71. Sulamī, *Ḥaqāʾiq*, 1:291.

72. Qushayrī, *Risāla*, 214.

73. Muḥāsibī, *Qaṣd*, 146–147.

74. Muḥāsibī, *Qaṣd*, 147.

75. The emphasis that Muḥāsibī lays on guarding oneself from pride (*kibr*) and conceit (*ʿujb*) is evident in the *Riʿāya* in which he devotes two significant subsections to these vices. Together they make up almost a sixth of the entire work. See *Riʿāya*, 397–507. For a brief analysis of Muḥāsibī's understanding of these vices, see Joseph van Ess, *Die Gedankenwelt*, 48–52.

76. Muḥāsibī, *Badʾ man anāba*, 26.

77. Muḥāsibī, *Bad' man anāba*, 27. See also idem, Muḥāsibī, *Iḥkām al-tawba*, fol. 8a.

78. Muḥāsibī, *Ādāb al-nufūs*, 135.

79. For brief remarks on *shahwa* in Muḥāsibī, see De Crussol, 230; Smith, *Early Mystic*, 113, 124; van Ess, *Die Gedankenwelt*, 35–39.

80. For a brief discussion of the differing opinions on both the spiritual benefits and dangers of hunger, see Muḥāsibī, *Kitāb al-makāsib* (published as *al-Rizq al-ḥalal wa ḥaqīqat al-tawakkul ʿalā Allāh*), ed. Muḥammad ʿUthmān al-Khisht (Cairo: Maktabat al-Qur'ān, 1984), 117–121.

81. Muḥāsibī, *Qaṣd*, 146. Muḥāsibī stipulates "making one's nourishment lawful (*iṣlāḥ al-qūt*)" as one of the conditions of *tawba*.

82. *Bad' man anāba*, 27.

83. I follow Chittick in my translation of *hawā* as "caprice." See *Sufi Path of Knowledge*, 20.

84. Muḥāsibī, *Bad' man anāba*, 29. For some brief remarks on *hawā* in Muḥāsibī, see De Crussol, 214, 229–230, 245; Picken, *Spiritual Purification*, 174–177; Smith, *Early Mystic*, 112; van Ess, *Die Gedankenwelt*, 35–39. For *mujāhada*, see De Crussol, 236–237; Picken, *Spiritual Purification*, 194–199; Smith, *Early Mystic*, 77, 154; van Ess, *Die Gedankenwelt*, 12, 32, 37, 93, 98, 188. The Hanbalite thinker, Abū al-Faraj al-Baghdādī (d. 1200), better known as Ibn al-Jawzī, seems to display a markedly Muḥāsibian influence in his discussion of the importance of making war against *hawā* in his *Dhamm al-hawā*. That such a prominent Hanbalite authority did not shy away even from quoting Muḥāsibī directly by name in this text should perhaps lead us to reconsider the extent and nature of early Hanbalite opposition to Muḥāsibī. See Joseph Bell, *Love Theory in Later Ḥanbalite Islam* (Albany: State University of New York Press, 1979), 15–18.

85. Muḥāsibī, *Bad' man anāba*, 28.

86. Muḥāsibī, *Ādāb al-nufūs*, 88. For more on the virtues of reciting and reflecting on the Qur'ān, see Muḥāsibī, *Waṣāya*, 96–97. For a more theological analysis of the Qur'ān, see Muḥāsibī's *Fahm al-qur'ān*.

87. Muḥāsibī, *Waṣāya*, 95.

88. Muḥāsibī, *Waṣāya*, 94. It should be noted here that since even the most pious of human beings cannot completely free themselves of sin, particularly in regards to the more subtle sins, Muḥāsibī's position should not be misunderstood to mean that one can never engage in supererogatory works. These works should be pursued once the individual has left those sins in which he was previously engrossed and that are clearly prohibited by the religious law.

89. Muḥāsibī, *al-Masā'il fī aʿmāl al-qulūb wa al-jawāriḥ*, ed. Khalīl ʿImrān (Beirut: Dār al-Kutub al-ʿIlmiyya, 2000), 72. According to ʿAbd al-Qādir Aḥmad ʿAṭā', there are four general reasons as to why Muḥāsibī privileges warding off sins to pursuing supererogatory deeds. First of all, says ʿAbd al-Qādir ʿAṭā', the human being is called to abandon all vices but not to perform all acts of virtue. The religious prohibitions are therefore more binding than the divine

call to pursue everything that is religiously esteemed. This excludes obligatory acts of worship (*farāʾiḍ*). Second, turning away from vices necessarily implies taking on virtues. The one who repents of fornication, for example, becomes chaste, while the one who turns away from pride becomes humble. *Tawba* does not simply lift the person from a morally objectionable condition to a neutral one, but its total opposite. Abandoning a particular vice adorns the *tāʾib* with a corresponding virtue. By focusing on warding off sin, the *tāʾib* is not therefore deprived of the merit of good deeds. The third reason he gives is that good deeds may not be accepted while the soul derives delight and sweetness from its persistence in other sins. These sins darken the heart so as to prevent the soul from performing righteous deeds marked by genuine sincerity and purity, qualities important to ensure God's acceptance of these works. Finally, says ʿAbd al-Qādir ʿAṭāʾ, there is little good, in Muḥāsibī's estimation, in a heart that is equally the source of both righteous and repugnant deeds. This mixture threatens to pollute and thereby tarnish good deeds themselves. See *al-Tawba*, 54–55. See also Muḥāsibī, *Ādāb al-nufūs*, 76.

90. Muḥāsibī, *Badʾ man anāba*, 46. For some brief remarks on *shukr* in Muḥāsibī, see De Crussol, 118–119, 123–124. For an analysis of *shukr* in Sufism, see my two articles, "On Cultivating Gratitude in Sufi Virtue Ethics," *Journal of Sufi Studies* 4 (2015): 1–26 and "The Embodiment of Gratitude (*Shukr*) in Sufi Ethics," *Studia Islamica* 111 (2016): 159–178.

91. Muḥāsibī, *Riʿāya*, 90.

92. Muḥāsibī, *Riʿāya*, 405–409.

93. He refers to this as a "knowledge based on nature and necessity" (*maʿrifa qāʾima bi al-ṭabʿ wa al-iḍṭirār*). See his *Riāʿya*, 405.

94. Muḥāsibī, *Riʿāya*, 405.

95. Muḥāsibī, *Masāʾil*, 79.

96. Muḥāsibī, *Riʿāya*, 416.

97. Muḥāsibī, *Riʿāya*, 416.

98. Muḥāsibī, *Riʿāya*, 90.

99. Muḥāsibī, *Riʿāya*, 90. ʿAbd al-Qādir ʿAṭāʾ draws attention in a footnote of the text to a similar interpretation ascribed to a member of the early Muslim community (*salaf*) in Abū Ṭālib al-Makkī's *ʿIlm al-qulūb*, in the chapter on wisdom (*bāb al-ḥikma*). For similar interpretations of this verse in early Sufism, see Sulamī, *Ḥaqāʾiq*, 1:340–341.

100. Muḥāsibī, *Riʿāya*, 96–100.

101. Muḥāsibī cites as evidence Q 33:23 and Q 9:75–77. In the former verse the Qurʾān praises those who have remained faithful to their oath to fight in the way of God. In the latter verses the Qurʾān condemns those who failed to live up to their promise to give charity if God provided for them from His bounty.

102. Muḥāsibī, *Riʿāya*, 97.

103. Muḥāsibī, *Riʿāya*, 88.

104. Muḥāsibī, *Riʿāya*, 88.

105. Muḥāsibī, *Riʿāya*, 88–89.

106. For more on *tawakkul* in Muḥāsibī, see Reinert, *Die Lehre vom tawakkul,* 59–64, 223–225, 264–265.

107. Qushayrī, *Risāla,* 210.

108. Hujwīrī, *Kashf,* 298.

109. Schimmel, *Mystical,* 110.

110. Cited in Schimmel, *Mystical,* 110.

111. See Q 12:87, where despair is presented as a quality of *kufr*. See also Q 39:53.

112. Abū Ḥāmid al-Ghazālī, *Minhāj al-ʿābidīn,* ed. ʿAbd al-ʿAzīz ʿIzz al-Dīn (Beirut: Muʾassasa Sīrawān, 1996), 36.

113. Ibn al-ʿArabī, *al-Futūḥāt al-makkiyya,* 3:212.

114. Ibn al-ʿArabī, *al-Futūḥāt al-makkiyya,* 3:212.

115. Muḥāsibī, *Mustarshidīn,* 80.

116. Muḥāsibī, *Mustarshidīn,* 65.

117. In a chapter on the ranks of God-fearingness (*taqwā*) in the *Riʿāya,* Muḥāsibī says that even the most realized of human beings are not entirely free of sin, but that their sins are the result of moments of inattentiveness (*sahwa*). For Muḥāsibī, their slips are not unlike those of the prophets and the truthful ones (*siddīqīn*). See *Riʿāya,* 63–64.

118. For more on *ghafla,* see Muḥāsibī, *Masāʾil,* 103–106.

119. Muḥāsibī, *Mustarshidīn,* 82. See also Smith, *Early Mystic,* 129.

120. Van Ess, *Die Gedankenwelt,* 61–63. The comparison with *jahl* is significant because Muḥāsibī appears to be drawing a correlation between the state of the pre-penitent sinner and the *jāhiliyya* of the pre-Islamic Arabs. Just as the advent of Islam caused the Arabs to emerge from a state of paganism and ignorance, *tawba,* like a descent of revelation into the heart of the sinner, takes him from a state of infidelity to submission.

121. Muḥāsibī, *Iḥkām al-tawba,* fol. 9a.

122. Van Ess, *Die Gedankenwelt,* 63.

123. He says that "persistence in minor sins is a major sin" (*iṣrār ʿalā ṣaghāʾir kabīra*). See Muḥāsibī, *Iḥkām al-tawba,* fol. 12a. Earlier in the same work he quotes the words of the second caliph, ʿUmar b. al-Khaṭṭāb: "[T]here is no minor sin (*ṣaghīra*) with persistence (*iṣrār*), and no major sin (*kabīra*) with seeking forgiveness (*istighfār*)." See fol. 9a. See also Smith, *Early Mystic,* 131.

124. *Waṣāyā,* 126–127. Van Ess notes that the distinction between the *aʿmāl al-jawāriḥ* and the *aʿmāl al-qulūb* was already present in the Muʿtazilite theologian, Abū Hudhayl (d. 849), who also gave precedence to the latter. See *Die Gedankenwelt,* 197.

125. *Waṣāyā,* 126. Among the "sins of the heart" some are more subtle than others.

126. *Waṣāyā,* 126.

127. Muḥāsibī, *Mustarshidīn,* 63. He couples this with being deluded by prolonged hopes (*ightirār bi ṭūl al-amal*).

128. Cited in Hujwīrī, *Kashf,* 109.

129. For more on the nature of the heart (*qalb*) in Muḥāsibī, see Smith, *Early Mystic*, 86–92; van Ess, *Die Gedankenwelt*, 35–36.

130. Muḥāsibī, *Ādāb al-nufūs*, 68.

131. The Arabic text of the *Kitāb al-ʿilm* appears in Leonard Librande, "Islam and Conservation: The Theologian-Ascetic al-Muḥāsibī," *Arabica* 30, no. 2 (1983): 141–146 (Arabic text).

132. Literally "sons," but *abnāʾ* can also mean "offspring" or "progeny."

133. Muḥāsibī is very explicit. He says that a person of this class has within him "internal vices for which he is not repentant" (*al-ʿuyūb al-bāṭina ghayr tāʾib minhā*). See *Kitāb al-ʿilm*, 143.

134. Muḥāsibī, *Kitāb al-ʿilm*, 142–143.

135. Librande, "Islam and Conservation," 131.

136. Muḥāsibī, *Kitāb al-ʿilm*, 143.

137. Muḥāsibī, *Kitāb al-ʿilm*, 142.

Chapter 7

1. Dhahabī, *Siyar aʿlām al-nubulāʾ*, 16:536–537.

2. Richard Gramlich, "Introduction," Abū Ṭālib al-Makkī, *Die Nahrung der Herzen*, trans. Richard Gramlich (Stuggart: F. Steiner, 1992), 1:11.

3. Knysh, *Islamic Mysticism*, 121; Renard, *Knowledge of God*, 34–35.

4. Abū al-ʿAbbās b. Khallikān, *Wafayāt al-aʿyān*, 4:303–304.

5. Knysh, *Islamic Mysticism*, 121.

6. Dhahabī quotes a rather peculiar anecdote about his death: "Abū al-Qāsim b. Bashrān said, 'I entered into the presence of our *shaykh*, Abū Ṭālib, who said, "if you know that my final state is good, then distribute sugar and almonds at my funeral [. . .] When I die, take my hand, and if I grasp yours, know that my final end has been good [. . . It so happened that] when he [Makkī] passed away, he grasped my hand with much strength, and so I [did as he asked, and] distributed sugar and almonds at his funeral.' " See Dhahabī, *Siyar aʿlām al-nubulāʾ*, 16:537. The passage was slightly mistranslated through a careless error on my part in my 2012 article on Makkī in *MW*, as well as in the abridged version of this chapter as it appeared in *JIS*.

7. Dhahabī, *al-ʿIbar fī khabar man ghabar*, ed. Fuʾad Sayyid (Kuwait: Dāʾirat al-Matbuʿat wa al-Nashr, 1961), 3:34; idem, *Siyar aʿlām al-nubulāʾ*, 16:536–537; Ibn Khallikān, *Wafayāt al-aʿyān*, 4:303–304.

8. Abū Bakr b. ʿAlī al-Khaṭīb al-Baghdādī, *Tarīkh baghdād* (Cairo: Maktabat al-Khānjī, 1931), 3:89; Ibn Khallikān, *Wafayāt al-aʿyān*, 4:303–304.

9. The *Iḥkām al-tawba* of Muḥāsibī, which we looked at in the previous chapter, is a much shorter work and concerned not so much with *tawba* as with the various sins the *tāʾib* must turn away from.

10. Arberry, *The Doctrine of the Sufis*, xii.

11. Schimmel, *Mystical Dimensions*, 18.

12. *Ibn ʿAbbād of Ronda*, 126. He also said that the *Qūt* is "for Sufism what the *Mudawwanah* is for legal science: It takes the place of all others and none can substitute for it." The *Mudawwana* of Saḥnūn (d. 854), on which Ibn ʿAbbād wrote a commentary, was "by all accounts the most influential work in North African jurisprudence." See Renard, "introduction," *Ibn ʿAbbād of Ronda*, 48.

13. For the influence of Makkī's *Qūt* on Ghazālī's *Iḥyāʾ*, see H. Lazarus-Yafeh, *Studies in Ghazzali* (Jerusalem: The Magnes Press, 1975), 34–35; Kojiro Nakamura, "Makkī and Ghazālī on Mystical Practices," *Oriens* 20 (1984): 83–91; Sherif, *Ghazali's Theory of Virtue*, 105–107.

14. Makkī, *Qūt*, 1:361.

15. For more on *tawakkul* in Makkī, see Reinert, *Die Lehre vom tawakkul*, 45–47, 85–90, 230, 264–268, 276–278, 285–289.

16. Even the sections of the *Qūt* that are of a more theoretical nature, such as its brief inquiries into the reality of the heart, inner light, and faith, relate in some manner or another to the pragmatic concerns of the aspirant. By setting aside esoteric matters, Makkī wishes to avoid diverting the attention of the amateur from the more pressing matters of the path. While the *ʿIlm al-qulūb* (ed. Aḥmad ʿAṭāʾ [Cairo: Dār al-Qāhira, n.d.]), authored sometime after the *Qūt*, and intended for more advanced mystics, has been ascribed to Makkī, recent scholarship has called into question the attribution. Karamustafa, basing his view largely on the scholarship of Pourjavadi, states that the *ʿIlm* is "likely a mid-fifth/eleventh century composition that relies heavily on the *Sustenance*." *Sufism*, 87–88. Yazaki followed this lead in her article, "A pseudo-Abū Ṭālib al-Makkī?: The authenticity of *ʿIlm al-qulūb*," *Arabica* 59 (2012): 1–35. Gramlich, however, did not have a problem accepting its attribution to Makkī. *Die Nahrung der Herzen*, 1:19–20.

17. There is little question that Makkī was influenced by as prominent a figure as Muḥāsibī in the development of his own psychology. Massignon stated that parts of the *Qūt* are "pale reflection[s]" of Muḥāsibī's *Riʿāya*. See *Essay*, 164. The exact nature and extent of this influence, however, has not yet been studied, and would require a close comparative analysis of the works of Muḥāsibī and the *Qūt* (a task that lies beyond the scope of this study). For the purposes of our analysis, it is sufficient to note that a Muḥāsibian influence does not seem to be definitively present in Makkī's discussion of *tawba*. Despite the liberty with which Makkī quotes his predecessors in his chapter on repentance, he makes no mention of Muḥāsibī. Nor does he draw in any obvious way from the sections in Muḥāsibī's works in which *tawba* is addressed (except in one possible case to be analyzed below). Despite some general conceptual overlaps between Muḥāsibī and Makkī's treatments of *tawba*, it remains difficult to know with any confidence whether these are due to Muḥāsibī's influence, a common source employed by both writers, or conclusions drawn through a similar process of reasoning. These overlaps will be noted over the course of this chapter.

18. Renard, *Knowledge of God*, 37.

19. Makkī, *Qūt*, 1:284.

20. Schimmel, *Mystical Dimensions*, 25.

21. By developing his ideas on the basis of past revelation, Makkī was an instrumental player in the formation of a distinct Islamic Sufi tradition. Eric Hobsbawm's remarks on the construction of tradition aptly apply to the manner in which Makkī sought to legitimate Sufism through the *Qūt*. "Inventing traditions," writes Hobsbawm, "is essentially a process of formalization and ritualization characterized by reference to the past." The "ritualization" component is evident in Makkī's extensive treatment of the various forms of prayer, fasting, and meditation he encourages the spiritual seeker to adopt, all of which have their precedent in some example from the life of the Prophet or his disciples. See Hobsbawm, "Inventing Traditions," in *The Invention of Tradition*, eds. Eric Hobsbawm and Terrence Ranger (Cambridge: Cambridge University Press, 1983), 4.

22. Ibn Kathīr, *al-Bidāya wa al-nihāya* (Beirut: Maktabat al-Maʿārif, 1966), 11:319–20.

23. Ibn Kathīr, *Bidāya*, 12:174. This was because Ghazālī himself drew *ḥadith*s from the *Qūt* in the composition of his own work.

24. Knysh, *Islamic Mysticism*, 121.

25. S.D. Goitein, "A Plea for the Periodization of Islamic History," *Journal of the American Oriental Society* 88, no. 2 (1968): 225.

26. This observation is also made by Nakamura, "Makkī and Ghazālī," 84; and Renard, *Knowledge of God*, 37.

27. Makkī, *Qūt*, 1:362.

28. Qushayrī unequivocally presents this as the interpretation of the verse in his own commentary. See *Laṭāʾif al-ishārāt*, 3:57. According to other interpretations found in the *tafsīr* tradition, the object of desire is anything from a "return to the world," "worldly pleasures," and "wealth and family," to "faith," "salvation [in the face] of punishment" and "paradise." See Gharnāṭī, *Tashīl*, 2:170; Shawkānī, *Fatḥ*, 4:386; Suyūṭī and Maḥallī, *Jalālayn*, 434; Rāzī, *al-Tafsīr al-kabīr*, 25:236. The most common interpretation cited by Ṭabarī is faith, though he also mentions the interpretation of Mujāhid—whom Makkī may have anonymously referred to—for whom the object of desire is a "return to the world so that they may repent" (*al-rujū ʿilā al-dunyāʾ li yatūbū*). See *Jāmiʿ*, 21:76.

29. Makkī, *Qūt*, 1:365.

30. Makkī, *Qūt*, 1:364. Cf. Muḥāsibī, *Iḥkām al-tawba*, fols. 9a–9b. For a treatment of the angel of death (*malak al-mawt*), see Jalāl al-Dīn al-Suyūṭī, *Sharḥ al-ṣudūr bi sharḥ ḥāl al-mawtā wa al-qubūr*, ed. Ṭaʿmā Ḥalabī (Beirut: Dār al-Maʿrifa, 1996), 61–96. On the importance of *tawba* before witnessing the angel of death, see 95–96.

31. Makkī, *Qūt*, 1:363–364.

32. Yazaki's recent monograph, *Islamic Mysticism and Abū Ṭālib al-Makkī: The Role of the Heart*, remains one exception, focusing—as the title indicates—on the theme of the heart. Only three of the nine chapters of the work, however, are devoted to this theme, with the remainder exploring the reception of Makkī in later tradition. For my review of this work, see *Journal of the Royal Asiatic Society* 25, no. 2 (2015): 357–360.

33. Majid Fakhry, *Ethical Theories in Islam* (Leiden: Brill, 1991), 35–57; idem, *A History of Islamic Philosophy* (New York: Columbia University Press, 1983), 42–55.

34. See Ghazālī, *Iḥyāʾ*, 4:8–11, and Ibn al-ʿArabī, *al-Futūḥāt al-makkiyya*, 3:208–214. For an overview of Sufi approaches to predestination and God's creation of human acts, see Richard Gramlich, "Mystical Dimensions of Islamic Monotheism," in *We Believe in One God: The Experience of God in Christianity and Islam*, eds. Annemarie Schimmel and Abdoldjavad Falaturi (New York: Seabury Press, 1976), 136–149. On the contested issue of the exact nature of predestination in Ghazālī, see Benjamin Abrahamov, "Al-Ghazāli's Theory of Causality," *Studia Islamica* 67 (1988): 75–98; Thérèse-Anne Druart, "Al-Ghazālī's Conception of the Agent in the *Tahāfut* and the *Iqtiṣād*: Are People Really Agents?," in *Arabic Theology, Arabic Philosophy: From the Many to the One: Essays in Celebration of Richard Frank*, ed. James Montgomery (Paris: Uitgeverig Peters, 2006), 426–440; Michael Marmura, "Ghazālian Causes and Intermediaries," *Journal of the American Oriental Society* 115 (1995): 89–100; idem, "Ghazālī and Ashʿarism Revisited," *Arabic Sciences and Philosophy* 12 (2002): 91–110. On Ibn al-ʿArabī's view of predestination, see Chittick, "Acts of God and Acts of Man," in *Sufi Path of Knowledge*, 205–211. For a general survey of the problem of predestination in *kalām*, see Wolfson, *Kalam*, 601–719.

35. Makkī cites the following saying from Aḥmad b. Ḥanbal: "The scholars of *kalām* are heretics (*zanādiqa*)." This is in a short section in which he raises his objections to the science of dogmatic theology. See Makkī, *Qūt*, 1:287.

36. Makkī, *Qūt*, 1:362.

37. For their views, see for example, Mānakdīm al-Qazwīnī, *Sharḥ al-uṣūl al-khamsa*, 794.

38. Makkī, *Qūt*, 1:385. Abū ʿAlī al-Daqqāq, the teacher of Qushayrī who was also a near contemporary of Makkī makes a similar point about the importance of a *tawba* that embraces all sins. He says that "nothing of this path is opened" for the one who "did not repent (*lam yatub*) at the hands of his *shaykh* or someone else, of all of his slips (*zallāt*), both hidden and open, both small and large." See ʿAbd al-Wahhāb al-Shaʿrānī, *al-Anwār al-qudsiyya fī bayān qawāʿid al-ṣūfiyya* (Beirut: Dār al-Ṣādir, 2004), 238.

39. Makkī, *Qūt*, 1:367.

40. Makkī, *Qūt*, 1:367. This view was held by some on the grounds that insofar as every sin is an offense against God, it cannot be trivialized. Thus Makkī states that "minor sins (*ṣaghāʾir*) in the eyes of the fearful ones (*khāʾifīn*) were major sins (*kabāʾir*)." The view that there are no minor sins was famously attributed to Ibn ʿAbbās when he said that "everything that God has prohibited is a major sin (*kabīra*)." Ghazālī, *Iḥyā*, 4:50. Ghazālī also quotes one of the gnostics as saying, "there is no such thing as a minor sin, for every act of disobedience is a major sin." See *Iḥyā*, 4:51. Fakhr al-Dīn al-Rāzī also observes that, from one perspective, every sin can indeed be seen as an enormity. "In its origin," he writes, "every sin is a major sin (*kabīra*), because the blessings of God are many, and to

transgress [against] the Benefactor (*al-mun'im*) is a great sin (*sayyi'a 'aẓīma*)." See *al-Tafsīr al-kabīr*, 29:8. The Ash'arite theologian Ibrāhīm b. Muḥammad al-Bājūrī (d. 1860) in his criticism of this view attributes it to the Khārijites, while ascribing the opposing view, that all sins are minor, to the Murji'ites. See his *Tuḥfat al-murīd 'alā jawharat al-tawḥīd*, ed. 'Abd al-Salām al-Shannār (Damascus: Dār al-Bayrūtī, 2002), 464. For more on Bājūrī, see Aaron Spevack's recent study, *The Archetypal Sunnī Scholar: Law, Theology, and Mysticism in the Synthesis of Al-Bājūrī* (Albany: State University of New York Press, 2014).

41. Cf. Ghazālī, *Iḥyā'*, 4:50.

42. Makkī, *Qūt*, 1:367.

43. Muḥāsibī, *Qaṣad*, 146–147.

44. Makkī, *Qūt*, 1:368.

45. Makkī, *Qūt*, 1:368.

46. Makkī, *Qūt*, 1:366. This is attributed anonymously to "one of the gnostics" (*ba'ḍ al-ārifīn*).

47. Makkī, *Qūt*, 1:366. This is attributed anonymously to "one of the early predecessors" (*ba'ḍ al-salaf*).

48. Makkī, *Qūt*, 1:366. This is attributed anonymously to "one of the learned ones" (*ba'ḍ al-ulāma'*).

49. Makkī, *Qūt*, 1:369.

50. Makkī, *Qūt*, 1:370. Interestingly, he quotes Sahl of all people to justify the view that in some circumstances of the initial journey, it may be in the aspirant's interest to forget his sins. Although Sahl is not taking the view that this "forgetting" is because of one's spiritual development, as in the case of Junayd, it nevertheless indicates that there are circumstances in which *tawba* need not be characterized by a remembrance of one's past wrongs.

51. Makkī, *Qūt*, 1:377.

52. I follow Sachiko Murata in translating *khāṭir* as "incoming thought" since it seems to most accurately convey the import of the term. The *khawāṭir* "are 'incoming,'" writes Murata, because "they come from some place." See Murata, *The Tao of Islam* (Albany: State University of New York Press, 1992), 293. We lose this sense of the term when *khāṭir* is rendered simply as "passing thought." See also note 57 below.

53. *Khaṭāyā* are literally "faults," "mistakes," or "errors." *Khaṭī'a* is a close equivalent of *vice*, whose primary meaning is "fault," "defect," or "flaw."

54. Makkī, *Qūt*, 1:379.

55. Compare with Hujwīrī, who proposes a slightly different order of psychological "events" that lead to the sin: "the devil cannot enter a man's heart until he desires to commit a sin; but when a certain quantity of passion appears the devil takes it and decks it out and displays it to the man's heart, and this is called suggestion (*waswas*). It begins from passion (*hawā*)." See Hujwīrī, *Kashf*, 208. The overriding concern of both authors is nevertheless with effacing the very origin of the offense.

56. Although Makkī does not address the origin of the thought itself, we can presume it may emerge either through an external stimulus or spontaneously from within.

57. The Sufi psychologists typically differentiate between four sources of the *khawāṭir*. They can either come from God, the angels, the self/soul, or satan. All *khawāṭir* that call to meritorious works are "divine" (*ilāhī*). See Kāshānī, *Iṣṭilāḥāt al-ṣūfiyya*, 177; idem, *Rashḥ al-zulāl*, 90; Murata, *Tao*, 294. For more on the *khāwāṭir* in Makkī see the thirtieth chapter of the *Qūt*, 1:238–268. See also Murata's brief discussion of Makkī's chapter and a few translated excerpts in the *Tao*, 294–295. For Makkī's analysis of the *khawāṭir* that arise in prayer, see *Qūt* 2:202–207. For one of the earliest Sufi discussions of the concept, see Kalābādhī, 62–63, 114. For more on the technical relation of the *khāṭir* to the *wārid* and *waswasa*, see Qushayrī, *Risāla*, 196, and Sells's translation in *Early Islamic Mysticism*, 142–146. See also Hujwīrī, *Kashf*, 208; Schimmel, *Mystical*, 256; Smith, *Early Mystic*, 126; Sulamī, *Darajāt al-ṣādiqīn (Stations of the Righteous)* trans. Kenneth Honnerkamp, in *Three Early Sufi Texts*, eds. Nicholar Heer and Kenneth Honnerkamp (Louisville, KY: Fons Vitae, 2003), 121, 125–126. These references illustrate the emphasis Sufis placed on discerning the origin of the incoming thoughts.

58. Muḥāsibī, *Bad' man anāba*, 29. Unlike Muḥāsibī, Makkī does not suggest that one deprive himself of permissible pleasures to punish the lower soul for its intransigent defiance. The self-lacerating mortification Muḥāsibī encourages for the *tā'ib*, though present in the *Qūt*, appears less pronounced.

59. In another context Makkī quotes Sahl al-Tustarī, "*tawba* is not made sound except by [their] leaving much of what is legally permissible (*kathīr min al-ḥalāl*) out of fear that it might take them into other than it [i.e., *ḥalāl*]," *Qūt*, 1:380. The saying also appears in the Tustarī *tafsīr* as a gloss on Q 25:70, where, instead of *kathīr min al-ḥalāl*, he speaks of *kathīr min al-mubāḥ*. Immediately after Sahl's aphorism in the *tafsīr*, ʿĀ'isha is quoted as saying, "Place a screen [or protection] of what is lawful (*sitr min al-ḥalāl*) between yourselves and what is unlawful." This scrupulousness is thereby legitimated by no less an authority than the wife of the Prophet himself. See Tustarī, *Tafsīr al-qur'ān*, 209.

60. For Makkī's discussion of *murāqaba*, see *Qūt* 1:188–200, 1:210–230. For *muḥāsaba*, see 162–174. See also Qushayrī's chapter on *murāqaba* in the *Risāla*, 353–356.

61. Makkī, *Qūt*, 1:369.

62. Makkī, *Qūt*, 1:369. Cf. Ghazālī, *Iḥyā'*, 4:64–65.

63. For biographical entries on him, see Hujwīrī, *Kashf*, 118–119; Sulamī, *Ṭabaqāt*, 91–94; Qushayrī, *Risāla*, 86–87.

64. There are no biographical entries on him in Hujwīrī, Sulamī, and Qushayrī. For more on him see Massignon, *Essay*, 150.

65. Makkī may be drawing a relation between *ṭuma'nīna* and *yaqīn* partly on the basis of Muḥāsibī's influence. In the *Kitāb al-mustarshidīn*, he states that "*yaqīn* has a beginning and an end: its beginning is *ṭuma'nīna* and its end is

finding sufficiency in being alone with God (*ifrād Allāh bi al-kifāya*)"; see 92. The relation between "certainty" and "repose" can be traced back to the Qur'ān, in which Abraham asks for a direct sign from God "so that my heart may be at rest (*li yaṭma'inna qalbī*)" (Q 2:260). According to Sahl al-Tustarī, Abraham was not troubled by doubt but asked for a direct unveiling that would increase his *yaqīn*. See Sulamī, *Ḥaqā'iq*, 1:79. The twelfth-century Maybudī saw in Abraham's request a desire that his "knowledge of certainty (*'ilm al-yaqīn*) might become the eye of certainty (*'ayn al-yaqīn*)." See Annabel Keeler, *Sufi Hermeneutics: The Qur'ān Commentary of Radhīd al-Dīn Maybudī* (Oxford: Oxford University Press and the Institute of Ismaili Studies, 2006), 227. For a similar explanation put forward by an earlier but anonymous Sufi, see Sulamī, 1:79. See also Qushayrī, *Laṭā'if al-ishārāt*, 1:120–121. Anṣārī defined *ṭuma'nīna*, to which he devoted an entire chapter in the *Manāzil al-sā'irīn*, as a "repose (*sukūn*) which is strengthened by a true security similar to direct experience." See Keeler, 227; Kamāl al-Dīn 'Abd al-Razzāq al-Kāshānī, *Sharḥ manāzil al-sā'irīn*, ed. Muḥsin Bidārfur, 2nd edition (Qum: Sharī'at, 1381 AH Solar), 371. Most importantly, *ṭuma'nīna* comes from the same quadrilateral root as *muṭma'inna*. This latter term is used in the Qur'ān to describe the "soul at peace," the *nafs al-muṭma'inna* of Q 89:27 which the Sufis considered to represent the most spiritually mature of souls.

66. Makkī, *Qūt*, 1:369. The debate was essentially one between the *'ulamā'* of Iraq and Syria, with the Basrans giving preference to the *mujāhid tā'ib*.

67. Makkī, *Qūt*, 1:369.

68. For a brief comparative analysis of the the contrasting views of Junayd and Ibn 'Aṭā' on this and other areas of the mystical path, see Massignon, *Essay*, 151; idem, *The Passion of Ḥallāj*, 1:91–93.

69. Susan Stark has succinctly expressed the proposition, which has been vigorously debated in Western philosophy from the time of Aristotle, namely, that "it matters not only that a person do the right action, but also that she feel the right way." See "Virtue and Emotion," *Nous* 35 (2001): 3:440–455. For further treatments of this question in Western ethical philosophy, see Jack Kelly, "Virtue and Pleasure," *Mind* 82 (1973): 401–408; Gabriele Taylor and Sybil Wolfram, "Virtues and Passions," *Analysis*, 31, no. 3 (1971): 76–83. The debate among the Sufis was centered on which action is more virtuous, while in Western ethical philosophy, the parallel debate was centered on determining whether a virtuous action requires a corresponding emotion. The relation between these two issues is drawn out in the following analysis.

70. Aristotle, *Nicomachean Ethics*, trans. David Ross (Oxford: Oxford University Press, 1980), 1104b4–b6; Taylor and Wolfram, "Virtues and Passions," 76.

71. The full passage in Aristotle runs, "We must take as a sign of states of character the pleasure or pain that supervenes upon acts; for the man who abstains from bodily pleasures and delights in this very fact is temperate, while the man who is annoyed at it is self-indulgent, and he who stands his ground against things that are terrible and delights in this or at least is not pained is

brave, while the man who is pained is a coward. For moral excellence is concerned with pleasures and pains" (1104b4–b10).

72. Aristotle, *Ethics*, 1104a–b.

73. Immanuel Kant, *Foundations of the Metaphysics of Morals*, trans. Lewis White Beck (New York: Liberal Arts Press, 1959), 14–15; Taylor and Wolfram, "Virtues and Passions," 76.

74. Kant, *Foundations*, 14–15.

75. This law for Kant is a rational law. Insofar as he places reason at the very center of morality, his ethical philosophy comes very close to that of the Muʿtazilites. For a recent study of Muʿtazilite ethics, see Sophia Vasalou, *Moral Agents and Their Deserts: The Character of Muʿtazilite Ethics* (Princeton, NJ: Princeton University Press, 2008). See also Richard Martin, Mark Woodward, and Dwi Atmaja, *Defenders of Reason in Islam: Muʿtazilism from Medieval School to Modern Symbol* (Oxford: Oneworld, 1997).

76. Kant, *Foundations*, 14–15. For Kant, the reasons that make it so difficult for us to understand the motives behind apparently virtuous actions are not unlike those that Ghazālī presents in the *Kitāb al-nīya wa al-ikhlāṣ wa al-ṣidq* of the *Iḥyāʾ*. Both Kant and Ghazālī provide four examples of human actions to illustrate the complexity of human intention; cf. Kant, *Foundations*, 9–14; Ghazālī, *Iḥyāʾ*, 5:112–114.

77. Makkī, *Qūt*, 1:362.

78. Makkī, *Qūt*, 1:362.

79. Muḥāsibī, *Iḥkām al-tawba*, fols. 8b–9a. Since this idea also prevails in the Qurʾān, there is no reason to presume that Makkī adopted it through Muḥāsibī's influence.

80. Makkī, *Qūt*, 1:380.

81. Makkī, *Qūt*, 1:380.

82. Makkī, *Qūt*, 1:362–363.

83. Makkī, *Qūt*, 1:362. Ṭabarī observes that the commentators differed on the nature of the *tabdīl* mentioned in the verse (*ikhtalafa ahl al-taʾwīl fī taʾwīl dhālik*). See Ṭabarī, *Jāmiʿ*, 19:29. According to Fakhr al-Dīn al-Rāzī, some of them understood the *tabdīl* to mean that the punishment that the *tāʾib* would receive in the next world would be transmuted, by *tawba*, into a corresponding reward (*innahu taʿāla yubaddilu al-ʿiqāb bi al-thawāb*). Following *tawba*, God would efface the sin and put in its place a good deed. See Rāzī, *al-Tafsīr al-kabīr*, 24:97–98. Rāzī's analytic tendency leads him to present these as two different but related interpretations. See also Ṭabarī, *Jāmiʿ*, 19:30. For Suyūṭī, the evil deeds are transmuted into good deeds in the next world (*ḥasanāt fī al-ākhira*). See Suyūṭī and Maḥallī, *Jalālayn*, 366. Commenting on this verse in his chapter on the *maqām al-tawba* in the *Futūḥāt*, Ibn al-ʿArabī explicitly adds that the reward will correspond to the magnitude of the averted punishment. The transmutation, which is the fruit of *tawba*, he argues, will render the wrongful killing of a soul tantamount to the saving of a life, and theft equivalent to charity. See *Futūḥāt*, 3:210–212. Rāzī attributes the

interpretation put forward by Makkī to Ibn ʿAbbās, Ḥasan, Mujāhid, and Qatāda. See *al-Tafsīr al-kabīr*, 24:98. Shawkānī quotes Ḥasan's explanation of this verse: "a group of people say that the *tabdīl* occurs in the next world, but it is not so. The *tabdīl* occurs in this world (*innamā al-tabdīl fī al-dunyā*). God transmutes for them faith in the place of associating others with God (*shirk*), sincerity (*ikhlāṣ*) for doubt (*shakk*), and good character (*iḥsān*) for debauchery (*fujūr*)." See Shawkānī, *Fatḥ*, 4:103. For more on this debate, see Gharnāṭī, *Tashīl*, 2:87.

84. Makkī, *Qūt*, 1:383.

85. For some insightful remarks on the concept of *kufr*, see Izutsu, *God and the Man*, 14–16.

86. Makkī, *Qūt*, 1:382–383. See my discussion of this theme in the context of Sufi notions of *shukr* in "The Embodiment of Gratitude (*Shukr*) in Sufi Ethics," *Studia Islamica* 111 (2016): 159–178.

87. Makkī, *Qūt*, 1:380.

88. Iṣfahānī, *Mufradāt*, 469.

89. If the prophets are mentioned, the more advanced Sufis invariably stand below them.

90. Makkī, *Qūt*, 1:380.

91. Qushayrī, *Risāla*, 213. This saying is attributed to Bunnān al-Ḥammāl in Sulamī, *Ḥaqāʾiq*, 2:69.

92. Sulamī, *Ḥaqāʾiq*, 1:312.

93. Qushayrī, *Risāla*, 213.

94. Makkī, *Qūt*, 1:388.

95. Makkī, *Qūt*, 1:389.

96. Makkī, *Qūt*, 1:389.

97. Makkī, *Qūt*, 1:389. An allusion to Q 9:102.

98. The four instances in which the verb is used are the following: "Lo those who turn their back after the guidance has been manifested to them. Satan has seduced them (*sawwala lahum*), and he gives them the rein" (Q 47:25); "And they came with false blood on his shirt. He [Jacob] said, 'your souls have beguiled you (*bal sawwalat lakum anfusukum*) into something' " (Q 12:18); "He [Jacob] said, 'Nay, but your souls have beguiled you (*bal sawwalat lakum anfusukum*) into something' " (Q 12:83); "[Moses] said, 'and what have you to say, O Sāmirī?' He said, 'I perceived what they perceive not, so I seized a handful from the footsteps of the messenger, and then threw it in. Thus my soul commanded me (*wa kadhālika sawwalat lī nafsi*)' " (Q 20:95–96). Some of the exegetes argue that the Sāmirī was well versed in Egyptian idolatry, and believed half-heartedly in the God of Moses. He used the "handful" of dust to make the golden calf, which was meant to serve as an idol, uttering a lowing sound while Moses went to the mountain. This negative use of *sawwala* in this case is consistent with the Qurʾān's other uses. It is worth noting that two of the word's instances appear to describe the deception of Joseph's brothers: they are not altogether evil, and they eventually repent.

99. Makkī, *Qūt,* 1:389–390.

100. This classification appears in the tenth chapter, entitled "on the differences of people in their quest for God-fearingness" (*bāb ikhtilāf al-nās fī ṭalab al-taqwā*). See Muḥāsibī, *Ri'āya,* 63–67.

101. ʿAbd al-Ḥalīm Maḥmūd, *Ustādh al-sā'irīn: al-Ḥārith ibn al-Muḥāsibī,* 121–124. See also Joseph van Ess's summary of these levels in *Die Gedankenwelt,* 63–64.

102. Muḥāsibī, *Riʿāya,* 66; Makkī, *Qūt,* 1:389. The words of the *ḥadīth* cited in the texts are slightly different. In the *Riʿāya,* Muḥāsibī quotes the Prophet as saying "the best of you are those who are tried and oft-repentant." In Makkī, the *ḥadīth* runs: "the believer is [the one who is] tried and oft-repentant."

103. There may also have been historical and intellectual circumstances (which I have been unable to identify) that led Makkī to expand Muḥāsibī's scheme.

104. Massignon, *Essay,* 164.

105. Ghazālī, *Iḥyā',* 4:67–72.

106. See Q 2:222. This is the only occasion in the Qur'ān where the human being is referred to by the emphatic *tawwāb.* In the other ten instances, the *mubālagha* form is used only of God (see chapter 2).

107. This, we can assume, would include shortcomings in *iṣlāḥ.*

108. Makkī, *Qūt,* 1:385.

109. Makkī, *Qūt,* 1:385.

110. Makkī, *Qūt,* 1:385.

111. Makkī, *Qūt,* 1:385–386.

112. Makkī, *Qūt,* 1:385.

113. Makkī, *Qūt,* 1:385.

114. Makkī, *Qūt,* 1:368. Cf. Ghazālī, *Iḥyā',* 4:65–66.

115. Ibn al-ʿArabī, *al-Futūḥāt al-makkiyya,* 3:215–216.

116. Ibn al-ʿArabī, *al-Futūḥāt al-makkiyya,* 3:216.

117. Ibd al-ʿArabī, *al-Futūḥāt al-makkiyya,* 3:215. See also the 241st *mawāqif* of ʿAbd al-Qādir al-Jazā'irī's *Kitāb al-mawāqif* (Dār al-Yaqẓa, 1966), 2:544. Jazā'irī is most likely citing Ibn al-ʿArīf indirectly through Ibn al-ʿArabī, whose influence on his own discussion of *tawba* is clear.

118. For biographical entries on him, see Hujwīrī, *Kashf,* 135–136; Iṣfahānī, *Ḥilyat,* 10:315–320; Sulamī, *Ṭabaqāt,* 147–151. For a survey of the source material on him, see Gramlich, *Alte Vorbilder des Sufitums,* 1:447–482.

119. Sarrāj, *Lumaʿ,* 43; Sells, *Early Islamic Mysticism,* 199–200. See also Qushayrī, *Risāla,* 213.

120. Kalābādhī, *Taʿarruf,* 64; cf. Arberry, *The Doctrine of the Sufis,* 83.

121. So common that even an astute modern scholar such as Renard restricts his explanation of Ruwaym's definition to this interpretation, when he writes, "others such as Ruwaym, emphasize that genuine repentance requires that one repent even of repenting itself, *as if warning of the danger of complacency and of*

self-congratulatory willingness to rest in this humble beginning" [italics mine]. See John Renard's excellent reference work, *Historical Dictionary of Sufism* (Oxford: Oxford University Press, 2005), 199–200.

122. For Ibn al-Qayyim, *tawba min al-tawba* can include repenting of witnessing one's repentance as if it were one's own and not the result of God's gift. See *Madārij al-sālikīn* (Riyadh: Dār Ṭība, 1423 AH) 1:374–375.

Conclusion

1. ʿAṭṭār, *Tadkhirat* (abridged), 247. I have very slightly modified Arberry's dated translation for idiomatic reasons.

2. Wensinck, 1:283.

3. Wensinck, 1:284.

4. The Basran Muʿtazilites argued that the repentant sinner deserved God's forgiveness due to merit (*istiḥqāq*), while those of Baghdad argued that the forgiveness stemmed from divine favor (*tafaḍḍul*). See Mānakdīm al-Qazwīnī, *Sharḥ*, 789–791; cf. al-Ashʿarī, *Maqālāt*, 270–272, 475–476; Abū Muḥammad b. Mattawayh, *Kitāb al-majmūʿ fī al-muḥīṭ bi al-taklīf*, ed. Jan Peters (Beirut: Dar el-Machreq, 1999), 392–394. See also Moucarry, *Search for Forgiveness*, 115.

5. He also cites the *ḥadīth*, a variant of which was cited above, that "every child of Adam is a sinner, and the best of sinners are those who seek the forgiveness of God." Makkī, *Qūt*, 1:379–380.

6. Michael Sells, *Mystical Languages of Unsaying* (Chicago: University of Chicago Press, 1994), 79.

7. Ibn al-ʿArabī, *Futūḥāt*, 3:212.

8. Jalāl al-Dīn al-Rūmī, *Signs of the Unseen: The Discourses of Rumi*, trans. W.M. Thackston (Boston: Shambhala, 1999), 139.

9. Ibn ʿAbbād, *Sharḥ al-ḥikam al-ʿaṭāʾiyya*, ed. Muḥammad al-Qahwajī (Damascus: Dār al-Farfūr, 2003), 241 [#95].

10. Ibid, 242 [#96].

11. Rūmī, *The Mathnawī of Jalāluʾddīn Rūmī: Edited from the Oldest Manuscripts Available: With Critical Notes, Translation and Commentary*, trans. R. Nicholson (London: E.J.W. Gibb Memorial and Messrs Luzac & Co. Ltd., 1972), 2:356–364. Translation slightly modified for idiomatic reasons.

12. Cited in Schimmel, *Mystical*, 110.

Bibliography

Primary Sources

ʿAbd al-Bāqī, Muḥammad Fuʾād. *al-Muʿjam al-mufahras li alfāẓ al-qurʾān al-karīm*. Beirut: Dār al-Maʿrifa, 1994.

al-Anṣārī, Abū Ismāʿīl ʿAbd Allāh b. Muḥammad. *Chemin de Dieu: trois traités spirituels*. Ed. and trans. Serge de Laugier de Beaurecueil. Paris: Sinbad, 1985.

Aristotle. *Nicomachean Ethics*. Trans. David Ross. Oxford: Oxford University Press, 1980.

Augustine. *Augustine of Hippo: Selected Writings*. Trans. Mary T. Clark. Mahwah, NJ: Paulist Press, 1988.

al-Ashʿarī, Abū al-Ḥasan. *al-Ibāna ʿan ʿuṣūl al-dīyāna*. Damascus: Dār al-Bayān, 1999.

———. *Maqālat al-islāmiyīn*. Ed. Helmut Ritter. Wiesbaden: Franz Steiner, 1980.

al-Baghdādī, ʿAbd al-Qāhir b. Ṭāhir b. Muḥammad. *al-Farq bayn al-firaq*. Ed. Muḥammad al-Ḥamīd. Beirut: al-Maktabat al-ʿAṣriyya, 1998.

al-Baghdādī, Abū Bakr Aḥmad b. ʿAlī al-Khaṭīb. *Taʾrīkh baghdād aw madīnat al-salām*. Cairo: Maktabat al-Khānjī, 1931.

al-Bājūrī, Ibrāhīm b. Muḥammad. *Tuḥfat al-murīd ʿalā jawharat al-tawḥīd*. Ed. ʿAbd al-Salām al-Shannār. Damascus: Dār al-Bayrūtī, 2002.

al-Bayḍāwī. *Tafsīr al-bayḍāwī*. Cairo, 1926.

al-Dhahabī, Shams al-Dīn Abū ʿAbd Allāh. *al-ʿIbar fī khabar man ghabar*. Eds. Salāḥ al-Dīn al-Munajjid and Fuʾād Sayyid. Kuwait: Dāʾirat al-Maṭbūʿāt wa al-Nashr, 1960–66.

———. *Siyar aʿlām al-nubulāʾ*. Ed. Shuʿayb Arnāʿuṭ. Beirut: Muʾassasat al-Risāla, 1996.

al-Fīrūzābādī. *al-Qāmūs al-muḥīṭ*. Damascus: Maktabat al-Nūrī, n.d.

al-Fayyūmī, Aḥmad b. Muḥammad b. ʿAlī. *al-Miṣbāḥ al-munīr fī gharīb al-sharḥ al-kabīr*. Beirut: Maktabat Lubnān, 1987.

al-Gharnāṭī, Muḥammad b. Aḥmad. *al-Tashīl li ʿulūm al-tanzīl*. Ed. ʿAbd al-Allāh al-Khālidī. Beirut: Dār al-Arqam, n.d.

al-Ghazālī, Abū Ḥāmid. *Iḥyāʾ ʿulūm al-dīn*. Aleppo: Dār al-Waʿī, 1998.

———. *The Incoherence of the Philosophers: A parallel English-Arabic text*. Trans. Michael Marmura. Provo, UT: Brigham Young University Press, 1997.

———. *Minhāj al-ʿābidīn*. Ed. ʿAbd al-ʿAzīz ʿIzz al-Dīn. Beirut: Muʾassasat Sīrawān, 1996.

al-Ḥallāj, Ḥusayn b. Manṣūr. *Kitāb al-ṭawāsīn*. Ed. Louis Massignon. Paris, 1970.

al-Hujwīrī, ʿAlī b. ʿUthmān al-Jullābī. *Kashf al-maḥjūb: The Oldest Persian Treatise on Sufism*. Trans. Reynold A. Nicholson. 1911. Reprint. Lahore: Islamic Book Service, 1992.

Ibn ʿAbbād, Muḥammad Ibrāhīm. *Letters on the Sufi Path*. Trans. John Renard. Mahwah, NJ; Paulist Press, 1986.

———. *Sharḥ al-ḥikam al-ʿaṭāʾiyya*. Ed. Muḥammad al-Qahwajī. Damascus: Dār al-Farfūr, 2003.

Ibn ʿAbbād, Ismāʿīl. *al-Muḥīṭ fī al-lugha*. Beirut: ʿĀlam al-Kutub, n.d.

Ibn ʿAjība, *Book of Ascension to the Essential Truths of Sufism: Miʿrāj al-tashawwuf ilā ḥaqāʾiq al-taṣawwuf [with Arabic text]*. Trans. Mohamed F. Aresmouk and Michael A. Fitzgerald. Louisville, KY: Fons Vitae, 2011.

Ibn al-ʿArabī, Muḥyī al-Dīn. *al-Futūḥāt al-makkiyya*. Ed. Aḥmad Shams al-Dīn. Beirut: Dār al-Kutub ʿIlmiyya, 1999.

Ibn ʿAṭāʾ Allāh al-Iskandarī. *Laṭāʾif al-minan*. Ed. Khālid ʿAbd al-Raḥmān al-ʿAkk. Damascus: Dār al-Bashāʾir, 1992.

———. *The Subtle Blessings*. Trans. Nancy Roberts. Louisville, KY: Fons Vitae, 2005.

Ibn ʿAyn, Khalīl. *Kitāb al-ʿayn*. Beirut: Dār Ḥayāʾ al-Turāth al-ʿArabī, n.d.

Ibn Durayd, Abū Bakr Muḥammad b. al-Ḥasan. *Kitāb jamharat al-lugha*. Ed. Ramzī Munīr Baʿalbakī. Beirut: Dār al-ʿIlm, 1987.

Ibn Fāris. *Muʿjam maqāyīs al-lugha*. Ed. ʿAbd al-Salām Muḥammad Hārūn. Cairo: Maktabat al-Bābī, 1969.

Ibn al-Jawzī. *Zād al-tafsīr*. Beirut: Maktabat al-Islāmī, 1965.

Ibn al-Kathīr. *al-Bidāya wa al-nihāya*. Beirut: Maktabat al-Maʿārif, 1966.

———. *Tafsīr al-qurʾān al-ʿaẓīm*. Riyadh: Dār al-Ṭayyiba li al-Nashr wa al-Tawzīʿ, 1997.

Ibn Khallikān, Abū al-ʿAbbās Shams al-Dīn Aḥmad. *Wafāyāt al-aʿyān*. Ed. Iḥsān ʿAbbās. Beirut: Dār al-Thaqāfa, 1968–1973.

Ibn Māja. *Sunan: Arabic–English edition*. Ed. and trans. M.T. Ansari. New Delhi: Kitāb Bhavān, 1994.

Ibn Mattawayh, Abū Muḥammad. *Kitāb al-majmūʿ fī al-muḥīṭ bi al-taklīf*. Ed. Jan Peters. Beirut: Dar el-Machreq, 1999.

Ibn Manẓūr. *Lisān al-ʿarab*. Ed. Muḥammad ʿAbd al-Wahhāb. Beirut: Dār al-Iḥyāʾ al-Turāth al-ʿArabī, 1997.

Ibn al-Qayyim al-Jawziyya, Abū Bakr. *Madārij al-sālikīn*. Riyadh: Dār Ṭība, 1423 AH.

Ibn Qudāma, Abū Muḥammad ʿAbd al-Allāh. *Kitāb al-tawwābīn*. Ed. ʿAbd al-Qādir al-Arnāʾūṭ. Damascus: Dār al-Bayān, 1969.

Ibn Rushd. *The Decisive Treatise and Epistle Dedicatory [with Arabic text]*. Trans. Charles E. Butterworth. Provo, UT: Brigham Young University Press, 2001.

Ibn Sīda. *al-Muḥkam wa al-muḥīṭ*. Ed. ʿAbd al-Ḥamīd Handāwī. Beirut: Dār al-Kutub al-ʿIlmiyya, 2000.

Ibn Taymiyya. *al-Risāla al-ṣafadiyya*. Beirut: Dār Ibn Ḥazm, 2002.

al-Iṣfahānī, Abū Nuʿaym Aḥmad b. ʿAbd Allāh. *Ḥilyat al-awliyāʾ wa ṭabaqāt al-aṣfiyāʾ*. Ed. Abd al-Qādir ʿAṭāʾ. Beirut: Dār al-Kutub al-ʿIlmiyya, 2002.

al-Iṣfahānī, al-Rāghib. *Mufradāt alfāẓ al-qurʾān*. Ed. Ṣafwān ʿAdnān. Beirut: Dār al-Shāmiyya, 1997.

al-Jāmī, ʿAbd al-Raḥmān b. Aḥmad. *Nafaḥāt al-uns*. Ed. and trans. (Arabic) Muḥammad Adīb. Beirut: Dār al-Kutub al-ʿIlmiyya, 2003.

al-Jawharī, Ismāʿīl b. Ḥammād. *al-Siḥāḥ*. Eds. Amīl Yaʿqūb and Nabīl Ṭarīfī. Beirut: Dār al-Kutub al-ʿIlmiyya, n.d.

al-Jazāʾirī, ʿAbd al-Qādir. *Kitab al-mawāqif*. Dār al-Yaqẓa, 1966.

al-Jīlānī, ʿAbd al-Qādir. *al-Ghunya*. Ed. Yūsuf Maḥmūd al-Ḥājj Aḥmad. Damascus: Maktabat al-ʿIlm al-Ḥadīth, 2001.

al-Junayd, Abū al-Qāsim. *The Book of Fanāʾ*. Trans. Sells in *Early Islamic Mysticism: Sufi, Qurʾan, Miʿraj, Poetic, and Theological Writings*, 259–265. Mahwah, NJ: Paulist Press, 1996.

al-Juwaynī. *Kitāb al-Irshād*. Ed. J.D. Luciani. Paris: Leroux, 1938.

al-Kafāwī. *al-Kulliyyāt: muʿjam fī musṭalaḥāt wa al-furūq al-lughawiyya*. Eds. Muḥammad al-Miṣrī and ʿAdnān Darwīsh. Beirut: Muʾassasat al-Risāla, 1996.

al-Kalābādhī, Abū Bakr Muḥammad b. Isḥāq. *al-Taʿarruf li madhhab ahl al-taṣawwuf*. Ed. Yuḥannā Ḥabīb Ṣādir. Beirut: Dār Ṣādir, 2001.

———. *The Doctrine of the Ṣūfis*. Trans. A.J. Arberry. Cambridge: Cambridge University Press, 1935.

al-Kāshānī, Kamāl al-Dīn ʿAbd al-Razzāq. *Iṣṭilāḥāt al-ṣūfiyya*. Ed. ʿAbd al-ʿĀl Shāhīn. Cairo: Dār al-ʿInār, 1992.

———. *Rashḥ al-zulāl*. Ed. Saʿīd ʿAbd al-Fattāḥ. Cairo: Maktabat al-Azharī li al-Turāth, 1995.

———. *Sharḥ manāzil al-sāʾirīn*. Ed. Muḥsin Bidārfar. Qum: Shariʿat, 1971.

al-Kharrāz, Abū Saʿīd. *The Book of Truthfulness (Kitāb al-Ṣidq) by Abū Saʿīd al-Kharrāz* [with Arabic text]. Ed. and trans. A.J. Arberry. Oxford: Oxford University Press, 1937.

al-Makkī, Abū Ṭālib Muḥammad b. ʿAlī. *Qūt al-qulūb fī muʿāmalat al-maḥbūb wa waṣf ṭarīq al-murīd ilā maqām al-tawḥīd*. Ed. Saʿīd Nasīb Makārim. Beirut: Dār Ṣādir, 1995.

———. *Qūt al-qulūb*. Ed. Saʿīd Makārim and ʿAbd al-Munʿim al-Ḥafinī. Cairo: Dār al-Rashshād, 1991.

———. *Die Nahrung der Herzen*. Ed. and trans. Richard Gramlich. Stuttgart: F. Steiner, 1992.

———. (attributed) *ʿIlm al-qulūb*. Ed. Aḥmad ʿAṭāʾ. Cairo: Dār al-Qāhira, n.d.

al-Muḥāsibī, al-Ḥārith b. Asad. *Ādāb al-nufūs*. In *Badʾ man anāba ilā Allāh wa yalīhi ādāb al-nufūs*, ed. Majdī Fatḥī al-Sayyid, 53–143. Cairo: Dār al-Islām. 1991.

———. *Badʾ man anāba*. In *al-Tawba*, ed. ʿAbd al-Qādir Aḥmad ʿAṭāʾ, 21–47. Cairo: Dār al-Iʿtiṣām. 1997.

———. *Fahm al-qurʾān*. In *al-ʿAql wa fahm al-qurʾān*, ed. Ḥusayn al-Quwwatī, 261–503. Dār al-Fikr. 1978.

———. *Fahm al-ṣalāt*. In *al-Waṣāya aw al-naṣā'iḥ al-dīniyya wa nafāḥāt al-qudsiyya*, ed. 'Abd al-Qādir Aḥmad 'Aṭā', 223–240. Beirut: Dār al-Kutub al-'Ilmiyya, 2003.

———. *Iḥkām al-tawba wa radd maẓālim al-'ibād wa khāliṣ minhā qabl al-ma'ād*. MS. Berlin. 1435.

———. *Kitāb al-'ilm*. In Leonard Librande, "Islam and Conservation: The Theologian-Ascetic al-Muḥāsibī." *Arabica* 30, no. 2 (1983): 141–146 (full Arabic text of treatise).

———. *Kitāb al-makāsib* (published as *al-Rizq al-ḥalal wa ḥaqīqat al-tawakkul 'alā Allāh*). Ed. Muḥammad 'Uthmān al-Khisht. Cairo: Maktabat al-Qur'ān, 1984.

———. *al-Masā'il fī a'māl al-qulūb wa al-jawāriḥ*. Ed. Khalīl 'Imrān. Beirut: Dār al-Kutub al-'Ilmiyya, 2000.

———. *al-Ri'āya li ḥuqūq Allāh*. Ed. 'Abd al-Qādir Aḥmad 'Aṭā'. Cairo: Dār al-Kutub al-Ḥadītha, 1970.

———. *Risālat al-mustarshidīn*. Ed. 'Abd al-Fattāḥ Abū Ghudda. Aleppo: Maktabat al-Maṭbū'āt al-Islāmiyya, 1964.

———. *al-Qaṣd wa al-rujū'*. In *al-Waṣāya aw al-naṣā'iḥ al-dīniyya wa nafāḥāt al-qudsiyya*, ed. 'Abd al-Qādir Aḥmad 'Aṭā', 145–205. Beirut: Dār al-Kutub al-'Ilmiyya, 2003.

———. *al-Tawahhum*. In *al-Waṣāya aw al-naṣā'iḥ al-dīniyya wa nafāḥāt al-qudsiyya*, ed. 'Abd al-Qādir Aḥmad 'Aṭā'. Beirut: Dār al-Kutub al-'Ilmiyya, 2003. 241–279.

———. *al-Waṣāya* (also known as *Naṣā'iḥ*). Ed. 'Abd al-Qādir Aḥmad 'Aṭā'. Beirut: Dār al-Kutub al-'Ilmiyya, 2003.

al-Niffarī, Muḥammad b. 'Abd al-Jabbār. *al-Mawāqif wa al-mukhāṭabāt*. Ed. and trans. A.J. Arberry. London: Cambridge University Press, 1935.

al-Nūrī, Abū al-Ḥasan. *Risālat maqāmāt al-qulūb*. In *Textes Mystiques Inedits d'Abū-l Ḥasan al-Nūrī (d. 295/907)*, ed. Paul Nwyia, 130–152. Beirut: Imprimerie Catholique, 1968.

al-Qazwīnī, Mānakdīm Aḥmad b. Abī Hāshim. *Sharḥ al-uṣūl al-khamsa* (incorrectly attributed to 'Abd al-Jabbār b. Aḥmad). Ed. 'Abd al-Karīm 'Uthmān. Cairo: Maktabat Wahba, 1965.

al-Qurṭubī, Muḥammad b. Aḥmad. *al-Jāmi' li aḥkām al-qur'ān*. Cairo: al-Maktabat al-'Arabiyya, 1967.

al-Qushayrī, Abū al-Qāsim. *Laṭā'if al-ishārāt*. Ed. 'Abd al-Laṭīf Ḥasan 'Abd al-Raḥmān. Beirut: Dār al-Kutub al-'Ilmiyya, 2000.

———. *Principles of Sufism* (The *Risāla* of Qushayrī). Trans. Barbara Von Schlegell. New York: Oneonta, 1990.

———. *Al-Qushayri's Epistle on Sufism: Al-Risala al-qushayriyya fī 'ilm al-tasawwuf*. Trans. Alexander Knysh. Berkshire: Garnet Publishing, 2007.

———. *al-Risāla al-qushayriyya*. Eds. 'Abd al-Ḥalīm Maḥmūd and Maḥmūd b. Sharīf. Damascus: Dār al-Fārfūr, 2002.

———. *The Risalah: Principles of Sufism*. Trans. Rabia Harris. Chicago: Kazi Publications, 2002.

al-Rāzī, Fakhr al-Dīn. *al-Tafsīr al-kabīr*. Beirut: Dār al-Kutub al-'Ilmiyya, 1990.

Rūmī, Jalāl al-Dīn. *The Mathnawī of Jalālu'ddin Rūmī: Edited from the Oldest Manuscripts Available: With Critical Notes, Translation and Commentary*. Trans. Reynold Nicholson. London: E.J.W. Gibb Memorial and Messrs Luzac & Co. Ltd., 1972.

———. *Signs of the Unseen: The Discourses of Rumi*. Trans. W.M. Thackston. Boston: Shambhala, 1999.

al-Ṣaghānī, al-Ḥasan b. Muḥammad b. al-Ḥasan. *al-Takmila wa al-dhayl wa al-ṣila*. Ed. ʿAbd al-ʿAlīm al-Ṭaḥāwī and ʿAbd al-Ḥamīd Ḥasan. Cairo: Maṭbaʿat Dār al-Kutub, 1970.

al-Sarrāj, ʿAbd Allāh b. ʿAlī. *Kitāb al-lumaʿ fī al-taṣawwuf*. Ed. Reynold Nicholson. Leiden: Brill, 1914.

———. *Kitāb al-lumaʿ fī al-taṣawwuf*. Ed. Kāmil Muṣtafā al-Hindāwī. Beirut: Dār al-Kutub al-ʿIlmiyya, 2001.

al-Balkhī, Shaqīq. (attributed) *Ādāb al-ʿibādāt*. In *Nuṣūṣ al-ṣūfiyya ghayr manshūra*, ed. Paul Nwyia, 17–22. Beirut: Dār el-Mashreq, 1972.

al-Shaʿrānī, Abū al-Mawāhib ʿAbd al-Wahhāb. *al-Anwār al-qudsīyya fī bayān qawāʿid al-ṣūfiyya*. Beirut: Dār Ṣādir, 2004.

———. *Lawāqiḥ al-anwār al-qudsiyya fī bayān al-ʿuhūd al-muḥammadiyya*. Ed. Muḥammad ʿAbd al-Raḥmān. Beirut: Dār Iḥyā' al-Turāth al-ʿArabī, 1996.

———. *al-Ṭabaqāt al-kubrā*. Ed. Khalīl Manṣūr. Beirut: Dār al-Kutub al-ʿIlmiyya, 1997.

al-Shawkānī, Muḥammad b. ʿAlī. *Fatḥ al-qadīr*. Damascus: Dār Ibn Kathīr, 1998.

al-Suhrawardī, Abū Ḥafṣ Shihāb al-Dīn. *ʿAwārif al-maʿārif*. Eds. Sayyid Aḥmad, Adīb al-Kimrānī and Maḥmūd Muṣṭafā. Saudi Arabia: al-Maktaba al-Makkīyya, 2001.

al-Sulamī, ʿAbd al-Raḥmān Muḥammad b. Ḥusayn. *Early Sufi Women: Dhikr an-niswa al-mutaʿabbidāt aṣ-ṣūfiyyāt*. Trans. Rkia E. Cornell. Louisville: Fons Vitae, 1999.

———. *Stations of the Righteous*. Trans. Kenneth Honnerkamp, in *Three Early Sufi Texts*. Eds. Nicholas Heer and Kenneth Honnerkamp, 118–128. Louisville: Fons Vitae, 2003.

———. *Stumblings of Those Aspiring*. Trans. Kenneth Honnerkamp, in *Three Early Sufi Texts*, eds. Nicholas Heer and Kenneth Honnerkamp, 129–154. Louisville: Fons Vitae, 2003.

———. *Subtleties of the Ascension: Early Mystical Sayings on Muhammad's Heavenly Journey*. Trans. and annotated by Frederick Colby. Louisville: Fons Vitae, 2006.

———. *Ṭabaqāt al-ṣūfiyya*. Ed. Abd al-Qādir Aḥmad ʿAṭā'. Beirut: Dār al-Kutub al-ʿIlmiyya, 2003.

———. *Tafsīr al-sulamī wa huwa ḥaqā'iq al tafsīr*. Ed. Sayyid ʿImrān. Beirut: Dār al-Kutub al-ʿIlmiyya, 2001.

———. *Ziyādāt ḥaqā'iq al-tafsīr (The Minor Qur'ān Commentary of Abū ʿAbd ar-Raḥmān b. al-Ḥusayn as-Sulamī [d. 412/1021])*. Ed. Gerhard Böwering. Beirut: Dār al-Machreq, 1997.

al-Suyūṭī, Jalāl al-Dīn and Jalāl al-Dīn al-Maḥallī. *Tafsīr al-jalālayn*. Eds. ʿAbd al-Qādir al-Arnāʾūṭ and Aḥmad Khālid Shukrī. Damascus: Dār Ibn Kathīr, 1998.

al-Suyūṭī, Jalāl al-Dīn. *al-Durr al-manthūr*. Beirut: Dār al-Kutub al-ʿIlmiyya, 2000.

———. *Sharḥ al-ṣudūr bi sharḥ ḥāl al-mawtā wa al-qubūr*. Ed. Ṭaʿmā Ḥalabī. Beirut: Dār al-Maʿrifa, 1996.

al-Ṭabarī, Abū Jaʿfar Muḥammad b. Jarīr. *Jāmiʿ al-bayān ʿan tafsīr al-qurʾān*. Beirut: Dār al-Maʿrifa, 1992.

al-Ṭabāṭabāʾī, ʿAllāma. *al-Mīzān fī al-tafsīr*. Beirut, 1971.

al-Ṭūsī, Muḥammad b. al-Ḥasan. *al-Tibyān fī tafsīr al-qurʾān*. Basra, 1963.

al-Tustarī, Sahl b. ʿAbd Allāh. *Tafsīr al-qurʾān al-karīm*. Eds. Ṭāhā ʿAbd al-Raʾūd Saʿd and Saʿd Ḥasan Muḥammad ʿAlī. Cairo: Dār al-Ḥaram li al-Turāth, 2004.

al-Zabīdī, Murtaḍā. *Tāj al-ʿarūs*. Kuwait: al-Turāth al-ʿArabī, 1966.

al-Zamakhsharī, Mahmūd b. ʿUmar. *Asās al-balāgha*. Ed. Mazīd Naʿīm and Shawqī al-Maʿarrī. Beirut: Maktaba Nāshirūn, n.d.

———. *al-Kashshāf*. Riyadh: Maktabat al-ʿAbīkān, 1998.

Secondary Sources

Abdel Kader, Ali Hasan. *The Life, Personality, and Writings of Junayd: A Study of a Third/Ninth Century Mystic with an Edition and Translation of his Writings*. London: Luzac & Company Ltd., 1976.

Abrahamov, Benyamin. "Al-Ghazālī's Theory of Causality." *Studia Islamica* 67 (1988): 75–98.

Addas, Claude. *Quest for the Red Sulphur: The Life of Ibn ʿArabi*. Trans. Peter Kingsley. Cambridge: Islamic Texts Society, 1993.

Andrae, Tor. *In the Garden of Myrtles: Studies in Early Islamic Mysticism*. Trans. Birgitta Sharpe. Albany: State University of New York, 1987.

Ansari, Muhammad Abdul Haq, "The Doctrine of One Actor: Junayd's View of *Tawḥīd*." *The Muslim World* 63, no. 1 (1983): 33–56.

Arberry, A.J. *Sufism: An Account of the Mystics of Islam*. 1935. Reprint. New York: Dover Publications, 2002.

———. "Preface." *The Book of Truthfulness (Kitāb al-Ṣidq) by Abū Saʿīd al-Kharrāz*. Trans. with preface by A.J. Arberry. Oxford: Oxford University Press, 1937.

———. "Junayd." *Journal of the Royal Asiatic Society* (1935): 499–507.

———. *Muslim Saints and Mystics: Episodes from the Tadhkirat al-Auliyaʾ*. Trans. A.J. Arberry. 1966. Reprint. London: Penguin Books, 1990.

ʿAṭāʾ, ʿAbd al-Qādir Aḥmad. *al-Tawba*. Cairo: Dār al-Naṣr, 1977.

Avery, Kenneth. *Shiblī: His Life and Thought in the Sufi Tradition*. Albany: State University of New York Press, 2014.

Aydinli, Osman. "Ascetic and Devotional Elements in the Muʿtazilite Tradition: The Sufi Muʿtazilites." *The Muslim World* 97 (2007): 174–189.

Ayto, John. *Dictionary of Word Origins: The Histories of Over 8,000 Words Explained*. London: Bloomsbury, 1990.

Ayoub, Mahmoud. "Repentance in the Islamic Tradition." In *Repentance: A Comparative Perspective*, 96–121, eds. Amitai Etzioni and David Carney. New York: Rowman and Littlefield, 1997.

Baldick, Julian. *Mystical Islam: An Introduction to Sufism*. London: I.B. Tauris & Co., 1989.

Bar-Asher, Meir M. *Scripture and Exegesis in Early Imāmī Shiism*. Leiden: Brill, 1999.

Barnhart, Robert, ed. *Chambers Dictionary of Etymology*. New York: Chambers, 1988.

Bell, Joseph. *Love Theory in Later Ḥanbalite Islam*. Albany: State University of New York, 1979.

Bell, Richard. "*Teshubah*: The Idea of Repentance in Ancient Judaism." *Journal of Progressive Judaism* 5 (1995): 22–52.

Bird, Norman. *The Roots and Non-Roots of Indo-European: A Lexicostatistical Survey*. Wiesbaden: Harrassowitz, 1993.

Blankinship, Khalid. "The Early Creed." In *The Cambridge Companion to Classical Islamic Theology*, ed. Tim Winter, 33–54. Cambridge: Cambridge University Press, 2008.

Böwering, Gerhard. "Early Sufism Between Persecution and Heresy." In *Islamic Mysticism Contested: Thirteen Centuries of Controversies and Polemics*, eds. Frederick De Jong and Bernd Radtke, 45–67. Leiden: Brill, 1999.

———. *The Mystical Vision of Existence in Classical Islam: The Qur'ānic Hermeneutics of the Ṣūfī Sahl al-Tustarī*. Berlin: Walter De Gruyter, 1980.

———. "The Qur'ān Commentary of Al-Sulamī." In *Islamic Studies Presented to Charles J. Adams*, eds. W.B. Hallaq and D.P. Little, 41–56. Leiden: Brill, 1991.

Brock, S.P. "Early Syriac Asceticism." *Numen* 20 (1973): 1–19.

Brohi, Allahbaksh K. "The Spiritual Significance of the Qur'ān." In *Islamic Spirituality: Foundations*, ed. S.H. Nasr, 11–23. New York: Crossroad, 1987.

Brown, Francis, S.R. Driver, and Charles A. Briggs. *A Hebrew and English Lexicon of the Old Testament: Based on the Lexicon of William Gesenius as Translated by Edward Robinson*. Oxford: Claredon, 1907.

Brown, Jonathan. "The Last Days of al-Ghazzālī and the Tripartite Division of the Sufi World: Abū Ḥāmid al-Ghazzālī's Letter to the Seljuq Vizier and Commentary." *Muslim World* 96, no. 1 (2006): 89–106.

Burton, John. Review of *Ethico-Religious Concepts in the Qur'an*, by Toshihiko Izutsu. *Bulletin of the School of African Studies* 31, no. 2 (1968): 391–392.

Chabbi, Jacqueline. "Fuḍayl b. ʿIyāḍ, un précurseur du ḥanbalisme." *Bulletin d'études orientales* 30 (1978): 37–55.

Chishti, Sadia Khawar Khan. "Female Spirituality in Islam." In *Islamic Spirituality: Foundations*, ed. S.H. Nasr, 199–219. New York: Crossroad, 1987.

Chittick, William. *Faith and Practice of Islam: Three Thirteenth Century Sufi Texts*. Albany: State University of New York, 1992.

———. *Sufism: A Short Introduction*. Oxford: Oneworld, 2000.

———. *The Sufi Path of Knowledge: Ibn al-ʿArabi's Metaphysics of Imagination*. Albany: State University of New York, 1989.

Chodkiewicz, Michel. "*Miʿrāj al-kalima*: de la *risāla qushayriyya* aux *futūḥāt makkiyya*." In *Reason and Inspiration in Islam: Theology, Philosophy, and Mysticism in Muslim Thought,* ed. Todd Lawson, 248–261. London: I.B. Tauris in association with the Institute of Ismaili Studies, 2005.

Clines, David. *The Dictionary of Classical Hebrew.* Sheffield: Sheffield Academic Press, 2001.

Coates, Peter. *Ibn ʿArabi and Modern Thought: The History of Taking Metaphysics Seriously.* Oxford: Anqa Publishing, 2002.

Cooperson, Michael. "Ibn Ḥanbal and Bishr al-Ḥāfī: A Case Study in Biographical Traditions." *Studia Islamica* 86, no. 2 (1997): 71–101.

Crossley, James. "The Semitic Background to Repentance in the Teaching of John the Baptist and Jesus." *Journal for the Study of the Historical Jesus* 2 (2004): 138–157.

Dakake, Maria Massi. "'Walking the Path of God Like Men?' Women and the Feminine in the Islamic Mystical Tradition." In *Sufism: Love and Wisdom,* ed. Jean-Louis Michon, 131–152. Bloomington, IN: World Wisdom Books, 2006.

Danner, Victor. "The Necessity for the Rise of the Term Sufi." *Studies in Comparative Religion* 6, no. 2 (1973): 71–77.

De Crussol, Yolande. *Le rôle de la raison dans la réflexion éthique d'Al-Muḥāsībī: ʿAql et conversion chez al-Muḥāsībī.* Paris: Consep, 2002.

Denny, Frederick. "The Qurʾanic Vocabulary of Repentance: Orientations and Attitudes." *Journal of the American Academy of Religion* (Thematic Issue S) 47, no. 4 (1980): 649–664.

Druart, Thérèse-Anne. "Al-Ghazālī's Conception of the Agent in the *Tahāfut* and the *Iqtiṣād*: Are People Really Agents?" In *Arabic Theology, Arabic Philosophy: From the Many to the One: Essays in Celebration of Richard Frank,* ed. James Montgomery, 426–440. Paris: Peeters, 2006.

Ernout, A., and A. Meillet. *Dictionnaire etymologique de la langue latin.* 3rd ed. Paris: Librairie C. Klincksieck, 1951.

Ernst, Carl. *Words of Ecstasy in Sufism.* Albany: State University of New York, 1985.

Ess, Joseph van. *Die Gedankenwelt des Ḥārith al-Muḥāsibī.* Bonn: Selbstverlag des Orientalischen Seminars der Universität Bonn, 1961.

———. *The Flowering of Muslim Theology.* Trans. Jane Marie Todd. Cambridge, MA: Harvard University Press, 2006.

———. "Sufism and Its Opponents: Reflections on Topoi, Tribulations, and Transformation." In *Islamic Mysticism Contested: Thirteen Centuries of Controversies and Polemics,* eds. Frederick De Jong and Bernd Radtke, 22–44. Leiden: Brill, 1999.

———. *Theologie und Gesellshaft im 2. und 3. Jahrhundert Hidschra. Eine Geschichte des religiösen Denkens in frühen Islam.* 6 Vols. Berlin: Walter de Gruyter, 1991–1997.

Etziono, Amitai, and David E. Carvey, eds. *Repentance: A Comparative Perspective.* New York: Rowman and Littlefield, 1997.

Fakhry, Majid. *Ethical Theories in Islam.* Leiden: Brill, 1991.

———. *History of Islamic Philosophy.* New York: Columbia, 1983.

Farhadi, Ravan. *Abdullah Ansari of Heart: An Early Sufi Master.* Surrey: Curzon, 1996.

Fenton, Paul. "Judaeo-Arabic Mystical Writings in the XIII-XIV Centuries." In *Studies in Muslim-Jewish Relations: Judaeo-Arabic Studies*, ed. Normal Golb, 87–103. Oxford: Harwood Academic Publishers, 1997.

———. "Judaism and Sufism." In *History of Islamic Philosophy*, eds. Oliver Leaman and S.H. Nasr, 755–768. London: Routledge, 1996.

Finn, Thomas M. *From Death to Rebirth: Ritual and Conversion in Antiquity*. Mahwah, NJ: Paulist Press, 1997.

Franke, Patrick. *Begegnung mit Khidr: Quellenstudien zum Imaginären im traditionellen Islam*. Stuttgart: Franz Steiner, 2000.

Friedmann, Yohanan. "Conditions of Conversion in Early Islam." In *Rituals and Ethics: Patterns of Repentance in Judaism, Christianity, Islam*, eds. Adriana Destro and Mauro Pesce, 95–106. Paris: Peeters, 2004.

Glock, Charles Y. "The Role of Deprivation in the Origin and Evolution of Religious Groups." In *Religion and Social Conflict*, eds. Robert Lee and Martin Marty, 24–36. New York: Oxford University Press, 1964.

Gramlich, Richard. *Abu l-ʿAbbās b. ʿAṭāʾ: Ṣūfī und Koranausleger*. Stuttgart: F. Steiner, 1995.

———."Abū Sulaymān ad-Dārānī." *Oriens* 33 (1992): 22–85.

———. *Alte Vorbilder des Sufitums*. 2 vols. Wiesbaden: Harrasowitz, 1995–1996.

———. "Mystical Dimensions of Islamic Monotheism." In *We Believe in One God: The Experience of God in Christianity and Islam*, eds. Annemarie Schimmel and Abdoldjavad Falaturi, 136–149. New York: Seabury Press, 1976.

Green, Nile. *Sufism: A Global History*. West Sussex, UK: Wiley-Blackwell, 2012.

Goitein, S.D. "A Plea for the Periodization of Islamic History." *Journal of the American Oriental Society* 88, no. 2 (1968): 224–228.

Goldziher, Ignaz. *Introduction to Islamic Theology and Law*. Trans. Andras and Ruth Hamori. Princeton, NJ: Princeton University Press, 1981.

Gutas, Dimitri. "Classical Arabic Wisdom Literature: Nature and Scope." *Journal of the American Oriental Society* 101, no. 1 (1981): 49–86.

Habil, Abdurrahman. "Traditional Esoteric Commentaries on the Qurʾān." In *Islamic Spirituality: Foundations*, ed. S.H. Nasr, 24–47. New York: Crossroad, 1987.

Hobsbawm, Eric. "Inventing Traditions." In *The Invention of Tradition*, eds. Eric Hobsbawn and Terrence Ranger, 1–14. Cambridge: Cambridge University Press, 1983.

Hawting, G.R. "The Tawwābūn, Atonement and ʿĀshūrāʾ." *Jerusalem Studies in Arabic and Islam* 17 (1994): 166–181.

Haywood, John. *Arabic Lexicography: Its History and its Place in the General History of Lexicography*. Leiden: Brill, 1960.

Heck, Paul. "Sufism—What Is It Exactly?" *Religion Compass* 1, no. 1 (2007): 148–164.

Hindsley, Leonard P. "Monastic Conversion: The Case of Margaret Ebner." In *Varieties of Religious Conversion in the Middle Ages*, ed. James Muldoon, 31–48. Gainesville: University of Florida Press, 1997.

Hodgson, Marshall. *The Venture of Islam: Conscience and History in a World Civilization*. 3 vols. Chicago: The University of Chicago Press, 1974.

Holladay, William L. *The Root Shub in the Old Testament*. Leiden: Brill, 1958.
Houghton, Louise Seymour. "The Cry of the Penitent: A Babylonian Prayer." *The Biblical World* 22, no. 1 (1903): 49–51.
Hourani, George. *Islamic Rationalism: The Ethics of ʿAbd al-Jabbār*. Oxford: Oxford University Press, 1971.
Hudson, Leila. "The Sufi Genealogy of Islamic Modernism in Late Ottoman Damascus." *Journal of Islamic Studies* 15, no. 1 (2004): 39–68.
Husain, Syed Muʿazzam. "Effect of *Tauba* (Repentance) on Penalty in Islam." *Islamic Studies* 8 (1969): 189–198.
Izutsu, Toshihiko. *Ethico-Religious Concepts in the Qurʾān*. 2nd ed. Montreal: McGill-Queen's University Press, 2002.
———. *God and Man in the Qurʾan: Semantics of the Qurʾanic Weltanschauung*. 2nd ed. Kuala Lumpur: Islamic Book Trust, 2002.
Kant, Immanuel. *Foundations of the Metaphysics of Morals*. Trans. Lewis White Beck. New York: Liberal Arts Press, 1959.
Karamustafa, Ahmet T. *Sufism: The Formative Period*. Berkeley: University of California Press, 2007.
———. "Walāya According to Junayd." In *Reason and Inspiration in Islam: Theology, Philosophy, and Mysticism in Muslim Thought*, ed. Todd Lawson, 64–70. London: I.B. Tauris in association with the Institute of Ismaili Studies, 2005.
Keeler, Annabel. *Ṣūfī Hermeneutics: The Qurʾān Commentary of Rashīd al-Dīn Maybudī*. Oxford: Oxford University Press in association with the Institute of Ismaili Studies, 2006.
Kelly, Jack. "Virtue and Pleasure." *Mind* 82 (1973): 401–408.
Khalil, Atif. "Abū Ṭālib al-Makkī (d. 996) and the *Qūt al-Qulūb* (*Nourishment of Hearts*) in the Context of Early Sufism." *Muslim World* 122 (2012): 331–356.
———. "Contentment, Satisfaction and Good Pleasure: *Rida* in Early Sufi Moral Psychology." *Studies in Religion/Sciences Religieuses* 43, no. 3 (2014): 1–19.
———. "Ibn al-ʿArabī (d. 1240) on the Three Conditions of *Tawba*." *Journal of Islam and Christian-Muslim Relations* 17 (2006): 403–416.
———. "Is God Obliged to Answer Prayers of Petition? The Response of Classical Sufis and Qurʾanic Exegetes." *Journal of Medieval Religious Cultures* 37, no. 2 (2011): 93–109.
———. "On Cultivating Gratitude in Sufi Virtue Ethics," *Journal of Sufi Studies* 4, no. 1–2 (2015): 1–26.
———. "The Embodiment of Gratitude in Sufi Ethics," *Studia Islamica* 111, no. 2 (2016): 159–178.
———. "The Interplay of Divine-Human Gratitude in the Non-Dualism of Ibn al-ʿArabī." In *Remembrance, Discourse, and Beauty in Islamicate Civilization*. Eds. Omid Ghaemmaghami and Sebastian Günther. Leiden: Brill (forthcoming).
———. Review of *Islamic Mysticism and Abū Ṭālib al-Makkī: The Role of the Heart*, by Saeko Yazaki. *Journal of the Royal Asiatic Society* 25, no. 2 (2015): 357–360.
———. Review of *Spiritual Purification in Islam: The Life and Words of al-Muḥāsibī* by Gavin Picken. *Journal of Medieval Religious Cultures* 42, no. 2 (2016): 278–280.

Kennedy, Philip. F. *The Wine Song in Classical Arabic Poetry: Abū Nuwās and the Literary Tradition*. Oxford: Oxford University Press, 1997.

Kilbourne, Brock, and James T. Richardson. "Paradigm Conflict, Types of Conversion, and Conversion Theories." *Sociological Analysis* 50, no. 1 (1988): 1–21.

Kinberg, Leah. "What Is Meant by *Zuhd*?" *Studia Islamica* 61 (1985): 31–36.

Klein, Ernest. *A Comprehensive Etymological Dictionary of the English Language*. London: Elsevier Publishing Company, 1967.

Knysh, Alexander. *Islamic Mysticism: A Short History*. Leiden: Brill, 2000.

Lane, Andrew. *A Traditional Mu'tazilite Qur'ān Commentary: The Kashshāf of Jār Allāh al-Zamakhsharī (d. 538/1144)*. Leiden: Brill, 2006.

Lane, Edward. *Arabic-English Lexicon*. Cambridge: Islamic Texts Society, 1984.

Lawson, Todd. "Note for the Study of a 'Shī'ī Qur'ān.'" *Journal of Semitic Studies* 36 (1991): 279–295.

———. Review of *Ṣūfī Commentaries on the Qur'ān in Classical Islam*, by Kristin Zahra Sands. *Journal of the American Oriental Society* 127, no. 4 (2007): 543–545.

Lazarus-Yafeh, Hava. "Is There a Concept of Redemption in Islam?" In *Some Religious Aspects of Islam*. Leiden: Brill, 1981. 48–57.

———. *Studies in Ghazzali*. Jerusalem: The Magnes Press, 1975.

Librande, Leonard. "Islam and Conservation: The Theologian-Ascetic al-Muḥāsibī." *Arabica* 30, no. 2 (1983): 125–146.

Liddell, Henry George and Robert Scott. *A Greek-English Lexicon*. 9th ed. Revised by Henry Stuart Jones, et al. Oxford: Clarendon Press, 1961.

Lobel, Diana. *Between Mysticism and Philosophy: Sufi Language and Religious Experience in Judah Ha Levi's Kuzari*. Albany: State University of New York, 2000.

———. *A Sufi-Jewish Dialogue: Philosophy and Mysticism in Baḥya Ibn Paqūda's Duties of the Heart*. Philadelphia: University of Pennsylvania Press, 2007.

Lumbard, Joseph. *Aḥmad al-Ghazālī, Remembrance, and the Metaphysics of Love*. Albany: State University of New York, 2016.

Maḥmūd, 'Abd al-Ḥalīm. *Ustādh al-sā'irīn: al-ḥārith b. al-muḥāsibī*. Cairo: Kitāb al-Sha'b, 1986.

Marmura, Michael. "al-Ghazālī on Bodily Resurrection and Causality in the Tahāfut and Iqtiṣād." *Aligarh Journal of Islamic Thought* 2 (1989): 46–75.

———. "Ghazālī and Ash'arism Revisited." *Arabic Sciences and Philosophy* 12 (2002): 91–110.

———. "Ghazālian Causes and Intermediaries." *Journal of the American Oriental Society* 115 (1995): 89–100.

Martin, David. "Fanā' and Baqā' in the Works of Abū al-Qāsim al-Junayd al-Baghdādī." PhD diss., University of California at Los Angeles, 1984.

Massignon, Louis. *Essay on the Origins of the Technical Language of Islamic Mysticism*. Trans. Benjamin Clark. Notre Dame, IN: University of Notre Dame Press, 1997.

———. *The Passion of Ḥallāj*. 4 vols. Trans. Herbert Mason. Princeton, NJ: Princeton University Press, 1982.

McAuliffe, Jane. *Qur'ānic Christians: An Analysis of Classical and Modern Exegesis*. New York: Cambridge University Press, 1991.

Meier, Fritz. "The Mystic Path." In *The World of Islam: Faith, People, Culture*, ed. Bernard Lewis, 117–128. London: Thames and Hudson, 1976.

Melchert, Christopher. "Baṣran Origins of Classical Sufism." *Der Islam* 82 (2005): 221–240.

———"The Transition from Asceticism to Mysticism at the Middle of the Ninth Century." *Studia Islamica* 83, no. 1 (1996): 51–70.

Mokdad, Arfa Mensia. "Théories du repentir chez théologiens musulmans classiques." In *Rituals and Ethics: Patterns of Repentance in Judaism, Christianity, Islam*, eds. Adriana Destro and Mauro Pesce, 125–139. Paris-Louvain: Peeters, 2004.

Mensia, Mongia Arfa. "L'acte expiatoire en Islam: *'Al Kaffāra.'*" In *Rituals and Ethics: Patterns of Repentance in Judaism, Christianity, Islam*, eds. Adriana Destro and Mauro Pesce, 125–139. Paris-Louvain: Peeters, 2004.

Mir, Mustansir. *Verbal Idioms of the Qur'ān*. Ann Arbour: University of Michigan, 1989.

Mojaddedi, Jawid A. *The Biographical Tradition in Sufism: The* ṭabaqāt *genre from al-Sulamī to Jāmi*. Surrey: Curzon, 2001.

———. "Getting Drunk with Abū Yazīd or Staying Sober with Junayd: The Creation of a Popular Typology of Sufism." *Bulletin of the School of Oriental Studies* 66, no. 1 (2003): 1–13.

———. "Legitimizing Sufism in al-Qushayrī's *Risāla*." *Studia Islamica* (2000): 37–50.

Molé, Marijan. *Les mystiques musulmans*. Paris: Presses Universitaires de France, 1965.

Montefiore, C.G. "Rabbinic Conceptions of Repentance." *Jewish Quarterly Review* 16 (1904): 209–257.

Moucarry, Chawkat. *The Search for Forgiveness: Pardon and Punishment in Islam and Christianity*. Nottingham: Inter-Varsity Press, 2004.

Mourad, Suleiman Ali. *Early Islam Between Myth and History: al-Ḥasan al-Baṣrī (d. 110 H/728 CE) and the Formation on His Legacy in Classical Islamic Scholarship*. Leiden: Brill, 2005.

Muldoon, James. "Introduction: The Conversion of Europe." In *Varieties of Conversion in the Middle Ages*, ed. James Muldoon, 1–10. Gainesville: University of Florida Press, 1997.

Murata, Sachiko. *The Tao of Islam*. Albany: State University of New York, 1992.

Nakamura, Kojiro. "Makkī and Ghazālī on Mystical Practices." *Oriens* 20 (1984): 83–91.

Nasr, Seyyed Hossein. *The Garden of Truth*. New York: Harper One, 2007.

———. "The Qur'ān as the Foundation of Islamic Spirituality." In *Islamic Spirituality: Foundations*, ed. S.H. Nasr, 3–10. New York: Crossroad, 1987.

———. *Sufi Essays*. Albany: State University of New York, 1991.

Nave, Guy D. Jr. *The Role and Function of* Repentance *in Luke-Acts*. Atlanta: Society of Biblical Literature, 2002.

Neuwirth, Angelika. "Orientalism in Oriental Studies." *Journal of Qur'anic Studies* 9, no. 2 (2007): 357–370.

Nicholson, Reynold. *The Mystics of Islam*. London: Routledge and Kegan Paul Ltd., 1963.

Nwyia, Paul. *Exégèse coranique et langage mystique: nouvel essai sur le lexique technique des mystiques musulmans*. Beirut: Dār el-Machreq, 1970.

———. *Ibn ʿAṭāʾ Allāh et la naissance de la confrèrie šaḏilite*. Beirut, 1973.

———. "Textes mystiques inédits d'Abū-l Ḥasan al-Nūrī (m. 295/907)." *Mélanges de l'université saint Joseph* 44 (1968): 117–143.

Oesterheld, Christina. "Nazir Ahmad and the Early Urdu Novel: Some Observations." *Annual of Urdu Studies* 16 (2001): 27–41.

Partin, Harry B. "Semantics of the Qurʾan: A Consideration of Izutsu's Studies." *History of Religions* 9, no. 4 (1970): 358–362.

Partridge, Eric. *A Short Etymological Dictionary of Modern English*. London: Routledge, 1961.

Penrice, John. *A Dictionary and Glossary of the Qur'ān: With Copious References and Explanations of the Text*. 1873. Reprint. Surrey: Gresham Press, 1985.

Peters, Rudolph, and Gert J.J. Vries. "Apostasy in Islam." *Die Welt des Islams* 17, no. 1 (1976–1977): 1–25.

Petuchowski, Jacob J. "The Concept of 'Teshuvah' in the Bible and Talmud." *Judaism: A Quarterly Journal* 17 (1978): 174–185.

Picken, Gavin. *Spiritual Purification in Islam: The Life and Words of al-Muḥāsibī*. London: Routledge, 2011.

Pomerantz, Maurice A. "Muʿtazilī Theory in Practice: The Repentance (*tawba*) of Government Officials in the 4th/10th century." In *A Common Rationality: Muʿtazilism in Islam and Judaism*, eds. Camilla Adang, Sabine Schmidtke and David Sklare, 463–4493. Würzburg: Ergon, 2007.

Radtke, Bernd. *The Concept of Sainthood in Early Islamic Mysticism: Two Works by al-Ḥakīm al-Tirmidhī*. Surrey: Curzon Press, 1996.

Renard, John. *Friends of God: Islamic Images of Piety, Commitment, and Servanthood*. Berkeley: University of California Press, 2008.

———. *Historical Dictionary of Sufism*. Oxford: Oxford University Press, 2005.

———. *Knowledge of God in Classical Sufism: Foundations of Islamic Mystical Theology*. Mahwah, NJ: Paulist Press, 2004.

Reinert, Benedikt. *Die Lehre vom tawakkul in der klassischen Sufik*. Berlin: De Gruyter, 1968.

Rizvi, Sajjad. "The Developed Kalām Tradition" (Part II). In *The Cambridge Companion to Classical Islamic Theology*, ed. Tim Winter, 91–94. Cambridge: Cambridge University Press, 2008.

Robinson, Francis. Review of *The Repentance of Nussooh (Taubat al-Nasuh)*, by Nazir Ahmad, trans. M. Kempson. *Journal of the Royal Asiatic Society* 14, no. 3 (2004): 285.

Robinson, Neal. *Discovering the Qur'ān: A Contemporary Approach to a Veiled Text*. 2nd ed. Washington, DC: Georgetown University Press, 2003.

Rosenthal, Franz. *Knowledge Triumphant*. Leiden: Brill, 1970.

Russell, Frederick H. "Augustine: Conversion by the Book." In *Varieties of Religious Conversion in the Middle Ages*, ed. James Muldoon, 13–30. Gainesville: University of Florida Press, 1997.

Rustom, Mohammed. "The Sufi Teachings of Dhuʾl Nūn." *Sacred Web* 24 (2009): 69–79.

Saab, Nada A. "Sufi Theory and Language in the Writings of Abū Saʿīd al-Kharrāz (d. 286/899)." PhD diss., Yale University, 2005.

Saleh, Walid A. *The Formation of the Classical Tafsīr Tradition: the Qurʾān Commentary of al-Thaʿlabī*. Leiden: Brill, 2004.

Sanders, E.P. *Paul and Palestinian Judaism*. London: SCM Press, 1977.

Sands, Kristin Zahra. *Ṣūfī Commentaries on the Qurʾān in Classical Islam*. London: Routledge, 2006.

Schacht, Joseph. Review of *Ethico-Religious Concepts in the Qurʾān*, by Toshihiko Izutsu. *Journal of the American Oriental Society* 83, no. 3 (1963): 366–367.

Schaub, Edward L. "The Consciousness of Sin." *Harvard Theological Review* 5, no. 1 (1912): 121–138.

Schimmel, Annemarie. "Abūʾl Ḥusayn al-Nūrī: 'Qibla of Lights.'" In *The Heritage of Sufism Vol. 1: Classical Persian Sufism from Its Origins to Rumi (700–1300)*, ed. Leonard Lewisohn, 59–64. London: Khaniqahi Nimatullahi Publications, 1993.

———. *My Soul is a Woman: The Feminine in Islam*. Trans. Susan H. Ray. New York: Continuum, 1995.

———. *Mystical Dimensions of Islam*. Chapel Hill: University of North Carolina Press, 1975.

Schuon, Frithjof. *Sufism: Veil and Quintessence*. Trans. William Stoddart. Bloomington, IN: World Wisdom Books, 1981.

Sejdini, Zekirija. *Die Nahrung der Herzen: Glaube und Wissen bei Abu Talib al-Makki*. Frankfurt am Main: Peter Lang, 2013.

Sells, Michael. *Early Islamic Mysticism: Sufi, Qurʾan, Miʿraj, Poetic, and Theological Writings*. Mahwah, NJ: Paulist Press, 1996.

———. "Heart-Secret, Intimacy, and Awe in Formative Sufism." In *The Shaping of an American Islamic Discourse: A Memorial to Fazlur Rahman*, eds. Earle H. Waugh and Frederick M. Denny, 165–188. Atlanta: Scholars Press for the University of South Florida, University of Rochester, and Saint Louis University, 1998.

———. "A Literary Approach to the Hymnic Sūras of the Qurʾān: Spirit, Gender, and Aural Intertextuality." In *Literary Structures of Religious Meaning in the Qurʾān*, ed. Issa J. Boullata, 3–25. London: Curzon, 1999.

———. "Sound, Spirit, and Gender in *Sūrat al-Qadr*." *Journal of the American Oriental Society* 11, no. 2 (1990): 101–139.

———. "Sound and Meaning in *Sūrat al-Qāriʿa*." *Arabica* 40 (1993): 403–430.

Shah-Kazemi, Reza. "The Notion and Significance of *Maʿrifa* in Sufism." *Journal of Islamic Studies* 13, no. 2 (2002): 155–181.

Sherif, Mohamed Ahmed. *Ghazali's Theory of Virtue*. Albany: State University of New York, 1975.

Siddiqui, Muzammil Husain. "The Doctrine of Redemption: A Critical Study." In *Islamic Perspectives: Studies in Honor of Mawlānā Sayyid Abul Aʿlā Mawdūdī*, eds. Khurshid Ahmad and Zafar Ansari, 91–102. London: Islamic Foundation, 1979.

Silvers, Laury. *A Soaring Minaret: Abu Bakr al-Wasiti and the Rise of Baghdadi Sufism*. Albany: State University of New York Press, 2010.

———. "Tawḥīd in Early Sufism: The Life and Works of Abū Bakr al-Wāsiṭī (d. 320/928)." PhD diss., State University of New York at Stony Brook, 2002.

———. "Theoretical Sufism in the Early Period: With an Introduction to the Thought of Abū Bakr al-Wāsiṭī (d. ca 320/928) on the Interrelationship between Theoretical and Practical Sufism." *Studia Islamica* 98/99 (2004): 71–94.

Sirāj al-Dīn, Abū Bakr. *The Book of Certainty: The Sufi Doctrine of Faith, Vision, and Gnosis*. Cambridge: Islamic Texts Society, 1992.

Sobieroj, Florian. "The Muʿtazila and Sufism." In *Islamic Mysticism Contested: Thirteen Centuries of Controversies and Polemics*, ed. Frederick de Jong and Bernd Radtke, 68–92. Leiden: Brill, 1992.

Smith, Margaret. *An Early Mystic of Baghdad: A Study of the Life and Teaching of Ḥārith B. Asad al-Muḥāsibī A.D. 781–857*. 1935. Reprint. London: Sheldon Press, 1977.

———. "The Forerunner of Ghazālī." *Journal of the Royal Asiatic Society* (1936): 65–78.

———. *Rabia the Mystic A.D. 717–801, and Her Fellow Saints in Islam*. Cambridge: Cambridge University Press, 1928.

———. "Al-Shaʿrānī the Mystic." *The Muslim World* 29, no. 3 (1930): 240–247.

Spevack, Aaron. *The Archetypal Sunnī Scholar: Law, Theology, and Mysticism in the Synthesis of Al-Bājūrī*. Albany: State University of New York Press, 2014.

Stark, Rodney. "Upper Class Asceticism: Social Origins of Ascetic Movements and Medieval Saints." *Review of Religious Research* 45, no. 1 (2003): 5–19.

Stern, Martin (Moshe) Stanley. *Al-Ghazzali on Repentance*. New Delhi: Sterling Publishers, 1990.

———. "Al-Ghazzālī, Maimonides, and Ibn Paqūda on Repentance: A Comparative Model." *Journal of the American Academy of Religion* 47, no. 4 (1979): 589–607.

———. "Notes on the Theology of Ghazzali's Concept of Repentance." *The Islamic Quarterly* 23, no. 2 (1979): 82–98.

Stark, Susan. "Virtue and Emotion." *Nous* 35, no. 3 (2001): 440–455.

Stuart, Douglas K. *The New American Commentary: An Exegetical and Theological Exposition of Holy Scripture: Exodus*. Nashville: B&H Publishing, 2006.

Straus, Roger. "Religious Conversion as a Personal and Collective Accomplishment." *Sociological Analysis* 40, no. 2 (1979): 158–165.

Sviri, Sara. "The Self and its Transformation in Ṣūfism, with a Special Reference to Early Literature." In *Self and Self-Transformation in History of Religions*, eds. David Shulman and Guy G. Stroumsa, 195–215. Oxford: Oxford University Press, 2002.

Taylor, Gabriele and Sybil Wolfram. "Virtues and Passions." *Analysis* 31, no. 3 (1971): 76–83.

Tirmingham, Spencer. *The Sufi Orders of Islam*. Reprint. Oxford: Oxford University Press, 1998.

Valpy, F.E.J. *An Etymological Dictionary of the Latin Language*. London: Baldwin and Co., 1838.

Watt, Montgomery. "Conversion in Islam at the Time of the Prophet." *Journal of the American Academy of Religion* (Thematic Issue S) 47, no. 4 (1980): 721–731.

———. Review of *God and Man in the Koran* and *The Concept of Belief in Islamic Theology*, by Toshihiko Izutsu. *Journal of Semitic Studies* 12, no. 1 (1967): 155–157.

Wensink, A.J. et al. *Concordance et indices de la tradition musulmane*. 4 vols. Leiden: Brill, 1962.

Wheeler, Brannon M. *Prophets in the Quran: An Introduction to the Quran and Muslim Exegesis*. London: Continuum International Publishing Group, 2002.

White, John, and Riddle, J.E. *A Latin-English Dictionary*. 4th ed. London: Longmans Green & Co., 1872.

Wilzer, Susan. "Untersuchungen zu Ġazzālis Kitāb al-Tauba [parts 1–3]." *Der Islam* 32 (1957): 237–309; 33 (1958): 51–120; 34 (1959): 128–137.

Winter, Michael. *Society and Religion in Early Ottoman Egypt*. New York: Transaction Books, 1982.

Winter, Tim. "The Chador of God on Earth: The Metaphysics of the Muslim Veil." *New Blackfriars* (2004): 144–157.

Wolfson, Harry Austryn. *The Philosophy of the Kalam*. Cambridge, MA: Harvard University Press, 1974.

Yazaki, Saeko. "A Pseudo-Abū Ṭālib al-Makkī?: The Authenticity of the *ʿIlm al-qulūb*." *Arabica* 59 (2012): 1–35.

———. *Islamic Mysticism and Abū Ṭālib al-Makkī: The Role of the Heart*. London: Routledge, 2013.

Zammit, Martin. *A Comparative Lexical Study of Qurʾānic Arabic*. Leiden: Brill, 2002.

Zilio-Grandi, Ida. "Return, Repentance, Amendment, Reform, Reconversion: A Contribution to the Study of *Tawba* in the Context of Islamic Ethics." *Islamochristiana* 39 (2013): 71–91.

Index

Abbasid(s), 3–4, 68
ʿAbd Allāh b. al-Mubārak, 2, 70
Abraham, 37, 54–55, 236n65
Abū ʿAbd Allāh b. Sālim, 100–101, 145
Abū al-Ḥasan Aḥmad b. Sālim, 101, 106, 113–115, 145, 219n84
Abū Ḥanīfa, 67
Abū Madyan, 123
Abū Saʿīd b. Abī al-Khayr, 82
Adam, 46, 131, 139, 176–178, 221n108
ʿAdawiyya, Rābiʿa al-, 89–90, 127, 163, 171, 210n75
ʿadhāb (punishment), 35–36, 42, 47, 50–58
Aḥmad b. Ḥanbal, 106, 151, 233n35
ʿAlī (Imām and Caliph), 79, 193n17
Ali, Yusuf, 56
ʿamila ṣāliḥan, 30
angel(s), 32–33, 37, 87, 149, 177–178, 180
Anṣārī, Abdullah, 82–83, 171
Arberry, A.J., 98, 107, 123, 146
Aristotle, 158–160
Ashʿarī, Abū al-Ḥasan al-, 106
Ashʿarite(s), 46, 106, 117, 119–120
ʿAṭṭār, 63, 66, 69–70, 97, 103–104, 175, 203n51
Augustine, 61, 198n3, 217n35
Awlāsī, Abū al-Ḥārith al-, 72

Baghdādī, Junayd al-, 2, 8–9, 66, 71–72, 82, 97, 103, 106–121, 123, 126, 145, 158, 170–172, 177, 218n56
Baḥya b. Paqūda, 124
Baldick, Julian, 125
Balkhī, Shaqīq al-, 69–70, 79–80, 89, 203n57
Baqlī, Ruzbihān, 101
Baṣrī, Ḥasan al-, 4, 124
Bayḍāwī, al-, 45
Bishr al-Ḥāfī, 72–73
Bisṭāmī, Abū Yazīd al-, 88, 92
Böwering, Gerhard, 62–63, 101, 105
Buddha, 63, 151
Buddhism, 69–70
Bunnān al-Ḥammāl, 91
Burger, Karl, 17
Būshanjī, al-, 89

Christ, 20, 61–62, 91, 176
conversion, 2, 7–8, 15, 53, 61–75, 77, 127, 168, 176, 197n1, 198n5, 199n14, 199n15
Covenant, the, 107–108, 110–111, 118, 177

ḍalāla, 47
Dārānī, Abū Sulaymān al-, 80, 157–158, 160
Daqqāq, Abū ʿAlī al-, 93, 138
Daqqāq, Ibrāhīm al-, 73–74
David, 54–56
Day of Judgment, 38, 68, 129
Denny, Frederick, 39, 49
Dhahabī, Shams al-Dīn, 106, 145

Dhū al-Nūn al-Miṣrī, 2, 80–82, 87, 91, 94, 98, 133, 204n70
disbelief (*kufr*), 25, 27, 30, 41, 47–48, 50, 57, 92, 106, 162, 171, 194

Ess, Joseph van, 124, 126

fasting, 29, 48, 115, 133, 141, 216n26
Fayyūmī, 15, 17
fiqh (Islamic jurisprudence), 2, 5, 191, 199
Fīrūzābādī, 15, 17
Fuḍayl b. ʿIyāḍ, 8, 66–67, 179

Ghazālī, al-, 41, 83, 86, 111, 123, 129, 139, 141, 146, 150–151, 166–167, 212n81
Gutas, Dimitri, 83–84

Ḥāfī, Bishr al-, 72–73
ḥāl (*see* states)
Ḥallāj, al-, 4, 106, 213n100, 220n93
Ḥammāl, Bunnān al-, 91
Ḥanbalite(s), 106, 123, 202n42, 219n84, 227n84
Hārūn al-Rashīd (caliph), 68
Ḥasan al- Baṣrī, 4, 124
hātif, 65–66, 138
Heck, Paul, 127
hidāya (guidance), 46–47
Hindsley, Leonard, 61
Ḥīrī, Abū ʿUthmān al-, 68–69, 86, 117, 133, 203n51
Hodgson, Marshall, 125
Holladay, William, 18
Hūd, 32
Hujwīrī, 3, 63, 65–66, 68–71, 73, 79–80, 83, 85, 89, 93, 113–115, 123, 125, 138
Ḥulūlīs (incarnationists), 114
Ḥusayn, (Imām), 93
hypocrisy (*nifāq*), 27–28, 35, 45, 47–48, 50, 57, 141, 161

Iblīs (*see* Satan)
Ibn ʿAbbād, 15, 17, 123, 125
Ibn Abī al-Ḥawārī, 157–158, 160
Ibn ʿAṭāʾ, 88
Ibn ʿAṭāʾ Allāh, 66, 123, 179
Ibn al-ʿArabī, 82, 94, 116, 120, 123, 139, 145, 177–178, 207n32, 212n83, 221n108
Ibn al-Jawzī, 45, 227n84
Ibn al-Kathīr, 45, 147
Ibn al-Mubārak, 2, 70
Ibn Bashshār, 64–65
Ibn Durayd, 15, 17
Ibn Fāris, 17
Ibn Khallikān, 145, 216
Ibn Manẓūr, 14–15, 17, 43
Ibn Nujayd, 68
Ibn Qayyim al-Jawziyya, 171
Ibn Qudāma, 72, 202n39
Ibn Sālim, 100–101, 145
Ibn Sīda, 15, 17
Ibrāhīm b. Adham, 2, 8, 63–64, 66–67, 69, 89, 179
īmān (faith), 25, 30, 45, 47, 140
Iṣfahānī, Abū Nuʿaym al-, 63–65, 68–70, 73
Iṣfahānī, al-Rāghib al-, 15, 26, 31, 40, 43, 47, 49, 52–54, 162, 192n8, 192n9
iṣlāḥ (rectification), 28–32, 38, 47–49, 51, 54, 56, 66, 88, 128–129, 161–162, 176–177
istighfār (forgiveness), 31–39, 42, 45–47, 49, 51, 54, 57, 87, 99–100, 128
Izutsu, Toshihiko, 7, 23–25, 36, 39, 191n6

Jāmī, ʿAbd al-Raḥmān, 63, 70
Jawharī, al-, 17
Jesus (*see* Christ)
Job, 55–56
Jonah, 131
Junayd (*see* Baghdādī, Junayd al-)

jurisprudence (see *fiqh*)

Kalābādhī, Abū Bakr al-, 2–3, 5, 81–82, 109–110, 116, 120, 148, 171
kalām (Islamic theology), 2, 45–46, 107, 123, 151, 176
Kant, Immanuel, 160, 237n75, 237n76
Karkhī, Maʿrūf al-, 71–72
Khalīl b. ʿAyn, 15, 17
Kharrāz, Abū Saʿīd al-, 2, 8–9, 23, 81, 97–100, 103, 111, 119, 132, 134, 214n11
Khawwāṣ, ʿAlī al-, 67, 71
Khiḍr, 66
Khuldī, Jaʿfar al-, 106
Knysh, Alexander, 79, 148
kufr (*see* disbelief)

Lofland, John, 63

maghfira (see *istighfār*)
Makkī, Abū Ṭālib al-, 3–5, 9–10, 23, 81–82, 89, 100–102, 105, 112–113, 115, 120, 126, 145–173, 177
manāzil (stages), 6, 78–80, 205. *See also* stations
Manichean(s), 70
maqam (*see* stations)
Maʿrūf al-Karkhī, 71–72
Massignon, Louis, 79–80, 98, 123–124, 220n93
Meier, Fritz, 6
miʿrāj (nocturnal ascent), 3
Miṣrī, Dhū al-Nūn al- (*see* Dhū al-Nūn al-Miṣrī)
muʿāmala (*see* praxis)
Muʿāwiya (caliph), 179
Muḥammad (*see* Prophet, the)
muḥāsaba, 9, 116–117, 124, 132, 141
Muḥāsibī, al-Ḥārith al-, 4, 8–10, 23, 80, 82, 89, 98–99, 102, 106, 116, 123–143, 145, 147, 149, 152–153, 156, 161, 163, 166–167, 177
Muḥibb, Sumnūn al-, 106
mujāhada (inner struggle), 6, 114–115, 150, 155–157, 159, 185n23
Mursī, Abū al-ʿAbbās al-, 66
Muʿtazilite(s), 45–46, 117, 135, 176, 212n90, 225n42

nadam (remorse), 15, 20–21, 49–51, 57–58, 81, 87, 99, 128, 133, 150, 152
Naṣrābādhī, al-, 90
nifāq (*see* hypocrisy)
Nīshābūrī, Abū Ḥafṣ, 90
Noah, 37, 50, 146
nocturnal ascent (*miʿrāj*), 3
Nūrī, Abuʾl Ḥusayn al-, 82, 106, 115
Nwyia, Paul, 79

Paul (apostle), 62
Petuchowski, Jacob, 19
praxis, 5, 10, 151, 177, 185n21
Promise and Threat, 127, 132, 165–166
Prophet, the, 2–3, 15, 31–32, 35, 37, 46–47, 49, 71, 84–85, 94, 119, 137, 147–148, 164, 166, 175, 192n17, 225n60

Qāsim (*see* Sayyārī, Abū al-ʿAbbās al-)
Qaṣṣāb, al-, 106
Qazwīnī, Mānakdīm al-, 152
Qurṭubī, al-, 45
Qushayrī, al-, 3, 63, 65–71, 82–83, 87, 93, 100, 109, 112, 120, 125, 138, 146

Rabāḥ b. ʿAmr al-Qaysī, 157
Rābiʿa (al-ʿAdawiyya), 89–90, 127, 163, 171, 210n75
Rāʾī, Ḥabīb al-, 67, 71
Rambo, Lewis, 63, 199n15
Rāzī, al-, 45–46, 237n83
remorse (see *nadam*)
Renard, John, 65, 74, 147
renunciation (see *zuhd*)

Rūmī, 146, 178–179, 221n108
Ruwaym b. Ahmad, 170–172

ṣabr (patience), 6, 81, 86, 98, 155–156
Ṣaghānī, al-, 17
Sahl al-Tustarī (*see* Tustarī, Sahl al-)
Ṣāliḥ, 32, 50
sālik (traveller), 79, 83, 110
Sālimiyya, 100, 106, 145, 219n84
Saqaṭī, Sarī al-, 2, 71, 73, 88, 106, 109
Sarrāj, Abū Naṣr al-, 3, 5, 23, 81–82, 101, 104–105, 112–113, 115–116, 120, 145, 148, 170–172
Satan, 64, 99, 139, 141, 165, 179, 221n108, 238n98
Sayyārī, Abū al-ʿAbbās al-, 93, 115
Schimmel, Annemarie, 138, 147
Sells, Michael, 2, 107, 124, 127, 178
Shaqīq al-Balkhī, 69–70, 79–80, 89, 203n57
Shaʿrānī, ʿAbd al-Wahhāb al-, 66–67
Shiblī, Abū Bakr al-, 106
Shīʿism, 2, 193n17
shirk, 15, 27, 37, 118, 225n42, 237n83
Shuʿayb, 29, 32, 54–55, 137
shukr (gratitude), 6, 81, 86
Silvers, Laury, 5, 119–120
Sin, Major (*kabāʾir*), 27, 140, 165, 167, 225n42, 233n40
Sin, Minor (*ṣaghāʾir*), 27, 140, 233n40
sincerity (*ikhlāṣ*), 28, 98, 161
Sīrjānī, Abū al-Ḥasan al-, 84, 92
Skonovd, Norman, 63
Solomon, 54–56
states (*aḥwāl*), 8, 77, 79–82, 90–91, 94, 111–112, 146, 169
stations (*maqāmāt*), 6, 8, 77–82, 86, 90–91, 146, 149, 152, 155
Suḥrawardī, Shihāb al-Dīn, 79, 83
Sulamī, ʿAbd al-Raḥmān al-, 63, 65, 68, 70, 80, 101, 107, 115–116, 120, 125
Sumnūn al-Muḥibb, 106
Suyūṭī, al-, 45

Ṭāʾī, Dāwūd al-, 67
tāʾib, 6, 10, 16, 26–27, 49, 57–58, 62, 67, 87–89, 92, 99, 102, 109–110, 117, 128–129, 132–143, 150–170, 172, 176–178, 221n108, 227n89
Tamīmī, ʿAbd Allāh al-, 92
Thawrī, Sufyān al-, 107
Tirmidhī, al-, 82, 98, 175–176
Tustarī, Sahl al-, 2, 8–10, 66, 92, 97, 100–108, 113–115, 145, 154

ʿulamāʾ, 97, 104
Umayyad(s), 3

vice, 18, 66, 90, 99, 134–135, 141–143, 147, 150, 158–159, 168, 177–178

Wāsiṭī, Abū Bakr al-, 8–9, 90, 97, 108, 115–120, 177, 212n83, 220n93, 220n97

Yāfiʿī, Afīf al-Dīn al-, 123

Zabīdī, al-, 14–15, 17
Zamakhsharī, al-, 15, 17, 45–46, 187n10
Zoroastrian(s), 69–70
zuhd (renunciation), 69–70, 80–81, 158
ẓulm (oppression), 47–48, 50, 141

www.ingramcontent.com/pod-product-compliance
Lightning Source LLC
Chambersburg PA
CBHW030533230426
43665CB00010B/872